EQUITABLE COMPENSATION AND DISGORGEMENT OF PROFIT

This collection of essays interrogates significant issues at the forefront of scholarship and legal practice in the field of money remedies in equity. Chapters address the contentious and developing field of equitable compensation, including: the nature of equitable compensation; the relevant causation inquiry for equitable compensation; whether notions of contribution apply to multiple agents; accessorial liability; the role of discretion in limiting equitable compensation; which wrongs yield equitable compensation; and the extent to which compensation in equity differs from money remedies at common law. Other chapters examine the remedy of disgorgement of profit, and specifically the theoretical basis of that remedy, its application in the context of fiduciary obligations, and third-party issues. A number of chapters also examine the interrelationship between loss- and gain-based money relief. In addressing these issues the book includes both doctrinal and theoretical perspectives, and brings together leading equity scholars and judges from across the common law world.

Volume 21 in the series Hart Studies in Private Law

Equitable Compensation and Disgorgement of Profit

Edited by
Simone Degeling and Jason NE Varuhas

•HART•
PUBLISHING
OXFORD AND PORTLAND, OREGON
2017

Hart Publishing
An imprint of Bloomsbury Publishing Plc

Hart Publishing Ltd
Kemp House
Chawley Park
Cumnor Hill
Oxford OX2 9PH
UK

Bloomsbury Publishing Plc
50 Bedford Square
London
WC1B 3DP
UK

www.hartpub.co.uk
www.bloomsbury.com

Published in North America (US and Canada) by
Hart Publishing
c/o International Specialized Book Services
920 NE 58th Avenue, Suite 300
Portland, OR 97213-3786
USA

www.isbs.com

First published 2017

British Library Cataloguing-in-Publication Data
A catalogue record for this book is available from the British Library.

ISBN: HB: 978-1-50990-145-6
ePDF: 978-1-50990-147-0
ePub: 978-1-50990-146-3

Library of Congress Cataloging-in-Publication Data

Names: Degeling, Simone, editor. | Varuhas, Jason, editor.

Title: Equitable compensation and disgorgement of profit / edited by Simone Degeling and Jason Varuhas.

Description: Oxford [UK] ; Portland, Oregon : Hart Publishing, 2017. | Series: Hart studies in private law ; volume 21 | Includes bibliographical references and index. | Description based on print version record and CIP data provided by publisher; resource not viewed.

Identifiers: LCCN 2016047435 (print) | LCCN 2016046247 (ebook) | ISBN 9781509901463 (Epub) | ISBN 9781509901456 (hardback : alk. paper)

Subjects: LCSH: Equity. | Trusts and trustees. | Compensation (Law) | Rescission (Law) | Restitution.

Classification: LCC K795 (print) | LCC K795 .E65 2017 (ebook) | DDC 346/.004—dc23

LC record available at https://lccn.loc.gov/2016047435

Series: Hart Studies in Private Law, volume 21

Typeset by Compuscript Ltd, Shannon
Printed and bound in Great Britain by Lightning Source UK Ltd

CONTENTS

CONTRIBUTORS

Elise Bant is Professor of Law at the University of Melbourne.

Matthew Conaglen is Professor of Equity and Trusts at the University of Sydney.

Simone Degeling is Professor of Law at UNSW Law.

The Hon Justice James Edelman is a Justice of the High Court of Australia, Adjunct Professor of Law at the University of Queensland and Conjoint Professor of Law at UNSW Law.

Jamie Glister is Associate Professor of Law at the University of Sydney.

Andrew S Gold is Professor of Law at DePaul University.

Matthew Harding is Professor of Law at the University of Melbourne.

Lusina Ho is Professor of Equity and Trusts at the University of Hong Kong.

Jessica Hudson is Senior Lecturer in Law at UNSW Law.

James Penner is Professor of Law at the National University of Singapore.

Pauline Ridge is Associate Professor of Law at the Australian National University.

PG Turner is University Lecturer in Law and a Fellow of St Catharine's College in the University of Cambridge.

Jason NE Varuhas is Associate Professor of Law at the University of Melbourne.

The Hon Justice Julie Ward is a Justice of the New South Wales Court of Appeal.

TABLE OF CASES

Australia

Brunei Darussalam

Canada

Gibraltar

Hong Kong

Isle of Man

Jamaica

Malaysia

New Zealand

Saint Lucia

Singapore

Turks and Caicos Islands

United Kingdom

United States of America

West Indies

TABLE OF LEGISLATION

1

Equity's Personal Monetary Remedies

SIMONE DEGELING AND JASON NE VARUHAS

I. Introduction

Money remedies are part of equity's arsenal available in cases of fiduciary or trustee malefaction, breach of confidence or other equitable wrong. The defendant may be vulnerable to a personal claim requiring her to surrender any gains or otherwise pay the plaintiff a sum of money, such as an award of equitable compensation or pursuant to an account in common form or on the basis of her wilful default. Relief may also be granted on terms, such that the court makes pecuniary awards and adjustments consequent on equitable rescission.[1]

Modern equity is still coming to grips with how internally to order and make sense of these money remedies. Since the House of Lords decision in *Target Holdings v Redferns*[2] (which itself came after the Supreme Court of Canada in *Canson Enterprises Ltd v Boughton & Co*[3]) brought under the spotlight the modern remedy of equitable compensation, there have been decisions of the High Court of Australia in *Youyang Pty Ltd v Minter Ellison Morris Fletcher*,[4] the Hong Kong Court of Final Appeal in *Libertarian Investments Ltd v Hall*[5] and the Supreme Court of the United Kingdom in *AIB Group (UK) plc Ltd v Mark Redler*.[6] We are therefore entering a stage of rapid development in which these money remedies are given shape and some of the deeper structural controversies of equity must be confronted. Our hope is that this book may in some way contribute to this process. The chapters of this collection are the result of a colloquium held at UNSW Law in August 2015. As a book with many contributors, it has been impossible to cover

[1] Note that this book does not consider awards pursuant to the Chancery Amendment Act 1858, 21 & 22 Vict c 27 and present Commonwealth provisions such as *Supreme Court Act 1970* (NSW) s 68.

[2] [1996] AC 421 ('*Target*').

[3] [1991] 3 SCR 534.

[4] (2003) 212 CLR 484 ('*Youyang*').

[5] [2013] HCKFA 93.

[6] [2015] AC 1503 ('*AIB*').

every facet of the various forms of account or equitable compensation. However, there are in-depth contributions written by experts dealing with critical issues in the field.

II. Themes and Controversies

In order to facilitate understanding of the material presented in the book, it is necessary briefly to sketch recurring themes and controversies underlying all of the chapters. For ease of exposition, these are reduced to the following list, albeit that all are interlinked: (A) the historical roots of the remedies; (B) the nature of the rights being enforced; (C) the architecture of the particular remedies; and (D) the future.

A. The Historical Root of the Remedies

This book is entitled *Equitable Compensation and Disgorgement of Profit* reflecting the shared historical root of equitable compensation and account of profits in equitable accounting procedures.[7] As stated by a majority of the High Court of Australia: '[b]efore a party can be ordered to account, liability to account must be established.'[8] The foundation on which equity's intervention rests is that the parties fall into a relationship in which one is responsible in equity to the other for due administration of a fund. This accounting relationship includes trustee and beneficiary or custodial fiduciary and principal and arises where one controls property that she must hold and apply for another person's (eg the beneficiary or principal's) benefit.[9] As vividly explained by Professor Getzler, one of the means by which equity supervises and enforces the obligations of the accounting party is to require that party to give an account or 'to *narrate* what happened to the assets or affairs entrusted [to it]: to give an account of what [the accounting party] did

[7] These are well documented elsewhere. See generally: M Conaglen, 'Equitable Compensation for Breach of Trust: Off *Target*' (2016) 40(1) *Melbourne University Law Review* (advance); S Elliott, *Compensation Claims against Trustees* (D Phil Thesis, University of Oxford, 2002); S Elliott, 'Remoteness Criteria in Equity' (2002) 65 *MLR* 588; S Elliott and C Mitchell, 'Remedies for Dishonest Assistance' (2004) 67 *MLR* 16; S Elliott, 'Personal Monetary Claims' in J McGhee (ed), *Snell's Equity* (London, Sweet & Maxwell, 2015), 543–56; J Glister 'Equitable Compensation' in J Glister and P Ridge (eds), *Fault Lines in Equity* (Oxford, Hart Publishing, 2012) 143; C Mitchell, 'Equitable Compensation for Breach of Fiduciary Duty (2013) 66 *CLP* 307.

[8] *Associated Alloys Ltd v ACN 001 452 106* (2000) 202 CLR 588, [56] (Gaudron, McHugh, Gummow and Hayne JJ).

[9] C Mitchell, 'Stewardship of Property and Liability to Account' [2014] 78(3) Conv 215, 219; *Ultraframe (UK) Ltd v Fielding* [2005] EWHC 1638 (Ch), [1516] (Lewison J); *Bairstow v Queens Moat Houses Plc* [2001] EWCA Civ 712, [53] (Robert Walker LJ); *Agricultural Land Management v Jackson [No 2]* [2014] WASC 102, [334] ('*Agricultural*') (Edelman J).

with [their] trust. On the other side of the relationship, to take an *audit* is to *hear* what is told of the assets.'[10]

The taking of an account thus allows the beneficiaries of the fund to obtain information about the state of the fund and the assets in which the value of the fund might reside. Importantly, the accounting procedure also discloses any deficit or surplus in the fund. However, the accounting procedure is more than mere information gathering, it also allows for substantive orders. As explained by Austin J in *Glazier v Australian Men's Health* (No 2)[11]

> [i]t is important to distinguish between two kinds of orders. One kind (... an order for account of administration) is made where the overall administration of a business enterprise or fund or other property is to be established or accounted for. Another kind (... an order for an account of profits) is made to provide a remedy for specific equitable wrongdoing.

The first category, an order for account of administration, is divided into accounts in common form and accounts on the basis of wilful default. The second category, account of profits, is dealt with separately below.

i. Accounts of Administration

An account of administration in common form is available as of right to the beneficiary or principal. This 'requires the defendant to account *only for what he or she has actually received*, and his or her disbursement and distribution of it.'[12] The defendant trustee or fiduciary prepares the accounts, which the other parties may challenge, choosing either to falsify items or surcharge the account.

> A surcharge is the showing of an omission for which credit ought to have been given, while a falsification is the showing of a charge which has been wrongly inserted, the falsifying party alleging that money shown in the account as paid was either not paid or improperly paid.[13]

Following the taking of the common account, a money remedy may be required if there is a deficit in the fund. Thus, for example, if a trustee has paid away trust funds on personal expenditure, those entries in the accounts may be falsified. Similarly, the beneficiary may demonstrate the trustee has received funds in her personal capacity which ought to have been credited to the trust and surcharge the account. Subject to any good discharge or acceptable reasons for these entries

[10] J Getzler, '"As If." Accountability and Counterfactual Trust' (2013) 91 *Boston University Law Review* 973, 977 (emphasis in the original); *Ultraframe (UK) Ltd v Fielding* [2005] EWHC 1638 (Ch), [1513] (Lewison J): 'The taking of an account is the means by which a beneficiary requires the trustee to justify his stewardship of trust property. The trustee must show what he has done with that property.'

[11] [2001] NSWSC 6, [36].

[12] ibid [38] (emphasis added). See also *Meehan v Glazier Holdings Pty Ltd* (2002) 54 NSWLR 146, [13] (Giles JA): '[u]nder such an order the accounting party accounts only for what has actually been received and disposed of'.

[13] *Bilyak v Pesor* [2012] NSWSC 193, [38] (Hallen AsJ).

in the records, a court may conclude that the trust accounts should be altered to reflect the state of affairs consistent with the defendant's equitable obligations. Actual balances in value must then match financial records, and any deficit is made up out of the trustee's own pocket.

An account on the basis of wilful default is by contrast concerned with what the accounting party has not received.[14] As explained by Austin J in *Glazier Holdings*:

> [t]he order is 'entirely grounded on misconduct', the defendant being required to account not only for what he or she has received, but also for what he or she might have received had it not been for the default.[15]

The misconduct in question is that the trustee has 'through breach of trust … failed to obtain for the trust that which would have been obtained if the trustees' duties had been discharged.'[16] Thus 'wilful default is not co-extensive with breach of trust: there may be a breach of trust which is not wilful default.'[17] The liability of the accounting party is therefore for what should have been received. The account may be surcharged and taken as if the funds had been received and the defendant will be required to make good the difference from her own pocket. In making this determination, the court may conduct a 'roving enquiry'[18] examining the entirety of the trustee's management and administration.

Modern equity has diverted from the pattern described above in two ways. First, some cases such as *Target Holdings Ltd v Redferns*[19] are argued and decided on 'the liability of a trustee who commits a breach of trust to compensate beneficiaries for such a breach.'[20] There is no intermediate accounting process and the orders of the court are thus not directed to that procedure. When we speak about equitable compensation therefore, the term potentially encompasses the orders following a common account, account on the basis of wilful default and the direct claim for equitable compensation. As discussed below, it is a matter of debate the extent to which the existence of the direct claim for equitable compensation carries with it any differences in substantive principles applied by the Court when assessing the money remedy.

Secondly, there is some evidence that equitable compensation may be available even outside the traditional accounting relationships. In particular, custodial

[14] We are grateful to Matthew Conaglen for forcefully drawing out this distinction. See M Conaglen, 'Equitable Compensation for Breach of Trust: Off *Target*' (2016) 40(1) *Melbourne University Law Review* (advance).

[15] *Glazier v Australian Men's Health (No.2)* [2001] NSWSC 6, [39], quoting *Partington v Reynolds* (1858) 4 Drew 253, 255–6; 62 ER 98, 98–9. See also: *Byrnes v Kendle* (2011) 243 CLR 253, [43] (Gummow and Hayne JJ).

[16] *Meehan v Glazier Holdings Pty Ltd* (2002) 54 NSWLR 146, [65] (Giles JA).

[17] ibid.

[18] See, eg: *Carantinos v Magafas* [2008] NSWCA 304, [135](Campbell JA). There are also references to 'roving commission'. See, eg: *Bartlett v Barclays Bank Trust Co Ltd [No 2]* [1980] 1 Ch 539, 546 (Brightman LJ).

[19] *Target* (n 2).

[20] ibid, 428 (Lord Browne-Wilkinson). In the same vein see *AIB* (n 6).

fiduciary relationships, in which the fiduciary has control of the fund for the benefit of the principal, fall into the traditional analysis. However, controversially, it may be that even outside these custodial relationships equitable compensation is also available. This is shown by cases on financial advisers and other pockets of cases in which the remedy has been awarded. In relation to financial advisers, an example is *ABN AMRO Bank NV v Bathurst Regional Council*.[21] Equitable compensation was claimed by local councils which had purchased Rembrandt Notes from, and on the advice of, a financial intermediary LGFS. The existence of a fiduciary relationship of adviser and advisee was found on the facts,[22] which was breached, there being a conflict of duty and self-interest. Equitable compensation for breach of fiduciary duty was held to be available.[23] It is not clear on the facts that LGFS stood in a custodial relationship to the plaintiff councils and this issue is not directly addressed in the Court's reasoning. Similarly in *CBA v Smith*[24] the bank manager of the branch of the bank where the plaintiff conducted his banking business gave financial advice to the plaintiff about the value and viability of a prospective investment in a hotel. The owner of the hotel was also a customer of the bank, thus bringing into play a duty-duty conflict of fiduciary duty. The failure of the bank manager to obtain informed consent to the conflicted engagement 'leads equity to afford its remedies for breach of duty, including that of compensation.'[25] Of course, it may be possible to argue that the bank had custody of the plaintiff's funds. However, the fiduciary relationship breached lay beyond the care and control of funds and arose in virtue of financial advice provided by the bank manager. Again, the need for a custodial relationship was not specifically addressed by the Court.

In addition, as discussed by Dr Turner in Chapter 14, considering that modern actions for breach of confidence outside of contract are wholly equitable, so are the available remedies. One of these is the equitable remedy of compensation.[26] This is despite the fact that the relationship of confidence may or may not mirror the traditional accounting relationship. As Turner points out, analogies with account and express trust are 'prone to collapse' since confidential information is not a trust asset and in relation to fiduciary analogies, not every fiduciary has custodial obligations. Similarly, Jessica Hudson in Chapter 11 points out that equitable compensation may be awarded as a remedial response to equitable estoppels. The equitable estoppels she examines include proprietary and promissory estoppel, the remit of neither being limited to accounting relationships. Thus, the money award following an equitable estoppel is another site of equitable compensation beyond

[21] [2014] FCAFC 65, [1084].
[22] ibid [1066], [1069].
[23] ibid [1090]–[1098].
[24] (1991) 42 FCR 390.
[25] ibid 394 (the Court).
[26] See, for example: *Smith Kline & French Laboratories (Aust) Limited v Secretary, Department of Community Services & Health* (1990) 22 FCR 73, 83 (Gummow J).

a breach of trust or custodial fiduciary obligation. Justice Ward in Chapter 4 also draws attention to this aspect of the modern remedy of equitable compensation, emphasising that the remedy is not confined to 'such breaches of trust or custodial fiduciary obligations.' She points out that equitable compensation has, amongst other claims, been awarded for unconscionable conduct[27] and undue influence.[28]

ii. Account of Profits for Equitable Wrongs

An account of profits is a process of accounting resulting in a monetary order requiring an equitable wrongdoer to surrender any gain made through misconduct. As explained by the High Court of Australia in *Warman International v Dwyer*[29] 'in determining the proper basis for an account of profits, it is of first importance … to ascertain precisely what it was that was acquired in consequence of the fiduciary's breach of duty'. Thus there may be discretionary adjustments to allow for the care and skill of the defaulting fiduciary[30] and other adjustments on the basis of equity's general commission to ensure a 'fair and equitable assessment' of the 'whole of the benefits acquired by [the defendant] through … breach of fiduciary duty.'[31] The list of equitable wrongs for which this form of personal liability is available is contentious. At the core are breach of fiduciary duty and those who knowingly assist or receive property through breach of fiduciary duty or trust. There is a debate beyond the scope of this book as to the nature and availability of this remedy to cover other civil wrongs, including breach of contract and property torts.[32]

[27] J Ward, 'Equitable Compensation-An Overview', Ch 4 of this book, fn 46 citing *Karam v ANZ Banking Group Ltd* [2001] NSWSC 709, [425]–[428] (Santow J) reversed on other grounds *Australia & New Zealand Banking Group Ltd v Karam* (2005) 64 NSWLR 149 but noting McLure J (as her Honour then was) expressed doubt as to the availability of the remedy in this context in *Australia & New Zealand Banking Group Ltd v Dzienciol* [2001] WASC 305, [413]. See also: *In the matter of Kevin Jocobsen Pty Limited* [2016] NSWSC 538, [47] (Black J) noting instances where equitable compensation had been awarded for unconscionable dealing albeit not needing to decide the issue to deal with the application before the court including *Tillett v Varnell Holdings Pty Ltd* [2009] NSWSC 1040, [101] in which Brereton J would have 'ordered equitable compensation for unconscionable dealing, had it been established, where other remedies were not appropriate.': *In the matter of Kevin Jocobsen Pty Limited* [2016] NSWSC 538, [47] (Black J).

[28] Ward, ibid, fn 47 citing *Smith v Glegg* [2005] 1 Qd R 561 and *Mahoney v Purnell* [1996] 3 All ER 61. There is a debate beyond the scope of this chapter as to the juridical nature of undue influence, in particular whether or not undue influence is a form of equitable wrongdoing or some other legal event. See generally: J Edelman and E Bant, *Unjust Enrichment*, 2nd edn, (Oxford, Hart Publishing, 2016) ch 10.

[29] (1995) 182 CLR 544, 565 (the Court) ('*Warman*').

[30] *Phipps v Boardman* [1964] 1 WLR 993 (Ch); *Warman*, 558. See generally: M Harding, 'Justifying Fiduciary Allowances' in A Robertson and Tang HW (eds), *The Goals of Private Law* (Oxford, Hart Publishing, 2009) 341.

[31] *Warman* 567–568 (the Court).

[32] In relation to contract, see: *Attorney-General v Blake* [2011] 1 AC 268; *Hospitality Group Pty Ltd v Australian Rugby Union Ltd* (2001) 110 FCR 157. In relation to tort, see: *Edwards v Lee's Administrator* 96 SW 2d 1028 (Ky Ct App, 1936); *Olwen v Nye & Nissen Co* 173 P 2d 652 (Wash, 1946). Note that

B. The Nature of the Rights Being Enforced

A fault line running through private law is the distinction between primary and secondary rights or between the primary rights which when infringed give rise to secondary remedial rights. For example, as explained by Lord Diplock in *Photo Production Ltd v Securicor Transport Ltd*[33] in relation to a claim for breach of contract:

> Leaving aside those comparatively rare cases in which the court is able to enforce a primary obligation by decreeing specific performance of it, breaches of primary obligations give rise to substituted or secondary obligations on the part of the party in default, and, in some cases, may entitle the other party to be relieved from further performance of his own primary obligations. These secondary obligations of the contract breaker and any concomitant relief of the other party from his own primary obligations also arise by implication of law—generally common law, but sometimes statute .... Every failure to perform a primary obligation is a breach of contract. The secondary obligation on the part of the contract breaker to which it gives rise by implication of the common law is to pay monetary compensation to the other party for the loss sustained by him in consequence of the breach...[34]

The distinction between primary and secondary rights has a pedigree stretching back to Austin and beyond.[35] However, modern debates rage about the nature of the relationship between rights and remedies.[36] In particular, the traditional 'monist' view which posits a high degree of correlation between a remedy and its associated right, such that the remedy is congruent or replicative of the primary right. The alternative is the 'dualist' position by which remedies are transformative based on a high degree of judicial discretion. Thus, once liability has been determined,

these are in relation to account of profits in the sense of disgorgement. The remedy 'strip[s] a profit' made by the defendant through wrongful conduct rather than restitutionary damages in the sense of 'the objective gain received by the defendant which has been wrongfully transferred from the claimant.' See J Edelman, *Gain-Based Damages: Contract, Tort, Equity and Intellectual Property* (Oxford, Hart Publishing, 2002), 1.

33 [1980] AC 827 (HL).

34 ibid 847–49.

35 J Austin, *Lectures In Jurisprudence*, 3rd edn,(R Campbell ed, London, John Murray, 1869), 44–7 and 795–800. See generally: B Rudden, 'Correspondence' (1990) 10 *OJLS* 288; P Birks, 'Definition and Division: A Meditation on *Institutes* 3.13' in P Birks (ed), *The Classification of Obligations* (Oxford, Oxford University Press, 1997), 23–4.

36 See generally: P Birks, 'Three Kinds of Objection to Discretionary Remedialism' (2000) 29 *University of Western Australia Law Review* 1; P Finn, 'Equitable Doctrine and Discretion in Remedies' in WR Cornish et al (eds), *Restitution: Past, Present & Future* (Oxford, Hart Publishing, 1998) 251; G Hammond, 'Rethinking Remedies: The Changing Nature of the Conception of the Relationship Between Legal and Equitable Remedies' in J Berryman (ed), *Remedies: Issues and Perspectives* (Toronto, Carswell, 1991) 1; R Zakrewski, *Remedies Reclassified* (Oxford, Oxford University Press, 2005); S Smith, 'Why Courts Make Orders (And What This Tells us About Damages)' (2011) 64 *Current Legal Problems* 51; S Smith, 'Duties, Liabilities and Damages' (2012) 125 *Harvard Law Review* 1272 and J Penner and K Quek, 'The Law's Remedial Norms' (2016) 28 *Singapore Academy of Law Journal* 768.

the court grants the most appropriate remedy according to the facts and circumstances of the case. There is an intermediate position by which analytical distinctions between primary rights and remedies are maintained, albeit that there is a strong but not absolute link between the primary and secondary right.[37]

Irrespective of one's views on the role of discretion in determining the appropriate remedy, an understanding of the distinction between a primary and secondary or a primary and remedial right is fundamental to understanding the landscape of equitable money remedies. It is imperative to distinguish between liabilities arising from breaches of equitable obligation, such as breach of trust or fiduciary duty and liabilities which arise independently of the equitable wrong. For example, it is relatively straightforward to conceive of the equitable remedy of specific performance as a means of exercising or fulfilling the plaintiff's primary right to performance of the underlying obligation. The same logic underpins the creditor who enforces a debt. The plaintiff seeks a money remedy, but the underlying right being enforced is the primary right to performance. This contrasts, for example, with the plaintiff who claims compensatory damages for breach of contract. Damages are also a monetary remedy, but in this instance the right to damages only arises because of the existence of the wrong of breach of contract. The right being realised is a secondary or remedial right.

Differentiating between primary rights and remedial rights is at the heart of the terminology which divides cases according to the labels 'substitutive compensation' and 'reparative compensation'. As explained by Edelman J in *Agricultural Land Management v Jackson [No 2]*[38] these terms are suggested by Dr Steven Elliott

> whose writing has shone light and brought much clarity to this area of the law … [Substitutive compensation is] based on the common account, [and] describes a claim for the substituted value of the asset dissipated without authority: it demands that the trustee perform his or her duty to maintain the assets or fund. [Reparative compensation is] based on the account on the basis of wilful default, [and] describes a claim for reparation for the loss suffered by breach of duty.[39]

The use of the terms reparative compensation and substitutive compensation is not without controversy.[40] However, leaving aside labelling what is vital is to engage with the substance of the remedies involved. The distinction between performance and loss, or debt and damage, is explored by Justice Edelman in Chapter 5, Professor Penner in Chapter 7 and Professor Ho in Chapter 8. The axis

[37] See generally: K Barker, 'Rescuing Remedialism in Unjust Enrichment Law: Why Remedies are Right' (1998) 57 *CLJ* 301, 323, 326–27.

[38] [2014] WASC 102.

[39] ibid [349].

[40] See, for example: JD Heydon, MJ Leeming and PG Turner, *Meagher Gummow and Lehane's Equity Doctrines and Remedies* 5th edn, (Sydney, LexisNexis Butterworths, 2015), [23-610]–[23-615] which does not support their use and M Congalen, 'Equitable Compensation for Breach of Trust: *Off Target*' (2016) *MULR* (advance), text to footnote 146, is of the view that the: 'new labels add little to a clear understanding of the principles'.

of debate in each chapter is the decision of the United Kingdom Supreme Court in *AIB Group (UK) plc v Mark Redler & Co.*[41] AIB agreed to lend £3.3 million to the borrowers to be secured by a mortgage on their home, at that time valued at £4.25 million. The property was already encumbered by an existing charge securing a debt of £1.5 million in favour of Barclays Bank, and it was a condition of AIB's loan that the existing charges be redeemed on or before completion of the AIB loan transaction. Mark Redler & Co was a firm of solicitors acting for both the borrower and AIB. AIB transferred the funds to Mark Redler to hold on trust pending completion of the transaction, including an instruction that Mark Redler obtain for AIB a fully enforceable first ranked legal charge over the property. In error, Mark Redler only paid Barclays £1.2 million which meant that the Barclays debt could not be fully discharged and AIB was registered as a second chargee. Further, Mark Redler released the balance of the £3.3 million to the borrower who subsequently defaulted on paying their debt and were declared bankrupt. Security over the property was enforced but property values had fallen, and in result AIB realised approximately £868,000, substantially less than the amount advanced.

AIB commenced proceedings against Mark Redler for the entire loan amount of £3.3 million, less the sale proceeds. AIB argued Mark Redler had acted in breach of trust and or fiduciary duty and sought equitable compensation to restore the fund. This obligation, it was argued, was not limited by questions of causation or remoteness but flowed from the trustee's duty to account and the beneficiary's corresponding right to falsify the account. Mark Redler counter argued by pointing out that AIB's actual loss was in the vicinity of £300,000. Mark Redler submitted that its liability should be limited to this figure, representing the actual loss suffered by AIB in Mark Redler not doing what it ought to have done in paying out the Barclays charge and obtaining for AIB a first ranked security. In result, the Supreme Court unanimously agreed with Mark Redler. The leading judgments were delivered by Lord Toulson and Lord Reed who each rejected reasoning founded on equity's accounting procedures and AIB's right to falsify the account. Instead, at least in a commercial context,[42] equitable compensation was limited by a causal link between the beneficiary's loss and the breach of duty.[43] The amount of compensation due to AIB was the difference between the value of the first ranking security and the value of security obtained, which was postponed to Barclays (approximately £273,777).

Justice Edelman postulates that the case did not follow a long established orthodoxy at common law, reflected also in like concepts in equity, which is the distinction between debt and damages. In so doing, he argues the case represents a misturning in the English law governing money awards in equity and considers reasons why other jurisdictions, principally Australian courts, might not take this

41 *AIB* (n 6).

42 *AIB* (n 6) [70] [102] (Lord Toulson JSC), [136] (Lord Reed JSC). Lord Neuberger PSC, Baroness Hale DPSC and Lord Wilson JSC agreed with Lord Toulson and Lord Reed JJSC.

43 *AIB* (n 6) [63]–[65], [73] (Lord Toulson JSC); [134], [140] (Lord Reed JSC).

path. He considers that the Supreme Court, following the manner in which the case was pleaded and argued, conceptualised as a claim for compensation for loss consequential upon breach of a primary duty that which could have been conceptualised as a claim akin to a debt—ie a claim for an order which would secure performance of a primary duty. Such conceptualisation is encouraged by appeal to an undifferentiated and generic notion of 'equitable compensation' to describe what may be quite different types of money award in equity. Some equitable awards such as those in cases of wilful default are properly characterised as loss-based, and thus implicate an inquiry into loss, factual and legal causation and mitigation. But other types of money award, such as that which may be ordered to follow an account of administration in common form, are in the nature of a debt in equity arising from an unauthorised disbursement. In order to make out his claims Edelman undertakes detailed analysis of both *AIB* and the earlier House of Lords decision in *Target Holdings v Redferns*,[44] and considers the prospects that those decisions may influence Australian law. He goes on to consider the legal position at law and in equity in a case where the unauthorised transfer is of an asset, such as shares, rather than money, and where a debt at common law cannot therefore be said to arise (and specific performance would be unavailable). He concludes that an equitable award which substitutes for performance of the duty to maintain the non-money asset—as opposed to a loss-based award—would be available.

Professor Penner in Chapter 7 and Professor Ho in Chapter 8 also engage with the reasoning of the court in *AIB*, but nonetheless attempt to justify and reconcile the outcome in that case by reference to established principle. One of the persistent criticisms of the case is that, had traditional falsification principles been applied, AIB would have been entitled to falsify the account when Mark Redler advanced the funds to Barclays and the borrower. This would potentially have resulted in an obligation binding Mark Redler in common account to restore the fund. Instead Mark Redler was held liable only to pay a lesser amount representing the loss in the value of AIB's security. However, Penner argues that, on a completely orthodox understanding of the principles of falsification, including the beneficiary's right to adopt a misapplication of trust funds by the trustee, Mark Redler should have escaped liability entirely. This analysis depends on a close reading of the facts of *AIB* and suggests that AIB adopted, accepted or later ratified the expenditure of funds to Barclays as a 'disbursement on [its] behalf'. To this extent, Penner argues that AIB's argument for restoration of the account was misconceived: there was no account to restore since by AIB's conduct in taking the disbursements to be applications of its own money, the trust was thereby brought to an end. Penner also points out that one of the difficulties post *AIB* is to know the limits of the ratio of that case, in particular whether a beneficiary is barred in all cases from falsifying the account, and being required to go down the path of proving loss. His chapter further explores the extent to which beneficiaries are generally disentitled from falsifying the account and only pursuing a claim for consequential loss.

[44] *Target* (n 2).

Professor Ho in Chapter 8 also considers the result in *AIB* and asks first whether the result in the case may nonetheless be justified by applying orthodox principles of falsification and secondly by examining the underlying policy justifications of the traditional accounting principles of surcharge and falsification in order to determine the extent to which these policies might be served by the case law post *AIB*. In relation to the application of orthodox principles, Ho points out that AIB could be regarded as having partially affirmed the unauthorised transfers and made a personal claim for the shortfall in the misapplied amount after affirmation. In this way, she attempts to reconcile the result in the case with traditional principles of falsification.

Ho's argument from policy rests on the observation that the principle articulated by Lord Toulson, that 'the basic purpose of any remedy [is] to put the beneficiary in the same position as if the breach had not occurred',[45] does not *of itself* compel compensation of but for losses. Thus, Ho interrogates whether what she identifies as equity's policies of protecting the beneficiary's expectation of performance and deterring trustee failures might be accommodated within this principle, such that a monetary award consonant with specific enforcement of the underlying obligation might also be available. Equally, she argues that there may be situations where specific enforcement might operate harshly on a trustee. For example, where the sole and absolute beneficiary has determined how a trust is to be invested, Ho argues the beneficiary should have some responsibility for 'bringing about a depletion' in the trust. In this instance, she argues an approach emphasising compensation of loss is sufficient.

There may also be third parties implicated in the wrong of breach of trust or breach of fiduciary obligation. This wrongful conduct by the third party similarly gives rise to a remedial or secondary right. The position of third parties is scrutinised by Associate Professor Glister in Chapter 9 and Associate Professor Ridge in Chapter 10. Glister focuses on the trustee or fiduciary required to disgorge a gain as having been received as a knowing recipient. He argues that care is required in the conclusion that knowing recipients are required to disgorge 'profits'. Drawing a distinction between 'traceable profits' and 'discrete profits', Glister suggests that it is not inherent in the finding of liability for knowing receipt that the defendant should be liable to disgorge discrete profits. Further, he argues that in contrast with the elements of liability based in assistance and procurement which ensure a sufficient level of blameworthiness, recipient liability arises on a relatively low level of knowledge and thus should not necessarily be subject to the same or automatic parallel remedial outcome of disgorging discrete profits.

Ridge considers money remedies for equitable participatory liability, encompassing within that term accessory liability for procuring, assisting or otherwise facilitating an equitable wrong and recipient liability, for knowing receipt

[45] *AIB* (n 6) [64].

of trust property for personal benefit in breach of trust or fiduciary duty.[46] She points out that the defendant's liability is derivative of the primary wrong in that the initial breach of duty is required in order to establish liability. However, the participant's liability does not duplicate that of the primary wrongdoer. In consequence, Ridge argues that it is not necessarily the case that the full range of remedies available against the defaulting trustee or fiduciary ought *or ought not* to be available against the participant. Rather, the answer will depend on the rationale and purpose of the participant's own liability. In so doing her chapter also highlights the joint and several nature of participatory liability for equitable compensation, in which the participant may share in the liability of the trustee or fiduciary.

The functional distinction between performance of an underlying obligation and the loss which flows from the failure to perform that obligation also forms the central plank of Jessica Hudson's examination in Chapter 11 of equitable compensation awarded in the area of equitable estoppels. Hudson bases her analysis on proprietary estoppel and promissory estoppel and argues that any pattern of variation in equitable compensation in these categories may be explained by the extent of the equity in each case and the form of relief considered appropriate. In particular, whether or not in awarding equitable compensation the court is purporting to compensate the plaintiff's loss or as a substitute for specific relief. Further, as is highlighted below, one important consequence of Hudson's analysis is that it allows the observation that the internal architecture of equitable compensation following an equitable estoppel does not need to accommodate limits on the defendant's liability through devices such as causation, since there are built into the prior step of satisfying the elements of the equitable estoppel mechanisms which do this work.

Dr Turner in Chapter 12 moves beyond narrow debates over the measures of equitable compensation to examine the availability and assessment of compensatory money awards for breach of equitable obligations of confidence. Through a detailed doctrinal exposition of case law drawn from across common law jurisdictions, Turner distils the fundamental principles governing such awards and argues the quantum of relief is that necessary 'to discharge the defaulting confidant's obligations of confidence' such that where a confider 'suffers a financial loss' by reason of the defendant's breach of an equitable obligation of confidence, 'the

[46] P Ridge, 'Monetary Remedies for Equitable Participatory Liability: General Principles and Current Questions' Ch 10 of this book, citing in fn 1: in relation to Australia *Farah Constructions Pty Limited v Say-Dee Pty Limited* (2007) 230 CLR 89; *Grimaldi v Chameleon Mining NL (No 2)* (2012) 200 FCR 296. In England, see in relation to accessory liability: *Twinsectra Ltd v Yardley* [2002] 2 AC 164 (adopting *Royal Brunei Airlines Sdn Bhd v Tan* [1995] 2 AC 378 (PC); *Abou-Rahmah v Abacha* [2007] Bus LR 220 (CA) (adopting subsequent clarification by the Privy Council in *Barlow Clowes International Ltd (in liquidation) v Eurotrust International Ltd* [2006] 1 WLR 1476 (PC)); and in relation to recipient liability: *Bank of Credit and Commerce International (Overseas) Ltd v Akindele* [2001] Ch 437 (CA).

confider ought to have a prima facie entitlement to recover compensation for those losses the confider would not have suffered had the obligation of conscience been kept.' Turner's chapter is a significant contribution to understanding of equitable compensation given the relatively recent development of the judge-made law protecting confidences in equity and, linked to this, the lack of general statements of principle by appellate courts. But through this doctrinal exegesis Turner also sheds light on the fundamental nature of the remedy as one that is (and ought to be) distinctly equitable in character. He finds that the reason why rules and principles governing the remedy have often been obscured is because of 'category errors'—compensatory awards for breach of the equitable duty of confidence have been confused with damages awards for common law wrongs which are underpinned by normative concerns distinct from those which underpin the equitable duty, while judicial flight to discretion has exacerbated the confusions that have often bedevilled this field.

The same fault line between primary right and secondary or remedial right may also explain an account of profits, at least as awarded against fiduciaries. Key to this argument is accepting the position that the fiduciary prohibition against conflicts stands separately to that against profit.[47] Additionally, it invites scrutiny of the conventional view which is that breach of prohibition against conflict and making a profit are each equitable wrongs. For example, Professor Lionel Smith elsewhere argues that the paramount fiduciary obligation is one of loyalty, which is necessarily imposed by law to control decision-making power held for or on behalf of another person.[48] On this view, the no-conflict and the no-profit rules exist to support and complete the requirement of loyalty. The no-conflict rules concern potentially tainted exercises in fiduciary judgement, and ensure that this judgement is not conflicted by self-interest or competing interests.[49] Smith controversially argues that the no-profit rule is a rule of primary attribution such that whenever property is acquired in relevant circumstances, the fiduciary is as a matter of primary obligation required to 'render the profit to the beneficiary'.[50] Thus on this model, the fiduciary obligation to account for a profit 'is not one that attaches a sanction to wrongdoing; it simply attributes the gain as a matter

[47] See generally: R Nolan, '*Regal (Hastings) Ltd v Gulliver*' in C Mitchell and P Mitchell (eds), *Landmark Cases in Equity* (Oxford, Hart Publishing, 2012), 499, 520–27. Nolan argues that the rule prohibiting unauthorised profit is a 'buttress' to the rules against conflict between duty and interest. Rather than adopt a rule, for example, which controls managerial discretion by open textured positive duties such as a duty to act in the best interests of the other, which are difficult to apply and may unduly inhibit decision making, Nolan suggests that managerial discretion should stand but is instead be curtailed if 'inherently risky'. The rule against unauthorised profit guards against the risk of latent and unarticulated conflicts which might otherwise go unremedied.

[48] L Smith, 'Fiduciary relationships: ensuring the loyal exercise of judgment on behalf of another' (2014) 130 *LQR* 608.

[49] The no-conflict rule is thus not on this model an equitable wrong, but rather a vitiated transfer voidable by the beneficiary and primarily remedied through rescission. See Smith ibid, 623–25.

[50] Smith (n 48) 628.

of primary right to the beneficiary.'[51] It is in the context of this debate that the following questions arise: what are the functions of the fiduciary prohibitions against conflict and profit and when may the plaintiff require the defendant to disgorge her gain? These questions are examined by Professor Harding in Chapter 2 and Professor Gold in Chapter 3.

Professor Harding seeks to carry forward our understanding of the no profit rule in fiduciary law by propounding and exploring a conception of fiduciary loyalty as fidelity. On an account of loyalty as fidelity, being loyal entails being true to one's pursuits and relationships by engaging in them according to their own terms; this conception of loyalty is distinct from conceptions that equate loyalty with partiality. Harding argues that loyalty as fidelity in the context of fiduciary relationships involves a true commitment, on the part of the fiduciary, to norms of selflessness, and among the applicable norms of selflessness is that one ought not to profit from the fiduciary relationship. On Harding's view the no profit rule in fiduciary law facilitates fidelity to norms of selflessness by helping to create conditions under which fiduciaries will be loyal. It does this by providing guarantees to principals that fiduciary action will, to an extent, conform to norms of selflessness and through the rule's expressive effects. Harding goes on to consider some implications of his argument, including its ramifications for deterrence-based rationales for the no profit rule, for our understanding of awards of equitable allowances to fiduciaries who breach the rule, and for the contentious question of whether fiduciary law ought to have no conflict disgorgement rules distinct from the no profit rule.

In his chapter Professor Gold takes the disgorgement remedy in fiduciary law as a basis for considering whether there may be circumstances in which it may be morally wrongful for a plaintiff to seek a remedy despite their claim for redress nonetheless being justified on the basis of principles of justice. Gold seeks to defend the counterintuitive thesis that it is indeed correct that justice can be wrongful and that norms of justice that authorise wrongful conduct may be legitimate. Thus, he considers that in some cases where a plaintiff claims the powerful remedy of disgorgement of profit for breach of fiduciary duty in circumstances where the defendant acted in good faith, was seeking to advance the plaintiff's interests, and caused the plaintiff no loss through their breach, the plaintiff may be at the same time seeking a remedy that is just and acting morally wrongfully in pursuing that remedy. Having established his claim Gold goes on to consider its implications, postulating that courts should countenance wrongful justice, but not in all cases.

[51] Smith (n 48) 630. See also: J Penner, 'Is Loyalty a Virtue, and Even If It Is, Does It Really Help Explain Fiduciary Liability' in A Gold and P Miller (eds), *Philosophical Foundations of Fiduciary Law* (Oxford, Oxford University Press, 2014), 159, 171 '… the law of fiduciary accountability is akin to the law of unjust enrichment. Both are cases of *primary, remedial* duties. … a fiduciary has no duty not to act in conflict of interest, but when they do and acquire a gain thereby, they fall under a duty to account for the gain to their principal.' (emphasis in original).

C. The Architecture of the Particular Remedies

Equitable compensation is an equitable money remedy which brings into view the court's need to undertake a valuation exercise. Connected to the question of whether or not the right being realised by the plaintiff is primary or secondary is therefore an understanding of the architecture of the remedy, and the choice of factors affecting the court's assessment. In particular, there is a debate as to whether and to what extent equity applies causation rules and related conceptual apparatus such as a doctrine of remoteness of loss to give shape to the remedy. Similarly, the extent to which an award of equitable compensation may be reduced on account of the plaintiff's own conduct via some type of apportionment and whether there is any obligation on the plaintiff to mitigate her loss.[52] In addition, all equitable money remedies occur within the realm of equitable discretion to award and fashion relief to meet the equity of the case.

In relation to factual causation, an approach which (contrary to that taken in *AIB*) separately identifies an obligation to perform the underlying duty (albeit in substituted form) from an obligation to make good loss allows for an observation that there is no causation inquiry in relation to substitutive compensation. As stated by Edelman J in *Agricultural*:

> that "but for" question [referring to causation] is irrelevant when the duty is to replenish a distribution of unauthorised trust funds. Like instances of payment of a debt, or of specific performance, it does not matter whether the funds would have been lost in any event.[53]

The position in relation to equitable compensation for loss is less coherent. In relation to breaches of an equitable obligation of care and skill[54] and breaches of fiduciary duty,[55] it is tolerably clear that a 'but for' test applies, pursuant to which on a common sense test of causation, the defendant is required to make good those losses which are caused by the breach of duty. As emphasised by Edelman J in *Agricultural*, 'it is difficult to see how "common sense" could be different in common law and equity'[56] and must in any case be approached with caution such

[52] The answers to these questions may in turn be informed by the view of the relationship between common law and equity, and the extent to which equity is permitted to develop 'by analogy' with the common law. See generally: *Harris v Digital Pulse* (2003) 56 NSWLR 298 (NSWCA); Sir A Mason, 'Fusion' in S Degeling and J Edelman (eds), *Equity in Commercial Law* (Sydney, Lawbook Co, 2005) 11; J Getzler, 'Am I My Beneficiary's Keeper?: Fusion and Loss-Based Fiduciary Remedies' in S Degeling and J Edelman (eds), *Equity in Commercial Law* (Sydney, Lawbook Co, 2005) 239; A Burrows, 'Remedial Coherence and Punitive Damages in Equity' in S Degeling and J Edelman (eds), *Equity in Commercial Law* (Sydney, Lawbook Co, 2005) 381.

[53] *Agricultural* (n 9) [344]. See also [337] and [395].

[54] *Permanent Building Society (in liq) v Wheeer* (1994) 11 WAR 187, [45] (Ipp J). Malcolm CJ and Seaman J agreed with the reasons of Ipp J.

[55] *Maguire v Makaronis* (1997) 188 CLR 449, 468 (Brennan CJ, Gaudron, McHugh and Gummow JJ); *Youyang* (n 4), [46] (the Court) quoting *Target* (n 2), 436 (Lord Browne Wilkinson).

[56] *Agricultural* (n 9) [396].

that the test is 'contextualised and supported by reasoned explanation so that it does not become a shroud which obscures teleological reasoning'.[57] The 'but for' test plays a role within a 'common sense approach' in excluding causes. Thus it is a negative criterion, satisfaction of which is a necessary but not sufficient connection demonstrating that 'the plaintiff's loss would not have been suffered but for the plaintiff's breach of duty.'[58] In relation to equitable compensation for equitable estoppels, Hudson argues that causation (and indeed remoteness, foreseeability and mitigation) are 'rendered functionally redundant' within equitable estoppels since irrespective the type of equitable estoppel in view, in order to establish the estoppel the plaintiff must demonstrate an unfulfilled expectation and the extent to which the defendant's conduct caused detriment to the plaintiff. Thus, there is no separate requirement for causation.

Part of the difficulty in understanding causation in equitable compensation for breach of fiduciary duty has been to accommodate an alternative approach to causation said to be rooted in a 'duty' binding the fiduciary to disclose material facts.[59] This approach is associated with the following advice given by Lord Thankerton (speaking for the Privy Council) in *Brickenden v London Loan & Savings Co*:[60]

> When a party, holding a fiduciary relationship, commits a breach of fiduciary duty by non-disclosure of material facts, which his constituent is entitled to know in connection with the transaction, he cannot be heard to maintain that disclosure would not have altered the decision to proceed with the transaction, because the constituent's action would be solely determined by some other factor, such as the valuation by another party of the property proposed to be mortgaged. Once the Court has determined that the non-disclosed facts were material, speculation as to what course the constituent, on disclosure, would have taken, is not relevant.[61]

Professor Conaglen in Chapter 6 directly addresses Lord Thankerton's dictum and its impact on the correct approach for causation when a plaintiff seeks equitable compensation for loss. Through a careful historical analysis of the case, Conaglen argues that the key to understanding *Brickenden* is to appreciate the significance of the counterfactual state of affairs against which the conduct of the fiduciary is to be measured. He posits that in a standard fiduciary breach case, there are at least two counterfactual scenarios to consider in identifying loss: one in which the fiduciary did not act in breach of duty and one in which the fiduciary obtains the informed consent of the principal. Relying on what he identifies as fiduciary

[57] ibid [393]. See generally: J Allsop, 'Causation in Commercial Law' in S Degeling, J Edelman and J Goudkamp (eds), *Torts in Commercial Law* (Sydney, LawBook Co, 2011), 269; J Stapleton, 'Reflections on Common Sense Causation in Australia' in S Degeling, J Edelman and J Goudkamp (eds), *Torts in Commercial Law* (Sydney, LawBook Co, 2011) 331.

[58] *Agricultural* (n 9) [394].

[59] *Short v Crawley (No 30)* [2007] NSWSC 1322, [427]–[428] (White J). The standing of *Brickenden* was not commented on on appeal: *Crawley v Short* [2009] NSWCA 410.

[60] [1934] 3 DLR 465 (PC).

[61] ibid 469.

doctrine's 'deterrent approach ... in implementing its subsidiary and prophylactic form of protection for non-fiduciary duties' he ultimately concludes equity prefers a posture according to which the fiduciary is kept to her duty by not being permitted to escape liability in accessing the alternate counterfactual according to which disclosure and the consent of the principal is obtained. Thus Conaglen argues Lord Thankerton's dictum requires that a fiduciary who has acted in breach of the prohibition against conflict(s) or profit cannot 'rely on the counterfactual which considers what would have happened if the fiduciary had made full disclosure.' Instead, the counterfactual which will apply is what would have happened if the fiduciary *had not* acted in a conflicted manner or *had not* taken the profit. In this way Conaglen's analysis attempts to integrate Lord Thankerton's dictum into analysis by locating it not as an exceptional case in which a different test of causation is applied, but rather as making explicit the counterfactual against which the assessment of the principal's loss should be measured.

The role of judicial discretion in awarding equitable compensation is addressed by Professor Degeling in Chapter 14. She separates her analysis into two functionally discrete inquiries. First, those factors traditionally analysed as bars to relief or considerations bearing on the exercise of equitable discretion in deciding whether and on what terms to award an equitable remedy. Discretion is notable here in that it often operates as a reason *in favour* of the award of compensation to the extent that compensation may be preferred over, for example, a proprietary remedy. Secondly, a particular exercise of equitable discretion in calculation of equitable compensation for loss of a chance. In this category Degeling argues that equity engages a principle directed to making certain the principal's loss and other adjustments reflecting the burdens which would have been incurred by the principal had the profit been pursued. In this respect her analysis separates certainty of loss from causation, thus articulating a discrete factor in the court's assessment. Discretionary considerations are also dealt with by Ridge, Turner and Hudson in their examinations respectively of participatory liability and equitable compensation for breach of confidence and equitable estoppels.

Professor Bant's chapter considers the nature of pecuniary awards and adjustments, including indemnity orders, consequent on equitable rescission. Her analysis illustrates that consideration of the proper role of compensatory ideas within equity cannot be decoupled from consideration of the proper role of gain-based measures, and thus serves as an important bridge between those chapters focused on restitutionary measures and those focused on loss-based measures. While courts approach such awards and adjustments on the basis that they are compensatory in nature, Bant argues that they can often be better analysed as restitutionary or gain-based in nature. Clarifying the nature of such awards or adjustments is important because it affects, among other things, when such awards may be made and the extent of relief that may be afforded. The chapter goes on to consider specific features of the jurisprudence arguing that though it is not always apparent the process of rescission involves bilateral or mutual restitution between plaintiff and defendant, change of position considerations are evident in the case law, and indemnity orders may at times and on closer analysis be explicable as restitutionary in nature. The chapter reinforces these conclusions through analysis of rescission-like orders under s 87 of the *Trade Practices Act 1974 (Cth)* and equivalent provisions of the *Australian Consumer Law*, and then goes on to consider the ramifications of this restitutionary analysis for our understanding of the doctrine of rescission and future legal development.

D. The Future

Justice Ward also places at the centre of her analysis in Chapter 4 the decision of the United Kingdom Supreme Court in *AIB*.[62] Locating *AIB* in parallel with its conceptual cousins and competitors from across the common law world, including *Target Holdings v Redferns*,[63] and *Youyang Pty Ltd v Minter Ellison Morris Fletcher*,[64] Ward points out that the following substantive questions (amongst others) remain. First, should restoration of money disbursed without authorisation be ordered irrespective of loss 'beyond that of the disbursement (ie substitutive compensation)'. Secondly, should equitable compensation depend on proof of loss beyond the fact of the disbursement itself and thirdly, the relevance and criteria by which a trust is classified as 'commercial'. Finally, Ward asks about the continuing role and availability of the equitable accounting procedures. Courts in Australia and the United Kingdom appear to be set on diverging paths in relation to the development of equitable compensation. It is hoped that this collection will assist in the law's development by pointing the way in relation to at least some of these issues.

In closing, we owe a debt of gratitude to those who participated in the colloquium held in August 2015. Presenters and non-presenters alike contributed to two days of rich discussion and debate and gave generously of their time and intellectual energy. We are grateful to UNSW Law for hosting and funding the colloquium, and to Whittens & McKeough for their generous donation in support of private law research at UNSW Law which in part assisted in the completion of this book. We also acknowledge the efforts of the team at Hart Publishing, in particular Bill Asquith. Simone Degeling thanks Maximus Jones for his invaluable research assistance and Jessica Hudson for her unstinting interest in this project. Jason Varuhas thanks Luke Chircop for his editorial assistance.

62 *AIB* (n 6).
63 *Target* (n 2).
64 *Youyang* (n 4).

2

Disgorgement of Profit and Fiduciary Loyalty

MATTHEW HARDING*

I. Introduction

It is well known that, in certain circumstances, fiduciaries are liable to disgorge profit obtained from a fiduciary relationship. In *Chan v Zacharia*, Deane J provided a now-classic formulation of the rule which imposes this liability:[1]

> [T]he principle of equity is that a person who is under a fiduciary obligation must account to the person to whom the obligation is owed for any benefit or gain … which was obtained or received by use or by reason of his fiduciary position or of opportunity or knowledge resulting from it.

Another now-classic formulation, this time from Lord Russell of Killowen in *Regal (Hastings) Ltd v Gulliver*, makes clear that the rule—which, in legal discourse, is typically called the 'no profit rule'—is strict in its application:[2]

> The rule of equity which insists upon those, who by use of a fiduciary position make a profit, being liable to account for that profit, in no way depends on fraud, or absence of bona fides; or upon such questions or considerations as whether the profit would or should otherwise have gone to the plaintiff, or whether the profiteer was under a duty to obtain the source of the profit for the plaintiff, or whether he took a risk or acted as he did for the benefit of the plaintiff, or whether the plaintiff has in fact been damaged or benefited by his action. The liability arises from the mere fact of a profit having, in the stated circumstances, been made. The profiteer, however honest and well-intentioned, cannot escape the risk of being called to account.

* An early version of this chapter was presented at the Fiduciary Law Roundtable held at the Melbourne Law School in July 2015; I am grateful to all the participants in that Roundtable for their thoughts and suggestions. Particular thanks are due to Andrew Gold, Rosemary Langford and Julian Sempill for reading and providing insightful comments on a draft.

1 (1984) CLR 154, 198 (HCA). The ellipsis stands in place of Deane J's description of a rule according to which fiduciaries must disgorge profits derived in a situation of conflict of interest and duty. My focus in this chapter is not on this 'no conflict' disgorgement rule, although, as I will suggest below (at 38–39), my arguments may have implications for our understanding of that rule.

2 [1967] 2 AC 134, 144–145 (HL).

It is fiduciary law's no profit rule, understood along the lines set out by Deane J and Lord Russell, that is my focus in this chapter.

Much has been written on the no profit rule: some have questioned its strictness; others whether it stands distinct in fiduciary law from a rule demanding that fiduciaries disgorge profit derived in a situation of conflict of interest and duty; others whether the rule is triggered by a breach of legal duty or is a primary liability rule. I will touch on these debates in what follows. But my aim in this chapter is not to engage in them head on. Rather, my aim is to explore the relation of fiduciary law's no profit rule and the notion of fiduciary loyalty. Much has been written on fiduciary loyalty, but the notion remains poorly understood. This may be because it bears more than one meaning in the fiduciary setting.[3]

In Section 2 of the chapter, I will develop an account of fiduciary loyalty using an understanding of loyalty that has been neglected in academic writings on fiduciary law: loyalty as fidelity. I will then explore the implications of loyalty as fidelity for our understanding of fiduciary relationships and fiduciary law. With a notion of fiduciary loyalty as fidelity in view, I will turn in Section 3 to fiduciary law's no profit rule. I will argue that the no profit rule facilitates fiduciary loyalty in the sense of fidelity, but at the same time recognises freedom of exit for fiduciaries who choose to 'opt out' of their commitment to a fiduciary relationship. In making these arguments, I will concentrate on certain guarantees that the no profit rule provides to principals, as well as the rule's expressive effects. In Section 4, I will consider briefly some implications for our understanding of fiduciary law that emerge from reflection on the relation of the no profit rule and fiduciary loyalty.

II. Fiduciary Loyalty

A. Loyalty as Fidelity

Philosophical literature on loyalty is not extensive, but it is extensive enough to discern at least two distinct understandings of its subject matter. The first I will call *loyalty as partiality*. This understanding of loyalty is prominent, for example, in the work of Simon Keller.[4] According to Keller, '[l]oyalty is the attitude and associated pattern of conduct that is constituted by an individual's taking something's side'.[5] Thus can we make sense of such ostensibly disparate instances of loyalty as loyalty to a football team, a designer brand, one's friends and one's country. Loyalty as partiality is an influential understanding of loyalty in philosophical

[3] See AS Gold, 'The Loyalties of Fiduciary Law' in AS Gold and PB Miller (eds), *Philosophical Foundations of Fiduciary Law* (Oxford, Oxford University Press, 2014) 176.
[4] S Keller, *The Limits of Loyalty* (Cambridge, Cambridge University Press, 2007) Ch 1.
[5] ibid, 21.

literature, and on the back of it philosophers have thought about the dilemmas of choosing between the demands of loyalty and the demands of justice,[6] or between conflicting loyalties.[7]

A second understanding of loyalty in philosophical literature might be called *loyalty as fidelity*. A short account of loyalty as fidelity is presented in Chapter 13 of Joseph Raz's celebrated book, *The Morality of Freedom*.[8] According to Raz, loyalty is a way of being committed to one's pursuits and relationships; it inheres in 'being true' to such pursuits and relationships by 'being engaged in them according to their terms'.[9] Thus we might make sense of the loyal public servant or even the loyal spouse.[10] The notion of loyalty as fidelity has not been especially influential in philosophical literature, but interestingly it emerges clearly from the definition of 'loyalty' in the Oxford English Dictionary: 'faithful adherence to one's promise, oath, word of honour, etc; conjugal faithfulness, fidelity.'[11]

There seems no reason to think that either of these understandings of loyalty fails to achieve plausibility on philosophical grounds. In particular, each understanding seems to pick out something ethically distinctive and interesting, and each seems to a degree consistent with ordinary language usage. Thus, each understanding seems a viable contender for developing an account of fiduciary loyalty. Much of the recent academic writing on fiduciary loyalty works with or assumes some conception of loyalty as partiality, and there seems no reason to doubt that loyalty as partiality promises to illuminate our understanding of fiduciary loyalty.[12] That said, I want to begin my own exploration of fiduciary loyalty from a different starting point: loyalty as fidelity. This perspective has been all but neglected in academic writing on fiduciary law. Bringing it into view, and considering its implications for fiduciary law, seems to me a worthwhile theoretical endeavour.

In order to see how loyalty as fidelity might figure in fiduciary relationships, and thus develop an account of fiduciary loyalty as fidelity, it is first necessary to gain a richer sense of loyalty as fidelity. Raz speaks of 'true' commitment to pursuits and relationships through 'being engaged in them according to their terms'.[13] What

[6] For example, R Rorty, 'Justice as a Larger Loyalty' in R Bontecoe and M Stepaniants (eds), *Justice and Democracy: Cross-Cultural Perspectives* (Honolulu, University of Hawaii Press, 1997) 9; J Gardner, 'The Virtue of Charity and Its Foils' in C Mitchell and SR Moody (eds), *Foundations of Charity* (Oxford, Hart Publishing, 2000) 1.

[7] For example, J Royce, *The Philosophy of Loyalty* (Nashville, Vanderbilt University Press, 1995) lecture 3.

[8] J Raz, *The Morality of Freedom* (Oxford, Clarendon Press, 1986) 353–357.

[9] ibid 354–355.

[10] It might be thought that an understanding of loyalty as partiality makes better sense of the loyal spouse. I do not agree. Take a core case of the disloyal spouse: a husband who is having an extra-marital affair. The moral failing of this man seems to me to be less a matter of not 'taking the side' of his wife in choosing a sexual partner and more a matter of not adhering to his marriage vows.

[11] 'Loyalty' in *Oxford English Dictionary*, available at www.oed.com.

[12] Although note JE Penner, 'Distinguishing Fiduciary, Trust, and Accounting Relationships' (2014) 8 *Journal of Equity* 202; JE Penner, 'Is Loyalty a Virtue, and if it is, Does it Really Help to Explain Fiduciary Liability?' in AS Gold and PB Miller (eds), *Philosophical Foundations of Fiduciary Law* (Oxford, Oxford University Press, 2014) 159.

[13] Raz (n 8) 354–355.

could this mean? I think what Raz is saying here begins with the thought that, by becoming committed to a pursuit or relationship, a person becomes subject to the operation of norms that did not previously apply to her but now do apply to her as a consequence of her commitment. In this way, by becoming committed, a person may take part in the creation of her normative world. Having become committed, to the extent that a person conforms to the norms made applicable to her situation by her commitment,[14] she is 'true' to that commitment and may be described as loyal to it. To the extent that the person does not conform to norms brought into view by her commitment, she fails to be loyal. Not that she is necessarily disloyal; the functional equivalent of loyalty is not invariably disloyalty and may—even much of the time—be the anodyne phenomenon best described as 'neither loyalty nor disloyalty'.[15] But even if she is not disloyal, the person who fails to conform to norms brought into view by her commitment might, depending on the circumstances,[16] fail morally in a significant way by not realising normative potential that is available for her to take up.[17]

Depending on their character, commitments bring different norms into view, and in different ways. In some cases, the identity of norms made applicable by a commitment may be ascertained only by careful reflection on the content and scope of the particular commitment. For example, friendship invariably generates norms,[18] but the precise demands of those norms vary from friendship to friendship; for example, what X owes to her best and oldest friends is likely to differ substantially from what she owes to casual acquaintances. In other cases, where a person makes a commitment by invoking a clearly delineated social practice, the identity of at least some of the norms brought into view by that commitment may be ascertained by reflection on the normative dimensions of that practice. For example, where X makes a promise to Y, X should now do what she has promised to do (all else being equal) because A has invoked a practice by which a person subjects herself to norms of promise-keeping.[19] And in other cases still, where X

[14] I say 'conform to' rather than 'act for' because sometimes taking a norm to be a reason for action is not the best way to conform to it. The friend who deliberates about whether or not to betray a confidence and decides that she should not do so for the sake of her friendship takes norms of friendship to be reasons for action; but she would conform better to those norms by never deliberating about the matter and simply not betraying the confidence. See further J Gardner and T Macklem, 'Reasons' in J Coleman and S Shapiro (eds), *The Oxford Handbook of Jurisprudence and Philosophy of Law* (Oxford, Oxford University Press, 2002) 440, 461–462.

[15] My description borrows from the description of 'neither trust nor distrust' in E Ullmann-Margalit, 'Trust, Distrust and In Between' in R Hardin (ed), *Distrust* (New York, Russell Sage Foundation, 2004) 60.

[16] The qualification is necessary because in some circumstances moral success depends on not being true to our commitments. A member of the Nazi Party has strong reasons not to be true to her commitment, because a commitment to the Nazi Party is a commitment to 'norms' that are a travesty of the real thing.

[17] See further M Harding, 'Responding to Trust' (2011) 24 *Ratio Juris* 75, 83–86.

[18] See further J Raz, *The Authority of Law*, 2nd edn (Oxford, Oxford University Press) 253–258.

[19] And we may see this irrespective of our view of the moral basis of those promise-keeping norms. For two different views on that further question: C Fried, *Contract as Promise* (Cambridge MA,

becomes committed by assuming some well-defined and widely understood social role, we may come to understand the norms whose operation X has now triggered by thinking in general terms about the normative dimensions of that social role. In such cases, X's commitment might best be thought of as a commitment to a 'pre-packaged' set of norms entailed in the social role in question and made applicable to X's case by X's occupation of the role. Thus, where X becomes a parent, she thereby makes available to her circumstances a set of norms that are entailed in the social role of parenthood.[20]

B. Fiduciary Loyalty as Fidelity

The understanding of loyalty as fidelity that I have just set out is not specific to fiduciary relationships; it is an understanding of loyalty that relates to commitments of all types, including commitments arising from contracts, promises, the assumption of social roles, and the panoply of human relationships and pursuits with which we engage in our daily lives. Understood in such general terms, loyalty as fidelity is unlikely to tell us much of specific interest about the no profit rule or other aspects of fiduciary law. In this part of the chapter, then, I want to narrow my focus and consider how we might understand loyalty as fidelity in the setting of a fiduciary relationship. My argument will be that fiduciary loyalty as fidelity entails, among other things, true commitment to norms of a certain type, *viz*, norms of selflessness. And I hope to show that this understanding of fiduciary loyalty as fidelity to norms of selflessness illuminates fiduciary law's no profit rule in certain ways.

As a helpful starting point, consider three questions that might be asked about fiduciary relationships. First, there is the question of what causes people to form a fiduciary relationship (the *causal question*). The causal question invites an account of fiduciary commitment, as well as an account that helps to explain why principals enter into fiduciary relationships.[21] Secondly, there is the question of what it means to say that people have formed a 'fiduciary' relationship (the *content question*). The content question is, in effect, that most intractable of all questions in

Harvard University Press, 1981) Ch 1; D Hume, *A Treatise of Human Nature* (ed EC Mossner, London, Penguin, 1985, first published 1739–1740) Book III, Part II.

[20] The case of parenthood shows that becoming committed is not always a matter of choice, even if in a liberal political order it often is. And this has implications for our understanding of fiduciary law: see further M Harding, 'Fiduciary Undertakings' in PB Miller and AS Gold (eds), *Contract, Status, and Fiduciary Law* (Oxford, Oxford University Press, 2016) (forthcoming).

[21] For some efforts in this direction, albeit from different methodological standpoints: FH Easterbrook and DR Fischel, 'Contract and Fiduciary Duty' (1993) 36 *Journal of Law and Economics* 425; J Edelman, 'When Do Fiduciary Duties Arise?' (2010) 126 *LQR Law* 302; J Edelman, 'The Role of Status in the Law of Obligations' in AS Gold and PB Miller (eds), *Philosophical Foundations of Fiduciary Law* (Oxford, Oxford University Press, 2014) 21; H Dagan and ES Scott, 'Reinterpreting the Status-Contract Divide: The Case of Fiduciaries' in PB Miller and AS Gold (eds), *Contract, Status, and Fiduciary Law* (Oxford, Oxford University Press, 2016) (forthcoming).

fiduciary law: what makes a relationship into a 'fiduciary' one? It has received a variety of answers over the years, none of which has gained universal support.[22] And thirdly, there is the question of what legal consequences flow from the fact that people have formed a fiduciary relationship (the *consequences question*). The consequences question invites consideration of the law's responses to fiduciary relationships, including, of course, the no profit rule of fiduciary law. The three questions are related, but distinct.[23] For the moment, I want to focus on the content question. But I will have more to say about the causal question and the consequences question later on.

What does it mean to say that people have formed a 'fiduciary' relationship? Part of the answer to the content question is to be located in certain factual incidents of the formation of such a relationship: one party exercises discretion in ways that affect the interests of another, one party relies on the other in some sense, and so forth. Another part of the answer to the question is to be located in certain norms to which a fiduciary becomes subject when she becomes committed to a fiduciary relationship; and, to this extent, answering the content question is the key to understanding in what fiduciary loyalty—in the sense of fidelity—consists from case to case. But of course, as I have said already, the content question has been the subject of much contestation over the years; as a result, the content of loyalty as fidelity in a fiduciary relationship is likely to be contested as well. For example, there is likely to be disagreement as to whether a loyal fiduciary must conform to norms of honesty or carefulness, for example, within the scope of the fiduciary relationship.[24]

For present purposes, I want to try to avoid controversy by focusing on just one proposition that I take to be uncontroversial: by becoming committed to a fiduciary relationship, a fiduciary becomes subject to norms of selflessness. Thus, Sarah Worthington speaks of relationships in which one party operates 'on the basis of self-denial'.[25] According to Paul Finn, '[i]t is accepted as axiomatic that a consequence of concluding that a relationship is fiduciary in whole or in part is that, to that extent, the fiduciary is obliged to act in the interests of the beneficiary, or in

[22] For an excellent recent survey: PB Miller, 'Justifying Fiduciary Duties' (2013) 58 *McGill Law Journal* 969.

[23] Failing to keep all three questions in view can lead to oversight. Thus the fact that a fiduciary undertakes to act in the interests of another is often thought to be relevant to the content question (as indeed it is), but its relevance to our understanding of fiduciary law is not exhausted by its relevance to the content question, because it is also relevant to the causal question. Equally, it is sometimes said that a fiduciary relationship is nothing more than a relationship to which fiduciary law's no conflict and no profit rules apply. To state that these rules apply to a fiduciary relationship is to give an answer to the consequences question but there is no reason to think that this also suffices as an answer to the content question: see further PB Miller, 'The Fiduciary Relationship' in AS Gold and PB Miller (eds), *Philosophical Foundations of Fiduciary Law* (Oxford, Oxford University Press, 2014) 63.

[24] On the extent to which fiduciary relationships entail such norms, see further JD Heydon, 'Are the Duties of Company Directors to Exercise Care and Skill Fiduciary?' in S Degeling and J Edelman (eds), *Equity in Commercial Law* (Sydney, Lawbook Co, 2005) 185.

[25] S Worthington, 'Fiduciaries: When is Self-Denial Obligatory?' (1999) 58 *CLJ* 500, 506.

their joint interest (as, for example, in the case of partnership) to the exclusion of his or her own self interest'.[26] And for Lionel Smith, 'if we think of a person who held the legal powers that go with any of the traditional fiduciary categories—a trustee, an agent, a partner—and we imagine that that person was free to use those powers exactly as they wished, in their own interests, then it would be impossible to say that they were a fiduciary'.[27] Of course, we must be careful not to overstate the point: many fiduciaries are permitted to, and do, pursue their own interests in substantial ways; this is true, for example, of cases where commercial contractual dealings generate partial, even interstitial, fiduciary relationships. But in every case where there is a fiduciary relationship, the fiduciary is to some extent, however small, subject to norms of selflessness, because that, at least in part, is what it means to be a fiduciary. Put simply, a fiduciary who is not subject to norms of selflessness is a contradiction in terms; thus Finn's description of the association of fiduciary relationships and selflessness as 'axiomatic'. From the perspective of loyalty as fidelity, then, it may be said with confidence that fiduciary loyalty entails selflessness. But from that perspective, the selfless fiduciary is loyal insofar as she is true to a commitment by which she has become subject to norms of selflessness, not insofar as she is partial to her principal.

To be subject to a norm of selflessness is to be subject to a reason, perhaps in the form of a standard or even an aspiration, and perhaps in the form of a duty,[28] stipulating the cultivation or achievement of selflessness in one or another way. In some circumstances, fiduciaries may become subject to such reasons in circumstances where conformity to them may be substantially achieved by the due performance of contractual and other 'non-fiduciary' duties owed within the scope of the fiduciary relationship. Take, for example, a limited fiduciary relationship arising out of a commercial contract. Prevailing social understandings of commercial contracts identify them as vehicles, first and foremost, for the pursuit of self-interest. Against this backdrop, norms of selflessness may not extend much beyond what is strictly entailed in the parties adhering to their bargain.[29]

[26] PD Finn, 'Fiduciary Reflections' (2014) 88 *Australian Law Journal* 127, 135 (see also PD Finn, 'The Fiduciary Principle' in TG Youdan (ed), *Equity, Fiduciaries and Trusts* (Toronto, Carswell, 1989) 1, 54). Finn's point is phrased as one about the 'consequence' of a fiduciary relationship arising, but I think it is plausibly read as a point about what it means to say that people have formed a 'fiduciary' relationship, *viz*, a response to the 'content' question.

[27] L Smith, 'Fiduciary Relationships: Ensuring the Loyal Exercise of Judgement on Behalf of Another' (2014) 130 *LQR* 608, 609.

[28] On the difference between the morality of aspiration and the morality of duty: LL Fuller, *The Morality of Law*, revd ed (New Haven, Yale University Press, 1969) Ch 1.

[29] The High Court of Australia has said that, against the backdrop of a commercial contract the terms of which do not provide for a fiduciary relationship, it will be 'very difficult' to identify such a relationship: *John Alexander's Clubs Pty Ltd v White City Tennis Club Ltd* (2010) 241 CLR 1, [92] (HCA). At the same time, though, 'in commercial bargains struck at arms length between sophisticated parties with equal bargaining power, the need to make one part of their agreement fiduciary may be the only means reasonably available to them if they are to be able to enter into a detailed commercial arrangement the principal object of which is to promote their separate—and non-fiduciary—interests' (Finn, 'Fiduciary Reflections' (n 26) 135–136).

And therefore fiduciary loyalty may be more or less a matter of contractual performance.[30]

That said, we should take care not to assume that fiduciaries may be loyal—in the sense of loyalty as fidelity—in all cases simply by duly performing 'non-fiduciary' duties.[31] In some cases fiduciaries become subject to norms of selflessness by becoming committed to fiduciary relationships in the setting of pre-contractual relationships;[32] in many other cases they become subject to such norms by assuming a social role.[33] In these cases norms of selflessness might be relatively diffuse; they might also be relatively extensive. Take, for example, cases where fiduciaries occupy social roles that entail adherence to particular sets of professional or ethical standards.[34] Such standards may deliver, to the fiduciaries in question, 'pre-packaged' norms mandating selflessness in ways that go beyond simply performing 'non-fiduciary' duties, say by cultivating a sense of disinterested duty or altruism in the discharge of the fiduciary role.[35] Now consider the position of the trustee of a family discretionary trust who has agreed to take on the trusteeship on an unremunerated basis. The norms of selflessness associated with this social role have been developed and refined over hundreds of years; they owe as much to culture as they do to the legal system.[36] Such a trustee might, by assuming this role, trigger the operation of norms not only demanding performance of her duties as a trustee, but also that she form selfless dispositions, express selfless attitudes and make discretionary decisions in selfless ways. She may therefore create a normative world for herself in which fiduciary loyalty—being true to her commitment to the fiduciary relationship—is a relatively demanding matter.[37]

Given the diversity of fiduciary commitments, it is difficult to generalise about the content of the norms of selflessness that arise in fiduciary relationships. That said, it does seem right to say that, at minimum, fiduciary norms of selflessness do

[30] See further the influential dissenting judgment of Mason J in *Hospital Products Ltd v United States Surgical Corporation* (1984) 156 CLR 41 (HCA).

[31] Compare M Conaglen, *Fiduciary Loyalty: Protecting the Due Performance of Non-Fiduciary Duties* (Oxford, Hart Publishing, 2010).

[32] *United Dominions Corporation Limited v Brian Pty Ltd* (1985) 157 CLR 1 (HCA).

[33] On this last possibility, see further Dagan and Scott (n 21); Harding, 'Fiduciary Undertakings' (n 20).

[34] For judicial recognition of the relevance of such standards to fiduciary law, see: *Farrington v Rowe McBride and Partners* [1985] 1 NZLR 83, 92 (NZCA) (Richardson J); *Hodgkinson v Simms* [1994] 3 SCR 377, 412 (SCC) (La Forest J); *Pilmer v Duke Group Limited (in liq)* (2001) 207 CLR 165, [138]–[144] (HCA) (Kirby J).

[35] For some reflections on the association of altruism and fiduciary loyalty: P Birks, 'The Content of the Fiduciary Obligation' (2000) 34 *Israel Law Review* 3.

[36] See further C Stebbings, *The Private Trustee in Victorian England* (Cambridge, Cambridge University Press, 2002); GS Alexander, 'A Cognitive Theory of Fiduciary Relationships' (2000) 85 *Cornell Law Review* 767, 774–775; M Graziadei, 'Fiduciary Law in Civil Law and Common Law Jurisdictions' in AS Gold and PB Miller (eds), *Philosophical Foundations of Fiduciary Law* (Oxford, Oxford University Press, 2014) 287, 287–288.

[37] We should not forget that such a trustee at the same time creates a normative world for herself in which she stands to succeed morally in new ways; just as her commitment imposes normative demands, it offers normative opportunities.

not permit those to whom they apply to seek to profit from the fiduciary relationship, including by seeking to keep profit obtained from that relationship. Just as it is axiomatic that fiduciary relationships are characterised by norms of selflessness, so is it axiomatic that a person who is subject to norms of selflessness cannot, consistently with such norms, seek to obtain or keep profit within the range of action to which the norms apply. In short, the loyal (faithful) fiduciary eschews profit-seeking, a proposition that helps us to understand the no profit rule for reasons to which I will return below.

Deliberation on the content question reveals one further feature of fiduciary relationships that is important for present purposes. When two people form a 'fiduciary' relationship, they do so against the backdrop of a liberal political order in which citizens are free, to a substantial degree, to choose their commitments, including their fiduciary commitments. Thus, a fiduciary relationship, including the norms of selflessness that are invariably entailed in it, is usually bounded by what might be called freedom of fiduciary exit. In particular, a fiduciary is usually free to vary or 'opt out' of norms of selflessness that might otherwise apply to her because of her commitment to the fiduciary relationship. This she is free to do at the point of becoming committed to the fiduciary relationship, perhaps by entering into contractual arrangements with her principal that limit the scope of the fiduciary relationship.[38] She is also free to vary or 'opt out' of norms of selflessness even after becoming committed to the fiduciary relationship, say by withdrawing from a social role that entails a fiduciary relationship,[39] or by obtaining the informed consent of her principal to acting in profit-seeking ways.[40] In no sense is such a fiduciary lacking in loyalty, from the perspective of loyalty as fidelity. We might instead say that such a fiduciary chooses, with the blessing of her principal, to diminish or suspend her commitment to the fiduciary relationship insofar as that commitment makes applicable norms of selflessness. To the extent that such a choice is successful, it renders questions of loyalty as fidelity no longer relevant to the case.[41]

III. The No Profit Rule and Fiduciary Loyalty

In this part of the chapter, I want to argue that fiduciary law's no profit rule facilitates fiduciary loyalty understood as fidelity to norms of selflessness, but at the

[38] For some thoughts on the extent to which such arrangements are possible: Finn, 'Fiduciary Reflections' (n 26) 140–143.

[39] In some circumstances such withdrawal might not be a straightforward matter: *Canadian Aero Service Ltd v O'Malley* (1973) 40 DLR (3rd) 371 (SCC).

[40] On what counts as informed consent: *Farah Constructions Pty Ltd v Say-Dee Pty Ltd* (2007) 230 CLR 89, 139–140 (HCA).

[41] In the same way, moral appraisal of the conduct of a divorced couple may no longer be a matter of loyalty as fidelity.

same time recognises freedom of exit for fiduciaries who choose to 'opt out' of those norms. At first glance, the proposition that fiduciary law's no profit rule facilitates fidelity to norms of selflessness might seem implausible. After all, if a fiduciary refrains from seeking to profit from her fiduciary relationship because she wishes to avoid liability under the no profit rule, then in what sense has she conformed to norms of selflessness that have been brought into view by her commitment to the fiduciary relationship? Surely the no profit rule is apt to distract the would-be loyal fiduciary, interrupting that person's engagement with the norms of selflessness to which she ought to be responsive if she is to be loyal, in the sense of loyalty as fidelity? There is some force to this point. The fiduciary who refrains from seeking profit because she does not wish to be liable under the no profit rule takes the no profit rule to be a reason for action. To that extent she does not conform to the norms to which she has become subject by her commitment. Earlier I noted that in some circumstances conforming to a norm is best achieved by not taking that norm to be a reason for action, but it seems implausible to suggest that this is true of the norms of selflessness entailed in a fiduciary commitment. Such norms tend to arise out of relational contracts or the occupancy of social roles or both, settings in which being true to commitments typically demands the achievement of some degree of deliberative engagement with those commitments.[42] So, for example, it seems right to say that a solicitor or trustee who simply adopted a policy of adherence to the law and never thought about the nature of her commitment as a solicitor or trustee would fail to be true to that commitment in a significant way.

Perhaps it might be said that taking the no profit rule to be a reason for action is itself a type of fidelity to norms of selflessness. In recent work, Lionel Smith describes the no profit rule as a 'primary' rule arising out of the 'nature' of the fiduciary relationship.[43] Smith's analysis might be thought to suggest that commitment to a fiduciary relationship triggers the operation of the no profit rule, a rule to which the loyal fiduciary may then be true by taking it to be a reason for action. But Smith's analysis does not go so far as to show that the no profit rule is a norm of selflessness. As is clear from the formulations of the no profit rule that I set out at the beginning of this chapter, that rule is oriented at the fiduciary who

[42] It has been argued that contracts do not demand the sort of ongoing deliberative engagement that I am talking about, and that it is precisely this that distinguishes them from fiduciary relationships: SR Galoob and EJ Leib, 'Intentions, Compliance, and Fiduciary Obligations' (2014) 20 *Legal Theory* 106. In response, I note that even if ongoing deliberative engagement is not required for contractual performance (and this may be doubted at least in the case of relational contracts), being true to the commitment entailed in the terms of a contract may require such engagement. One might perform a contract, for example by accident, and yet not be true to the commitment it entails.

[43] L Smith, 'Deterrence, Prophylaxis and Punishment in Fiduciary Obligations' (2013) 7 *Journal of Equity* 87; Smith, 'Fiduciary Relationships' (n 27); L Smith, 'Can We Be Obliged To Be Selfless?' in AS Gold and PB Miller (eds), *Philosophical Foundations of Fiduciary Law* (Oxford, Oxford University Press, 2014) 141. The quotations in the text come from 'Fiduciary Relationships' at 628. In 'Can We Be Obliged?' (at 150), Smith talks of the no profit rule as arising from the 'logic' of the fiduciary relationship.

has profited from her fiduciary relationship and not yet disgorged that profit. A rule that is oriented in this way can scarcely be described as a norm of selflessness; it is, rather, a norm requiring a fiduciary who has not acted selflessly now to act in ways consistent with selflessness. I will return to this point below. Moreover, Smith's powerful argument that the no profit rule is a 'primary' rule shows only that the rule does not presuppose that a fiduciary who is liable to it has acted in breach of a legal duty;[44] that argument is consistent with the proposition that a fiduciary who is liable under the no profit rule has failed to conform to a norm that has arisen from her commitment to the fiduciary relationship but does not take the form of a legal duty. Overall, Smith's account of the no profit rule is consistent with the proposition that the no profit rule, while a primary legal norm, arises to serve remedial and other objectives in circumstances where a fiduciary has failed to be true to her commitment.[45]

We may thus accept the proposition that the fiduciary who refrains from seeking profit because she wishes to avoid liability under the no profit rule is not, to that extent, a loyal fiduciary, in the sense of loyalty as fidelity.[46] Notwithstanding this, I think that fiduciary law's no profit rule facilitates fiduciary loyalty understood as fidelity to norms of selflessness, even as it accommodates fiduciaries who choose to 'opt out' of those norms. This it does in at least two ways. First, the no profit rule provides guarantees to principals that fiduciary action will, to a certain degree, be consistent with fidelity to norms of selflessness, guarantees that help to create conditions under which fiduciaries may be loyal generally speaking. Secondly, via its expressive effects, the no profit rule helps to produce cultural conditions of fidelity to norms of selflessness. I will consider each theme in turn.

A. The No Profit Rule's Guarantees

Consider the no profit rule from the perspective of the principal who would like to enter into a fiduciary relationship.[47] To think from this perspective is to take as one's focal concern the causal question to which I alluded earlier, ie, the question

44 This argument is also associated with Lord Millett (see, eg, Lord Millett, 'Bribes and Secret Commissions Again' (2012) 71*CLJ* 583) although, as Smith points out, there are differences between his view and Lord Millett's: 'Fiduciary Relationships' (n 27) 628, n 81.

45 James Penner describes the law of fiduciary accountability as constituted by '*primary, remedial* duties': 'Is Loyalty a Virtue?' (n 12) 171 (emphasis in original). Leaving to one side the difficult question whether or not fiduciary law's no profit rule picks out legal duties, Penner's description seems an apt one when applied to that rule.

46 Significantly, this includes the fiduciary who wishes to obey the law as well as the fiduciary who fears legal sanction. Of course, for the fiduciary who has made a commitment to obey the law, taking the no profit rule to be a reason for action may amount to loyalty as fidelity to *that* commitment, even if it does not amount to *fiduciary* loyalty as fidelity. This possibility raises questions about the circumstances in which it might be said that a citizen has made a commitment to obey the law, questions that cannot be traversed here.

47 This and the next paragraph draw on my earlier work in 'Manifesting Trust' (2009) 29 *OJLS* 245; 'Trust and Fiduciary Law' (2013) 33 *OJLS* 81.

of what causes people to form a fiduciary relationship. A would-be fiduciary is in view. Will this person be loyal, in the sense of loyalty as fidelity? In particular, will this person conform to the norms of selflessness entailed in committing to the fiduciary relationship in question? Perhaps, in the circumstances, the principal has reasons to think that the would-be fiduciary will be true to applicable norms of selflessness: she has known and trusted the would-be fiduciary for years; the would-be fiduciary occupies a social role in respect of which the principal has generalised expectations of loyalty; the would-be fiduciary has a reputation for selfless and diligent service in whatever she decides to do. But perhaps the principal lacks such reasons, and simply has no grounds for forming relevant beliefs about the fidelity of the would-be fiduciary to applicable norms of selflessness. The no profit rule of fiduciary law provides reasons for such a principal to enter into the fiduciary relationship notwithstanding her lack of relevant beliefs about fiduciary loyalty as fidelity.

To see this more clearly, take first the case of a principal who lacks relevant beliefs about fiduciary loyalty as fidelity but who believes that the would-be fiduciary knows of the existence and demands of the no profit rule. The no profit rule guarantees to this principal that the non-loyal fiduciary who wishes to avoid legal liability will not seek to profit from the fiduciary relationship or will seek the blessing of the principal to 'opt out' of her commitment so as to be free to seek profit.[48] These are precisely the ways in which a loyal (faithful) fiduciary would act. Now of course the no profit rule cannot provide any such guarantee in circumstances where the non-loyal fiduciary does not wish to avoid legal liability.[49] But if the guarantee is not perfect, it is nonetheless there in relation to non-loyal fiduciaries who do wish to avoid legal liability. And even in the case where the non-loyal fiduciary does not wish to avoid legal liability, the no profit rule provides a further guarantee to the principal who lacks relevant beliefs about fiduciary loyalty as fidelity: the rule guarantees that the non-loyal fiduciary who seeks to keep profit from the fiduciary relationship will be made to act as though she were loyal by disgorging any profit she has obtained.[50] Again, this guarantee

[48] On this aspect of the no profit rule, see further R Nolan, '*Regal (Hastings) Ltd v Gulliver*' in C Mitchell and P Mitchell (eds), *Landmark Cases in Equity* (Oxford, Hart Publishing, 2012) 499; M Bryan, '*Boardman v Phipps*' in C Mitchell and P Mitchell (eds), *Landmark Cases in Equity* (Oxford, Hart Publishing, 2012) 581; RS Sitkoff, 'An Economic Theory of Fiduciary Law' in AS Gold and PB Miller (eds), *Philosophical Foundations of Fiduciary Law* (Oxford, Oxford University Press, 2014) 197, 207.

[49] Lionel Smith has argued that the no profit rule is ill-suited to causing fiduciaries to wish to avoid legal liability: 'The Motive, Not the Deed' in J Getzler (ed), *Rationalizing Property, Equity and Trusts: Essays in Honour of Edward Burn* (London, Lexis-Nexis Butterworths, 2003) 53; 'Deterrence' (n 43). I will return below to Smith's argument: see 36–37.

[50] In cases where a fiduciary diverts to herself profit that she should have made for the principal, disgorgement to the principal mimics closely the demands of fiduciary loyalty. In cases where a fiduciary receives a bribe or a secret commission, disgorgement *to the principal* does not closely reflect the demands of fiduciary loyalty, because the fiduciary should not have received the bribe or secret commission at all. In those cases, the no profit rule could guarantee that non-loyal fiduciaries will be made to act as though they were loyal without, at the same time, requiring disgorgement to the principal (for example, by requiring disgorgement to the state).

is not perfect—it may ultimately be relied upon after the stress and expense of litigation—but it is there.

In several ways it is desirable that a principal have reasons to enter into a fiduciary relationship notwithstanding a lack of relevant beliefs about fiduciary loyalty as fidelity. Most obviously, this enables the principal and the fiduciary to coordinate their action for their individual benefit in ways that might not be possible otherwise. More importantly for present purposes, though, it enables the principal and the fiduciary to form a relationship and thus shape and direct their normative world, making available new ways to engage with value, and to succeed (and fail) morally. In particular, where a principal enters into a fiduciary relationship, that principal contributes to the creation of conditions under which the fiduciary becomes committed to that fiduciary relationship, thereby making applicable to her circumstances norms that would not otherwise apply to her. None of the normative potential of such a commitment is even on the horizon unless the principal enters into the fiduciary relationship in question. Thus, to the extent that the guarantees provided by fiduciary law's no profit rule give a principal reasons to enter into a fiduciary relationship even though she lacks relevant beliefs about fiduciary loyalty as fidelity, those guarantees place that normative potential within reach of the fiduciary notwithstanding that the principal does not believe that the fiduciary will be loyal.

Of course, the guarantees of the no profit rule do not mean that the normative potential of a fiduciary commitment will be realised: the no profit rule does not guarantee that fiduciaries will be faithful to the norms entailed in their commitments; it guarantees only that fiduciaries will act as though they were loyal in this way, and only loyal by eschewing profit-seeking at that.[51] But by helping to bring about conditions under which fiduciaries become committed to fiduciary relationships, the no profit rule helps to bring about conditions under which fiduciaries are situated so as to conform to the norms entailed in their commitments. And in this sense fiduciary law's no profit rule facilitates fiduciary loyalty as fidelity; without the no profit rule there might be fewer fiduciary relationships, and without fiduciary relationships there can be no fiduciary loyalty as fidelity.

Could fiduciary law facilitate fiduciary loyalty as fidelity in this way even in the absence of the particular guarantees provided by the no profit rule? On the one hand, it seems plausible to think that conditions under which principals are prepared to enter into fiduciary relationships notwithstanding a lack of relevant beliefs about fiduciary loyalty as fidelity might be generated even in the absence of those guarantees. For example, fiduciary law might guarantee that fiduciaries will

[51] Indeed, in a liberal political order, part of the attraction of the guarantees of the no profit rule is that they enable people to form and then benefit from fiduciary relationships even though the fiduciary may never be loyal and even though the principal may only trust the fiduciary to be motivated by a wish to avoid legal liability. Such detached relationships play their role in serving personal autonomy. See further Harding, 'Trust and Fiduciary Law' (n 47) 101–102; H Dagan and S Hannes, 'Managing our Money: The Law of Financial Fiduciaries as a Private Law Institution' in AS Gold and PB Miller (eds), *Philosophical Foundations of Fiduciary Law* (Oxford, Oxford University Press, 2014) 91, 102–104.

disgorge profit only in circumstances of exploitation, dishonesty or neglect of the principal's interests, and not when that profit has been obtained in the course of honest, good faith efforts for the benefit of the principal; such a guarantee might well be sufficient to cause a principal to enter into a fiduciary relationship.[52] On the other hand, there are reasons to think that such a reform of fiduciary law's no profit rule might do more than simply effect a change to the legal consequences of being in a fiduciary relationship. Such a reform might bring about changes to what it means for people to form a 'fiduciary' relationship in the first place. In a world where the no profit rule of fiduciary law allowed fiduciaries to keep profits obtained from a fiduciary relationship, this might change legal and social understandings of the content of commitment to a fiduciary relationship. In particular, legal and fiduciary communities who work with and interpret fiduciary relationships and fiduciary law might cease to regard it as 'axiomatic'—to repeat Finn's phrase—that fiduciary relationships entail commitment to norms of selflessness.[53] In this world, legal and fiduciary communities would still speak of 'fiduciary' relationships but they would mean something other than we do when we use that term; fiduciaries would still be loyal by being true to the normative dimensions of their commitments, but they would be true to commitments that we do not currently recognise as fiduciary in nature.

B. The No Profit Rule's Expressive Effects

Arguably, then, fiduciary loyalty as fidelity, as we know it, depends on the particular guarantees provided by the no profit rule, because legal and social understandings of 'fiduciary' relationships are likely to be informed in key ways by those guarantees. The content question is affected by the consequences question. And this brings me to a further way in which the no profit rule facilitates fiduciary loyalty understood as fidelity to norms of selflessness. Our starting point here is to highlight the expressive effects of law, effects that are often overlooked but nonetheless important.[54] To the extent that law has expressive effects, law may provide normative guidance to citizens not via its usual techniques of coercion

[52] An argument for such a reform of fiduciary law has been presented by J Langbein, 'Questioning the Trust Law Duty of Loyalty: Best Interest or Sole Interest?' (2005) 114 *Yale Law Journal* 929. And see also G Jones, 'Unjust Enrichment and the Fiduciary's Duty of Loyalty' (1968) 84 *LQR* 472; *Chan v Zacharia* (1984) 154 CLR 178, 204–205 (HCA) (Deane J); *Murad v Al-Saraj* [2005] EWCA Civ 959, [82] (Arden LJ), [122]–[123] (Jonathan Parker LJ).

[53] It is conceivable that a fiduciary community might believe that fiduciary relationships entail commitment to norms of selflessness in circumstances where fiduciary law did not, in important ways, reflect such norms. Such a scenario might suggest that the fiduciary community in question was alienated from that body of law, with worrisome implications for the rule of law: M Harding, 'Equity and the Rule of Law' (2016) 132 *LQR* 278. At the same time, though, fiduciary law might pre-empt such alienation via strategies of accommodation: AS Gold, 'Accommodating Loyalty' in PB Miller and AS Gold (eds), *Contract, Status, and Fiduciary Law* (Oxford, Oxford University Press, 2016) (forthcoming).

[54] For an overview of the literature on the expressive function of law: MD Adler, 'Expressive Theories of Law: A Skeptical Overview' (2000) 148 *University of Pennsylvania Law Review* 1363.

and facilitation, but instead by a technique of communication. In some cases law is characterised by a communicative technique independent of any of its other usual techniques. In other cases, a communicative technique is packaged with other techniques, coercive or facilitative, so that the one legal rule performs more than one function. I think that fiduciary law's no profit rule reflects just such a packaging of techniques for providing normative guidance; the rule is coercive—of that there can be no doubt—but it is also communicative. It produces expressive effects to that extent.[55]

In thinking about what the no profit rule communicates, we might start by noticing the obvious. As I discussed earlier, insofar as it is coercive the no profit rule is directed at fiduciaries who have sought to keep profit from the fiduciary relationship and, to that extent, have failed to conform to the norms of selflessness entailed in their commitment. Because the coercive technique of the no profit rule presupposes this non-conformity, the no profit rule is an apt vehicle for communicating certain normative messages to fiduciary communities. For one thing, it communicates the basic message that fiduciaries are subject to norms of selflessness. Moreover, because the no profit rule applies to fiduciaries irrespective of considerations like good faith or harm to the principal, the no profit rule communicates that fiduciary norms of selflessness are not norms of good faith or harm-avoidance, and this helps to isolate their distinctive character as norms of selflessness. Furthermore, to the extent that it guarantees that non-loyal fiduciaries will either act or be made to act as though in conformity with norms of selflessness, the no profit rule communicates messages about what is entailed in that conformity. Specifically, the no profit rule signals that conformity entails not seeking to keep profit obtained from the fiduciary relationship; by implication it also signals that norms of selflessness enjoin fiduciaries from seeking to profit from the fiduciary relationship in the first place. At the same time, because the coercive technique of the no profit rule is not invoked against the fiduciary who has, with her principal's blessing, 'opted out' of norms of selflessness ex ante, ex post or against the backdrop of an extant fiduciary relationship, the no profit rule communicates that a fiduciary is free to 'opt out' in any of these ways.

In short, by tracking the demands of fiduciary norms of selflessness, and by noticing and highlighting the freedom of fiduciary exit that circumscribes the operation of those norms, fiduciary law's no profit rule reflects the communicative technique that is associated with the expressive effects of law. To the extent that such a communicative technique is successful, the no profit rule assists in educating users of fiduciary law about what it means to be in a fiduciary relationship. More specifically, the rule educates fiduciary communities about what it means to be committed to a fiduciary relationship and how, consistent with loyalty as fidelity, a fiduciary may free herself from such a commitment. This education is

55 For an account emphasising in insightful ways the expressive effects of fiduciary law: I Samet, 'Fiduciary Loyalty as Kantian Virtue' in AS Gold and PB Miller (eds), *Philosophical Foundations of Fiduciary Law* (Oxford, Oxford University Press, 2014) 125.

no guarantee of fiduciary loyalty, but it is a condition of such loyalty. The person who has become committed but lacks knowledge of or misunderstands the norms brought into view by that commitment is not situated so as to conform to those norms; in contrast, the person who knows and understands what her commitment entails is in a position to be loyal, even if there is no certainty that she will be. Thus, to the extent that the communicative technique of the no profit rule is successful, we may assert that the rule facilitates fiduciary loyalty not only by guaranteeing that fiduciaries will act in certain ways, but also by helping fiduciaries to grasp what is required if they are to be true to their commitments.[56]

The educative potential of the no profit rule, insofar as it has expressive effects, seems worth emphasising. Many fiduciaries (think for example of trustees or company directors) undertake activities whose purpose is to generate profit; moreover they do so against the backdrop of a public culture, and commercial subcultures, in which making profit is widely regarded as a valuable pursuit. Given that fiduciaries act under these pressures and within these general norms, it seems significant that the no profit rule communicates that, because of their commitments, they are subject to specific norms preventing them from doing what they might otherwise regard as proper or natural given their circumstances and orientation.[57]

A question now arises: to what extent is the communicative technique of fiduciary law's no profit rule successful? The answer to this question depends on the extent to which knowledge of the no profit rule causes fiduciary communities to better understand the normative dimensions of fiduciary relationships. In looking for such effects, we should be careful not to assume that members of fiduciary communities have highly technical and specialised knowledge of the no profit rule of the type possessed by expert equity lawyers. Some members of fiduciary communities—in particular, those with legal training—may well have such knowledge. But many do not. At the same time, though, we should be open to the possibility that the no profit rule may achieve indirect, diffuse, expressive effects via cultural channels. High profile court cases involving corporate fraud and fiduciaries 'on the take' produce and reinforce an association of fiduciary relationships and norms of selflessness in public culture; so do depictions of such events in fiction, in film and on television.[58] An account of the extent to which the no profit rule succeeds in educating fiduciary communities, and indeed the wider

[56] Paul Finn writes, '[The fiduciary principle] originates, self-evidently, in public policy: in a view of desired social behaviour for the end this achieves. To maintain the integrity and the utility of those relationships in which the (or a) role of one party is perceived to be the service of the interests of the other, it insists upon a fine loyalty in that service': 'The Fiduciary Principle' (n 26) 27. My arguments about the communicative technique of the no profit rule seek to illuminate how fiduciary law pursues the public policy objective described by Finn.

[57] I am grateful to Julian Sempill for helping me to grasp this point.

[58] The extent to which the Bernie Madoff affair has captured popular imagination may be cited as a case in point. A Google search reveals that in the US, at the time of writing, the ABC plans to produce a television miniseries starring Richard Dreyfus as Madoff; HBO has been planning a feature length film on Madoff starring Robert de Niro; and the History Channel has produced a documentary film on Madoff's Ponzi scheme, freely available on Youtube.

community, about the nature of commitment to a fiduciary relationship should have something to say about such indirect, diffuse effects.

For present purposes I want to focus on one particular way in which the communicative technique of the no profit rule may succeed. As is well known, fiduciary law assumes that relationships within certain categories are fiduciary:[59] the relationships of trustee-beneficiary; solicitor-client; agent-principal; company director-company; and partner-partner are usually given in this connection.[60] One way of thinking about relationships in these categories is that they entail (at least) one party to them occupying what might be called a fiduciary role.[61] The work of constituting such fiduciary roles by assuming that certain categories of relationship are fiduciary has traditionally been and continues to be performed by members of the legal community—primarily the judiciary—who interpret and shape fiduciary law. By constituting fiduciary roles, interpreters of fiduciary law associate those roles and the no profit rule of fiduciary law. Moreover, via the no profit rule, such interpreters associate fiduciary roles and the norms of selflessness that are presupposed and reinforced by the no profit rule. Fiduciary communities may then draw on these associations when working out the normative dimensions of the roles in question and thereby educating themselves about the demands of fiduciary loyalty.

None of this is to say that such associations will be made by each and every occupant of a fiduciary role. As I said earlier, it cannot be assumed that every fiduciary has detailed knowledge of fiduciary law. Rather, the associations may be made at certain key moments by those members of fiduciary communities who are charged with defining a social role that is at the same time a fiduciary role. One such moment might be the adoption, by a body representing a fiduciary community of professional service providers, of a professional code of conduct or a set of ethical standards. Similarly, the associations might be made by those who are responsible for educating occupants of fiduciary roles about the practices and standards of conduct expected of occupants of those roles. By being exposed to and constrained by the outputs of role-defining activities, as well as educated about what is expected of them as role-occupants, members of fiduciary communities may come to view themselves as subject to norms of selflessness because they occupy a particular social role that interpreters of fiduciary law have identified as a fiduciary role. In these circumstances, the communicative technique of fiduciary law may play its part in successfully educating members of fiduciary communities about their commitments, even though those members of

59 Although these relationships are often assumed to be fiduciary in general terms, it seems clear enough that they are fiduciary only to the extent that there is scope for one of the parties to them to exercise discretionary powers in relation to the interests of the other: see further Penner, 'Distinguishing' (n 12) 214–223.

60 These categories (and the employee-employer relationship) are described as 'accepted fiduciary relationships' by Mason J in *Hospital Products Ltd v United States Surgical Corporation* (1984) 156 CLR 4, 96 (HCA).

61 See further Harding, 'Fiduciary Undertakings' (n 20).

fiduciary communities may lack specific knowledge about fiduciary law and its no profit rule.

IV. Implications

In this final part of the chapter, I want to consider some implications for our understanding of fiduciary law that emerge from reflection on the relation of the no profit rule and fiduciary loyalty as fidelity. I stress at the outset that I do not claim to have provided anything like a complete theoretical account of the no profit rule; rather, my aim in this chapter has been to illuminate just one dimension of that rule. Nonetheless, I think that my arguments may illuminate that dimension of the rule sufficiently to justify some tentative observations about fiduciary law.

I think that reflection on the relation of the no profit rule and fiduciary loyalty as fidelity opens up a new way of viewing old arguments to the effect that at least part of the justification of the no profit rule is to be found in deterrence. Deterrence arguments, which are familiar both in the case law and in the academic literature,[62] have been subjected to trenchant criticism in recent years. Most notably, Lionel Smith has argued that, for two reasons, the no profit rule is a poor vehicle for achieving deterrence.[63] First, Smith thinks that the no profit rule under-deters because it requires disgorgement of no more than the profit obtained from a fiduciary relationship.[64] And secondly, Smith thinks that the no profit rule's method of deterring fiduciary misconduct is unjust because the rule imposes liability on fiduciaries whose own conduct is not of the type that the rule seeks to deter.[65] These two objections are forceful ones. But in response to them, two points might be made in light of the relation of the no profit rule and fiduciary loyalty as fidelity.

First, Smith's first objection seems relevant only to arguments that view deterrence as a function of the coercive effects of the no profit rule and therefore focus on the rule's propensity to cause fiduciaries to fear legal liability and act accordingly. It seems less relevant to arguments that view deterrence as a function of the expressive effects of the no profit rule and therefore focus on the rule's propensity to cause fiduciary communities better to understand the normative dimensions of fiduciary relationships.[66] It is true that deterrence arguments about the no profit

[62] See, eg, *Harris v Digital Pulse Pty Ltd* (2003) 56 NSWLR 298, [161] (Mason P); [305], [414] (Heydon JA) (NSWCA); *Grimaldi v Chameleon Mining (No 2)* (2012) 200 FCR 296, [576] (FCAFC); J Edelman, *Gain-Based Damages: Contract, Tort, Equity and Intellectual Property* (Oxford, Hart Publishing, 2002) 83–85, 212; S Worthington, *Equity*, 2nd edn (Oxford, Oxford University Press, 2006) 131, 134.

[63] Smith, 'The Motive' (n 49); Smith, 'Deterrence' (n 43).

[64] Smith, 'The Motive' (n 49) 60; Smith, 'Deterrence' (n 43) 91–93.

[65] Smith, 'Deterrence' (n 43) 93–94.

[66] To borrow terms from James Penner, Smith's first objection seems more relevant to the no profit rule in its 'prudential' mode, and less relevant to the rule in its 'epistemic' mode: 'Is Loyalty a Virtue?' (n 12) 175, n 45.

rule have traditionally focused on its coercive effects; but I think that reflection on the relation of the rule and fiduciary loyalty as fidelity shows that deterrence arguments that focus on the rule's expressive effects are also available.

Secondly, Smith directs his second objection against arguments to the effect that the no profit rule seeks to deter conduct that is harmful to the principal or that constitutes a breach of legal duty.[67] When understood in this way, the rule certainly does, as Smith says, impose liability on fiduciaries whose own conduct is not of the type that it seeks to deter; we have already seen that a fiduciary may be liable under the rule even where she has caused no harm to—indeed has benefited—her principal and even though her conduct has not placed her in breach of any relevant legal duty.[68] But an account of fiduciary loyalty as fidelity allows us to view the conduct that the no profit rule seeks to deter in a new way. Rather than being oriented against harmful or wrongful conduct, we may see the no profit rule as oriented against non-conformity with norms of selflessness entailed in a fiduciary commitment. And, to the extent that the no profit rule is so oriented, it never seeks to deter non-conformity with norms of selflessness except in cases of such non-conformity, precisely because, as a rule that demands the disgorgement of profit, it presupposes that non-conformity. A rule that deters harmful or wrongful conduct by imposing liability on one who has done no harm or wrong seems clearly unjust. Not so a rule that deters non-conformity with norms of selflessness by imposing liability on one who has failed to conform to such norms.[69]

Reflection on the relation of the no profit rule and fiduciary loyalty as fidelity seems to yield implications for our understanding of another aspect of fiduciary law as well: the award of equitable allowances to fiduciaries who are liable under the no profit rule but have expended time and skilled labour in generating the profit that stands to be disgorged.[70] At first glance, such allowances seem difficult to justify to the extent that the no profit rule has a deterrent function; after all, they render the operation of the rule less harsh than it otherwise would be.[71] But the difficulty arises only to the extent that the deterrence of the no profit rule is viewed as a function of its coercive effects; to the extent that the rule deters because of its expressive effects, the practice of awarding allowances to fiduciaries who are liable under the no profit rule appears well-suited to achieving practical justice from

[67] Smith, 'Deterrence' (n 43) 90–91.

[68] The *ne plus ultra* is, of course, *Boardman v Phipps* [1967] 2 AC 46 (HL).

[69] Some argue that a private law rule is necessarily unjust to the extent that it serves any sort of deterrent function: see, eg, EJ Weinrib, *The Idea of Private Law*, revd edn (Oxford, Oxford University Press, 2012) chs 1–2. This chapter is not the place to consider that view, except to say that I do not share it: see further M Harding, '*Forgotten Justice* and Private Law Theory' (2015) 40 *Australian Journal of Legal Philosophy* (forthcoming).

[70] See, eg, *Phipps v Boardman* [1964] 1 WLR 993 (Ch); *Warman International Ltd v Dwyer* (1995) 182 CLR 544 (HCA); *Chirnside v Fay* [2007] 1 NZLR 433 (NZSC).

[71] Some have sought to explain allowances as reflecting a causal inquiry into which profit has been obtained in breach of fiduciary duty and which has not. Elsewhere I have argued that there are reasons not to accept these explanations: M Harding, 'Justifying Fiduciary Allowances' in A Robertson and Tang HW (eds), *The Goals of Private Law* (Oxford, Hart Publishing, 2009) 341, 345–348.

case to case, consistent with deterrence. The award of allowances presupposes liability under the no profit rule; and it is a matter within the discretion of the court. In these ways, the award of allowances enables the guarantees of the no profit rule to operate in all their strictness; that practice also allows the expressive effects of the no profit rule to be achieved unambiguously while at the same time alleviating harsh consequences of the operation of the no profit rule in individual cases. Elsewhere, I have argued that the moral basis for such intervention to alleviate harsh consequences is desert-based justice,[72] but it is not necessary to accept that further argument to see how, in light of the arguments of this chapter, equitable allowances are consistent with the no profit rule performing a deterrent function via its guarantees and its expressive effects.

A final implication for fiduciary law relates to the individuation of disgorgement rules that apply to fiduciaries. Deane J's judgment in *Chan v Zacharia* refers to two, related but distinct, disgorgement rules: the no profit rule; and a rule according to which fiduciaries must disgorge profits derived in a situation of conflict of interest and duty (a 'no conflict' disgorgement rule).[73] Although the view that there are two disgorgement rules is widely applied in Australian case law, largely due to its authoritative formulation in leading cases like *Chan v Zacharia*,[74] it is much debated in academic literature. Some argue that there is, or should be, just one disgorgement rule; moreover, among those who favour the recognition of just one disgorgement rule, there is debate as to what that disgorgement rule should be: no conflict or no profit?[75] A range of considerations, some of them tending to the prosaic, may bear on the question of the optimal individuation of fiduciary law's disgorgement rules; Richard Nolan, for example, has argued convincingly that one reason to recognise a no profit rule in addition to a no conflict disgorgement rule is that in litigation there are particular difficulties associated with pleading and proving conflicts.[76]

I think there are reasons for fiduciary law to have a distinct no conflict disgorgement rule; as I have argued elsewhere, I think that these reasons have to do with the ways in which a no conflict rule aims, by a prophylactic strategy,

[72] ibid 350–360.

[73] It has been recognised in the case law that non-conformity with a no conflict rule may also lead to rescission or the award of compensation: see, eg, *Maguire v Makaronis* (1997) 188 CLR 449 (HCA) (rescission); *Canson Enterprises Ltd v Boughton* [1991] 3 SCR 534 (SCC) (compensation); *Pilmer v Duke Group Limited (in liq)* (2001) 207 CLR 165 (HCA) (compensation). Whether non-conformity with a no conflict rule should lead to compensation is, however, a matter of debate: see L Smith, 'The Measurement of Compensation Claims against Trustees and Fiduciaries' in E Bant and M Harding (eds), *Exploring Private Law* (Cambridge, Cambridge University Press, 2010) 363; Smith, 'Fiduciary Relationships' (n 27) 621–623.

[74] For a sensitive account of the treatment of the individuation of disgorgement rules in the case law: Conaglen (n 31) 114–125.

[75] For instance, Penner seems to take the view that fiduciary law needs only a no conflict disgorgement rule: 'Distinguishing' (n 12) 230–233; Smith, on the other hand, takes the view that the only disgorgement rule in fiduciary law should be the no profit rule, and that the no conflict rule should deal with cases of rescission: 'Fiduciary Relationships' (n 27) 625.

[76] Nolan (n 48) 522–523.

to maintain conditions under which a fiduciary is unlikely to resolve conflicts of interest and duty in morally wrongful ways.[77] Now I want to add that I also think that reflection on the relation of the no profit rule and fiduciary loyalty as fidelity points to reasons (in addition to other reasons such as those provided by Nolan) for fiduciary law to have a distinct no profit rule. The guarantees of the no profit rule, as well as its expressive effects, depend on the ways in which the rule tracks the demands of norms of selflessness that are entailed in commitment to a fiduciary relationship. Seeking to keep profit obtained from the fiduciary relationship is, in and of itself, action that fails to conform to those norms, and this is clearly reflected in the no profit rule. Assume, for the sake of argument, that a rule demanding the disgorgement of profit derived in circumstances of conflict of interest and duty could achieve disgorgement in every situation to which a no profit rule applies.[78] Even so, a no conflict rule is likely to draw attention away from the demands of fiduciary norms of selflessness, and towards the existence and normative significance of the conflicts to which the rule refers. And this may interrupt and complicate the guarantees and the expressive effects that are achieved by a straightforward no profit rule. This is not to say that conflicts are irrelevant to fiduciary loyalty in the sense of fidelity: a fiduciary commitment is feasibly viewed as entailing commitment to norms of respect that, in my view at least, ground the moral duty underpinning the no conflict rule. But it is to say that fiduciary loyalty in the sense of fidelity is a matter of more than avoiding conflicts; it is a matter of being true to all of the norms brought into view by commitment to a fiduciary relationship, including the norms of selflessness to which a stand-alone no profit rule, uniquely, relates.

V. Conclusion

Perhaps the best way to conclude is to point to some general propositions that seem to emerge from my analysis of the relation of fiduciary loyalty and the no profit rule. These propositions might be viewed as starting points for further inquiry into the themes of this chapter, or indeed as points of potential divergence from the arguments or underpinning commitments of the chapter. First, an account of fiduciary loyalty need not rest on a conception of loyalty as partiality; such an account may proceed from a different, and equally philosophically plausible, understanding of loyalty: loyalty as fidelity. Secondly, fiduciary loyalty as fidelity is distinctive not because of any feature of loyalty as fidelity per se, but instead because of the content of norms that are entailed in a fiduciary

[77] Harding, 'Trust and Fiduciary Law' (n 47) 89–95.

[78] Although there are reasons to doubt that this assumption can be made: see further RP Austin, 'Fiduciary Accountability for Business Opportunities' in PD Finn (ed), *Equity and Commercial Relationships* (Sydney, Lawbook Co, 1987) 141, 146–147.

commitment and to which a loyal (faithful) fiduciary is true. Thirdly, fiduciaries are always committed, in some way, to norms of selflessness; such norms may take the form of or be entailed in legal duties, but equally they may not. And finally, the no profit rule has a social orientation, providing guarantees to principals who seek to enter into fiduciary relationships, and educating fiduciary communities and lending social meaning to fiduciary roles.

3

Justice, Redress, and the Right to Do Wrong

ANDREW S GOLD*

I. Introduction

This chapter concerns the morality of redress, and in particular the morality of redress where a right to redress is legitimate. In such cases, it is entirely possible that redress ought not to be pursued, either because the results would be overly harsh or because it would be better to forgive. At the same time, if an individual nonetheless seeks redress, that individual may bring about a type of justice by doing so. The evident result is that it can be morally wrongful to obtain justice. One of the best illustrations arises when plaintiffs seek disgorgement of gains acquired by conflicted fiduciaries, and I will start with that example.

The disgorgement remedy is one of the more interesting features of fiduciary law. In part, this is because disgorgement is available even where the plaintiff has not been made worse off by the fiduciary's conduct. It is also because the defendant can be liable even if she acted in complete good faith, attempting to advance the interests of her beneficiary. And these features are especially striking because the disgorgement remedy is so powerful.[1] We may rightly wonder if the defendant deserves to face this remedy under these circumstances—perhaps, the plaintiff may have a moral duty to let the defendant off the hook. Can it nonetheless be just for the plaintiff to bring suit under these circumstances? The answer is yes, or so I will argue. It can be just for a plaintiff to act wrongfully.

* I am grateful to Elise Bant, Sam Bray, Richard Brooks, Matthew Conaglen, James Edelman, Kim Ferzan, Stephen Galoob, John Gardner, Matthew Harding, Tonja Jacobi, Marin Levy, Paul Miller, James Penner, Deborah Tuerkheimer, and Peter Turner for helpful comments on ideas contained in this chapter. I also benefitted from participants' comments at the Remedies Discussion Forum held at Université Paris-Dauphine, at an Obligations workshop held at the University of Melbourne, and at the Conference on Equitable Compensation and Disgorgement of Profit at the UNSW Law School. Any errors are my own.

[1] See PB Miller, 'Justifying Fiduciary Remedies' (2013) 63 *University of Toronto Law Journal* 570, 570 (noting that '[r]emedies for breach of fiduciary duty are notoriously potent').

Let's begin with an illustration from the case law. A classic example is *In re Will of Gleeson*.[2] In that case, Mary Gleeson had owned farmland, which she leased on a yearly basis to a partnership in which Con Colbrook was a partner. Colbrook was also a trustee for Gleeson's estate (which included the farmland), and she passed away 15 days before the 1952 farming year began. Acting as trustee, Colbrook allowed the partnership to continue leasing the property for that year. There was apparently no secrecy to Colbrook's actions, he claimed that he wished to advance the best interests of the estate, and the timeline meant it would be difficult to successfully find another tenant.[3] In addition, the trust allegedly suffered no financial loss as a result of the transaction.[4] Even so, the court found the trustee's good faith and honesty irrelevant, and it was unmoved by the possibility that the trust suffered no losses.[5] Disgorgement was the remedy: Colbrook had to turn over the profits he earned from farming the Gleeson land under the new lease.[6]

Commentators have suggested a variety of justifications for such disgorgement remedies in fiduciary law, ranging from deterrence to a rightful claim on the disgorged assets.[7] My concern is not to assess the overall merits of this legal doctrine. Instead, my concern is with the justice of this remedy. The puzzle I will start with is whether fiduciary law's disgorgement remedy can be squared with leading philosophical accounts of private law. Corrective justice theory is an obvious candidate, but it often focuses on the duties of defendants in a way that fits poorly with the legal point of view. I will focus on two alternative, rights-based understandings: the civil recourse and redressive justice accounts. As will be developed, these accounts can help make sense of the disgorgement remedy in fiduciary law, and in combination, they suggest a way that justice is done in disgorgement settings. In short, there is a type of justice that fits disgorgement.

This interpretive exercise, however, is a backdrop for the real topic of this chapter. My ultimate concern is with the relation between moral duties and theories of

[2] *In re Will of Gleeson*, 124 NE2d 624 (Ill App Ct 1955).

[3] ibid 626.

[4] ibid.

[5] ibid 627.

[6] While cases like *Gleeson* (n 2) are raised as examples of the harshness of the disgorgement remedy, it should be noted that the effects of this doctrine can be alleviated by legal rules that permit the fiduciary to seek authorisation for the relevant conduct. See M Conaglen, 'The Extent of Fiduciary Accounting and the Importance of Authorisation Mechanisms' (2011) 70 *CLJ* 548, 560–562. Likewise, equitable allowances may limit some of the effects of disgorgement: at 568–569. On the other hand, some of these cases implicate unsophisticated and poorly counseled trustees. For suggestions on how the law should address such cases, see MB Leslie, 'In Defense of the No Further Inquiry Rule: A Response to Professor Langbein' (2005) 47 *William and Mary Law Review* 541, 582–586.

[7] Compare R Cooter and BJ Freedman, 'The Fiduciary Relationship: Its Economic Character and Consequences' (1991) 66 *New York University Law Review* 1045, 1051–1052 (analysing the disgorgement remedy in deterrence terms) with L Smith, 'Deterrence, Prophylaxis and Punishment in Fiduciary Obligations' (2013) 7 *Journal of Equity* 87 (providing a prophylaxis-based account of the conflicts rules, but suggesting disgorgement involves enforcement of primary rights); Miller (n 1) (suggesting a beneficiary's interest in her means supports disgorgement); S Worthington, 'Reconsidering Disgorgement for Wrongs' (1999) 62 *MLR* 218, 236–237 (suggesting that disgorgement is justified as a means of protecting particular types of relationships).

justice. There are cases in which it is morally wrongful for a plaintiff to seek the disgorgement remedy, especially given a fiduciary's good faith and the absence of losses.[8] Yet, if this chapter is correct, this disgorgement is explicable in justice-based terms. How can these two premises be reconciled? It may seem strange to think that a claim that ought not to be brought can nonetheless be just. I will argue that, even where bringing a legal claim is morally wrong, the claim can still be just: justice, in other words, can be wrongful. This insight, in turn, has bearing on the way we structure private law and on the various remedies available to plaintiffs who have been wronged.

Part I of this chapter will assess a common approach to corrective justice. Part II will introduce the civil recourse alternative. Part III will introduce the redressive justice approach. As will be developed, civil recourse and redressive justice theories can account for most cases of disgorgement in fiduciary law. Part IV will draw connections between justice and a right to do wrong. This Part will indicate how certain types of justice—including redressive justice—can incorporate sound norms even where those norms allow wrongful conduct. Part V will discuss legal implications.

II. Corrective Justice

Corrective justice is a type of justice that governs allocations back—that is, it governs the undoing of transactions.[9] If, for example, A owns an apple, and B wrongly takes that apple from A, corrective justice governs the return of the apple. In Aristotle's famous account, corrective justice thus involves an arithmetic relation.[10] The details of corrective justice, however, are debated. Theorists disagree whether the losses that corrective justice is concerned with must be wrongful; they disagree whether corrective justice is concerned with rectifying wrongful losses, or wrongs as such; and they disagree as to what counts as a wrong.[11]

For present purposes, I will assume that while corrective justice governs allocations back, it does so without a necessary link to wrongs or wrongful losses.[12] This

[8] Or, to be more precise, the absence of losses other than the gains that are to be disgorged. Since these gains may not have been available to the beneficiary but for the challenged transaction, from a certain perspective there may be no losses for disgorgement to remedy.

[9] For helpful analysis of the idea of 'allocation back', see J Gardner, 'What is Tort Law For? Part 1: The Place of Corrective Justice' (2011) 30 *Law and Philosophy* 1. For application in the fiduciary setting, see M Harding, 'Constructive Trusts and Distributive Justice' in E Bant and M Bryan (eds), *Principles of Proprietary Remedies* (Pyrmont, Lawbook Co, 2013) 20–24.

[10] See Aristotle, 'Nicomachean Ethics', Book V, s 4, in Jonathan Barnes (ed), *The Complete Works of Aristotle* (Princeton, Princeton University Press, 1984) 1786.

[11] See JL Coleman, 'The Practice of Corrective Justice' (1995) 37 *Arizona Law Review* 15, 19.

[12] Although there is controversy on this point, this premise is well within the range of mainstream corrective justice theories. See, eg, Gardner (n 9) 34 (noting that some transactions 'need not be wrongful in order to call for correction').

broad definition makes it much more plausible to claim that corrective justice can help explain disgorgement in fiduciary law. On some accounts, fiduciary law's disgorgement remedy applies in cases that do not involve wrongs.[13] In turn, if disgorgement is applicable in the absence of a wrong, a wrongs-based account of corrective justice is a poor fit for the legal doctrine. I will sidestep this concern for present purposes, for, as we will see, even with this more congenial starting point disgorgement is challenging for some of the leading corrective justice theories.

The distinctive aspects of fiduciary law pose various hurdles for these corrective justice theories. As Paul Miller notes, there are several scenarios that raise questions: '[t]he first kind of case is that in which the fiduciary has (wittingly or not) acted under a conflict of interest but manifestly did so with the intention and for the primary purpose of benefitting the beneficiary';[14] '[t]he second case is that in which the fiduciary has (again, knowingly or not) acted in conflict of interest and gained from doing so, but the gain in question is not one the beneficiary had any reasonable expectation of securing';[15] '[t]he third and last kind of case is that in which the fiduciary has, knowingly or not, acted in conflict of interest and realized gains shared with the beneficiary but in achieving the gains has invested personal resources ... without compensation.'[16]

These features are difficult for corrective justice theories that require the existence of a wrong, and they are also problematic if corrective justice is thought to involve the reversal of losses. Depending on how one reads these fact patterns, however, they may also raise concerns that the plaintiff in such cases is getting a windfall; he or she may appear to get more than she properly has a right to, or properly deserves. In what respect is the plaintiff in such cases getting his or her due?

Miller's answer is to focus on an ownership-like relation between the fiduciary's powers and the beneficiary.[17] On his view, '[t]he conflict rules proscribe appropriation by the fiduciary of a means belonging to the beneficiary. The fiduciary may not treat fiduciary power as a personal means.'[18] The beneficiary has an exclusive

[13] See L Smith, 'Can We Be Obliged to Be Selfless?' in AS Gold and PB Miller (eds), *Philosophical Foundations of Fiduciary Law* (Oxford, Oxford University Press, 2014) 141, 150 (indicating that the no-profit rule applies as a matter of primary right); J Penner, 'Is Loyalty a Virtue?, and Even If It Is, Does It Really Help Explain Fiduciary Liability?', AS Gold and PB Miller (eds), *Philosophical Foundations of Fiduciary Law* (Oxford, Oxford University Press, 2014) 159, 171 (indicating that the law of fiduciary accountability involves primary remedial duties). Compare Miller (n 1) 617 (describing the beneficiary's implied primary right to gains made from the execution of a fiduciary mandate, but also indicating that disgorgement 'rectifies the wrong of disloyalty').

[14] See Miller (n 1) 588.

[15] ibid.

[16] ibid 588–589.

[17] ibid 600 (noting that '[t]his approach is appealing because ... disgorgement is least controversial in respect of wrongs involving appropriation of property.'). Compare EJ Weinrib, 'Restitutionary Damages as Corrective Justice' (2000) 1 *Theoretical Inquiries in Law* 1, 32–33 ('[a]lthough restitutionary damages do not ... respond to the violation of what is strictly speaking a proprietary right, the relationship between the parties can give rise to an interest sufficiently property-like to allow this kind of award.').

[18] See Miller (n 1) 611.

claim over the exercise of fiduciary power—whether that power is derived from the beneficiary's personality, or from a benefaction—and where the fiduciary uses that means for her own purposes, the law steps in. If we adopt this view, there is also an explanation for the disgorgement remedy: '[t]he exclusivity of the beneficiary's claim over fiduciary power necessarily extends to gains associated with its exercise.'[19] As Miller suggests, '[t]here are deep parallels between the wrongs of disloyalty and conversion that reflect parallels in the content and justification of primary rights to loyalty and private property.'[20]

It is reasonable to conclude that a theory along these lines will be called for if corrective justice is to underpin the fiduciary law disgorgement remedy. Yet even if this perspective is taken, some corrective justice theories still run into a major difficulty: these corrective justice theories often suggest that courts are bringing about defendants' compliance with their corrective duties. To the extent that a corrective justice approach adopts this view, it is a mismatch with private law, as courts tend not to act on a defendant's behalf when they rule against the defendant and order damages (or disgorgement). And, although not all corrective justice theories claim that the court is acting on behalf of the defendant in this way, this is a common understanding of how courts do corrective justice.[21]

Consider John Gardner's formulation of corrective justice as an example. On his view:

> The question of corrective justice is not the question of whether and to what extent and in what form and on what ground [something] should be allocated among [two parties] *full stop*, but the question of whether and to what extent and in what form and on what ground it should now be allocated *back* from one party to the other, reversing a transaction that took place between them.[22]

This is a clear exposition of the idea that corrective justice involves allocation back.

Yet Gardner also concludes that: 'a norm of corrective justice only regulates the actions of the person from whom the transfer back is to be made *or another person acting on behalf of that person*.'[23] Since the court is forcing the allocation back in the typical case, the second clause is important. The court, on Gardner's view, is acting on behalf of the party who must allocate back.[24] Gardner rightly notes

[19] ibid 616.

[20] ibid 617. For a somewhat similar account that draws on primary rights rather than secondary rights, see Smith (n 13). Smith, however, suggests a distinctive perspective from Miller's, given that he does not view disgorgement under the no-profit rule as a response to disloyalty. See Smith (n 13) 150 fn 50 (noting the apparent distinction). For present purposes, it will not matter which account is right on this point.

[21] Miller's account of corrective justice suggests a view that can avoid this concern. See Miller (n 1) 580 (indicating that a court order 'novates a primary right and duty into a secondary duty to redress the wrong in the manner ordered').

[22] See Gardner (n 9) 9–10 (emphasis in original).

[23] ibid 10. Gardner is not alone in thinking that corrective justice is concerned with the corrective obligations of duty bearers. Other theories of corrective justice share this emphasis. See, eg, J Coleman, *Risks and Wrongs* (Oxford, Oxford University Press, 1992) 303–324; SR Perry, 'The Mixed Conception of Corrective Justice' (1992) 15 *Harvard Journal of Law and Public Policy* 917.

[24] See Gardner (n 9) 10–11.

some hard problems in figuring out how the court could be acting on behalf of the defendant in a corrective justice case.[25] Even assuming these conceptual puzzles are resolved, however, the difficulty is more basic. This duty-based picture is simply not a fit with the legal point of view.

If courts are acting on behalf of anyone when they order disgorgement, they are acting on behalf of the plaintiff. Returning to the *Gleeson* case as an example, the court there was not trying to do Colbrook a favor when they ordered him to turn over all profits to the trust beneficiaries. The court assisted the plaintiff in enforcing his rights, and it acted on his behalf. Accordingly, we should be looking for accounts that will fit this feature—ie, accounts that treat the court as acting on behalf of the plaintiff when a remedial order is issued. As it is defined by Gardner and others, corrective justice will not adequately capture the legal point of view.[26] There are, fortunately, private law theories that do emphasise the right holder's private right of action, and these theories understand the court to be acting on behalf of the plaintiff in ordering damages or otherwise remedying wrongs or undoing transactions. The next Section will turn to these right-based theories.

III. Civil Recourse Theory

One of the most prominent right-based accounts is civil recourse theory. Civil recourse theory was first developed as a way to explain core features of tort law, and its early formulations reflect this focus. As Benjamin Zipursky explains the core idea:

> By recognizing a legal right of action against a tortfeasor, our system respects the principle that the plaintiff is entitled to act against one who has legally wronged him or her. I call this the principle of civil recourse. The legal principle that the victim of a tort has a right of action against the tortfeasor is an instance of this more general idea.[27]

The principle of civil recourse can explain several doctrinal features of tort law. These include the substantive standing doctrine (the doctrine under which only a party whose rights were violated will have a private right of action);[28] the

[25] ibid 11 ('To explain how corrective justice can be done as between two parties without the co-operation of the party from whom the transfer back is to be made we need to explain the possibility of vicarious agency: how there can be an agent who acts on my behalf, such that on occasions I can be regarded as having conformed to norms of corrective justice even though it was someone else that did the allocating back for me').

[26] It should be noted that some corrective justice theories have a very different conceptual structure from Gardner's account. See, eg, EJ Weinrib, *The Idea of Private Law* (Harvard, Harvard University Press, 1995); A Ripstein, 'As If It Had Never Happened' (2007) 48 *William and Mary Law Review* 1957. I will bracket these accounts for the present discussion.

[27] See BC Zipursky, 'Civil Recourse, Not Corrective Justice' (2003) 91 *Georgetown Law Journal* 695, 735.

[28] ibid 714–716.

variability in tort law remedies (from nominal damages, to compensatory damages, to punitive damages);[29] and certain doctrinal details that indicate that a tort defendant does not have a remedial duty prior to an actual court order.[30] Civil recourse theory readily accounts for each of these features.

Under the conventional understanding of civil recourse, recourse involves holding someone accountable, or 'getting satisfaction'.[31] Civil recourse thus allows the wronged party to respond to the affront of being wronged.[32] As applied to tort law, this account also has much to recommend it, particularly when we consider the difficulty of explaining remedies like nominal damages and punitive damages under a corrective justice rubric. Yet the private rights of action emphasised by civil recourse theorists are prominent throughout private law: we can see similar features in cases involving contracts, fiduciary law, and unjust enrichment.[33] And this raises a challenge. As we move away from tort law, the tie between getting satisfaction and legal remedies is increasingly strained.

When we turn to contract law, there are notable difficulties with the conventional civil recourse picture. The expectation remedy holds pride of place, and it is standardised in a way that does not seem well-suited for responding to an affront or for holding someone accountable.[34] It is true that breaches of contract may be taken as affronts,[35] but in many cases a contract plaintiff will have no particular interest in getting satisfaction. What she may want is simply to have what was promised to her, or the next best thing.

When we reach fiduciary law, the problem is significantly greater. Disgorgement is an unusual remedy if one's aim is to hold someone accountable—the amount available to the plaintiff will not vary in proportion to the degree of affront to the plaintiff. Yet this standard remedy is only part of the problem. Why should someone want to get satisfaction from a trustee like Colbrook? Here, the defendant was

[29] ibid 710–713.

[30] ibid 719–720. See also SA Smith, 'Duties, Liability, and Damages' (2012) 125 *Harvard Law Review* 1727, 1727–1728. But note that there is debate over the civil recourse view on this issue. See, eg, J Gardner, 'Torts and Other Wrongs' (2011) 39 *Florida State University Law Review* 43, 58 fn 56.

[31] See JCP Goldberg and BC Zipursky, 'Tort Law and Moral Luck' (2007) 92 *Cornell Law Review* 1123, 1162 (describing tort victims who have been 'injured in a way that warrants their thinking that someone else is responsible for mistreating them and that their wrongdoer is an appropriate person from whom to demand redress or satisfaction'). See also JM Solomon, 'Equal Accountability through Tort Law' (2009) 103 *Northwestern University Law Review* 1765 (adopting an accountability-based understanding of civil recourse).

[32] See BC Zipursky, 'Rights, Wrongs, and Recourse in the Law of Torts' (1998) 51 *Vanderbilt Law Review* 1, 87 ('The answer is that entitlement to recourse does not spring from the need precipitated by injury. It springs from the affront of being wronged by another').

[33] A point which Goldberg and Zipursky recognise. See JCP Goldberg and BC Zipursky, 'Civil Recourse Revisited' (2011) 39 *Florida State University Law Review* 341, 349 ('Civil recourse … is, we think, a broad concept that can and does encompass not only torts, but contracts and other domains of private law').

[34] See AS Gold, 'The Taxonomy of Civil Recourse' (2011) 39 *Florida State University Law Review* 65, 72 (noting that 'an enforcement account of recourse explains the standardization of remedies prevalent in certain private law fields').

[35] Compare T Wilkinson-Ryan and DA Hoffman, 'Breach is for Suckers' (2010) 63 *Vanderbilt Law Review* 1003 (studying the psychological impact of contractual breaches).

actively trying to help the plaintiff, and the plaintiff has suffered no financial loss as a result. If civil recourse is about responding to the affront of being wronged, is this a plausible setting to recognise an affront?

This challenge is especially striking if we conclude that these settings do not truly involve wrongs, as some have argued. For example, James Penner has recently suggested that being in a conflict isn't in itself a wrong.[36] Drawing on the case of *Boardman v Phipps*, he argues that it would be morally problematic to say that fiduciaries have a duty to remove a conflict when they in good faith don't realise they are in that conflict.[37] His argument extends to the question of legal wrongs as well. As Penner claims: 'In this respect the law of fiduciary accountability is akin to the law of unjust enrichment. Both are cases of *primary*, *remedial* duties.'[38]

Lionel Smith describes similar features in his analysis of the no-profit rule. As he notes:

> Any benefit or advantage acquired by the fiduciary in the exercise of his or her duty-bound management is attributed, as a matter of primary right, to the beneficiary by the no-profit rule. This applies even to a benefit whose acquisition was unauthorized, if the beneficiary so chooses. When I say "as a matter of primary right," I mean that this rule is not a sanction for wrongdoing. It does not depend on proof of the breach of any duty. This is why, like the no-conflict rule, it can apply to people who are in perfectly good faith.[39]

On this view, disgorgement may be an important remedy in fiduciary law without being a remedy for a wrong.[40]

Absent a wrong, an affront is hard to locate.[41] Yet even if there are genuine legal wrongs in these cases, civil recourse theorists should still care about a range of salient details: whether the fiduciary was trying to help the beneficiary; whether the fiduciary in good faith even realised a conflict existed; and whether the beneficiary suffered any losses. With these concerns in mind, the disgorgement remedy in fiduciary law is remarkably inflexible; it applies to fact patterns that do not implicate a need to get satisfaction, or to hold someone accountable, or apparently to respond to an affront. Only the hypersensitive could recognise a significant affront in some of these cases. To the extent affronts may exist, moreover, the legal remedy does not vary with the seriousness of the affront. The only answer for this fit problem—assuming that civil recourse is to apply broadly to private rights of action outside of tort law—is to recognise that civil recourse involves more than one norm.

36 See Penner (n 13) 171.

37 ibid.

38 ibid.

39 See Smith (n 13) 150. See also L Smith, 'Fiduciary Relationships: Ensuring the Loyal Exercise of Judgement on Behalf of Another' (2014) 130 *LQR* 608, 628.

40 It may also be that some cases involve wrongs, and others do not. See Gardner (n 30) 49–50 (comparing trustee liability to disgorge a profit and nontrustee fiduciary cases).

41 Note also that a legal wrong may not be a moral wrong. Compare P Birks, 'The Concept of a Civil Wrong' in David Owen (ed), *Philosophical Foundations of Tort Law* (Oxford, Oxford University Press, 1995) 29, 37 (noting that a wrong must be understood with respect to a duty within the normative system in question, and indicating that '[a] legal wrong cannot be understood except as a breach of legal duty'). The affront stemming from a bare legal wrong may be different from the affront attached to a moral wrong.

In prior work, I have argued that several distinct norms fall under the civil recourse umbrella.[42] Civil recourse theorists ordinarily emphasise accountability, but civil recourse may also implicate enforcement rights, or even private revenge.[43] And, if civil recourse is understood to support enforcement rights, we can readily account for contract remedies in civil recourse terms. By the same token, we can make sense of the disgorgement remedy in fiduciary law. If, for example, a beneficiary has an ownership-like interest like the one Paul Miller describes, it will be quite reasonable to see the private right of action as a means to enforce the beneficiary's primary right to the gains associated with a means that belongs to her.

Unfortunately, there is still a potential difficulty, for civil recourse theorists sometimes appear to distance civil recourse from norms of justice.[44] To the extent they just mean to distinguish civil recourse from corrective justice, they are right to do so.[45] On the other hand, to the extent civil recourse theorists may deny conceptual links between private rights of action and justice of any type, their theory goes awry. Private law adjudication is ordinarily taken to be a mechanism for doing justice.[46] A key component of private law reasoning is that the private right of action is a pathway to just results, and if an interpretive accounts aims to take legal concepts seriously this means that it should at least indicate how courts might think a private law remedy is doing justice.[47] If the conceptual linkage between recourse and justice is removed, the plausibility of the civil recourse interpretation is diminished.[48] The next Section will therefore consider what type of justice might underpin civil recourse in the disgorgement setting.

[42] See Gold (n 34).

[43] ibid 68–78; AS Gold, 'A Theory of Redressive Justice' [2014] 64 *University of Toronto Law Journal* 159, 182. Zipursky has since endorsed the view that civil recourse can involve enforcement rights. See BC Zipursky, 'Civil Recourse and the Plurality of Wrongs: Why Torts are Different' [2014] *New Zealand Law Review* 145, 158.

[44] See BC Zipursky, 'Substantive Standing, Civil Recourse, and Corrective Justice' (2011) 39 *Florida State University Law Review* 299, 339–340 (noting the perception that the tort system 'is a system that corrects injustices', and suggesting that '[d]oing corrective justice is one of many things that tort law sometimes accomplishes,' while adding that 'its capacity to do so is not basic to the account of private rights of action').

[45] Some corrective justice theorists, however, have argued that corrective justice and civil recourse theories can be reconciled. See, eg, A Ripstein, 'Civil Recourse and Separation of Wrongs and Remedies' (2011) 39 *Florida State University Law Review* 163. See also S Hershovitz, 'Corrective Justice for Civil Recourse Theorists' (2011) 39 *Florida State University Law Review* 107 (suggesting civil recourse may be consistent with a type of corrective justice that focuses on 'getting even').

[46] On adjudication and its relation to norms of justice, see J Gardner, 'The Virtue of Justice and the Character of Law' in *Law as a Leap of Faith* (Oxford, Oxford University Press, 2012) 238; SA Smith, 'Why Courts Make Orders (and What This Tells Us about Damages)' (2011) 64 *Current Legal Problems* 51, 82–83.

[47] For further thoughts on this interpretive criterion, see AS Gold, 'Private Rights and Private Wrongs' *Michigan Law Review* (forthcoming) (reviewing A Ripstein, *Private Wrongs* (Cambridge, Harvard University Press, 2016)).

[48] This is not to say that civil recourse norms must actually be just, but rather that they must plausibly be just from the perspective of the law. Compare SA Smith, *Contract Theory* (Oxford, Oxford University Press, 2004) (describing a morality criterion for private law interpretation under which courts could plausibly think that a given set of legal concepts is moral).

IV. Redressive Justice

Redressive justice is, in some respects, the flip side of corrective justice. We can see how if we return to the idea of allocation back. Suppose we revisit 'the question of whether and to what extent and in what form and on what ground [something] should now be allocated back from one party to the other, reversing a transaction that took place between them.'[49] On Gardner's account, it will be a matter of corrective justice if the relevant norms govern the conduct of a duty bearer, or someone acting on the duty bearer's behalf. Notice, however, that there is conceptual space left over if we adopt this understanding of corrective justice. Not all norms that govern allocation back concern the conduct of a duty bearer, or someone acting on a duty bearer's behalf. Some norms govern the conduct of right holders, or someone acting on a right holder's behalf.

Redressive justice is the type of justice concerned with allocation back from the right holder's perspective. It addresses the question of whether and how something may be allocated back by a right holder from a duty bearer, reversing a transaction between them. To the extent the state is involved, redressive justice governs the actions of the state taken to reverse such transactions on behalf of a right holder. In other words, redressive justice is the type of justice that governs a right holder's enforcement rights when she seeks to undo a transaction.

One might think that this is effectively the same thing as corrective justice (using Gardner's definition of corrective justice), but it is not. There are important cases in which a duty bearer will have an obligation to undo a transaction, yet the right holder cannot legitimately force this to happen.[50] A breach of an ordinary promise offers a good illustration, as the promisor will have a duty to correct, but the promisee cannot legitimately make this happen. These are cases where corrective justice is apt, but redressive justice would be improper. There are also important cases in which a duty bearer will have an obligation to undo a transaction by a certain means, and a right holder will have a legitimate right to undo that transaction, but only by a different means.[51] For example, a services contract may implicate a promisor's duty to perform after the fact, while the promisee can only legitimately seek damages. Here, both corrective justice and redressive justice apply, but with different remedies attaching. And there may also be cases in which a defendant has no duty to allocate back, but a right holder can nevertheless legitimately force a reversal of the transaction.[52] Certain instances of unjust enrichment suggest

[49] See Gardner (n 9) 9–10 (using this formulation to describe the question of corrective justice).

[50] See Gold (n 43) 188 (describing an example in the promissory setting).

[51] ibid 191 (describing an example in the contractual setting).

[52] ibid 189–190 (describing a potential example in the unjust enrichment setting). For further analysis of the issues raised in this type of context, see SA Smith, 'Justifying the Law of Unjust Enrichment' (2001) 79 *Texas Law Review* 2177, 2194.

this result. In those cases, redressive justice would be apt, but corrective justice no longer fits. In short, the legitimacy of enforcement does not perfectly correspond to a duty bearer's remedial duties—and the divide between corrective and redressive justice reflects this asymmetry.[53]

Redressive justice is a good match for many applications of civil recourse in the forms it takes outside of tort law. To the extent private rights of action are available in contract law, unjust enrichment law, and fiduciary law, those rights of action are often concerned with a plaintiff's enforcement rights, not with getting satisfaction.[54] Redressive justice, with its focus on the legitimacy of a right holder's enforcement, is an excellent fit. Whether or not there is a wrong involved when fiduciary law calls for disgorgement, there is usually an allocation back, and courts understand the legal remedy to constitute a type of justice.[55] Once redressive justice is added to the picture, this understanding makes sense.

Civil recourse can be a mechanism for redressive justice, and accordingly we have now taken several steps toward explaining the connection between private rights of action, legal norms of justice, and the disgorgement remedy. We have made progress in terms of understanding the legal point of view. What if instead we are speaking in moral terms? This will be our next concern, for the legal and moral perspectives on justice might diverge in this setting. Perhaps from a moral perspective plaintiffs ought to avoid lawsuits against defendants who were trying in good faith to help them, and who caused them no losses.[56] One might object that, in such a case, it is not really justice that is being done through a private right of action, since the plaintiff is acting contrary to her moral obligations in seeking disgorgement. These issues will be discussed in the next Sections.

V. The Moral Challenge

What if it is morally dubious for the right holder to stand on her rights? It may be the case—and in cases of especially strong remedies, it often will be the

[53] Authorship of an allocation back is also relevant to the moral status of a wrongdoer. See Gold (n 43) 192–195.

[54] But see N Oman, 'Consent to Retaliation: A Civil Recourse Theory of Contractual Liability' (2011) 96 *Iowa Law Review* 529.

[55] In exceptional cases, there may not be an allocation back. Matthew Harding suggests that in bribery cases, for example, no allocation back occurs. In these settings, the disgorgement remedy may be doing a local form of distributive justice. See Harding (n 9) 31–33.

[56] It should also be noted that concerns with the morality of bringing suit are by no means limited to fiduciary disgorgement cases. Compare Ripstein (n 47) 272 ('If I defraud you, you are entitled to demand compensation, but you might think it more important to forgive, or you might be too embarrassed that you fell for a such a ridiculous scam that you don't want to be reminded, or have others learn, of your gullibility').

case—that the plaintiff, morally speaking, ought to forgive and forget, or at least ought to settle for a less powerful remedy than the law provides. Redressive justice may not mirror corrective justice, but it is still a type of justice, and we may question whether it is sound in cases where a right holder seeks onerous remedies against a good faith defendant whose conduct caused no losses.

A. The Kind of Wrongful Conduct at Issue

A redressive justice theory thus faces a distinctive concern: sometimes the private right of action is permitted in cases where the right holder ought not to insist on disgorgement. In these cases, there is a certain awkwardness in describing the conduct of the plaintiff as just, because, given our premises, the plaintiff is acting wrongfully in pursuing her claim in court. There is cause to question whether it can really be just when a plaintiff insists on his rights against a good faith defendant who caused no financial losses.

There are several types of 'wrong' behaviour that could be at issue, however, and I should clarify at the outset what I have in mind. As David Owens suggests, we may divide up wrong behaviour in multiple ways.[57] When used as a noun, 'a wrong' tends to 'render blame apt.'[58] One can nonetheless engage in various forms of conduct that are unwise without meriting blame—to use Owens' example, one may make the wrong move in a chess game.[59] We can also divide up blameworthy conduct depending on whether it violates rights, or is simply immoral. For purposes of this chapter, I will be interested in cases where conduct is morally improper, yet not in violation of anyone's rights. I will be interested in cases where a plaintiff is acting wrongfully in pursuing a claim, but not wronging the counterparty when they do so because not violating their rights.

I recognise that some wrongful behaviour that enforces rights is inconsistent with redressive justice. Like preventive justice, legitimate applications of redressive justice are subject to various constraints, including a proportionality constraint.[60] Where these constraints aren't met, there is wrongful behaviour that takes us outside of sound norms of redressive justice. I will be concerned with the possibility of wrongful behaviour that is actually consistent with such norms of justice. In certain cases, I will suggest that examples of redress involve the exercise of a right holder's discretion to act wrongfully. In these settings, redressive justice allows for wrongful conduct where the plaintiff is exercising a legitimate right to do wrong.

[57] See D Owens, *Shaping the Normative Landscape* (Oxford, Oxford University Press, 2012). Owens' particular approach is not the only way to divide up the relevant concepts and terminology. Compare Coleman (n 23) 329–332 (distinguishing wrongdoing from wrong). It appears that Owens' notion of a wronging corresponds to Coleman's notion of a wrong.

[58] Owens (n 57) 45.

[59] ibid.

[60] Gold (n 43) 201–202.

B. Sound and Unsound Categories of Justice

In arguing for wrongful justice, there is also an easy answer that I wish to avoid. Justice is often thought to be concerned with allocative questions.[61] Various norms govern our behaviour, but only some of them are allocative—this distinguishes norms of justice from a range of other norms. Norms that govern allocations can be extraordinarily wide-ranging, however. For example, laws tell legal officials to allocate in a variety of ways, and it is possible to say that justice is done whenever these legal guidelines are followed correctly. This possibility suggests a simple way to explain how justice could be wrongful: we could refer to norms of justice without caring about their moral merits. We could take an allocation to be a just allocation if it merely follows legal rules.

This type of justice is not the type of justice I am concerned with here. If we take norms of justice simply to be norms that govern allocative questions—and nothing more—then it is quite straightforward to say that such norms can be wrongful in application. Undesirable norms of justice are evident with regrettable frequency in legal systems, and they provide grounds for legal reform. The possibility that legal norms of justice will be undesirable, and that their exercise will be morally wrongful, is an important but relatively mundane possibility. My real concern is with those norms of justice that are desirable, or sound.

The distinction between desirable and undesirable norms of justice is well-recognised. For example, John Gardner argues that it is not enough to simply say that tort law instantiates corrective justice. As he indicates, we will also want to know if such corrective justice is sound:

> You may be tempted to say in response that norms of justice are sound by definition. But that is a subtle distortion of the truth. It is true that whatever is just is to that extent and in that respect analytically worth pursuing. It is admittedly contradictory to say: That solution is just but it has nothing going for it, morally speaking. But this is because a solution is just if and only if it is in conformity with a sound norm of justice. … "Sound norm of justice" is no tautology; "unsound norm of justice" is no oxymoron.[62]

In other words, when we talk of a norm of justice, we will want to know 'what the norm has going for it'.[63]

[61] For suggestions that norms of justice are allocative norms, see Gardner (n 9) 6 ('Norms of justice are moral norms of a distinctive type. They are norms for tackling *allocative* moral questions, questions about who is to get how much of what'); HLA Hart, *Punishment and Responsibility: Essays in the Philosophy of Law*, 2nd edn (Oxford, Oxford University Press, 2008) ('It is clear that like all principles of Justice [retributive justice] is concerned with the adjustment of claims between a multiplicity of persons'). The reader who rejects the view that justice is concerned with allocating may, with suitable adjustments, still accept the arguments in this chapter.

[62] Gardner (n 9) 14. See also Gardner (n 46) 247 (indicating that Aristotle 'argues at some length that there are unsound principles as well as sound ones, on both the distributive front and the corrective front'). Indeed, '*some* [norms of justice] must be mistaken or there is no such thing as the vice of injustice': at 248.

[63] Gardner (n 9) 15.

My claim will be that sound norms of justice can be wrongful when applied. This is not to say that morality and sound norms of justice require different things. Nor is it to argue, as Gardner has, that the virtue of justice will sometimes pull in different directions from other moral virtues.[64] We need not go this far for present purposes. It is not that justice requires wrongful conduct, but that wrongful conduct can be just. In the following sections, I will suggest that sound norms of justice—at least when norms of justice have certain features—can implicate rights to do wrong. This feature is what makes wrongful justice a realistic possibility. To begin, then, it may be helpful to assess the meaning and significance of the right to do wrong.

C. The Right to Do Wrong

A right to do wrong is sometimes seen as a counterintuitive idea, or at least this is the case when both the right and the wrong at issue occupy the same normative terrain. The existence of a legal right to commit moral wrongs is unsurprising. Legally speaking, it is foreseeable that our legal rights will sometimes conflict with morality, as we can readily have a legal right to commit a moral wrong if the law says so. Likewise, depending on the legitimacy of our legal system and the exigencies of our circumstances, it is plausible to recognise a moral right to commit a legal wrong. In the case of illegitimate governments, such moral rights may be commonplace. It is far less obvious what it means to have a moral right to commit a moral wrong.

On one account, a moral right to do moral wrong involves a Hohfeldian claim right to non-interference, but not a privilege.[65] This is correct in a sense, but only if we modify certain aspects of the Hohfeldian scheme. For Hohfeld, duties always by definition have correlative rights; they are directed duties,[66] and this is a matter of stipulation. If we take the Hohfeldian worldview seriously, a privilege may be exactly what a right to do wrong involves, since wrongful behaviour need not violate any directed duties. In that case, the person exercising a right to do wrong will not be violating any duties at all, per Hohfeld's account. She has a privilege, combined with a claim right to non-interference.

Yet, an insistence on the full Hohfeldian picture is an uncomfortable fit with the moral realm. As Jeremy Waldron notes: 'Hohfeld's account of privileges was designed to cope with the analysis of normative systems in which duties were perfectly correlative with claim rights, as they are, for the most part, in contract, tort, and property law.'[67] When we turn to morality, it is quite plausible for there to

[64] See Gardner (n 46) 244–246 (comparing the just person with the humane person).

[65] See OJ Herstein, 'Defending the Right to Do Wrong' (2011) 31 *Law and Philosophy* 343, 345 fn 6.

[66] See WN Hohfeld, 'Fundamental Legal Conceptions as Applied in Judicial Reasoning' (1917) 26 *Yale Law Journal* 710.

[67] See J Waldron, 'The Right to Do Wrong' in *Liberal Rights: Collected Papers 1981–1991* (Cambridge, Cambridge University Press, 1993) 67.

be duties that do not have correlative claim rights, at least if the word 'duties' is permitted its common extra-legal meaning. It is very possible, for example, to owe a duty of charity without anyone having a claim to that charity.[68] Or, depending on one's understanding of duties, there may be a duty that one owes to oneself.[69] Likewise, and of particular relevance to this chapter, there may be cases in which one has a duty to forgive or to show mercy, but no one can legitimately demand these things as a matter of right. If these duties are counted when we assess whether a privilege exists, then the right to do wrong means there is a right to do certain things without interference, but no privilege to do them. With the above caveats on Hohfeld, I will adopt the view that a moral right to do wrong implicates a claim right to non-interference but no privilege.[70]

Waldron argues that, as a conceptual matter, it is quite reasonable to recognise a moral right to commit a moral wrong. As he notes: 'To assent to the proposition that I have a right to perform some action is not thereby to acknowledge any reason for my performing that action.'[71] The key effect of a right to perform an action is that others may not prevent performance of that action.[72] And this feature brings us to an important insight: 'the wrongfulness of an act does not by itself entail the moral permissibility of interfering with it.'[73] Rights to do wrong are possible because the moral undesirability of a course of conduct is distinct from the legitimacy of preventing that conduct.

That said, the mere conceptual possibility of a moral right to do wrong does not mean that such rights exist as a matter of morality.[74] There are arguments that morality incorporates such rights, but it should not be assumed that such rights are automatically present. Waldron suggests reasons for thinking that they do exist, however. He argues that '[t]here are certain types of choices, certain key areas of decision-making, which have a special importance for individual integrity and self-constitution.'[75] In his view, if only morally permissible actions were subject to such rights, the results would be undesirable or counterintuitive. One possibility would be a range of discretion that only applied to trivial choices.[76]

[68] This is admittedly a disputed view. Compare MH Kramer, 'Rights Without Trimmings' in *A Debate Over Rights* (Oxford, Clarendon Press, 1998) 25 fn 11 (suggesting ways in which a duty of charity can be squared with the correlativity thesis).

[69] See D Enoch, 'A Right to Violate One's Duty' (2002) 21 *Law and Philosophy* 355, 359 (noting the possibility of a moral duty owed to oneself, 'for instance, leading a reasonably healthy life').

[70] It should be noted that here are additional ways to conceptualise a right to do wrong. Enoch (n 69) 371 ('When we talk of a right to Φ, we attribute a cluster right, and the exact components of that cluster right vary with context'). For present purposes, I am focusing on the bare minimum structure—a claim right but no privilege.

[71] See Waldron (n 67) 71.

[72] ibid 73 ('The cutting edge of the claim that P has a right to do A is the correlative claim that other people are morally required to refrain from interfering with P's performance of A').

[73] ibid 74.

[74] For discussion on this point, see Enoch (n 69) 378–380.

[75] See Waldron (n 67) 81.

[76] ibid 83 ('But what would be left over when the morality of rightness and wrongness had had its say? The answer seems to be: the banalities and trivia of human life'). But see WA Galston, 'On the

This is the outcome if moral rightness and wrongness are resolved prior to any question of moral rights. Alternatively, the morality of rights might come first, with moral duties delimited so that there is no conflict. Waldron concludes that this would be implausible; morality must have its say as to how we should act, and as a consequence, 'it is necessary to insist that wrong actions as well as right actions and indifferent actions can be the subject of moral rights.'[77]

Individual integrity is not the only justification offered for a right to do wrong. Ori Herstein has recently emphasised the importance of autonomy as a basis for moral rights to do moral wrong.[78] Here, the concern is that individuals should be part authors of their own lives.[79] On this view, the right to do wrong means that people will have an adequate range of choices, such that they are truly autonomous individuals. This is not an uncontested perspective, however. Arguably, individuals will have a sufficient range of self-constituting choices even in the absence of rights to do wrong: once a certain threshold of choices is available, the availability of further choices may be unnecessary, and this may obviate the need for a right to do wrong.[80] This latter possibility raises empirical questions concerning the range of choices individuals face.

Yet perhaps we shouldn't just be worried about self-constitution in general, for self-constitution has more than one aspect. It may be that *moral* self-constitution calls for a right to do wrong. As Herstein argues: 'The autonomous self-development of an integral moral (or immoral) identity mandates … allowing a measure of choice between good and evil, right and wrong, virtue and vice.'[81] Here, too, there are potential counterarguments. It may be that autonomy is not valuable when

Alleged Right to Do Wrong: A Response to Waldron' (1983) 93 *Ethics* 320, 322 ('This argument rests on a misconception. To say that moral considerations do not dictate a choice among A, B, … N in specific circumstances is *not* to say that the subject matter of this choice is humanly unimportant').

[77] See Waldron (n 67) 85. In David Enoch's view, Waldron has not adequately shown that one can have a moral right to violate one's duty, but rather a moral right to do what is not morally optimal. See Enoch (n 69) 365 ('This becomes clear as soon as one realizes that the moral status of actions does not divide neatly into the three categories Waldron seems to assume—impermissible, required, and indifferent'). As Enoch argues: 'the thesis that one can have a right to violate one's duty can be rejected without trivializing rights, as long as it is acknowledged that one can have a moral right to do something it is morally better not to do': at 366. Enoch makes a convincing case that moral rights to violate moral duties are nonetheless conceptually possible: at 366–378.

[78] See Herstein (n 65). Compare Enoch (n 69) 379–380 ('A right to violate one's duty is not merely, then, a conceptual possibility. A moral theory that fails to justify such rights fails to take autonomy seriously'). Enoch, however, does not develop the view that a moral theory should justify rights to violate one's duty; he is, rather, clarifying what is at stake.

[79] See J Raz, *The Morality of Freedom* (Oxford, Oxford University Press, 1986) 369 ('The autonomous person is a (part) author of his own life. The ideal of personal autonomy is the vision of people controlling, to some degree, their own destiny, fashioning it through successive decisions throughout their lives').

[80] See Herstein (n 65) 355–356.

[81] ibid 358. As Herstein notes, an objector might respond that even in the absence of a right to do wrong, many moral choices to do wrong 'would go unchecked and even unnoticed': at 359. In other words, people would still be effectively free to do wrong. Herstein responds that a *de facto* right to do wrong may do less to further personal autonomy than a genuine right: at 359–360.

good people are faced with a choice between good and evil; perhaps that is not a real choice for them.[82] In turn, Herstein responds that self-transformation then becomes a key concern. As he suggests: 'where moral choice seems most significant to determining one's moral self is where one's moral makeup is not fully formed in relation to the issue at hand, or where an immoral person is given the choice of moral self-transformation.'[83]

As this discussion should make clear, there is great complexity involved in determining the quantity and type of choices needed for an autonomous self. While this is cause for caution, it is at least plausible to think that there are moral rights to do moral wrong given autonomy values. And, if we are willing to accept that such moral rights exist, then it is a relatively short step to the idea that moral rights to do moral wrong are implicated by private rights of action in tort, contract, or fiduciary law. While the choices a potential plaintiff makes in these settings are not always central to her identity, it is clear that such choices often will be. Personal integrity and autonomy values extend to the pursuit of legal remedies, just as they extend to the rights that those remedies are there to protect. Furthermore, it is quite reasonable to think that sometimes the choice to bring suit will be a morally dubious one. These conclusions do not, however, yet show that justice can implicate a right to do wrong. In order to see how that is possible, it will help to look more closely at conceptions of justice.

D. Mandatory and Permissive Norms of Justice

While there are many ways to categorise types of justice, I will suggest the answer lies along a particular divide. We can split types of justice into two categories: those types of justice that, as a matter of duty, moral agents ought to bring about; and those types of justice that, as a matter of right, moral agents are legitimately permitted to bring about. The latter case involves a justified permission. While justice that governs permitted but not mandated conduct receives somewhat less attention, this category of justice is most relevant here. Norms of justice that govern permissible conduct can implicate a right to do wrong.

In a common formulation, corrective justice falls within the first category. Corrective justice governs the conduct of duty bearers, or parties acting on their behalf, with respect to the undoing of a transaction. So understood, in the corrective justice setting we are often concerned with a wrongdoer's compliance with his or her remedial duties: where corrective justice is apt, the wrongdoer ordinarily ought to bring it about. This duty-focused type of justice poses a challenge for the idea that justice can be sound and at the same time wrongful. One might doubt that there can be wrongful justice where a sound norm of justice grounds a

[82] ibid 361 (suggesting a possible objection that autonomous pursuit of the bad is valueless, and citing Raz (n 79) 380, 412).

[83] ibid 364.

party's remedial moral duties, on the theory that complying with moral duties is not wrongful behaviour.[84]

The second category is exemplified by norms of preventive justice and redressive justice. These are norms of justice that govern the exercise of a right to perform certain actions, but in settings where these norms apply the conduct at issue is optional.[85] Characteristically, this conduct is also protected by duties of non-interference. Accordingly, these are norms of justice that may implicate the right to do wrong. It is conceptually possible to have a moral right to do moral wrong where the moral right at issue is grounded in norms of justice of this type. It is also plausible to think that permissive norms of justice are sound. The justice in self-defence, for example, is usually considered legitimate in its core applications. Yet acting in self-defence is typically seen as an optional but protected choice, rather than a response to a threatened wrong that the potential victim morally has to take.

Some examples may be helpful. Consider first preventive justice—this is the type of justice involved in self-defence and property defence. Preventive justice operates ex ante, before a wrong has occurred, and it is ordinarily concerned with liability rather than desert.[86] If the party against whom an individual acts in self-defence deserved to be subject to preventive justice, we might well conclude that the person acting in self-defence has a corresponding duty to engage in self-defence. Yet we need not think this. Self-defence is often seen as optional, and an individual doesn't automatically fail to comply with her moral duties if she decides to risk harm to herself rather than cause harm to, say, an attacker.[87] Perhaps our judgment would be different if we were in her shoes—we might exercise our discretion to defend ourselves—but her choice not to do so does not demonstrate that she has shown a moral failing.

Preventive justice gives us nice examples of conduct that is permissible yet not morally required. Indeed, it gives us examples of permissible conduct that nevertheless ought to be avoided. John Goldberg has recently offered a useful illustration. Goldberg contends that there is some conduct that is permitted—and justified—but which nonetheless ought not to occur. Here is his example:

> [S]uppose Dave knows that his friend Paul is going through a very difficult time, and that he (Dave) has just given Paul some advice that is very hard for Paul to accept. Dave

[84] A potential exception arises where a third party is acting on behalf of the wrongdoer. There may well be cases in which a third party acts wrongfully in assisting a wrongdoer in complying with the wrongdoer's remedial moral duties.

[85] At times, these permissive norms of justice may also overlap with duties to perform the relevant acts. For example, one might have a moral duty to act in self-defence in order to subsequently protect others for whom one holds responsibility. These duties, however, are contingent on facts that need not exist in such preventive justice contexts.

[86] See J McMahan, 'Self-Defense and the Problem of the Innocent Attacker' (1994) 104 *Ethics* 252, 259–260 (discussing a justice-based account of self-defence which 'is concerned with liability rather than desert').

[87] Compare McMahan (n 86) 261 (suggesting that a deontological account of self-defence is consistent with self-defence being optional, as the potential victim's reasons for action can be cancelled out by a choice not to defend).

> perceives that Paul is very angry with him, and indeed is about to spit on him. In this situation, it might be right for Dave to endure the indignity of being spat upon by Paul, even though Dave is surely permitted to take certain steps (for example, lightly pushing Paul) to avoid being spat upon.[88]

Depending on the friendship, and on the current state of Paul's psyche, it may well be that Dave as a good friend has a moral duty to allow Paul to spit on him. And yet if Paul did lightly push Dave to prevent that outcome, this could still be a legitimate application of preventive justice. If so, it would be a case of justice that is both sound and wrongful in application.

Now consider redressive justice. A similar point applies to acts of redress. We can imagine a case like the following:

> Ann negligently damages Brian's expensive antique vase while picking it up. The vase is shattered due to Ann's carelessness, and Brian has a viable claim in tort against Ann for the value of the vase. Ann is going through a difficult period in her life, she is poor, she has family to take care of, and she is also sincerely apologetic for her carelessness. Brian is rich and could replace the vase without noticing the financial cost. Brian can see that Ann is genuinely sorry for what happened, and the value of the vase far exceeds the degree of carelessness that Ann showed.[89]

Brian can legitimately bring his claim, given that the vase belonged to him and he had a right to Ann's care in handling it. Yet, morally speaking, he ought not to exercise this right. Here, too, there is a type of justice—redressive justice—that is apt and, if we grant Brian the legitimacy of his rights, also sound. Exercise of Brian's right of redress would be perfectly consistent with redressive justice norms; this is not a case in which redressive justice would fail to ground his conduct. Yet, were Brian to seek redress, it could be morally wrongful.[90]

This kind of fact pattern is also applicable to fiduciary settings, including those contexts in which disgorgement applies. In an agent-principal relationship, for example, it may be that the principal has a genuine moral right to disgorgement of profits that resulted from the agent's good faith yet conflicted behaviour. Should the principal seek a disgorgement remedy, this allocation back would be just. It does not follow that the principal has a moral duty to seek this remedy, and in fact the principal may be acting morally wrongfully in pursuing

88 See JCP Goldberg, 'Inexcusable Wrongs' (2015) 103 *California Law Review* 467, 472 fn 14.

89 This is a variant on a vase-breaking fact pattern discussed by Arthur Ripstein. For his account, see A Ripstein, 'As If It Had Never Happened' (2007) 48 *William and Mary Law Review* 1957, 1980.

90 Precisely when conduct of this type is morally wrongful may depend on additional facts, including the motivation of the plaintiff, the difficulty of the defendant's situation, etc. Broadly speaking, such cases often involve someone who is a 'stickler' for their rights. Compare Gardner (n 30) 57 (discussing a rights stickler in the tort setting). In some cases, but not all, a rights stickler may be an opportunist as well. See HE Smith, *Equity as Second-Order Law: The Problem of Opportunism*, available at: http://ssrn.com/abstract=2617413. Whether being a stickler for one's rights is good or bad may nonetheless depend on context. See D Klimchuk, 'Equity and the Rule of Law' in LM Austin and D Klimchuk (eds), *Private Law and the Rule of Law* (Oxford, Oxford University Press, 2014) 257–260 (noting both possibilities).

disgorgement. Disgorgement may be both just and—at least with respect to the plaintiff—wrongful.[91]

VI. Implications

The idea of wrongful justice has several implications, and while there is not space here to fully develop their significance, I will highlight a few. To begin with, it is often thought that the aim of adjudication is to do justice between the litigants.[92] From that perspective, the occasional harshness of a remedy like disgorgement could be beside the point.[93] Even if we are convinced in some cases that a plaintiff ought not to seek disgorgement, the plaintiff's claim is quite possibly still just, and the court's responsibility to order disgorgement may then follow. Whether this is so depends on an analysis of the plaintiff's right to the disgorged profits, not to mention our account of the justice at issue. Yet, under the right circumstances, disgorgement can be just even if the plaintiff is acting wrongfully in litigating the case.

On the other hand, we have cause to revisit what is at stake when legal claims are brought. It is easy to think that if an outcome is just, we should wholeheartedly endorse an individual party's effort to bring that outcome about. That doesn't follow. There are some cases in which we should hope that a plaintiff will not seek redress, even if that redress constitutes a genuine form of justice. The difficulty is in telling when this is the case.

When a plaintiff is a stickler for her rights, this may or may not be a good thing. Sometimes, litigants should avoid being rights sticklers. Aristotle speaks of someone being a 'stickler for justice in a bad sense',[94] and he is right do so. In some of the more egregious cases, people who insist on their rights are being opportunistic.[95] Courts address these concerns in a variety of ways. Courts sometimes issue nominal damages as a way of showing contempt for claims that are valid but ought not to have been brought.[96] And equity responds to some of the more glaring

[91] Note that, even in cases where the plaintiff is wrongful in seeking disgorgement, it need not follow that the court is acting wrongfully in enforcing the remedy. The reasons for action that apply to courts are not identical to the reasons for action that apply to litigants, and the all-things-considered duties of courts may differ from those of the plaintiff.

[92] See Gardner (n 46) 259 ('Any adjudicative institution, whether or not it is administering a system of rules, ought to be just above all').

[93] Compare JH Langbein, 'Questioning the Trust Law Duty of Loyalty: Sole Interest or Best Interest?' (2005) 114 *Yale Law Journal* 929, 990 ('In a case such as *Boardman v. Phipps* …, the sole interest rule takes away a benefit from the trustee who earned it and awards it to the trust beneficiary. In these cases trust law works unjust enrichment, in ugly tension with the equity tradition of preventing unjust enrichment').

[94] See Aristotle (n 10) 1796.

[95] See Smith (n 90).

[96] See Gardner (n 30) 57.

cases. The doctrine of unclean hands, for example, means that in certain instances an equitable remedy won't be available in light of a claimant's prior misconduct. Estoppel can similarly limit a misuse of rights, as can the doctrine of *laches*.[97] Each of these doctrines circumscribes the possibility that a plaintiff's claim will be morally wrongful.[98]

Yet being a rights stickler is not uniformly bad. As Dennis Klimchuk notes: 'Sometimes, one might argue, one ought to be a stickler for one's rights. "Do not let others tread with impunity on your rights", says Kant, in a list of injunctions issuing from the duty to treat oneself with respect.'[99] Those who insist on their rights may be demonstrating a form of dignity, rather than showing bad faith, opportunism, or other moral failings. And, if people who strictly insist on their rights are sometimes doing what they ought to do, we have added reason to make room for their claims.

Nevertheless, some viable suits will still be morally wrongful for the plaintiff to bring. With this in mind, it is noteworthy that the pursuit of causes of action is optional. Litigants have significant discretion in resolving a dispute. Private law theory tends not to focus as much on the settlement of claims, but settlement is an important legal institution. We can be glad that in some cases viable suits are not brought, and we can also be glad that litigation is often settled for amounts that are less than the full amount potentially available.[100] The availability of nonsuits and settlements allows for legal recognition of a plaintiff's rights while giving plaintiffs an opportunity to avoid excessive insistence on them.[101]

Even so, the possibility of wrongful justice also gives us cause to revisit the judicial role. Courts sometimes develop legal doctrines in a way that minimises opportunities for wrongful justice.[102] It is worth asking whether courts should do this,

[97] Compare Klimchuk (n 90) 262–263 (describing a type of estoppel that 'prevents persons from being sticklers in a bad way'); '[Laches] protects [the defendant] against a particular sort of exploitation, or at least inequitable advantage-taking, by the plaintiff': at 263.

[98] It is an interesting question whether our understanding of a private law field should take into account the application of equity in this respect. For example, Arthur Ripstein's account of tort law appears to assess tort law without incorporating such considerations. See Ripstein (n 47) 15 ('The law does not make a global assessment of whether you should stand on your rights; it leaves that question to you').

[99] ibid 260 (citing I Kant, *The Metaphysics of Morals*, trans M Gregor (Cambridge, Cambridge University Press, 1996) 188 (6:436)).

[100] For further analysis of cases in which plaintiffs may exercise forbearance, see SV Shiffrin, *Speech Matters: On Lying, Morality, and the Law* (Princeton, Princeton University Press, 2014) 165–166 (noting contexts in which plaintiffs do not sue due to compassion, or in which plaintiffs' attorneys advise clients not to seek damages that exceed insurance coverage out of a sense that the remedy will be too harsh). In the tort setting, one concern may be that the remedy at issue is out of proportion to the degree of negligence involved. Compare J Waldron, 'Moments of Carelessness and Massive Loss' in DG Owen (ed), *Philosophical Foundations of Tort Law* (Oxford, Oxford University Press, 1995).

[101] Note that the incomplete allocation back that results from settlement may not only be a morally desirable outcome, but also an example of justice. Compare Gold (n 43) 174–176 (describing contexts in which a partial allocation back still qualifies as a type of corrective justice).

[102] Or, courts may act leniently by quietly contradicting a legal rule when deciding a case. Compare E Sherwin, *Formal Elements of Contract and Fiduciary Law*, available at: http://ssrn.com/

and if so, when. Disgorgement is an area where courts enable plaintiffs to bring suit when, perhaps, those plaintiffs are being sticklers for justice in a bad way. Not every private law doctrine looks this way, or at least not to this degree. In some circumstances, legal doctrine is designed so that otherwise enforceable rights will be left unprotected by the courts.[103] This, in turn, may limit the available range for instances of wrongful justice.

Consider an example from contract law. As Seana Shiffrin has argued, unconscionability doctrine may be a mechanism courts use to avoid assisting parties in immoral conduct.[104] As Shiffrin notes, 'unless we assume that one must ensure that others' obligations are met, the promisor's genuine responsibility does not entail that unaffected parties or the community at large must take it upon themselves to enforce promises.'[105] In cases of unfairness, a court's refusal to enforce a contract could stem from paternalistic motivations. Shiffrin, however, suggests another possibility: 'Instead, the motive may reasonably be a self-regarding concern not to facilitate or assist harmful, exploitative, or immoral action.'[106] So construed, a court that refuses to enforce an unconscionable contract is looking to make sure that it doesn't help someone in their pursuit of an immoral choice.[107]

Let's assume that the unconscionability doctrine is motivated by a judicial desire to avoid assisting in immoral conduct, and let's also assume that this is a good thing. It is far from clear that this type of reasoning should apply to every case in which a plaintiff ought not to bring suit. There are an uncountable number of cases in which a plaintiff may sue when she ought in an ideal world to forgive, or show mercy, or demonstrate tolerance. If only for epistemic reasons—how readily can a court assess the full complexity of a plaintiff's moral duties?—the vast majority of these cases are good candidates for legal enforcement. Moreover, if a plaintiff's suit involves a genuine moral right to do moral wrong, it is plausible to think that courts at least sometimes have a responsibility to assist the plaintiff.[108]

abstract=2634109 (forthcoming in PB Miller and AS Gold (eds), *Contract, Status, and Fiduciary Law* (Oxford, Oxford University Press, 2016)).

[103] For present purposes, it is not relevant whether the rights are thought to be present but unenforced, or instead shaped so that they do not extend to the particular context under dispute. Compare Klimchuk (n 90) 267–68 (noting the distinction). In either case, the law has developed in such a way so that opportunities for wrongful justice are limited.

[104] This is by no means the only account of the unconscionability doctrine. For a very different picture, see RA Epstein, 'Unconscionability: A Critical Reappraisal' (1975) 18 *Journal of Law and Economics* 293 (providing a near-fraud account). This chapter makes no claims about what actually justifies the unconscionability doctrine.

[105] See SV Shiffrin, 'Paternalism, Unconscionability Doctrine, and Accommodation' (2000) 29 *Philosophy and Public Affairs* 205, 222.

[106] ibid 224.

[107] It should be noted that Shiffrin allows for the possibility that there should be judicial accommodation of behaviour with which courts disagree: Shiffrin (n 105) 245–250. She does not believe the enforcement of unconscionable contracts falls into this category, however: at 249–250.

[108] Whether one shares this view may depend on one's theory of the private right of action. There are different ways to develop the basis for a private right of action. For an influential approach, see B Zipursky, 'Philosophy of Private Law' in J Coleman and S Shapiro (eds), *The Oxford Handbook of Jurisprudence and Philosophy of Law* (Oxford, Oxford University Press, 2002) 623, 637–642.

Existing work tells us very little about when courts should assist plaintiffs in immoral behaviour. We should recognise that courts sometimes do assist, and, if justice is truly at stake, that perhaps they sometimes should assist. It does not follow that courts should facilitate all morally wrongful behaviour, however, even if doing so is consistent with a type of justice. There is an important line-drawing problem here, and it is worth considering whether the line is drawn in the right place.

VII. Conclusion

The notion of wrongful justice may sound oxymoronic, or at least perverse. The aim of this chapter is to suggest otherwise. Acts that are just can be morally wrongful, without any contradiction in terms. In addition, norms of justice that authorise wrongful conduct can be perfectly legitimate, sounds norms of justice. The disgorgement remedy in fiduciary law gives us an illustration of how this can work.

Disgorgement is available as a remedy in cases where a fiduciary has acted in good faith, in the best interests of her beneficiary, without converting any of the beneficiary's property, and without causing any financial losses. In at least some such cases, the beneficiary ought not to seek disgorgement; she acts wrongfully in doing so. But, if she nevertheless seeks disgorgement, the remedy will also be a just remedy. Norms of justice can govern the exercise of rights, and—at least on one prominent account of the moral landscape—moral rights can be exercised wrongfully. The moral right to do moral wrong can thus intersect with norms of justice, and it is this possibility that opens up space for wrongful justice.

It is helpful to recognise this possibility, as it better clarifies what is at stake when courts order certain remedies. It is a separate question when, if ever, courts should countenance wrongful justice. In my view they should, but perhaps not in all cases. Drawing the line between desirable and undesirable judicial involvement is a particularly tricky puzzle. That puzzle, however, is best resolved in another paper. For the present, I will simply claim that disgorgement can be both just, and morally troubling.

4

Equitable Compensation—An Overview

JULIE WARD*

I. Introduction

The latest edition of that iconic point of reference for scholars of equity, *Meagher, Gummow and Lehane's Equity: Doctrines and Remedies*, refers to the term 'equitable compensation' as having become 'a category of concealed multiple reference.'[1] The varying circumstances in which courts of equity will grant money awards against defaulting trustees and fiduciaries amply bear out such a description. The attempt to categorise those circumstances more precisely has seen the adoption of nomenclature ranging from the substitutive/reparative distinction[2] to the five-fold classification suggested by Edelman J and Dr Elliott[3] which includes, as well as substitutive/reparative compensation, disgorgement damages (ie the remedy of account of profits), restitutionary damages and punitive damages (the latter not available in equity, at least in New South Wales, following *Harris v Digital Pulse*).[4] Therefore, the notion that the term 'equitable compensation' conceals more than it reveals is not surprising.

Perhaps it is the air of mystery evoked by descriptions of the kind appearing in *Meagher, Gummow and Lehane*, or the perceived flexibility of the remedy[5] that

* I wish to acknowledge the insightful contribution by Jessica Hudson, Lecturer, UNSW Law, in reviewing and discussing this chapter in draft and the diligent research of my tipstaff, Lucy Moclair-Adams in the preparation of this chapter.

[1] J D Heydon et al, *Meagher, Gummow and Lehane's Equity: Doctrines and Remedies* 5th edn (Sydney, LexisNexis Butterworths, 2015) [23-015] ('*Meagher, Gummow & Lehane*').

[2] Sourced by Edelman J back to a D Phil thesis of Steven Elliott (S Elliot, *Compensation Claims Against Trustees* (DPhil Thesis, University of Oxford, 2002) and adopted since then in a variety of academic articles by Dr Elliot, J Edelman and Professor Mitchell, culminating in the exposition of the terms in *Agricultural Management Ltd v Jackson (No 2)* [2014] WASC 102, [333]–[359] (Edelman J) ('*Agricultural*').

[3] S Elliot and J Edelman, 'Money Remedies against Trustees' (2004) 18 *Trust Law International* 116.

[4] [2003] NSWCA 10; (2003) 56 NSWLR 298 [5], [44], [57], [63], [233], [470].

[5] *Cole v Manning* [2002] NSWCA 150, [63] (Bergin J).

explains the otherwise inexplicable appearance from time to time of claims for such relief in areas well removed from equity's exclusive jurisdiction. For example, a claim for loss suffered as a result of an alleged breach of an implied contractual duty of care in the context of a building consultant's pre-purchase property inspection.[6] No suggestion of a trust or a fiduciary relationship arose. There was no plea based on breach of an equitable obligation. There was simply an allegation of breach of contract by reason of an alleged failure to comply with an implied duty of care and skill. This was hardly the context in which one would expect to see a claim for equitable monetary relief. How then to explain the claim for equitable compensation baldly appearing in the prayers for relief?

Perhaps as some form of catch-all, in case (as was evident from a cursory appreciation of the facts) the contractual claim did not succeed. Perhaps in the vain hope that some equitable obligation might emerge as a source of relief during the conduct of the case (it being run at first instance as an unpleaded claim in negligence rather than for breach of a contractual duty of care); or perhaps because the notion of equitable compensation as a developing area of the law[7] offered hope for a remedy based on an unspecified form of wrongdoing that would extend equitable relief to an otherwise straightforward negligence claim.

A not dissimilar disconnect between the claim pleaded and the relief sought was dealt with in *Anderson v McPherson [No 2]*[8] where Edelman J, sitting as his Honour then was in the Supreme Court of Western Australia, recounts that equitable compensation had been identified in the pleading as part of the relief claimed but Counsel for the plaintiffs accepted, in opening the case, that there was nothing to support such a claim.[9] Following delivery of his Honour's principal reasons, the plaintiffs sought (not surprisingly, unsuccessfully) to maintain a claim for equitable compensation supported by reference to the 'minimum equity principle' alone.[10] Apart from anything else, such an attempt ignores what was said by Dixon CJ in *Mayfair Trading Co Pty Limited v Dreyer*[11] to the effect that in the Court of Chancery it was necessary for a plaintiff to show an equity to relief and that what constituted an equity to relief was determined by the doctrines of equity.[12] What this suggests is that, for some, the term 'equitable compensation' is not so much a term of concealed reference but a remedy that is sadly misunderstood. Lest I be thought to be uncharitable in that regard, I concede at the outset that the component parts of the term, at least when combined, may themselves be apt to mislead.

Equitable compensation is not a remedy available wherever it may be considered 'fair' (and in that sense 'equitable') as that adjective is used, say, when considering

[6] *Delaney v Winn* [2015] NSWCA 124.

[7] *Beach Petroleum NL v Kennedy* [1999] NSWCA 408; (1999) 48 NSWLR 1 (Spigelman CJ), [430] (Sheller and Stein JJA). See also *Aequitas v AEFC* [2001] NSWSC 14; (2001) 19 ACLC 1006, [443] (Austin J) ('*Aequitas*').

[8] [2012] WASC 19.

[9] ibid [3].

[10] ibid. See particularly: [6], [36]–[49].

[11] [1958] HCA 55; (1958) 101 CLR 428.

[12] ibid [19].

claims for damages or other relief for unconscionable conduct claims. Nor does the remedy necessarily amount to 'compensation' in the sense that an award of damages at common law compensates for loss or injury suffered by the breach in question (though it has been suggested that, at least in some contexts, the scope of equitable compensation is the same at law and in equity;[13] for example, in *Bristol and West Building Society v Mothew,*[14] Millett LJ expressed the view that the remedy of equitable compensation for losses caused by breach by a fiduciary of the duty of skill and care resembled common law damages).[15] The remedy is available when the breach itself constitutes the 'loss' and the beneficiaries may have suffered no immediate or other readily identifiable loss. In that sense it is a substitute for specific relief—to keep trustees up to their duty[16] or to vindicate the duties owed by a fiduciary, rather than to recoup loss. In *Maguire v Makaronis,*[17] for example, the remedy was available in lieu of rescission. Thus the remedy does not always have a compensatory function in the sense in which that is generally understood as being focused on loss.[18]

In *Salvation Army (South Australia Property Trust) v Rundle,*[19] Basten JA explained the use of the term 'compensation' as being to avoid the inference that the same temporal element or other principles relevant to the award of damages under common law apply to the remedy of equitable compensation.[20] Edelman and Elliott, in contrast, embrace the notion of 'damages' as encompassed in the remedy of equitable compensation in its reparative sense, describing it in that context as a claim seeking compensation damages irrespective of its jurisdictional provenance.[21] Unsurprisingly, therefore, equitable compensation has been recognised as a remedy the application of which is not readily able to be encapsulated in a simple formula.[22]

But I digress. This chapter serves as a general overview and addresses the topic: which equitable wrongs generate a remedy of equitable compensation, and why. The 'which', one might have thought, is relatively simple to articulate. The 'why' perhaps less so, having regard to the way in which the law on equitable compensation has developed in the UK. If the 'why' remains the same as that reflected by the

[13] Lord Toulson's discussion in *AIB Group (UK) plc v Mark Redler & Co Solicitors* [2014] UKSC 58, [71] ('*AIB v Redler*') expressing agreement with the view of Professor Hayton in this regard in his chapter 'Unique Rules for the Unique Institution, the Trust' in S Degeling and J Edelman (eds), *Equity in Commercial Law* (Sydney, Lawbook Co, 2005), 279–308. See also *Libertarian Investments Ltd v Hall* [2013] HKCFA 93, [170] per Lord Millett NPJ, likening equitable compensation in the context of a wilful default accounting as akin to the payment of damages as compensation for loss.

[14] [1998] Ch. 1 ('*Bristol v Mothew*').

[15] ibid 17.

[16] *Youyang Pty Ltd v Minter Ellison Morris Fletcher* [2003] HCA 15; (2003) 212 CLR 484, [39] ('*Youyang*').

[17] [1997] HCA 23; (1997) 188 CLR 449.

[18] See C Mitchell, 'Equitable Compensation for Breach of Fiduciary Duty' [2013] *Current Legal Problems* 307.

[19] [2008] NSWCA 347.

[20] ibid [129].

[21] Elliot and Edelman (n 3) 120–121.

[22] C Rickett, 'Equitable Compensation: the giant stirs' (1996) 112 *LQR* 27 32; *Meagher, Gummow and Lehane* (n 1) [23–015].

orthodox or traditional explanation for equitable compensation, as conditioned by its derivation from the equitable remedy of account, the 'how' now appears to have clearly diverged as between this jurisdiction and the UK. As Lord Neuberger has charitably put it, have our equitable wires become crossed?[23]

Against the background of the academic debate (that has perhaps not quite 'raged' but has certainly proliferated) as to taxonomy and the usefulness of drawing a distinction between what have been labelled the substitutive and reparative functions of the remedy, the current question of interest is as to whether, in the context of bare commercial trusts or bare trusts arising as an incident of a commercial arrangement, or perhaps any commercial trusts at all, there remains room for notions of substitutive compensation. Does it assist, when considering the remedy of equitable compensation and the principles applicable to a claim for equitable compensation, to distinguish between 'substitutive' and 'reparative' compensation (as has been suggested by various academics and judges)? Is the focus on the nature of the particular obligation (primary or secondary of the trustee/fiduciary) or the commercial or other character of the relationship giving rise to the obligation (or should it be)?

Should a 'loss-focused'[24] concept of equitable compensation, along the lines of that expressed by Lord Browne-Wilkinson in *Target Holdings Ltd v Redferns*[25] (and approved in *AIB Group (UK) Plc v Mark Redler & Co Solicitors*)[26], be adopted in New South Wales or does that approach fail to give appropriate recognition to the historical development of the remedy? And if the remedy is divorced from its roots in the nineteenth century remedy of account, will that pave the way for consequential loss for breaches of trust, as has been suggested?[27] Insofar as posing the question 'why' equitable compensation is available for particular equitable wrongs points to 'how' it is to be assessed, that may be the real lesson to be learnt from the *Target Holdings* and *AIB v Redler* judgments in the UK.

In *Youyang Pty Ltd v Minter Ellison Morris Fletcher*[28] their Honours posed the question, in *obiter*, with reference to *Target Holdings* as to:

> ... whether the unique foundation and goals of equity, which has the institution of the trust as its heart, warrant any assimilation even in this limited way with the measure of compensatory damages in tort and contract. It may be thought strange to decide that the precept that trustees are to be kept by courts of equity up to their duty has an application limited to the observance by trustees of some only of their duties to beneficiaries in dealing with the funds.[29]

[23] Lord Neuberger, 'Equity—The soul and spirit of all law or a roguish thing?' (Speech delivered at the Lehane Lecture 2014, Supreme Court of New South Wales, Sydney, 4 August 2014) See www.supremecourt.uk/docs/speech-140804.pdf [34].

[24] As so characterised by Rickett when welcoming of his Lordship's analysis as the 'loss-focused nature of equitable compensation': Rickett (n 22) 29.

[25] [1996] 1 AC 421 ('*Target Holdings*').

[26] *AIB v Redler* (n 13).

[27] J Glister, 'Breach of trust and consequential loss' (2014) 8 *Journal of Equity* 235.

[28] *Youyang* (n 16).

[29] ibid 39.

Strange or otherwise as it may be, that is now the result of the way in which equitable compensation principles have been applied in the UK at least in the context of bare commercial trusts.[30]

II. The Remedy of Equitable Compensation

As has been explained in academic and judicial writing, the term 'equitable compensation' in the context of a breach of trust was used to denote relief that was derived from the equitable remedy of account but was able to be obtained without the need for an order for an account first to be made.[31] I note in discussion below the suggestion by Associate Professor Glister that it may be misleading to 'short-circuit' the process by going straight from the 'wrong' of breach of trust to the 'remedy' of equitable compensation because equitable compensation for breach of trust cannot extend to consequential losses (even though surcharging an account has a compensatory aim) and that the process of going straight to the remedy may hide the point that the trustee's obligation is limited to the protection and management of the trust fund.[32]

The purpose of an order for equitable compensation has been described as that of effecting restitution.[33] Parallel examples include *Ex Parte Adamson*[34] where the claim was in the context of the misappropriation of partnership property and *Nocton v Lord Ashburton*[35] where the allegation was one of fraud on the part of the plaintiff's solicitor. In these cases the relevant obligation was to restore the value of that which was lost as a result of the breach of the equitable obligation in question.[36] Viscount Haldane LC, in an oft-quoted statement in *Nocton v Lord Ashburton*, referred to the purpose being to put the plaintiff in as good a position from a pecuniary perspective as that in which the plaintiff was before the injury or wrong.[37] The remedy is not confined to cases where there has been a breach of trust[38] (whether of a primary duty to maintain the trust or a secondary duty to

30 See *AIB v Redler*, where solicitors holding funds on trust were not 'kept up to their duty', at least in the sense considered in *Youyang*, in the performance of the trust.

31 *Meagher, Gummow and Lehane* (n 1) [23–015]. See also: Glister (n 27); S Elliott, *Compensation Claims Against Trustees* (n 2); *Agricultural* (n 2); *AIB v Redler* (n 13).

32 Glister (n 27).

33 *Re Dawson dec'd* [1966] 2 NSWR 211, 214 (Street J, as his Honour then was). The obligation of the defaulting trustee was said to be essentially one of effecting restitution to the estate.

34 (1878) 8 Ch D 807, where the claim available in the Court of Chancery for fraudulent conduct or breach of trust was described not as a suit for damages but as a suit for 'an equitable debt or liability in the nature of debt … a suit for restitution of the actual money or thing, or value of the thing, of which the cheated party had been cheated': 819 (per James and Baggallay LLJ).

35 [1914] AC 932 (HL) ('*Nocton*').

36 *O'Halloran v R T Thomas & Family Pty Ltd* (1998) 45 NSWLR 262, 272–273 ('*O'Halloran*').

37 *Nocton* (n 35) 952.

38 Though an example of a case where it was awarded for breach of trust was *Youyang*.

make good losses sustained by a breach of a primary duty).[39] It is also available where there has been a breach by a custodial fiduciary.[40]

Nor is the remedy confined to such breaches of trust or custodial fiduciary obligations. In *Nocton,* relief was granted by way of monetary compensation for breach of fiduciary duty where a solicitor had advised his client to release part of a mortgage security in circumstances where the solicitor thereby obtained a personal benefit. In the Court of Appeal, damages had been awarded for deceit. However, in the House of Lords it was made clear that the compensation ordered was in the exercise of the jurisdiction of the Court of Chancery, as a court of conscience, for breach of an obligation within equity's exclusive jurisdiction.[41]

Since *Nocton*, equitable compensation has been made available for breach of a variety of non-custodial fiduciary or equitable obligations, including breach of the equitable obligation of confidence;[42] breach of the obligation of a fiduciary to avoid a potential conflict of interest;[43] breach of fiduciary duty by failure to make full disclosure;[44] breach of the obligation of a fiduciary to act in good faith;[45] and in other instances: for unconscionable conduct;[46] claims of undue influence;[47] for liability under the two limbs of the rule in *Barnes v Addy;*[48] and for equitable

[39] *Mitchell*, for example, distinguishes between proscriptive rules that preclude or disable fiduciaries from acting in certain ways and prescriptive rules that require fiduciaries to perform certain duties, breaches of which trigger secondary obligations to disgorge profits or pay compensation, and suggests that breach of a primary duty 'is conceptualised as a civil wrong that triggers a secondary duty to account for unauthorised gains, or to pay compensation for loss': Mitchell (n 19) 317 (and the cases there cited).

[40] An example is *Madoff Securities International Limited v Raven* [2013] EWHC 3147 (Comm), [291]. See also *Hill v Rose* [1990] VR 129 143; *McKenzie v McDonald* [1927] VLR 134 ('*McKenzie*').

[41] See *Nocton* (n 35) 952 (per Viscount Haldane LC).

[42] See, for example *Ithaca Ice Works Pty Ltd v Queensland Ice Supplies Pty ltd* [2002] QSC 222, though I note that the term 'equitable damages' was used seemingly interchangeably with the term 'equitable compensation'. See also the obiter remarks of Gummow J in *Smith Kline & French Laboratories (Aust) Limited v Secretary, Department of Community Services & Health* (1990) 22 FCR 73 83.

[43] Ian Davidson refers, for example, to *Holmes v Walton* [1961] WAR 96 where a solicitor negligently represented that his client invest in a company with which he was associated; *McKenzie* (n 40) where the fiduciary breached an obligation of full disclosure; and *Coleman v Myers* [1977] 2 NZLR 225. See I Davidson, 'The Equitable Remedy of Compensation' (1982) 13 *Melbourne University Law Review* 349, 374, 376–377. Indeed in *Nocton* Viscount Haldane postulated a third form of procedure being the 'old bill in Chancery to enforce compensation for breach of a fiduciary obligation' (n 35) 946. See also *Aequitas* (n 7) where there was a failure to make full disclosure where there was a conflict of interest and duty.

[44] *Aequitas* (n 7) [453] in which Austin J held all losses were there recoverable in equity, and *Fico v O'Leary* [2004] WASC 215; (2004) ATPR (Digest) 46–259, [282] per EM Heanan J. Both cases are cited by Glister as an example of the award of consequential loss by way of equitable compensation. See Glister (n 27) 239.

[45] *Bristol v Mothew* (n 14).

[46] *Karam v ANZ Banking Group Ltd* [2001] NSWSC 709, see particularly [425]–[428] (reversed on other grounds, *Australia and New Zealand Banking Group Ltd v Karam* (2005) 64 NSWLR 149) (though I note that McLure J (as her Honour then was) expressed doubt as to the availability of the remedy in this context in *Australia & New Zealand Banking Group Ltd v Dzienciol* [2001] WASC 305, [413]).

[47] *Smith v Glegg* [2005] 1 Qd R 561; *Mahoney v Purnell* [1996] 3 All ER 61. See also the discussion in J Heydon, 'Equitable compensation for undue influence' 113 *LQR* 8.

[48] See, eg: *Greater Pacific Investments Pty ltd (in liq) v Australian National Industries Ltd* (1996) 39 NSWLR 143, 153 (McLelland AJA); *New Cap Reinsurance Corporation Ltd v General Cologne Re*

fraud.[49] Returning for one moment to the claim for equitable compensation in the pre-purchase building inspection case to which I referred earlier, had that been framed as a claim for fraudulent misrepresentation, then this might have fallen within the class of case where equitable compensation was in the past made available.[50]

Nevertheless, it is usually accepted that the remedy is not available for breach of all non-custodial fiduciary duties, such as the no profits rule.[51] Similarly we query its availability for duties of skill and care owed by fiduciaries whether or not these duties are properly described as fiduciary duties. The explanation for this in relation to breaches of the no profits rule is that the focus of the complaint in such cases is on the gain made by the fiduciary, not the loss to the principal.[52] I say 'usually' because in prefatory comments made by Lord Neuberger in handing down the decision of the UK Supreme Court in *FHR European Ventures LLP v Mankarious,*[53] in the context of considering whether a bribe or secret commission received by an agent is held on trust for the principal, reference was made to the well-established principle that an agent receiving a benefit in breach of fiduciary duty is obliged to account to the principal for such a benefit and it was said that this was in effect the payment of 'a sum equal to the profit by way of equitable compensation.'[54]

III. Why Equitable Compensation?

For those equitable wrongs where equitable compensation is available, in the words of the late Professor Julius Sumner Miller (which will be memorable probably only to those going to school in Australia in the 60s): 'Why is this so?'

Australia Ltd [2004] NSWSC 781, [34] per Young CJ in Eq, as his Honour then was, which I considered in *George v Webb* [2011] NSWSC 1608—a case where there was a wrongful expropriation of a fund the subject of a Quistclose trust. As a recent example of the award of equitable compensation following the finding of liability for knowing receipt of under the rule in *Barnes v Addy*, the decision in *Cassegrain v Cassegrain* [2015] NSWSC 851 to which I refer below.

49 See, eg: *Houghton v Immer (No 155) Pty Ltd* (1997) 44 NSWLR 46, 56 (fraud on a power).

50 See, eg: *Colt v Wollaston* (1723) 2 P. Wms 154; 24 ER 579, to which Ian Davidson SC has referred when considering the availability of equitable compensation outside of fiduciary obligations though he had found no examples since *Derry v Peek* of compensatory relief in equity's concurrent jurisdiction where deceit could be established at common law: Davidson (n 44) 356.

51 J Glister, 'Equitable Compensation' in J Glister and P Ridge (eds), *Fault Lines in Equity* (Oxford, Hart Publishing, 2010) 158, nn 63–64. I note that the position in respect of fiduciary dealing rules is less clear. It has been suggested that the equitable compensation remedy is available for breach of fiduciary dealing rules—see eg: M Conaglen, 'Equitable compensation for breach of fiduciary dealing rules' (2003) 119 *LQR* 246; *Gwembe Valley Development Company Ltd v Koshy* [2003] EWCA Civ. 1048. See also R Nolan, 'A fiduciary duty to disclose?' (1997) 113 *LQR* 220, 222.

52 Glister, ibid, 158.

53 [2015] AC 250.

54 ibid [6], reference there being made to *Regal (Hastings) Ltd v Gulliver (Note)* [1967] 2 AC 134, 144–145.

In the context of equitable compensation for breaches involving the misapplication, or unauthorised disbursement, of trust property, the orthodox explanation for the imposition of a strict standard on the trustee (at least with a traditional trust) was explained by Spigelman CJ in *O'Halloran* as the vulnerability of the beneficiaries with respect to the disposition of property by a trustee who has control over such disposition.[55] The same strict (some say unforgiving) standard applies, for the same reasons, to a custodial fiduciary. Hence the reason for the remedy in these contexts appears to be a combination of equity's general attitude of suspicion towards trustees, who have in their hands the wherewithal to abuse their position of trust, and its correspondingly solicitous or protective attitude to beneficiaries.[56] The strict standard so imposed is thus reflected in the requirement that the trustee or custodial fiduciary make good the trust fund without enquiry as to loss beyond the fact of the misapplication of the trust property. The loss is constituted by the misapplication itself.

In *O'Halloran*, his Honour endorsed the statement by McLachlin J in *Canson Enterprises v Boughton*[57] as to the concern of equity being 'not only to compensate the plaintiff but to enforce the trust which is at its heart'.[58] Hence, there exists an analogy in this context between equitable compensation and an order for specific performance (see James and Baggallay JJ in *Ex parte Adamson*).[59] By reference to the historic roots of the equitable compensation remedy in the equitable remedy of account, this is explained by the requirement that the trustee or fiduciary 'account' on a common account basis for what has been disbursed or dissipated without authorisation out of the relevant trust fund.[60] By contrast, when the account is taken on the wilful default basis then the trustee or fiduciary must account for what would have been received but for the breach.[61] Where an account of profits is available in equity (the third of the accounting processes that could traditionally be brought in equity and by its very description a gains-based remedy), the focus is instead on the profits made by the trustee or fiduciary.

The above explanation, based on the historical remedy of account, does not address the availability of the award of equitable compensation for non-custodial fiduciary breaches. The explanation cannot account for claims arising on breach of the no conflicts rule, unless the breach in question can be formulated as, say, the misapplication of an opportunity available to the entity to whom the duty is owed. However, it is capable of explaining why a claim for equitable compensation

[55] *O'Halloran* (n 36) 277.

[56] See N D'Angelo, 'The trust as a surrogate company: The challenge of insolvency' (Speech delivered at the Journal of Equity Conference 2014, 29 August 2014) later published as 'The trust as a surrogate company: The challenge of insolvency' (2014) 8 *Journal of Equity* 299, 317.

[57] [1991] 3 SCR 534; (1991) 85 DLR (4th) 129 ('*Canson*').

[58] ibid 154, cited in *O'Halloran* (n 36) 277.

[59] *Ex Parte Adamson* (1878) 8 Ch D 807, 819.

[60] See *Meagher, Gummow and Lehane* (n 1) [23-020]–[23-160]; *Agricultural* (n 2), [334]–[349]; S Elliot, *Compensation Claims Against Trustees*, (n 2); Rickett (n 22); Mitchell (n 18).

[61] ibid.

for breach of trust may be framed alternately as both a substitutive and reparative claim, since there may be an unauthorised application of trust property that involves a wilful breach and hence straddles both types of claim.[62]

The explanation for equity's intervention, as a court of conscience, to award monetary relief by way of compensation outside the trust or custodial fiduciary context has instead been said to be derived from the inherent power of the court exercising equitable jurisdiction over fiduciaries.[63] A failure to distinguish between the different types of claim for which equitable compensation is available has been decried by Professor Mitchell as leading some courts 'incorrectly to assume that all claims for equitable compensation are the same.'[64] Mitchell criticises the adoption of a 'one-size-fits-all model of equitable compensatory award that derives from the rules governing the reconstitution of trust funds', those rules being inapt in his opinion to resolve the issues raised by compensatory claims for breach of fiduciary duty.[65] He says that:

> Treating an action to recover equitable compensation for breach of fiduciary duty as though it were an action to reconstitute a trust fund makes as little sense as treating an action for damages for breach of contract as though it were an action for debt.[66]

Professor Mitchell is similarly critical of the approach adopted in the UK in *AIB v Redler* of what is in effect the converse proposition—the Supreme Court, in a case of unauthorised disbursement of funds held in trust, there not applying the rules governing reconstitution of trust funds in favour of the application of rules governing compensatory claims for breach of non-custodial fiduciary duties.[67]

IV. The Substitutive/Reparative Distinction

I have referred above to the distinction between the substitutive and reparative functions of the equitable compensation remedy. The distinction has been the subject of comprehensive analysis by a number of academics[68] and was explained by Edelman J in *Agricultural Land Management Ltd.*[69] That analysis was considered and its erudition commended by the Supreme Court of the United Kingdom in *AIB v Redler.*[70]

[62] As recognised in *Agricultural* (n 2).
[63] *Markwell Bros Pty Ltd v CPN Diesels (Qld) Pty Ltd* (1982) 7 ACLR 425 (there using the term 'equitable damages').
[64] Mitchell (n 18) 309.
[65] ibid.
[66] ibid.
[67] ibid 323–324, (n 82) therein.
[68] See Elliot, *Compensation Claims Against Trustees,* (n 2); Rickett, (n 23); Glister, 'Equitable Compensation' (n 51).
[69] *Agricultural* (n 2) [333]–[375].
[70] *AIB v Redler* (n 13) [53] (per Lord Toulson JSC).

For present purposes it is not necessary to do more than to note that the '*substitutive compensation*' label has been applied to claims for equitable compensation which historically would have followed the taking of a common account by which the plaintiff could 'falsify' the account and require the monetary equivalent of performance. Such claims were not dependent on proof of a loss but, instead, treated the 'loss' as being the unauthorised disbursement of the funds and required the trustee or custodial fiduciary to pay the money equivalent of performance of his or her duty. The '*reparative compensation*' label is applied to claims for equitable compensation which would have followed the taking of an account on the wilful default basis (which *was* dependent on proof of a loss), to require the trustee or fiduciary to account for the value of the rights that the custodial fiduciary would have obtained had the duty not been breached.[71] Whereas the former type of claim involved a 'falsification' of the account, the latter enabled the plaintiff to 'surcharge' the account so as to require the trustee or custodial fiduciary to make good the loss resulting from the relevant breach.[72]

The adoption of such labels is seen by various equity scholars as important in order to distinguish between the different types of claim and hence the rules applicable thereto. In *Agricultural Land Management*, Edelman J agreed with the observation by Dr Elliott and Professor Mitchell that the use of the term 'equitable compensation' in modern cases conceals the distinction between the two types of claim.[73] Professor Glister, as already noted, has similarly suggested that it may be misleading to 'short-circuit' the process and go straight from the 'wrong' of breach of trust to the remedy of equitable compensation.[74]

In contrast, while acknowledging that the labels 'substitutive' and 'reparative' may facilitate private understanding, particularly in respect of the older law on accounting, the authors of *Meagher, Gummow and Lehane* caution that the public use by the courts of such labels:

> … in applying the modern law can only be useful if the terms correspond with the observable realities of the law. Too many decisions of courts, including the ultimate appellate and intermediate appellate courts of several jurisdictions, have worked out the principles incompatibly with the terms "substitutive compensation" and "reparative compensation", so defined, for the courts to find these terms to be of any assistance.[75]

The fundamental distinction between substitutive and reparative compensation lies in the function to be performed by an award of equitable compensation in each case: the former, being as a substitute for performance; the latter, as compensation for loss. However, the practical relevance of the distinction, at least in the

[71] *Agricultural* (n 2): see from [334]–[347] there citing S Elliot and C Mitchell, 'Remedies for Dishonest Assistance' (2004) 67 *MLR* 16; Rickett (n 22) and Mitchell (n 18).

[72] ibid.

[73] *Agricultural* (n 2) [348]–[349] citing Mitchell (n 18) 322; Elliot and Mitchell (n 71); Rickett (n 22); Elliot (n 2).

[74] Glister (n 27).

[75] *Meagher, Gummow and Lehane* (n 1) [23–610].

Australian jurisdiction, lies in the requirement of proof of loss for a claim of the latter kind (which is not necessary, in the substitutive context, beyond the fact of the unauthorised disbursement or dissipation of trust funds).[76] Its significance can be seen most clearly in the academic debate that was sparked by the judgment of Lord Browne-Wilkinson in *Target Holdings*, which has now been resolved in the UK by the decision of the Supreme Court in *AIB v Redler*.

To put that debate in context, and to address what seems to me to be the issue of principle now posed by the *Target Holdings/AIB v Redler* approach, I propose briefly to revisit those decisions, as well as the High Court's decision in *Youyang*, and the decision of Edelman J, sitting in the Supreme Court of Western Australia, in *Agricultural Land Management*, which preceded (and was considered in) *AIB v Redler*.

A. *Target Holdings Ltd v Redferns*

The first of the decisions in this context (recognised as controversial by Lord Neuberger when delivering the John Lehane memorial lecture at a time when *AIB v Redler* was still under consideration by the UK Supreme Court)[77] is *Target Holdings*.

A claim was made against a firm of solicitors who had acted for both borrower and finance company and who wrongly released to the borrower moneys received from their finance company client prior to completion of the conveyance and execution of the charge required in order to secure those moneys. The conveyance was nevertheless completed and the charge executed some days later. To all intents and purposes, therefore, the breach had on a practical level been rectified. Subsequently, the borrower defaulted and was wound up in insolvency. The finance company sued for fraud as well as for breach of trust and negligence in releasing funds when the solicitors had no authority to do so.

In the Court of Appeal,[78] the approach of Peter Gibson LJ, with whom Hirst LJ agreed, accorded with the analysis subsequently outlined in *Agricultural Land Management*: it was recognised that the liability of a trustee was to restore to the trust fund that which had been lost to it; payment of the moneys caused an immediate loss and an immediate duty to restore; hence there should be summary judgment for the finance company in the amount advanced less the amount it had subsequently recovered.

In the House of Lords, Lord Browne-Wilkinson referred to the dissenting judgment of McLachlin J in *Canson* where her Honour said that, in assessing an award of equitable compensation, 'it is essential that the losses made good are only those

[76] See further: Elliot (n 2); Rickett (n 22), Glister (n 51); *Agricultural* (n 2) [249].
[77] Neuberger (n 23) [5].
[78] *Target Holdings* (n 25).

which, on a common sense view of causation, were caused by the breach.'[79] His Lordship was of the view that:

> ... equitable compensation for breach of trust is designed to achieve exactly what the word compensation suggests: to make good a loss in fact suffered by the beneficiaries and which, using hindsight and common sense, can be said to have been caused by the breach.[80]

Lord Browne-Wilkinson said:

> ... it is in any event wrong to lift wholesale the detailed rules developed in the context of traditional trusts and then seek to apply them to trusts of quite a different kind. In the modern world the trust has become a valuable device in commercial and financial dealings. The fundamental principles of equity apply as much to such trusts as they do to traditional trusts in relation to which those principles were originally formulated. But in my judgment it is important, if the trust is not to be rendered commercially useless, to distinguish between the basic principles of trust law and those specialist rules developed in relation to traditional trusts which are applicable only to such trusts and the rationale of which has no application to trusts of quite a different kind.[81]

Lord Browne-Wilkinson went on to say:

> I do not intend to cast any doubt on the fact that moneys held by solicitors on client account are trust moneys or that the basic equitable principles apply to any breach of such trust by solicitors. But the basic equitable principle to breach of trust is that the beneficiary is entitled to be compensated for any loss he would not have suffered but for the breach. *I have no doubt that, until the underlying commercial transaction has been completed, the solicitor can be required to restore to client account moneys wrongly paid away. But to import into such trust an obligation to restore the trust fund once the transaction has been completed would be entirely artificial.*[82] (emphasis added)

The last proposition is what gave rise to what has been referred to as the alternative justification for the conclusion his Lordship reached; namely that propounded by Lord Millett in 'Equity's Place in the Law of Commerce'[83] that *Target Holdings* is an authorised application of what must be treated as trust money notionally restored to the trust estate on the taking of the account.

B. Criticism of *Target Holdings*

Criticism of Lord Browne-Wilkinson's judgment was based on the proposition that in its substitutive function an award of equitable compensation does not depend on causation of loss beyond the 'loss' constituted by the unauthorised

[79] ibid 163.
[80] ibid 438.
[81] ibid 435.
[82] ibid 436.
[83] P J Millett, 'Equity's Place in the Law of Commerce' (1998) 114 *LQR* 214.

disbursement of the funds held in trust or in a custodial fiduciary capacity. It was said, in effect, that to hold otherwise would be to ignore the significance of the requirement to account for the misapplied funds and the entitlement of the beneficiary or principal to enforce the primary duty of maintenance and preservation of the trust property.

Similarly, Elliott and Edelman accept that equitable compensation for 'loss' is awarded in the sense of a monetary equivalent to injury or harm when the claim is for mismanagement by the trustee of the fund or where there is a breach consisting of fiduciary disloyalty.[84] They consider that, viewed as a case where the misapplication of property had been notionally restored by the time of the hearing, Lord Browne-Wilkinson's requirement of a sufficient causal connection between breach and loss was appropriately applied.[85]

They nevertheless maintain that:

> ... "loss" and "compensation" are used in a different sense where the claim in equity is for replacement or due application of misapplied trust property. Instead of seeking reparation for the harm sustained by his interest under the trust, here the beneficiary calls on the trustee to account for his fund and, if that accounting shows that there have been unauthorised dispositions, to make good the shortfall with his own money. This sum is sometimes called "compensation", but it is compensation in the sense of an equivalent to the misapplied property rather than any injury the trust or beneficiaries may have suffered. Similarly, the only relevant "loss" is the literal loss of the property that occurred when it passed into unauthorised hands; and causation of loss is only apposite insofar as it establishes the trustee's responsibility for that disposition (*Target Holdings Ltd v Redferns* [1994] 1 W.L.R 1089 at p.1102 *per* Peter Gibson L.J.; *Pelly's* Case (1882) 21 Ch.D. 492 at p.506 *per* Brett L.J.). Remoteness and mitigation of loss do not fit with this concept. Indeed, the term "loss" may be better avoided altogether in this connection. Lord Hanworth M.R. said that the misapplied fund in *Re Windsor Steam Coal Company* [1929] 1 Ch. 151 at p.156 "was not lost. The liquidator received it, and having received it paid it away to the wrong person."[86]

Not all academics were critical of the decision in *Target Holdings*. Rickett, for example, was initially in favour of the articulation of the 'loss-focused nature of equitable compensation', seeing the aim of the remedy as the same as the aim of compensatory damages.[87] However Rickett saw as troubling the distinction drawn between 'traditional trusts' (which he described as subsisting trusts with indeterminate or contingent beneficial interests) and bare trusts or bare commercial trusts (under which beneficiaries are absolutely entitled).[88]

[84] S Elliot and J Edelman, '*Target Holdings* considered in Australia' (2003) 119 *LQR* 545, 546.

[85] ibid.

[86] ibid 548.

[87] Glister (n 51) 150, citing C Rickett, 'Where are We Going with Equitable Compensation?' in A Oakley (ed), *Trends in Contemporary Trust Law* (Oxford, Oxford University Press, 1996). See also Rickett (n 22) and A Burrows, 'We Do This at Common Law But That in Equity' (2002) 22 *OJLS* 1.

[88] Rickett (n 22).

Others, such as Lord Millett and Glister, argued that the result in *Target Holdings* was correct because the fund was effectively reconstituted when the charge was belatedly executed, Glister arguing that the eventual execution of the charge could be seen as the belated performance of the trustee's primary duty.[89] The Hon JD Heydon AC QC suggested that it was questionable whether *Target Holdings* should, in truth, be regarded as a 'breach of trust case' rather than as an example of kind of case where equitable compensation is available for breach of a fiduciary duty to hold and apply money in a particular way without the fiduciary being subject to many of the duties of trusteeship, such as the duties in relation to investment. In effect, this would seem to support a distinction between bare trusts and other trusts.[90]

Glister has suggested that it would be correct to distinguish between different types of trusts but not on their commercial or non-commercial character; rather, by reference to whether there is an ongoing relationship that would allow one party to call on the other for an account.[91]

C. *Youyang Pty Ltd v Minter Ellison Morris Fletcher*

In *Youyang* the High Court considered a not dissimilar situation. The firm of solicitors were in breach of an express trust by having paid out certain subscription moneys otherwise than in compliance with a term requiring a bearer certificate of deposit to be lodged, which would have provided security for the moneys. They were held liable to compensate the investor for the total amount of the subscription moneys paid out plus interest.

The High Court (Gleeson CJ, McHugh, Gummow, Kirby and Hayne JJ) observed that the appeal concerned the provision of a money remedy for breach of an express trust and noted that the nature of that remedy may vary to reflect the terms of the trust and the breach of which complaint is made. In that regard, their Honours warned against generalisations that may mislead.[92] Their Honours noted that this was not a case of providing a remedy to restore or replenish funds that were thereafter to be held on trusts yet to be fully performed (contrasting this with the position in *Maguire v Makaronis*)[93] and that the solicitors did not hold the moneys for indeterminate or contingent beneficial interests.[94]

Their Honours further noted that the complaint was not merely one of imprudent exercise of a power (or mal-administration) of the trust as was the case in *Bristol v Mothew*. Reference was made to *Bank of New Zealand v New Zealand*

[89] Glister (n 51) 150; Millett (n 83).

[90] J D Heydon, 'Causal Relationships between a Fiduciary's Default and the Principal's Loss' (1994) 110 *LQR* 328, 335. See also Rickett (n 22) 31.

[91] Glister (n 51) 157.

[92] *Youyang* (n 16) [36].

[93] (1997) 188 CLR 449.

[94] *Youyang* (n 16) [37].

Guardian Trust Co Ltd[95] which approved the view taken in *Bristol* on the basis that the stricter view of liability for breaches of trust or fiduciary duty was not required for breach of a fiduciary duty of loyalty or fidelity where the complaint concerned failure to exercise the necessary degree of care and diligence.[96] Their Honours referred to the observations of McLachlin J in *Canson* to the effect that the essence of the fiduciary relationship was that one party pledges to act in the best interest of the principal and has trust, not self-interest, at its core; hence when breach occurs the balance favours the wronged person.[97]

Their Honours emphasised that *Youyang* was not a case where the complaint was in breach of the no profit or no conflict rules; rather, the essence of the complaint was the misapplication of moneys held on trust.[98] In the course of argument, Jackson QC had put Youyang's case[99] on the basis that the solicitors were obliged to restore the sum misapplied, indicating that the courts of equity ordered both restoration and an account which required defaulting trustees to be called upon to account for any deficiency and citing *Partington v Reynolds.*[100]

Target Holdings was distinguished by the Court on the basis that Youyang was not the client of the solicitors in question and that the proposed commercial transaction, unlike that in *Target Holdings*, was not completed (an argument reminiscent of the alternative justification propounded by Lord Millett for *Target Holdings*). The Court noted that the trust was concerned (as was that arising in the *AIB v Redler* matter later) with the application of moneys in completion of a larger commercial transaction. Their Honours expressly disavowed the suggestion that they were thereby embracing 'any theory of reductionism whereby, notwithstanding the rigour of the rule requiring observances of the terms of the trust, in certain events 'commercial' trusts do not provide for their beneficiaries the full panoply of personal and proprietary rights and remedies designed by equity'[101] as the *Target Holdings* decision was suggested to have done.[102]

Rather, their Honours emphasised that, in the administration of the pecuniary remedy Youyang sought for the misapplication of its funds by the solicitors, regard should be had to the scope and purpose of the trust which bound the solicitors. Their Honours considered that those considerations lent force to the application of the proposition in *Target Holdings* that an accrued cause of action for breach did not mean that the quantum of compensation was ultimately fixed as at the date the breach occurred on the basis that 'stopping the clock' may lead to compensation for loss which, on the facts as known at trial, had never been suffered.

[95] [1999] I NZLR 664.
[96] ibid 681.
[97] *Youyang* (n 16) [40].
[98] Ibid [42]–[43].
[99] *Youyang* (n 16) 486.
[100] (1858) 4 Drew 253 at 255–256, 62 ER 98, 99.
[101] ibid [49].
[102] See R Austin, 'Moulding the content of Fiduciary Duties' in T Oakley (ed), *Trends in Compulsory Trust Law* (Oxford, Oxford University Press, 1996) 153, 167–167 as cited in *Youyang* (n 16) at fn 47.

Relevantly, the High Court rejected the proposition that no compensable loss had been suffered, stating that the trust moneys were lost when paid out in breach of trust and that '[t]hat is the injuria with which equity is concerned, not the failure of the investment transaction'.[103] The award so made in favour of Youyang was described as restitutionary or restorative by the High Court in the later decision *Alexander v Perpetual Trustees WA Ltd*.[104]

D. *Agricultural Land Management v Jackson (No 2)*

This case involved, relevantly, a claim for equitable compensation by the responsible entity and trustee of a managed investment scheme (Agricultural Land Management) against two of its directors and another company of which they were also directors (Bunbury Centro). It involved the sale to Agricultural Land Management by Bunbury Centro of a property in Western Australia for the purpose of development, in connection with which a licence was granted to it. The development resulted in a loss. Proceedings were brought against the two directors and Bunbury Centro. The claims against the directors included a claim for equitable compensation for breach of their fiduciary duty to avoid placing themselves in a position where their duties to the company conflicted with their duties to Bunbury Centro. Also alleged was breach of a duty not to prefer their own interests to those of the company.

Edelman J found that no actual conflict of interest was proved because the company failed to prove that the directors had preferred their own interests to those of the company. However, his Honour found that there was a breach of the no conflict rule because of the potential conflict of the directors' duties to the respective companies. His Honour noted that the claim for equitable compensation was framed in two ways: compensation for loss suffered (ie, reparative compensation) and compensation, in the absence of loss, to restore any unauthorised disposition of assets (ie, substitutive compensation).[105]

It was in this context that Edelman J analysed the mechanism by which, historically, courts of equity gave effect to monetary remedies against custodial fiduciaries. His Honour noted that the manner in which an account was taken reflected the nature of the duty which was allegedly breached and affected the nature of the claim for equitable compensation.[106] His Honour further suggested that where the loss complained of occurred by reference to the trustee making unauthorised investment, the question was not whether loss was caused by or flowed from the breach; rather, the loss (in the sense of the disposition of the asset) occurred by reason of the breach.[107]

[103] *Youyang* (n 16) [69] (Gleeson CJ, McHugh, Gummow, Kirby and Hayne JJ).
[104] [2004] HCA 7; (2004) 216 CLR 109, [44] (Gleeson CJ, Gummow and Hayne JJ).
[105] *Agricultural* (n 2) [333].
[106] ibid [334].
[107] Referring to the Hon William Gummow's analysis in 'Compensation for Breach of Fiduciary Duty' in TG Youdan (ed), *Equity, Fiduciaries and Trusts* (Toronto, Carswell Limited, 1989) 57, 89.

Edelman J referred to the separate policies underlying the recognition of liability of custodial fiduciaries to make substantive compensation where there was unauthorised dissipation of assets, on the one hand, and the reparation of losses suffered by a principal caused by breaches of duty by the fiduciary on the other hand. Agricultural Land Management did not succeed on its reparative compensation claim because it could not prove that it had suffered loss.[108] It did not succeed on its substitutive compensation claim for three reasons: the payment of the money could not be treated as unauthorised when it was paid under a contract that was never rescinded; to have required 'falsification' would have required the whole transaction to be considered (both the disallowed disbursement and the receipt of the property); and no claim for restoration of the trust asset *in specie* had been pleaded.[109]

E. *AIB Group (UK) plc v Mark Redler & Co Solicitors*

In the UK the debate over the decision in *Target Holdings* has been put to rest by the decision in *AIB v Redler*, the facts of which bore a close similarity to those in *Target Holdings*, the relevant difference being that in *AIB v Redler* the breach was not 'put right', so to speak, before loss was incurred by the party seeking equitable compensation.

As in *Target Holdings*, the solicitors acted for both the borrowers and the bank. The solicitors were in breach of their custodial fiduciary duties in releasing loan funds obtained from the bank to the borrowers contrary to their instructions (which were to the effect that, on completion of the loan transaction, the bank required a fully enforceable first charge over the property by way of legal mortgage, and that all existing charges be redeemed on or before completion).

There was an existing first registered charge over the property to another bank. The solicitors sought advice from that bank as to the redemption amount required in relation to that charge and released the loan funds before the charge was released, acting on a wrong understanding as to the redemption amount. In the result, the plaintiff bank was only able to obtain a second registered charge over the property. When the borrowers subsequently defaulted on its debt to the bank and the bank enforced its charge, the value of the bank's security on sale of the property was insufficient to cover the amount outstanding after the first ranking charge holder was satisfied.

The bank sued the solicitors claiming the full amount of the loan that had been advanced, less the amount recovered by it on the sale of the property (after satisfaction of the first registered charge). The solicitors maintained that their liability was limited to the amount by which the bank had suffered loss by comparison with the position in which it would have been had the full amount covered by the

[108] *Agricultural* (n 2) [386]–[385].
[109] ibid [376]–[430].

first registered mortgagee been paid out at the time of the loan, as it should have been. The bank's claim included both a claim for reconstitution of the fund paid away in breach of trust and breach of fiduciary duty and alternative claims for equitable compensation and damages for breach of contract and negligence.

At first instance, it was held that the solicitors acted in breach of trust in making payment contrary to authority but the breach of trust lay in paying out (and failing to retain and then apply to discharge the debt covered by the first registered charge) the £300,000 difference between the actual redemption amount and the amount the solicitors wrongly believed was necessary to redeem the first registered charge.[110] Equitable compensation was awarded on that basis (ie, for the amount secured by the first charge that had remained in priority to the second ranking charge).[111]

The Court of Appeal held that the breach of trust consisted of paying out the whole of the loan funds to the borrowers since the solicitors had no authority to release any part of the funds without the first registered charge having been redeemed.[112] However, applying *Target Holdings*, the Court of Appeal found that it was necessary for the bank to identify a 'proper causal connection' between the breach of trust and the eventual loss in order to be entitled to the amount it sought by way of equitable compensation. The primary judge had found that the bank would have proceeded with the transaction irrespective of the breach. Therefore, on the basis that the bank would still have been exposed to the losses it ultimately suffered, the Court of Appeal affirmed the quantum of equitable compensation awarded at first instance.

The Supreme Court dismissed the bank's appeal. Both Lords Toulson and Reed, with whom the rest of the Court agreed, adopted a qualitative approach to the analysis of the trust relationship. Lord Toulson expressly affirmed the approach taken by Lord Browne-Wilkinson in *Target Holdings.*

Lord Toulson summarised the approach of Lord Browne-Wilkinson in *Target* as being that, while the fundamental principles of equity apply to all trusts, certain detailed rules applicable to one form of trust (a traditional trust) do not necessarily have to be applied to other forms of trust (a commercial trust) if the rationale does not sensibly apply to the latter.[113] Lord Reed similarly agreed that it would be mistaken to think that all different types of trust must be governed in every respect by identical rules, saying that:

> In particular, as Lord Browne-Wilkinson pointed out, commercial trusts, usually arising out of contractual relationships rather than the transfer of property by way of gift, differ in a number of respects from the more traditional trust. That is not to say that there is a categorical distinction between trusts in commercial and non-commercial relationships, or to assert that there are trusts to which the fundamental

[110] *AIB Group (UK) Plc v Mark Redler & Co Solicitors* [2012] EWHC 35 (Ch); [2012] PNLR 16.
[111] ibid.
[112] *AIB Group (UK) Plc v Mark Redler & Co Solicitors* [2013] EWCA Civ 45; [2013] PNLR 19.
[113] *AIB v Redler* (n 13) [33] (Lord Toulson).

principles of equity do not apply. It is, on the other hand, to recognise that the duties and liabilities of trustees may depend, in some respects, on the terms of the trust in question and the relationship between the relevant parties (cf *Kelly v Cooper* [1993] AC 205, 214–215).[114]

Lord Toulson addressed the criticism that had been made of the passage by Lord Browne-Wilkinson to the effect that it would be 'wrong to lift wholesale the detailed rules developed in the context of traditional trusts' and apply them to a bare trust which was 'but one incident of a wider commercial transaction involving agency'.[115] His Lordship said:

> … it is a fact that a commercial trust differs from a typical traditional trust in that it arises out of a contract rather than the transfer of property by way of gift. The contract defines the parameters of the trust. Trusts are now commonly part of the machinery used on many commercial transactions, for example across the spectrum of wholesale financial markets, where they serve a useful bridging role between the parties involved. Commercial trusts may differ widely in their purpose and content, but they have in common that the trustee's duties are likely to be closely defined and may be of limited duration. Lord Browne-Wilkinson did not suggest that the principles of equity differ according to the nature of the trust, but rather that the scope and purpose of the trust may vary, and this may have a bearing on the appropriate relief in the event of breach …. Lord Browne-Wilkinson … identifi[ed] the basic equitable principles. In their application, the terms of the contract may be highly relevant to the question of fact whether there has been a loss applying a "but for" test, that is, by reference to what the solicitors were instructed to do.[116]

Their Lordships both separately referred to the fact that *Target Holdings* concerned a bare trust that arose as an 'incident of a commercial transaction involving agency'[117] the purpose of the moneys paid to the solicitor being 'to achieve the bank's commercial objective … it [was] but one aspect of the arrangements between the parties, such arrangements being for the most part contractual.'[118]

Lord Reed concluded that one of the principal ideas in *Target Holdings* was that where a solicitor holds money on trust as an incident of a commercial transaction, the solicitor can be required to restore any money paid away up until the point that the underlying commercial transaction has been completed, but not after that point, 'since it would be artificial to impose the same obligation once the transaction has been completed.'[119] However, Lord Toulson considered that, as a commercial matter, the transaction was executed or 'completed' when the loan moneys were released to the borrower; since at that moment the relationship between the

114 ibid [102] (Lord Reed).
115 ibid [70] (Lord Toulson).
116 ibid [70] (Lord Toulson).
117 ibid [34] (Lord Toulson), [103] (Lord Reed).
118 ibid.
119 ibid [106] (Lord Reed). That analysis appears to accord with the so-called alternative justification for the decision.

borrowers and the bank became one of contractual borrower and lender, and that was 'a fait accompli'.[120]

Lord Toulson concluded that the extent of equitable compensation, specifically in circumstances such as those in *Target Holdings*:

> … should be the same as if damages for breach of contract were sought at common law. That is not because there should be a departure in such a case from the basic equitable principles applicable to a breach of trust, whether by a solicitor or anyone else. … Rather, the fact that the trust was part of the machinery for the performance of a contract is relevant as a fact in looking at what loss the bank suffered by reason of the breach of trust, because it would be artificial and unreal to look at the trust in isolation from the obligations for which it was brought into being. I do not believe that this requires any departure from proper principles.[121]

Lord Reed, in the context of considering cases in other common law jurisdictions, noted the High Court decision in *Youyang* which he referred to as a case on broadly analogous facts to that of *Target Holdings*,[122] and to the observation by the High Court 'that the nature of the remedy for breach of trust could vary to reflect the terms of the trust and the breach of which complaint was made.'[123] His Lordship said that the focus on the obligations of the trustee is 'the most important point' in determining the availability of equitable compensation.[124]

There is thus a clear divergence in the position as between Australia and the UK on this issue[125]—another instance perhaps of equity being 'a roguish thing' (as Lord Neuberger contemplated); I hesitate to describe it as an instance of equitable wires being crossed. Unsurprisingly, those who criticised the failure to apply substitutive compensation principles in *Target Holdings* remain critical of the decision in *AIB v Redler*. Adam Shaw-Mellors, for example, argues that, however pragmatic the outcome in *AIB v Redler* might be, it defies principled analysis and is not easy to reconcile with the more favourable treatment afforded to lenders in similar contexts.[126] Most recently, Associate Professor Paul Davies has written on the issue noting that the decision in *AIB v Redler* elides falsification and surcharge; and pointing to difficulties that may arise in considering concurrent liability in this context.[127]

120 ibid [74] (Lord Toulson).

121 ibid [71] (Lord Toulson).

122 With the important distinction that the security—which would have been good—was never provided and that the plaintiff investor was not the client of the solicitor trustee: *AIB v Redler* (n 13) [124] (Lord Reed).

123 *AIB v Redler* (n 13) [125] (Lord Reed).

124 ibid [93] (Lord Reed).

125 See A Shaw-Mellors, 'Equitable Compensation for Breach of Trust: Still Missing the Target?' (2015) 2 *Journal of Business Law* 165, where the author laments that the decision in *AIB v Redler*—unlike *Target Holdings*—cannot be rescued by any alternative analysis, the consequence of which he describes as being that the language of equitable compensation has been allowed to stray into a claim that should properly be analysed as one to enforce the strict obligations of the trustee.

126 ibid 172.

127 See P Davies, 'Remedies for Breach of Trust' (2015) 78 *MLR* 672.

V. Where to from Here?

What does that tell us, from the perspective of the question 'why' equitable compensation is available, for wrongs of the kind that occurred in the abovementioned cases?

If equitable compensation is available in order to protect beneficiaries from unauthorised application of moneys held on trust then on the orthodox view, AIB should have recovered the moneys paid out in breach of its instructions (after taking into account whatever had been able to be recovered). Whether described as substitutive compensation or not, this was a case where there was a misapplication of trust property. If, as has been recognised, equity applies a strict standard to trustees and custodial fiduciaries to whom their beneficiaries are vulnerable, there is no reason not to apply that standard even if the moneys are held in the capacity of bare trustee; and even though the context in which the moneys were held was a commercial context. To the extent that the contractual arrangements between the parties may confine the parameters of the trust or fiduciary obligations, the solicitors could presumably have made provision for their liability in the event of a misapplication of moneys.

The loss was suffered, in the sense made clear in *Youyang*, when the money was disbursed. The failure of the commercial transaction for which the moneys had been held does not affect that proposition. The basis on which the *AIB v Redler* decision proceeded was that there was a relevant distinction to be made between bare commercial trusts or those arising as an incident to a commercial transaction.[128] Why should such a distinction be drawn?[129] To the extent that there is a policy decision to draw such a distinction, whether that should be followed in this jurisdiction is obviously a matter for the High Court to determine if and when such a matter comes before it. Certainly, *Youyang* would not provide support for such a distinction in this jurisdiction.

There can be seen to be considerations in favour of such a distinction. Some of the arguments posed by D'Angelo may support this.[130] Similarly, to the extent that the Court of Appeal decision in *Target Holdings* was described by Heydon as 'harsh', 'chancy' and difficult to formulate,[131] the approach favoured in *AIB* may address at least the first two criticisms. The harshness to which Heydon referred was the perception that the trustee has to bear the burden of loss arguably created

[128] Lord Toulson citing Professor Hayton's argument that there are sufficient policy reasons to oust traditional trust law principles as to consequential losses in cases where there is a bare trust that is 'merely incidental to the furtherance of a contractual agreement' in D Hayton, 'Unique Rules for the Unique Institution, the Trust' in S Degeling and J Edelman (eds), *Equity in Commercial Law* (Sydney, Lawbook Co, 2005), 279–308: *AIB v Redler* (n 13) [71] (Lord Toulson).

[129] Davies points out that professional trustees acting for financial reward under a contract may be more likely to have the benefits of an exclusion clause than, say, a lay trustee acting gratuitously and hence do not need sympathetic treatment from the court: Davies, (n 127) 688.

[130] See D'Angelo (n 56).

[131] Heydon (n 90) 329.

not so much by breach of trust but by the actual commercial decision to enter into the transaction. The element of chance was that it was adventitious that acts constituting breach of trust preceded by a relatively short period rather than coincided with the happening of an event the client had always contemplated.[132]

D'Angelo argues that the 'corporatised trust'[133] is an anomalous accident of history and is, in effect, a surrogate company. He notes that the strict attitude of equity towards trustees applied in this context may therefore risk the compounding of breaches. For example, where directors of the trustee company, unaware that the trustee is in breach, continue to apply trust assets to an unauthorised transaction.[134] However, as a matter of principle, the fact that the trust arises in the context of a commercial transaction should not lessen the strictness of the standard applied to trustees or custodial fiduciaries in relation to the holding of funds over which a trust is impressed. It may well be that the commercial arrangement encompasses contractual provisions that define the parameters of the trust[135] but then it will be a relatively simple question of the parties' contractual promises moulding or shaping the trust. Absent contractual provisions dealing with this issue, why should there be a less onerous obligation on persons holding funds as trustee or in a fiduciary capacity simply because they do so in the commercial context, irrespective of whether or not that may be an incident of some wider commercial transaction?

The focus of equity in unauthorised disbursement cases has traditionally been to uphold the core obligation of the trustee—to preserve the trust fund—and hence to require the trustee in effect to perform the trust by restoring that which has been misapplied. Why should a commercial trustee be in any different position in this regard? Similarly, how is a 'commercial' trust to be defined in this context? There has been criticism of such a distinction[136] and the suggestion that an account should only be available where there is continuous and custodial trusteeship.[137] Ultimately, Davies suggests that *AIB v Redler* may be seen as another step in the 'contractualisation of trust'.[138]

The distinction itself seems apt to produce room for further debate. How does one treat, say, a corporate trustee of a self-managed family superannuation fund? Or a professional trustee performing solely custodial (not investment) functions? Or a family business run through a trust vehicle? Is 'commercial' to be understood

[132] ibid.

[133] D'Angelo defines 'corporatised trusts' as trading trusts and managed investment schemes configured as unit trusts with a limited liability company as trustee. See D'Angelo (n 56) 301.

[134] D'Angelo, Conference Proceedings, (n 56) 33, n 130. See also the published version, 333, n 127.

[135] See *AIB v Redler* (n 13) [70] (Lord Toulson).

[136] See, eg: Davies (n 127) to the querying of the 'novel distinction' drawn by Lord Browne-Wilkinson, in particular, by Robert Walker LJ in *Bairstow v Queens Moat Houses Plc* [2001] EWCA Civ 712; [2002] BCC 91 at [53].

[137] Davies (n 127) n 42 referring there to J Getzler, 'Equitable Compensation and the Regulation of Fiduciary Relationships' in P Birks and F Rose (eds) *Restitution and Equity Volume 1: Resulting Trusts and Equitable Compensation* (London, Mansfield Press, 2000) 249–250.

[138] ibid 693.

in the sense of the function of profit generation or does it encompass family estate planning or wealth management?

There have been difficulties in assessing equitable compensation where the duty arises in a commercial (rather than 'traditional') trust or fiduciary context. In *BigTinCan Pty Ltd v Ramsay*,[139] for example, the courts have had to grapple with how to value the loss of an opportunity to raise capital when determining the equitable compensation payable for breach of a fiduciary duty of loyalty by the director in question. In that case the director of a 'start up' smart phone app company, who had worked on raising capital for the company was held to have breached his statutory and fiduciary duties as a director by formulating a plan to raise capital for another company which necessarily put him in a position of conflict: he had an interest in seeking the failure of the task that it was his duty to the plaintiff company to pursue (ie, to raise capital).[140] Ball J found that there was a clear causal connection between the director's breaches and the loss of the plaintiff company's opportunity to raise capital.[141] His Honour awarded equitable compensation in an amount assessed by valuing the lost opportunity of the company to raise capital by reference to profit projections that had been made. On appeal the Court found that there was error in treating the loss of an opportunity to obtain funding as, of itself, a substantial financial loss.[142]

Macfarlan JA, with whom McColl and Gleeson JJA agreed on this issue, stated that:

> … the raising of funds would only have been of benefit to BTC if it could have done something useful with them. Otherwise, whilst the company would have received money, it would have incurred a liability to the investor to repay an equivalent amount, either as a debt due to a creditor or as share capital ultimately to be returned to a shareholder. If the evidence established that funding would, or might, have enabled BTC to earn profits, the absence of that funding might fairly be regarded as causally related to a financial loss. Otherwise, it could not be so regarded.[143]

Query whether the loss of the interest that would have been received while the findings were in the company's bank account, or the reduction in interest payable on its borrowings in that period, might itself have been a sufficient financial loss for the purpose of causation (the case being one of reparative compensation on the substitutive/reparative dichotomy, such that loss was required to be shown as causally connected to the breach).

More recently, *Dennis Cassegrain v Gerard Cassegrain & Co Pty Ltd (in liquidation)*,[144] *Target Holdings*, *Youyang* and *AIB v Redler* (among others) were considered

[139] [2013] NSWSC 1248.
[140] ibid [80], [89].
[141] ibid, [89], [99].
[142] *Ramsay v BigTinCan Ltd* [2014] NSWCA 452.
[143] ibid [69]. His Honour referred to authorities 'confirm[ing] the correctness of this view', including the decision of French J, then sitting in the Federal Court of Australia, in *Adelaide Petroleum NL v Poseidon Ltd* (1990) 98 ALR 431, 530–2.
[144] [2015] NSWSC 851.

in determining the question whether the referee (to whom the equitable compensation enquiry was referred) had erred in valuing the shares in question at the date of their transfer rather than the date of the trial. The liability to pay equitable compensation in that case arose on the finding of accessorial liability for knowing receipt of trust property and was thus not a case of substitutive compensation by the third party recipient of trust property. Bergin CJ in Eq, considering whether to adopt the referee's report, did not have cause to consider the question whether substitutive compensation was available in the context of a commercial trust; and applied the authorities that recognised that there may be circumstances in which the court is justified in departing from the general rule as to the date of assessment of equitable compensation for breach of fiduciary duty.[145]

Replacing a remedy of substitutive compensation (in a case of unauthorised disbursement) with a remedy of reparative compensation for commercial trusts does not make the task easier nor does it provide certainty for the parties.

And, finally, does the treatment in *AIB v Redler* suggest anything as to the fate of the strict causation rule in *Brickenden*?[146] Heydon's commentary to which I have earlier referred saw the Court of Appeal decision in *Target Holdings* as conformable with that rule.[147] Heydon considered that if the *Brickenden* principle exists, its operation without reference to issues of causation would support by analogy the recoverability of damages as trustees independent of a causal link between breach and loss.[148] If so, then the decision in *AIB v Redler* would not confirm to the rule. That, however, is another topic altogether.

VI. Conclusion

Like the editors of the current edition of *Meagher, Gummow and Lehane*, I suspect that the usefulness of labels such as substitutive compensation and reparative compensation lies only when they are commonly understood and consistently applied. The issue on which the paths of equity in Australia and the UK seem to be divided in the area discussed in this chapter is not so much a taxonomical one, but on the more substantive question as to whether restoration of moneys disbursed without authorisation should be ordered irrespective of the question of any loss beyond that of the disbursement; ie, whether substitutive compensation is or should be available for breach of trust/custodial fiduciary duty in the context of a bare commercial trust or a trust arising as an incident of a broader commercial relationship, or whether in those circumstances the remedy of equitable compensation is dependent on proof of a loss beyond the fact of the disbursement itself.

[145] ibid [73]–[74].
[146] *Brickenden v London Loan & Savings Co* [1934] 3 DLR 465.
[147] Heydon (n 990) 333.
[148] ibid, 331.

And, if substitutive compensation is not to be available in such a case, how are the boundaries between commercial and traditional trusts to be defined? If the more relevant distinction is between a bare trust, a trust where active duty arise, how does that accommodate the central core of the trustee's obligation (to perform the trust and preserve the trust fund). How does this keep the trustees up to their duty (in the words of their Honours in *Youyang*)?

From a practitioner's viewpoint, other issues arise. How does *AIB v Redler* square with the continuing availability of the equitable remedy of account? Perhaps that is the real elephant in the room in this analysis. If AIB had formally sought the remedy of account, rather than in effect short circuiting this by claiming equitable compensation, would it not, subject to the fact that account is a discretionary remedy, have been entitled to an account; and, on a common account (falsification) basis would it not have been entitled to require the solicitors to account for the whole of that which had been disbursed without authority? Or would *AIB v Redler* have been decided in the same way on a discretionary basis (and if so why)?

It seems that equity in this context will remain, in the words adopted by Lord Neuberger as part of the title for his 2014 John Lehane memorial lecture, to be seen by some at least as 'a roguish thing' and that the spectre of dissension between distinguished equity judges and scholars is set to continue.

5

An English Misturning with Equitable Compensation

JAMES EDELMAN

I. Introduction: Debt and Damages

A and B enter an agreement. For consideration, B promises to hold $1 million on trust for A. B promises to repay $1 million to A if the money is not used for a particular purpose. The money is not used for the particular purpose. Is B required to repay it to A as he had promised?

For at least the last three centuries, the same answer to this question would be given at common law as in equity. At common law there is a contract. B promised to repay the money to A if it was not used for a purpose. It had not been used for that purpose. A debt arose. Loss need not be proved. A claim could be brought for the debt. Similarly, in equity, a bill could be brought against B as a trustee requiring him to account for the $1 million. Since B cannot prove an authorised disbursement, B would be liable to reconstitute the fund.

In equity, the language of 'account' was misleading in one significant respect. It concealed the different types of accounting process and the different types of liability that could arise. Those different types of account, and different types of liability, were based upon (i) an account of administration in common form, (ii) an account on the basis of wilful default, and (iii) an account of profits. The first was the claim for debt in equity that I have described, where a debt arose from an unauthorised disbursement. The second was a claim for loss caused by default, even where the conduct was authorised provided there was fault including carelessness. The third was a claim for profits made by the trustee.

Whilst trials of liability were separate from the taking of an account in equity, the three forms of account, and the rules governing them, were unlikely to cause difficulty. When liability to account was found, the attention of all the parties was squarely focused upon the rules for accounting and the basis upon which the account was taken. These rules were well known. In the opening words of Lord Selborne's speech in *Speight v Gaunt*,[1] the Lord Chancellor said:

> the principles of equity, with respect to the duties and responsibilities of trustees, and the distinction between those losses of trust funds for which they are, and those for which they are not, liable, are so well settled, and are of such great general importance, that the present case, in which two Courts have differed as to their application, has naturally been considered by your Lordships with some anxiety.

Two developments led to change. The first was the movement after the Judicature Acts from the expensive and time consuming process of splitting trials of liability and quantum. What began to vanish was a split which had occurred in Chancery, particularly in cases of wilful default accounting. The split had involved the separate questions of (i) whether a defendant was accountable from (ii) the taking of the account.[2] Split trials still occur but they are no longer frequent for good reasons which the High Court of Australia has explained.[3] Without a split trial, the attention of the parties is often heavily focused upon liability at the expense of the rules governing remedy. The three forms of account that would have been crystal clear to a nineteenth-century chancery practitioner began to be neglected.

The second development was that during the twentieth century, the old language of account became modernised. Lawyers began to speak instead of claims for 'equitable compensation'. In one sense this was more accurate since parties would often prove a loss in the same suit as the trial of liability. No account was needed. But the language of equitable compensation has also led to real difficulty. The difficulty arises because to almost any lawyer or layperson, the word 'compensation' is associated with 'loss'. Dictionary definitions also associate 'compensation' with 'loss'. There is an immediate tendency to forget that there are two other remedial forms because the use of an undifferentiated label of 'equitable compensation' encourages attempts to shoehorn at least three different principles into the same analytical framework. As equity textbooks that had previously been very closely focused on historical remedies were 'updated', this attempt to modernise by a unitary label has had unfortunate consequences.

On occasion, even from the early nineteenth century, there were lawyers and judges who used 'damages' in this same way as a unitary term to describe money awards in equity. As late as 1998, Sir Peter Millett said that:

> Woe betide a Chancery Junior who spoke of "damages for breach of trust" or "damages for breach of fiduciary duty". The judges knew that misuse of language often conceals a confusion of thought. Nowadays these misleading expressions are in common use. It is time that the usage was stamped out.[4]

[1] (1883) 9 App Cas 1, 4.

[2] *Sleight v Lawson* (1857) 3 K & J 292.

[3] *Tepko Pty Ltd v Water Board* (2001) 206 CLR 1, 55 [168]–[170] (Kirby and Callinan JJ), 18 [52] (Gaudron J), 27 [90] (McHugh J).

[4] P Millett, 'Equity's Place in the Law of Commerce' (1998) 114 *LQR* 214, 225.

Just as the attempt to unify money awards in equity by the single, undifferentiated label 'damages' was problematic, it was also inevitable that the attempts to shoehorn three different remedies into a single, undifferentiated notion of 'compensation' would cause problems. Three examples can be given of the dangers of the use of 'equitable compensation' as an undifferentiated label now common in equity texts and some judicial decisions.

First, it is sometimes said that a plaintiff who has suffered no loss can obtain 'equitable compensation' for a breach of duty which has caused profit to a defendant.[5] But as a matter of nomenclature, it is very awkward to speak of disgorgement of a defendant's profits as 'compensating' a plaintiff who has suffered no loss. As Professors McFarlane and Mitchell rightly say, '[n]o good can come of describing a gain-based liability as though it were a liability to compensate for loss. We must hope that the courts do not use this language in future cases.'[6]

Secondly, it has been said that 'equitable compensation' can be subject to a 'defence' of 'no causation'.[7] Taken literally, this would mean that, subject to defences, a plaintiff is entitled to recover any losses suffered from a defendant who did not cause them provided that the money claim can be described as 'equitable compensation'. On this approach, the defendant could sometimes, but not always on this view (although it is unclear when), defend that claim by saying 'I did not cause your loss'. No case has adopted this principle in such terms. This second point is closely related to the third point below which is to assume that all cases that are today described as 'equitable compensation' should be seen as claims for loss. This is both ahistorical and unprincipled.

Thirdly, and most relevantly to this chapter, the language of equitable compensation tends to lead to a denial of the existence of a claim for equitable debt, which would historically have been based on the common account. That was the conclusion reached in a powerful essay by Professor Chambers.[8] The language of 'equitable compensation', undifferentiated, invites this conclusion. A debt is a claim for a payment which is due. It is not compensation for a loss.

Chambers' argument, which is by far the most cogent exposition of this thesis, goes as follows. The 'equitable debt' claims all involve some form of 'default' by the trustee. Therefore these claims must all be based on trustee wrongdoing. Therefore these claims must all be concerned with loss. The false step in this argument is the assumption that because these claims involve a 'default' by a trustee they must therefore be claims for wrongdoing and not for debt. It is akin to an assertion that

[5] See for instance *FHR European Ventures LLP v Cedar Capital Partners LLC* [2014] 3 WLR 535, [1] (Lord Neuberger).

[6] B McFarlane and C Mitchell, *Hayton and Mitchell's Text, Cases and Materials on the Law of Trusts and Equitable Remedies*, 14th edn (London, Sweet and Maxwell, 2015) [13.067].

[7] Eg P Turner, 'The New Fundamental Norm of Recovery of Losses to Express Trusts' (2015) 74 *CLJ* 188.

[8] R Chambers, 'Liability' in P Birks and A Pretto (eds), *Breach of Trust* (Oxford, Hart Publishing, 2002) 1, 9–10.

there can be no claim for a contractual debt because every failure to pay a debt is a breach of contract.

The argument is ahistorical. The cases of accountability are not concerned with trustee default or breach. They contrast with the accountability on the basis of wilful default which *was* concerned with loss, and *was* based on a breach by the trustee. As Kindersley VC said in *Partington v Reynolds*:

> The one [common account] is a decree compelling him to account only for what he has received … the other is a decree compelling him to account, not only for what he has received, but also for what he might, without his wilful neglect or default, have received, although he has not received it … They proceed upon totally distinct grounds. The one supposes no misconduct; the other is entirely grounded on misconduct.[9]

Chambers accepts the historical characterisation of common accountability, but he argues that the claim must be based on wrongdoing because the trustee is exempted from liability in cases where the trust property is stolen or where the bank where it is invested becomes insolvent. The case commonly cited for this proposition is a decision from 1894: *Re Gasquoine*.[10] As Chambers recognises, however, the principle existed for centuries before 1894.[11] None of those cases conceived of these circumstances as a 'defence'. They were merely the boundaries of the trustee's primary duty to account. The cases concerned the rules for calculating the debt owed, not the loss suffered. The principle was that the trustee must account, as a debt, for the value of the trust fund that she holds at the time of the account. The fund might have increased by payments of interest. Just as, today, a bank's debt to its customer might be reduced by fees payable to the bank, so too the trustee's debt could be reduced by matters which were legitimate debits. One legitimate debit was where the fund was stolen or subject to insolvency, entirely independently of any act by the trustee. The trustee will still have performed her obligation to maintain the trust fund.[12]

In contrast, the trustee *was* accountable for the full debt, and reductions would be falsified, if the reduction arose as a result of an act or omission by the trustee, even if the trustee was entirely without fault. For instance, trustees were liable when they paid over the trust fund to the wrong persons because they relied upon a marriage certificate which turned out to be a forgery which the Master of the Rolls said would have deceived anyone not looking for fraud.[13] The Master of the Rolls simply said that the trustee is 'bound to pay the trust fund to the right

[9] (1858) Drew 253, 255–256; (1858) 62 ER 98, 98–99.

[10] *Re Gasquoine* [1894] 1 Ch 470.

[11] *Morley v Morley* (1678) 2 Ch Cas 2; (1678) 22 ER 817; *Jones v Lewis* (1750) 2 Ves Sen 240; (1750) 28 ER 155.

[12] *Jones v Lewis* (1750) 2 Ves Sen 240, 241; (1750) 28 ER 155, 155.

[13] *Eaves v Hickson* (1861) 30 Beav 136; (1861) 54 ER 840.

person'.[14] The cases involving theft were cited but disregarded. Again, the cases involving theft were disregarded when a trustee handed over trust property to a solicitor, chosen carefully, but who turned out to be fraudulent. The Master of the Rolls said that the 'case is too clear for argument'.[15] These were not novel decisions. A century earlier, the Lord Chancellor had said, in a case involving a forged transfer, that:

> 'if the transfer is made without the authority of the owner the act is a nullity, and in consideration of law and equity the rights remain as before. This is such plain, clear reasoning, that I need do no more in order to give the plaintiff complete relief…'[16]

The simplest lesson from this chapter is that the greatest danger of treating all equitable awards as 'compensation' or 'damages' is that it ignores a basic distinction between a claim for compensation/damages and a claim for debt. The former is a claim based on *breach* of a right. The latter is a claim for the enforcement of the right by an order that the defendant do something as close as possible to the promised performance.

The academic view that abandons claims for debt in an attempt to create a unified award of 'compensation' might have easily been rejected were it not supported by a recent decision of the United Kingdom Supreme Court in *AIB Group (UK) Plc Ltd v Mark Redler*.[17] The remainder of this chapter focuses heavily upon that decision. The difficulty with the decision is really the manner in which it was pleaded and argued. The focus of counsel, and therefore the Court, was upon compensation following breach. This is a powerful illustration of the grave danger in using the language, undifferentiated, of 'equitable compensation'.

The *AIB* case was not pleaded or argued at trial as one involving a debt. Had the case been pleaded or argued as one about debt then the result might have been different. For instance, in the simple example with which I commenced this chapter, A could argue that B's obligation to repay was a debt subject to a condition precedent. If the condition occurred then the debt arose. It matters not what A would otherwise do with the money or what events might otherwise have happened. This obvious truth was unfortunately obscured by the fact that the case was argued as one involving 'equitable compensation' for breach of trust. More broadly, it is a truth that is often misunderstood because of a focus on notions of 'causation' which have no place in this area of discourse. Once this truth is recognised it is possible to consider the same issues which arise where the obligation is not to repay money but to transfer other rights such as shares.

14 ibid 842.
15 *Bostock v Floyer* (1865) LR 1 Eq 26, 27.
16 *Ashby v Blackwell* (1765) 2 Eden 299, 302; (1765) 28 ER 913, 914.
17 [2014] 3 WLR 1367.

II. The Decision in *AIB Group (UK) Plc Ltd v Mark Redler*

AIB agreed to lend £3.3 million to borrowers so that they could re-mortgage their home. AIB retained the solicitors, Mark Redler & Co, for the transaction. AIB required a first charge over the borrowers' home, which had been valued at £4.25 million. As it turned out, this security sought by AIB was 'hopelessly inadequate'.[18]

The contract between AIB and Mark Redler consisted of a letter of instruction which incorporated the Council of Mortgage Lenders' Handbook. AIB would pay the loan monies to Mark Redler. Mark Redler would hold the money on trust for AIB until completion of the transaction. The contract (by the Handbook) included a term that upon completion the mortgage lender required a fully enforceable first charge over the property by way of legal mortgage. It also required all existing charges to be redeemed on or before completion. The contractual clause at the heart of *AIB Group* was as follows: 'You must hold the loan on trust for us until completion. If completion is delayed, you must return it to us when and how we tell you.'[19]

Although the clause only referred to a delayed completion, it must also have included a complete failure to complete. A failure to complete would include a delay in the completion. In any event, by necessary implication, if the client had terminated the contract so that there would never be completion, the solicitors could not possibly claim to retain the money.

AIB paid £3.3 million to Mark Redler. Mark Redler *should* then have attended a settlement at which it paid £1.5 million to Barclays to refinance the borrowers' existing loan with the remainder being paid to the borrowers. The payment of £1.5 million would have been in exchange for a simultaneous undertaking either by Barclays or its solicitors that the money would be applied to redeem its first charge. Unfortunately, Mark Redler made a mistake. It only paid £1.2 million to Barclays. So it did not receive a discharge of the first charge held by Barclays. The transaction never completed.

In the lower courts, there had been some dispute about whether the transaction had completed. Mark Redler argued that the transaction had completed when it released the loan money even though the money was released without a solicitors' undertaking and without confirmation from Barclays that the money would be applied to redeem the first charge. The Court of Appeal accepted the argument by AIB[20] that completion did not occur. In the leading judgment, Patten LJ said:

> I accept Mr Cousins' submission that the completion of the remortgage transaction required [Mark Redler] to be in receipt of a solicitors' undertaking, or unconditional

[18] ibid [140] (Lord Reed JSC).
[19] ibid [4].
[20] *AIB Group (UK) Plc v Mark Redler & Co Solicitors* [2013] EWCA Civ 45, [11] (Patten LJ).

> confirmation from Barclays that the advance monies would be applied by it in redemption of its charge, before releasing the advance.[21]

In the United Kingdom Supreme Court, it appears that Mark Redler did not challenge this finding.

However, there were references in each of the judgments of Lord Toulson JSC and Lord Reed JSC to the transaction having been completed 'commercially', albeit without AIB ever obtaining what it regarded as essential to completion: a first charge.

Lord Toulson said:

> The solicitors did not complete the transaction in compliance with the requirements of the CML Handbook. But as a commercial matter the transaction was executed or completed when the loan moneys were released to the borrowers. At that moment the relationship between the borrowers and the bank became one of contractual borrower and lender, and that was a fait accompli. The Court of Appeal was right in the present case to understand and apply the reasoning in *Target Holdings* as it did.[22]

Lord Reed said:

> If Redler had performed their trust, they would on completion have held a registrable first charge which secured a debt of £3.3m. In the event, on completion they held a second charge in respect of that debt; but Barclays continued to hold a first charge.[23]

This must simply have been a loose use of the term 'completion'. To paraphrase the words of Lord Toulson, the transaction was completed 'as a commercial matter' but it was not completed as required by the contractual documents. The reason why there cannot have been completion in the sense in which the term was used in the parties' contract is because if completion had occurred then the act of releasing the funds would have been authorised. It might have been careless but it would have been an authorised act. But, as I have said, the Court of Appeal rejected this argument and there was no dispute in the Supreme Court that the release of funds was unauthorised.

Therefore, under the key contractual clause, and in the absence of completion (within its contractual meaning), Mark Redler was under a continuing obligation in equity to hold the £3.3 million on trust for AIB as well as an obligation to pay £3.3 million to AIB 'when and how' AIB told them.

The Supreme Court held that Mark Redler was not required to pay the £3.3 million to AIB. Lord Toulson JSC said:

> This involves effectively treating the unauthorised application of trust funds as creating an immediate debt between the trustee and the beneficiary, rather than conduct meriting equitable compensation for any loss thereby caused.[24]

21 ibid [43].
22 *AIB* (n 17) 1402 [74].
23 ibid 1402 [139].
24 ibid 1383 [61].

With respect, this is correct. But the Supreme Court apparently considered that no debt had been created. This may be because the most obvious debt claim would be at common law. But no claim for debt had been brought at common law. It is hard to understand why AIB did not do so. AIB brought four claims: breach of trust, breach of fiduciary duty, breach of contract and negligence. Breach of contract and negligence were admitted by the solicitors.[25] But AIB never brought a claim which was of the form 'repay the money which you promised to repay under the conditions which occurred'.

The existence of a trust would not have precluded AIB from bringing a common law claim for debt. The rights arising as a result of a trust do not exclude common law debt obligations. For instance, trustees often borrow money to invest to obtain returns for a trust. The trustee cannot say to a lender of funds 'I am not required to repay the money to you because I hold the benefit of it on trust'.

The obvious advantage of a claim in *AIB* for debt (rather than 'compensation') is that matters concerning causation, loss, and remoteness would have been irrelevant. As Millett LJ (Otton LJ and Sir Stephen Brown P agreeing) said in *Jervis v Harris*,[26] there is a clear distinction between a claim for payment of a debt and a claim for damages for breach of contract. A plaintiff 'who claims payment of a debt need not prove anything beyond the occurrence of the event or condition on the occurrence of which the debt became due. He need prove no loss; the rules as to remoteness of damage and mitigation of loss are irrelevant'.

III. The Decision in *Target Holdings* and the Traditional Approach in Equity

Central to the Supreme Court's decision in *AIB v Redler* was an earlier decision of the House of Lords in *Target Holdings Ltd v Redferns*.[27] The cases were similar but there was one critical difference. In *Target*, a purchaser had been lent £1.5 million by Target Holdings. The money was paid by Target Holdings to the purchasers' solicitors, Redferns. The terms on which the money was paid to Redferns was that the money was to be held on trust and not to be distributed until Redferns had obtained a mortgage over the property. Redferns distributed most of the money before the mortgage was executed. After the purchaser defaulted, Target sold the property for £450,000. Target claimed the difference from Redferns. Redferns defended the claim on the basis that they had not caused Target's loss. The loss had been caused because the property (on the assumed facts) had been overvalued as a result of fraud. On the analysis above, and on these facts only,

[25] ibid [9]
[26] [1996] Ch 195, 202.
[27] [1996] AC 421.

Target Holdings should have succeeded against Redferns in a claim for debt, either at common law or in equity.

In the House of Lords, the claim by Target Holdings was brought only in equity. In the leading speech, Lord Browne-Wilkinson acknowledged the traditional equitable approach required the trustee to account for the money that it held.[28] Where a trustee undertook responsibility for trust assets, the trustee was accountable for those assets as an administrator. If the trustee paid them away without authority then the payment entry was falsified in the accounts and he remained liable to the beneficiary for the assets. This meant that he had to pay the cost to ensure that those assets were maintained as promised.[29] The cost of performing the trust duty was usually calculated by the value of the notional trust assets at the date of trial because the trustee's undertaking usually continued until trial.[30] As Lord Millett explained in *Libertarian Investments Ltd v Hall*:

> If the account discloses an unauthorised disbursement the plaintiff may falsify it, that is to say ask for the disbursement to be disallowed. This will produce a deficit which the defendant must make good, either *in specie* or in money. Where the defendant is ordered to make good the deficit by the payment of money, the award is sometimes described as the payment of equitable compensation; but it is not compensation for loss but restitutionary or restorative. The amount of the award is measured by the objective value of the property lost determined at the date when the account is taken and with the full benefit of hindsight.[31]

In other words, this account of administration required the trustee to pay the cost of performing his duty to preserve the fund. This was a duty assumed by every express trustee. Even the trustee of a bare trust was required to perform his duty to preserve the trust property. As the High Court of Australia explained in *CGU Insurance Limited v One.Tel Limited (In Liquidation)*:

> One obligation of a trustee which exists by virtue of the very office is the obligation to get the trust property in, protect it, and vindicate the rights attaching to it. That obligation exists even if no provision of any statute or trust instrument creates it. It exists unless it is negated by a provision of any statute or trust instrument.[32]

The obligation to maintain the property, and the liability to account for it, was described in some cases as 'equitable debt'.[33] Like claims for common law debt, in a claim for equitable debt questions of remoteness or mitigation of loss were

[28] ibid 434.

[29] *Magnus v Queensland National Bank* (1888) 37 ChD 466, 471–472 (Halsbury LC), 477 (Cotton LJ) 480 (Bowen LJ).

[30] *Re Dawson (deceased); Union Fidelity Trustee Co Ltd v Perpetual Trustee Co Ltd* [1966] 2 NSWR 211; *Hagan v Waterhouse* (1991) 34 NSWLR 308, 345–346; *Canson Enterprises Ltd v Boughton & Co* [1991] 3 SCR 534; *Target Holdings Ltd v Redferns* [1996] AC 421, 437; *Youyang Pty Ltd v Minter Ellison Morris Fletcher* (2003) 212 CLR 484, [35].

[31] [2013] HKCFA 93; [2014] 1 HKC 368, [168].

[32] (2010) 242 CLR 174, [36].

[33] *Ex p Adamson* (1878) 8 ChD 807, 819.

irrelevant.[34] Hence, it did not matter that the ultimate cause of the loss was the dishonesty of a third party.[35] As Lord Lyndhurst said in *White v Baugh*:

> The Court says, "You cannot be relieved from your liability unless your conduct has been strictly regular, whether the loss has been occasioned by the irregularity of your conduct or not."[36]

On the facts of *Target*, involving a modern commercial trust, Lord Browne-Wilkinson rejected the traditional approach. The reason why he considered that the traditional approach should not apply was his concern that the traditional approach requiring performance by trustees would render modern commercial arrangements useless. Lord Browne-Wilkinson therefore insisted that, in this commercial context, the claimant could only recover for losses which had been caused by Redferns' breach.

IV. Earlier Doubts Concerning *Target Holdings*

In *Bairstow v Queens Moat Houses plc*,[37] Robert Walker LJ had considered a case involving a director's liability for a knowingly wrongful distribution of dividends. His Lordship considered that the same principles should apply to directors as those that apply to trustees, saying that custodial directors 'were not strictly speaking trustees, as title to the assets was not vested in them; but they had trustee-like responsibilities, because they had the power and the duty to manage the company's business in the interests of all its members'.[38] His Lordship then raised doubts about the reasoning in *Target*. His Lordship said that:

> It may be that a more satisfactory dividing line is not that between the traditional trust and the commercial trust, but between a breach of fiduciary duty in the wrongful disbursement of funds of which the fiduciary has this sort of trustee-like stewardship and a breach of fiduciary duty of a different character (for instance a solicitor's failure to disclose a conflict of interest...[39]

His Lordship distinguished *Target*, and applied the traditional accounting approach on the basis that the unlawful distribution in that case had been

[34] *Pelly's Case* (1882) 21 ChD 492, 506; *Re Windsor Steam Coal Company* [1929] 1 Ch 151, 156; *Target Holdings Ltd v Redferns* [1994] 1 WLR 1089, 1102 (CA).

[35] *Target Holdings* (n 27) 434 citing *Caffrey v Darby* (1801) 6 Ves 488; *Clough v Bond* (1838) 3 M & C 490. See also *Magnus v Queensland National Bank* (1888) 37 ChD 466.

[36] (1835) 3 C and F 44, 66; 6 ER 1354, 1363.

[37] [2001] EWCA Civ 712.

[38] ibid [53].

[39] ibid.

deliberate rather than negligent. This is a distinction of fact but not of relevant principle. His Lordship said:

> It is sufficient, in my view, to observe that this is a wholly different case from *Target Holdings*, in which (so far as concerned the application for summary judgment) the solicitors were shown to have done no more than to have acted imprudently in disbursing their client's funds before they obtained their client's security. In this case the former directors are liable for deliberately and (at least in relation to the 1991 accounts) dishonestly paying unlawful dividends out of the company's funds which were in their stewardship. Those unlawful payments have never been reimbursed. Queens Moat's case does not depend on any artificial exercise in 'stopping the clock'. The judge (at p.42 of the dividends judgment) rejected the submission that there was no loss because lawful dividends could and would have been paid, had the 1991 accounts reflected the true position. But even in the absence of such a finding, the submission was in my view bound to fail.[40]

Subsequently, the decision of the House of Lords in *Revenue and Customs Commissioners v Holland, In Re Paycheck Services 3 Ltd*[41] also appeared to revert to the traditional accounting approach. In that case, composite companies in a complicated network of companies had paid dividends on the basis that the company was not liable for higher rate corporation tax. The structure had been established to avoid the higher rate tax and the defendants knew that the composite companies had become liable for the higher rate. When the composite companies went into liquidation there was a substantial deficiency of assets. The Revenue argued that the defendants were de facto directors who were in breach of their directors' duties, and that the distribution of dividends was unlawful. The trial judge held that one defendant (Mr Holland) was a de facto director. The Court of Appeal, and the Supreme Court (by majority) held that Mr Holland was not a de facto director.

Although Mr Holland was held not to be liable as a de facto director, in the course of the reasoning the Court of Appeal and Supreme Court made observations about the alternative arguments run by Mr Holland. One of those alternative arguments concerned the compensation for which Mr Holland was liable to pay. It was accepted that directors are under an unqualified duty not to cause an unlawful and ultra vires payment of a dividend.[42] But, it was argued for Mr Holland, in reliance upon *Target*, that if Mr Holland was in breach of a duty as a director then the correct measure of recovery was damages for that breach which required an investigation into whether the net position of the companies was worse by continued trading and payment of dividends than if trading had

40 ibid [54].

41 [2010] UKSC 51; [2010] 1 WLR 2793.

42 *Re Paycheck Services 3 Ltd* [2010] Bus LR 259, [82]. See *In re Exchange Banking Company, Flitcroft's Case* (1882) 21 ChD 591; *Re Lands Allotment Company* [1894] 1 Ch 616, 638; *In re Sharpe, Masonic and General Life Assurance Company v Sharpe* [1892] 1 Ch 154; *Selangor United Rubber Estates Ltd v Cradock and Others (No 3)* [1968] 1 WLR 1555, 1575; *Belmont Finance Corp v Williams Furniture Ltd and others (No 2)* [1980] 1 All ER 393, 404; *Bairstow v Queens Moat Houses plc and others* [2000] 1 BCLC 549, 555; *Re Loquitur Ltd, Inland Revenue Commissioners v Richmond and another* [2003] 2 BCLC 442, 471–472.

stopped. In the Court of Appeal, Rimer LJ (with whom Elias and Ward LJJ agreed on this point) rejected this argument saying:

> the basic remedy is one of restitution. That is because directors of a company, if not trustees in the strict sense (because its assets are not vested in them), owe a like duty as a trustee not to misapply the company's assets and a like duty to make restitution to the company if they do.[43]

In the Supreme Court, the approach of Rimer LJ was endorsed by Lord Clarke[44] and Lord Walker.[45] Lord Hope also said that:

> The obligation is to restore the moneys wrongfully paid out. This, as the deputy judge accepted, is the established remedy. Where dividends have been paid unlawfully, the directors' obligation is to account to the company for the full amount of those dividends.[46]

The desire to distinguish the reasoning of the House of Lords in *Target* appears to have been motivated by doubts concerning whether there should be a distinction between commercial and non-commercial trusts. Lord Browne-Wilkinson's assertion that the commercial trust would be rendered 'commercially useless' was unsupported by any reference to any empirical study which suggested that the equitable approach to performance, tempered by the power to excuse trustees or directors who have acted honestly, reasonably and ought fairly be excused.[47]

V. Lord Millett's Re-explanation of *Target Holdings*

Some commentators observed that the reasoning in *Target* was unorthodox.[48] One attempt to justify the result in *Target* without departing from the traditional approach of equity was made by Sir Peter Millett. In an extrajudicial article in 1998, Lord Millett argued that even on the traditional approach the solicitors ought not to have been liable because they had performed their obligations: 'the acquisition of the mortgage or the disbursement by which it was obtained… was an authorised application of what must be treated as trust money notionally restored to the trust estate'.[49]

I have previously argued that there is a difficulty with this explanation of *Target*.[50] The central difficulty is that it involves a fiction. It treats as retrospectively

[43] *Re Paycheck Services 3 Ltd* [2010] Bus LR 259.
[44] [2010] 1 WLR 2793, 2839 [146].
[45] ibid 2835 [124].
[46] ibid 2813–2814 [49].
[47] Now contained in s 61 of the Trustee Act 1925 and s 1157 of the Companies Act 2006.
[48] P Birks, 'Equity in the Modern Law: An Exercise in Taxonomy' (1996) 26 *UWALR* 1; Millett (n 4); S Elliott, 'Remoteness Restrictions in Equity' (2002) 65 *MLR* 588.
[49] Millett ibid 227.
[50] J Edelman, 'Money Awards of the Cost of Performance' (2010) 4 *Journal of Equity* 122.

authorised a transaction which was unauthorised. There was no finding that the solicitors were authorised to receive the mortgage a month after the money had been dissipated. The moment Redferns paid out the money without having first obtained the mortgage they came under a duty to reimburse the trust fund. When they later obtained the mortgage, Target Holdings could have refused to accept the mortgage. Any explanation of the result in *Target* needs to acknowledge that the unauthorised transaction had not been immediately cured. A better explanation may be that Target Holdings waived its right to refuse the mortgage when it ultimately accepted the mortgage and relied upon it in the sale of the property. Hence, the disbursement of trust funds would not be treated as unauthorised on the ground that it had been paid out without having obtained the mortgage.

Irrespective of whether *Target* should be re-explained, or the manner in which it should be re-explained, the case was very different from *AIB v Redler.* The fundamental difference is that in *Redler* the obligation to obtain the first charge (and complete the transaction) was *never* fulfilled and was *never* waived. The effect of *AIB v Redler* must now be that in English law claims against a trustee can no longer be brought as an equitable debt claim. Claimants will need to be careful not to neglect a possible claim for common law debt. The position in other jurisdictions, notably Hong Kong and Australia, may still permit the claim for equitable debt.

VI. Is the Position Different in Cases where there is No Money Debt?

I began this chapter with an example where A promises, for consideration, to pay $1 million to B on trust and B promises to use the money only for a particular purpose and otherwise to repay it to A. As I have explained, if the money is paid to B, but the condition is not satisfied, then a debt arises.

A difficult question arises where the subject matter is something other than money. Would it make a difference if the subject matter transferred to B is publicly traded shares? In other words, if B had promised to transfer publicly traded shares to A then can A demand that B pay to A the *money value* of the shares irrespective of any loss that A has suffered? The difficulty for A is that at common law a money debt has not arisen and the obligation to transfer the shares would not be the subject of an order for specific performance.

A. Common Law

At common law, a claim in the circumstances above was never expressed as a claim for debt. Debt was an obligation to pay money. Historically, however, the claim at common law would have been brought as a claim for an account. Indeed, in *Jones v Lewis*,[51] the Lord Chancellor explained that the principle exempting a trustee from accounting for goods that had been stolen was derived from the account at common law, requiring a bailee to account for goods that the bailee held. The liability of the bailee was to account as promised that care would be taken of the goods. This account required no proof of fault by the bailee. Nor did it require proof that the bailee caused any loss. So when goods are bailed to a bailee, the bailee was, and still is, liable to account for the careless loss of the goods even where she acts honestly and reasonably by entrusting the safekeeping to an apparently competent independent contractor.[52] As Professor Stevens explains, the 'duty assumed is that care will be taken of the claimant's goods, not a duty that the bailee will personally take care'.[53]

But, at common law, the claim for the money value of a promise to maintain an asset is no longer expressed in the language of account. The language used is 'damages' which carries with it the same connotations of loss. Hence, there are cases where the result appears inexplicable. Damages without loss. A case which illustrates this point, deriving from a line of older English authority,[54] is the decision in *Joyner v Weeks*.[55] A lessor sued a lessee for breach of a lease covenant to leave the demised premises in good repair. The lessor claimed as 'damages' the full cost of repair. However, this was not a real loss because the lessor had granted a lease to another person which required the demolition of part of the premises. The lessee was still required to pay damages for a failure to repair that part of the premises which was to be pulled down. The Court of Appeal gave different reasons why causation of loss was disregarded. Lord Esher MR was 'strongly inclined' to think that an award of the cost of repair for breach of a covenant to repair was 'an absolute rule applicable under all circumstances'.[56] In contrast, Fry LJ relied on 'a general rule … that, where a cause of action exists, the damages must be estimated with regard to the time when the cause of action comes into existence'.[57]

The decision in *Joyner v Weeks* was approved by the High Court of Australia in *Graham v The Markets Hotel Pty Ltd*.[58] This decision involved a different situation in which the state of repair had rendered the premises unlettable at the end of the lease because they were disqualified from a liquor licence. But the High Court rejected the submission of Barwick KC that *Joyner v Weeks* should be confined to its 'special facts'.[59] Latham CJ described *Joyner v Weeks* as creating a 'general rule',[60]

[51] (1750) 2 Ves Sen 240, 241; (1750) 28 ER 155, 155.
[52] *Morris v C W Martin & Sons Ltd* [1966] 1 QB 716; *York Products Pty Ltd v Gilchrist Watt & Sanderson Pty Ltd* [1970] 1 WLR 1262.
[53] R Stevens, *Torts and Rights* (Oxford, Oxford University Press, 2007) 115.
[54] See the cases cited at [1891] 2 QB 31, 45 (Lord Esher).
[55] ibid.
[56] ibid 43.
[57] ibid 48.
[58] (1943) 67 CLR 567.
[59] ibid 576.
[60] ibid 582.

and Starke J described it as the 'true measure'.[61] The effect of the decision in *Joyner v Weeks* was ameliorated in England and Wales by s 18 of the *Law of Property Act 1925* (UK), and in New South Wales, by s 133A of the *Conveyancing Act 1919* (NSW). But it remained a common law rule and remains an illustration of a case where the award of damages at common law is quantified by the money value of the obligation of a non-money performance.

The leading decision in Australia is now the decision of the High Court of Australia in *Clark v Macourt*.[62] In that case, the purchaser of defective straws of sperm was held to be entitled to recover the value that the straws would have had if the contract had been performed, even though the purchaser had acquired new straws and defrayed much of that cost by sale to patients using the new straws. The judgments focused on the nature of the award as representing the money value of the obligation of performance. As Hayne J said, the compensation 'reflects a normative order in which contracts must be performed'.[63] And, as Keane J said:[64]

> it is the general intention of the law that, in giving damages for breach of contract, the party complaining should, so far as it can be done by money, be placed in the same position as he would have been in if the contract had been performed.[65]

The same concept of a money award to substitute for the value of the promised performance at common law was the issue that divided the House of Lords in *Alfred McAlpine Construction Ltd v Panatown Ltd*.[66] McAlpine promised Panatown that it would build an office block and car park. For tax reasons, the owner of the land upon which McAlpine would build was not Panatown but was a company related to Panatown called UIPL. McAlpine undertook, by deed with UIPL, to take reasonable care in performing the work. McAlpine performed the work defectively and Panatown sought recovery of the cost of repair. A minority of the House of Lords would have dismissed the appeal because no financial loss had been suffered by Panatown. However, a majority considered, or assumed, that despite the absence of financial loss, a contracting party is generally entitled to recover the cost of performance. Lords Goff and Millett considered that such an award should have been available. Lord Browne-Wilkinson also assumed that the cost of performance award should be available but he dismissed the appeal because McAlpine had entered a duty of care deed to UIPL, which could recover the cost. For Lord Browne-Wilkinson, this meant that McAlpine had no interest in performance because the purpose of the whole contractual scheme was to ensure that it was UIPL which was the party which would enforce any right to performance.[67] A majority of their Lordships, therefore, recognised or assumed that, absent a duty

[61] ibid 588.
[62] (2013) 88 ALJR 190.
[63] ibid [11].
[64] ibid [130].
[65] Quoting from the Privy Council in *Wertheim v Chicoutimi Pulp Co* [1911] AC 301, 307–308.
[66] [2001] 1 AC 568.
[67] ibid 577–578.

of care deed, Panatown had a right to recover the cost of repair to ensure that it obtained the performance it had been promised.[68] All their Lordships assumed that this remedy was subject to 'reasonableness', a notion which Lord Millett assimilated with 'legitimate interest'.[69] The reasoning of Lords Goff and Millett in *Panatown* has been applied by lower courts.[70] However, the principle remains controversial. In one case it was said that to the extent that such a principle exists it should be confined to services cases and that it does not apply to sales of goods.[71]

Commentators such as Professor Coote have referred to this type of award as performance interest damages.[72] The label is important. It reminds us that the award focuses on the value of performance rather than loss. As Dr Winterton has explained:[73]

> the claimant has not suffered any loss in the sense in which this term is typically understood. Rather, to the extent that any "loss" was suffered, it was a loss of the performance that the innocent party was entitled to under the contract … references to "loss" should be confined to describing deteriorations in a party's factual position.

Dr Winterton explains that the justification for an award of this nature is not a desire to compensate for loss but a desire to undo, as far as possible, a breach by requiring a payment of the cost of achieving performance of the duty. The award is designed to achieve 'next best conformity': it is the next best thing to being awarded the performance that was promised. As Lord Neuberger MR said of a doctor's negligence in *Wright (A Child) v Cambridge Medical Group (A Partnership)*,[74] 'it is the nearest the law can get to putting the patient into the position that she should have been if the doctor had not been negligent'. So understood, in contract the money award of the value of performance is little more than the money cost of specific performance. 'Specific performance' is really a misnomer. It is also an award that aims for next best conformity because specific performance almost never involves the precise performance of the promised duty. Almost inevitably, the claimant for specific performance of a contractual right will bring the claim because the defendant has failed to perform at the time required.

B. Equity

It might have been thought that equity would take the same approach as the common law, requiring a monetary payment, essentially as a debt, which represents

[68] This is also how the House of Lords decision was understood on the remitter: [2001] EWCA Civ 485, [20].

[69] *Panatown* (n 66) 592.

[70] *Mirant Construction (Hong Kong) Ltd v Ove Arup & Partners International Ltd* [2007] EWHC 918 (TCC); *Technotrade v Larkstore Ltd* [2006] 1 WLR 2926.

[71] *DRC Distribution Ltd v Ulva Ltd* [2007] EWHC 1716, [70].

[72] See B Coote, 'Contract Damages, *Ruxley* and the Performance Interest' [1997] *CLJ* 537; and IN Duncan Wallace, 'Third Party Damage: No Legal Black Hole?' (1999) 115 *LQR* 394.

[73] D Winterton, *Money Awards in Contract Law* (Oxford, Hart Publishing, 2015) 163.

[74] [2013] QB 312, [60].

the substitute for the cost of obtaining the promised performance by a trustee, or other custodial fiduciary. Indeed, equity was more generous than the common law in recognising claims for debt. The absence of a common law debt is not an obstacle to an order in equity. Even if the contract right had not accrued for a debt to arise at common law, equity would require that the money be paid. In *M'Intosh v The Great Western Railway Company*,[75] Mr M'Intosh agreed to do work for the Great Western Railway Company. Mr M'Intosh was only entitled to be paid upon the issue of a certificate of completion by the company's engineer. The engineer refused to provide a certificate; this was not found to be fraudulent. The Lord Chancellor accepted that the certificate was a condition 'without the performance of which it is provided that no right under the contract shall arise.'[76] But, affirming the decision of the Vice Chancellor, he held that the claim was not demurrable. He rejected the argument that Mr M'Intosh was confined to a claim for damages for breach of contract. Mr M'Intosh was held to be entitled to an account in equity of the value that was due to him even though no right to it had accrued.

Historically in equity it also did not matter if the obligation was non-monetary. In Dr Elliott's doctoral research on this subject he used the label 'substitutive compensation' to differentiate these claims from those for loss (which he called 'reparative compensation')[77] and which were based on a different type of account concerned with wilful default.[78] That distinction reappears in the chapter on equitable compensation written by Dr Elliott in the leading English text on equity.[79]

As I have explained above, that English approach had a long historical lineage up until the decision in *Target*. That approach cannot now have survived the decisions in *Target* and *AIB*. It would be incoherent for equity to *refuse* a claim that the trustee pay a money award based on performance of a duty to maintain money but to *allow* a claim that the trustee pay a money award as a substitute for the performance of a duty to maintain a non-money asset.

VII. Conclusion

The focus of this chapter has been on English rather than Australian law. The reason for this is that, unlike Australian law, English law has now twice confronted, and rejected, a long established orthodoxy in equity, including a very recent decision last year. The purpose of this chapter has been to consider any reasons why this path might not be taken by Australian lawyers.

75 (1850) 2 M & G 74; 42 ER 29.

76 (1850) 2 M & G 74, 96; 42 ER 29, 38.

77 S Elliott, *Compensation against Trustees* (DPhil Thesis, University of Oxford, 2002). See also S Elliott and C Mitchell, 'Remedies for Dishonest Assistance' (2004) 67 *MLR* 16.

78 D Yale, *Lord Nottingham's Chancery Cases Vol 2* (London, Selden Society, 1961) 141.

79 S Elliott, 'Equitable Compensation' in J McGhee (ed), *Snell's Equity*, 33rd edn (London, Sweet and Maxwell, 2015) 550–551 [20–028].

There are reasons to believe that Australian law might not follow the new English path. The leading Australian case on this subject is *Youyang Pty Ltd v Minter Ellison Morris Fletcher.*[80] In *Youyang* the agreement was between an investment company and solicitors. The investment company paid money to the solicitors. The first half of the money was only to be released for investment by the solicitors when they had obtained a bearer deposit certificate. Once they obtained the certificate then the other half of the money was to be invested in speculative activities on the international money market. The solicitors released all the money to a prime bank without obtaining a certificate. The solicitors later reinvested the money on the instructions of the investment company but still no bearer deposit certificate was obtained. The money was all lost in bad investments. A majority of the New South Wales Court of Appeal held that Youyang's claim should fail for reasons of causation. As Handley JA explained, if the director who acted on behalf of Youyang 'had been told about the form of the certificate he would not have been concerned and would have proceeded with the investment'.[81]

The appeal to the High Court of Australia was argued as a case of compensation for loss. Senior counsel for the solicitors in breach submitted that the 'issue is whether the required causal connection between breach and loss was established'.[82] The submission was that 'a trustee in breach of trust is not obliged to restore to the trust fund, or pay by way of equitable compensation to the beneficiaries, moneys which would have been lost if the breach had not occurred'.[83] The High Court applied this causal reasoning but reached the opposite conclusion, endorsing the comments of Hodgson JA who dissented in the New South Wales Court of Appeal saying:

> [I]f a trustee wishes to assert that a breach of trust caused no damage for the reason that the beneficiary would, if asked, have authorised the very action which constituted the breach of trust, then there is at least an evidentiary onus on the trustee to make good that proposition.[84]

The case was argued, and therefore decided, by the High Court on these causal principles. But, the High Court nevertheless made a number of remarks that can be read as endorsing, in some contexts, the accounting liability approach described extrajudicially by Lord Millett. For instance, the High Court referred to Lord Millett's explanation of *Target* that:

> The plaintiff could not object to the acquisition of the mortgage or the disbursement by which it was obtained; it was an authorised application of what must be treated as trust money notionally restored to the trust estate on the taking of the account.[85]

[80] Above n 30.
[81] ibid 506 [60].
[82] ibid 488.
[83] ibid 488–489.
[84] ibid 506 [60].
[85] ibid 502 [45], citing Millett (n 4) 227.

The High Court also distinguished *Target* on two grounds, one of which was that 'the proposed commercial transaction, involving the provision of security to Youyang, was not after delay, as in *Target*, completed; the security was never provided and Minters should not have disbursed Youyang's moneys'.[86] Precisely the same point could have been made about *AIB v Redler*.

[86] ibid 503 [48].

6

Brickenden

MATTHEW CONAGLEN*

This chapter considers the meaning of the Privy Council's advice in *Brickenden v London Loan & Savings Co.*[1] Specifically, it is concerned with the correct approach to causation where a plaintiff seeks equitable compensation for loss caused by a breach of fiduciary duty. What link, if any, must be shown between the breach of fiduciary duty and the loss for which the plaintiff seeks compensation? In order to answer that question, one needs to address *Brickenden* because of the following dictum of Lord Thankerton in that case:

> When a party, holding a fiduciary relationship, commits a breach of fiduciary duty by non-disclosure of material facts, which his constituent is entitled to know in connection with the transaction, he cannot be heard to maintain that disclosure would not have altered the decision to proceed with the transaction, because the constituent's action would be solely determined by some other factor, such as the valuation by another party of the property proposed to be mortgaged. Once the Court has determined that the non-disclosed facts were material, speculation as to what course the constituent, on disclosure, would have taken, is not relevant.[2]

The meaning of that dictum is difficult to decipher, not least because it seems to rely on a notion akin to estoppel in the first sentence ('he cannot be heard'), apparently preventing the calling of evidence as to what the plaintiff would have done, but then in the second sentence states that 'speculation' as to what the plaintiff would have done will not be permitted, which is the very thing that evidence

* I am grateful, with the usual caveats, to Jamie Glister and Richard Nolan for helpful comments on earlier drafts of this chapter. I am also very grateful to Peter Turner, who kindly shared photographs he took at the Lincoln's Inn Library of the Privy Council Record for the *Brickenden case* (Lincoln's Inn Library, 1934/25), which contains the Case for the Appellant and the Case for the Respondents in the Privy Council, as well as the Record of Proceedings in the lower courts in the case. These have helped to clarify some points which are left unclear by the incomplete reports of the earlier decisions in the case.

[1] [1934] 3 DLR 465 (PC) ('*Brickenden*').

[2] ibid 469.

would help to avoid.[3] Numerous courts have grappled with the dictum's meaning, although generally without considering the issue from the perspective of fundamental principles. This chapter considers a number of possible interpretations of the dictum, and assesses the extent to which these have found favour in the case law since *Brickenden* was decided.

The dictum appears to draw upon principles applied in the context of trust accounting and other fiduciary relationships involving the stewardship of assets. It is suggested that such considerations are inapposite in non-stewardship fiduciary cases. However, what was said in *Brickenden* can be justified when it is borne in mind that the context in which it was uttered involved a claim for compensation rather than the profit-stripping remedies that are more commonly associated with fiduciary doctrine. Where a profit-stripping remedy is sought, it is irrelevant to consider what the plaintiff would have done if there had been no breach of duty.[4] But this is not so where compensation is sought, as compensatory remedies are assessed by resort to a counterfactual analysis to determine where the plaintiff would have stood had the breach not occurred.

While the meaning of the *Brickenden* dictum is obscure, it is suggested that it makes most sense if it is understood as identifying the relevant counterfactual against which the plaintiff's loss properly falls to be assessed. It is suggested that what *Brickenden* requires is that a fiduciary who has acted with a conflict between duty and interest (or between duties), or has taken an unauthorised profit, cannot rely on the counterfactual which considers what would have happened if the fiduciary had made full disclosure, but is instead held liable for loss determined by reference to the counterfactual of what would have happened if the fiduciary had not acted with the relevant conflict or taken the unauthorised profit.

I. Context

It is instructive to consider the context of the *Brickenden* dictum, including the various judgments before the case reached the Privy Council.

[3] JD Heydon, 'Causal Relationships between a Fiduciary's Default and the Principal's Loss' (1994) 110 *LQR* 328, 332.

[4] See, eg, *Gray v New Augarita Porcupine Mines Ltd* [1952] 3 DLR 1, 15 (PC); *Murad v Al-Saraj* [2005] EWCA Civ 959, [2005] WTLR 1573. See also M Conaglen, 'The Extent of Fiduciary Accounting and the Importance of Authorisation Mechanisms' [2011] *CLJ* 548.

George Arthur Porte Brickenden
(Photograph used with the kind permission of The Law Society of Upper Canada Archives)

George Arthur Porte Brickenden was born on 3 February 1896. Before the events which generated the Privy Council decision, he had served in WWI, and in 1918, he married Catharine McCormick, the granddaughter of a wealthy biscuit maker. The events relevant to the case took place in the 1920s, while he was a solicitor, practising under the firm name GAP Brickenden & Co. He later also served in WWII, holding the rank of Wing Commander in the Royal Canadian Air Force, for which work he was mentioned in despatches.[5] He subsequently became a county judge,[6] and died on 3 December 1971. The Brickenden name lives on, apart from the Privy Council decision, in the Brickenden Awards, which celebrate independent theatre in London, Ontario, those awards being named after his wife, Catharine Brickenden.

In November 1924, Walter Herbert Biggs and his wife, Eva Viola Biggs, already owed $30,000 to the London Loan & Savings Co of Canada, those debts being secured by mortgages over their properties. The Biggs then granted mortgages

[5] Canada Gazette, Vol 79, 14 June 1945, p 8. The commendation was for 'untiring efforts in determining the causes of obscure accidents' as Command Flying Accidents Investigation Officer: http://rcafassociation.ca/uploads/airforce/2009/07/ALPHA-BR.2.html.

[6] See http://images.ourontario.ca/Partners/ClaPL/CLaPL002714675pf_0013.pdf; www.brantford-expositor.ca/2014/12/08/flashback-dec-8.

over the same properties as security for further loans, to the value of $13,500, made by London Loan & Savings. The Biggs brought an action in the Ontario Supreme Court seeking redemption of the mortgages securing the $13,500 loans by repayment of the principal but without interest, arguing that the loans contravened the Interest Act, RSC 1927, c 102. Wright J referred the claim to Master Blackburn, who concluded (based on recent Supreme Court authority)[7] that the mortgages were enforceable, both as to interest and principal. Mr and Mrs Biggs appealed, but Raney J upheld this decision.[8]

The claim which led to the Privy Council decision was a counterclaim brought in these proceedings by the loan company (and its successors) against Brickenden, and against George McCormick. McCormick had been President of the loan company at the time the loans were made to the Biggs, and was also Brickenden's father-in-law,[9] being Catharine McCormick's father. As noted, in 1924, before the grant of the mortgages to secure the further loans of $13,500, London Loan & Savings already held mortgages over the Biggs' properties for debts amounting to $30,000. It had also already refused a request from the Biggs, in 1923, for a further loan of $8,400. Faced with that refusal in 1923, the Biggs had instead borrowed three sums from Brickenden, also secured by registered mortgages against their properties: one loan of $5,000, one of $2,000 and another of $1,200. These three loans are critical to the claim that ultimately succeeded against Brickenden.

By 1924, the Biggs were behind in their interest payments to London Loan & Savings, but had been paying interest on Brickenden's loans in a timely manner. It was Brickenden who made an application on their behalf to London Loan & Savings for the new loans totalling $13,500. The loan documentation revealed that the properties to be mortgaged were already encumbered, by the mortgages securing the $30,000 already owed to London Loan & Savings but also by other mortgages securing debts owed to other creditors, apart from Brickenden, totalling a further $17,000.

Raney J considered that London Loan & Savings could probably have successfully sued its directors for its loss on the $13,500 loan transaction.[10] As Crocket J said in the Supreme Court of Canada, Raney J's finding that there was no equity in the mortgaged properties suggested that the new mortgages were worthless, which pointed 'to a marked laxity and dereliction of duty on the part of the managing director and the other officers of the Company'.[11] The 'transaction was highly improvident and one which was fraught with disaster to both Biggs and the Loan Company'.[12] However, the managing director had died before the proceedings

[7] *London Loan & Savings Co of Canada v Meagher* [1930] SCR 378.

[8] *Biggs v London Loan & Savings Co* (1930) 39 OWN 126, 127 (Ont SC) ('*Biggs*'); Record of Proceedings, *Privy Council Record: Brickenden v London Loan etc* (Lincoln's Inn Library, 1934/25), pp 198–199 & 203.

[9] *London Loan & Savings Co of Canada v Brickenden* [1933] SCR 257, 260 ('*London Loan*').

[10] *Biggs* (n 8) 127.

[11] *London Loan* (n 9) 265.

[12] ibid 266.

came to trial, and McCormick had not given evidence, so Raney J held that there was insufficient evidence to make clear findings of breach by the directors. That claim therefore failed.

That left the other counterclaim, against Brickenden. In addition to acting on behalf of the Biggs in the $13,500 loan transaction, Brickenden had also acted as solicitor for London Loan & Savings in that transaction. The counterclaim relied, not on the conflicting duties that he owed to the Biggs on the one hand and to London Loan & Savings on the other,[13] but rather on the conflict between his duty to London Loan & Savings, as its solicitor, and his personal interest in the $13,500 loan transaction. Brickenden's interest in the transaction lay in how the new loan monies were used.

London Loan & Savings retained $1,000 as a bonus, and another $1,636.14 was used to clear the outstanding interest on its previous loans. A further $5,000 was used by London Loan & Savings to acquire the $5,000 mortgage from Brickenden. The fact that Brickenden's $5,000 mortgage would be transferred to London Loan & Savings was mentioned in the loan documentation that Brickenden prepared for London Loan & Savings. However, his documentation did not mention the other mortgage debts of $2,000 and $1,200 that he held over the Biggs' property, nor that he had arranged with the Biggs that they would pay him the amounts outstanding on those other two loans from the $13,500 loan monies. The new mortgages were dated 8 November 1924, and on the same date Brickenden took a cash order from Biggs sufficient to clear his $2,000 and $1,200 mortgages. Those mortgages were discharged on 12 November, on which date Brickenden signed the certificate of title for London Loan & Savings, without reference to them. Brickenden presented the order for payment on 13 November. The board of London Loan & Savings did not authorise the new loan until 17 November, but it seems the managing director must have earlier consented to the loan, without authorisation from the board,[14] as the funds were credited to Biggs on 13 November.[15] Brickenden did not give evidence at trial, and so the discrepancy in dates and the non-disclosure of his two mortgages was not explained,[16] but by this means he had effectively disguised the fact that the new loan monies would be used to pay off two mortgages which he held and which were not revealed to London Loan & Savings.[17] As Raney J said, the mortgages that Brickenden had held were doubtful securities, and so his interest was to have those mortgage debts paid off.[18] The new loan ensured that the

[13] See generally M Conaglen, 'Fiduciary Regulation of Conflicts Between Duties' (2009) 125 *LQR* 111.

[14] *London Loan* (n 9) 265.

[15] *Brickenden* (n 1) 468.

[16] *London Loan* (n 9) 262 and 264–265.

[17] The fact that it was the $13,500 loan monies which were used to repay the two mortgages did not become clear until the Appellate Division hearing: see Record of Proceedings, *Privy Council Record: Brickenden v London Loan etc* (Lincoln's Inn Library, 1934/25), p 214.

[18] *Biggs* (n 8) 128.

Biggs' indebtedness to him personally was fully satisfied, while London Loan & Savings was left with an indebtedness for which it held insufficient security.

Further, Brickenden also received a fee of $500 for arranging the loan, despite his disbursements amounting to a mere $8.85. Brickenden's loan documentation also made no mention of this further bonus of $491.15, over and above his costs.[19]

Raney J held that Brickenden's conflict between duty and interest meant 'he is responsible for whatever loss the company may suffer.'[20] His reasons for judgment explained that:

> There will be judgment for the plaintiffs by counterclaim against Brickenden for whatever balance the Master may find owing on the $13,500 mortgages according to the terms of those mortgages allowing credit for payments that have been made by the mortgagors [21], and upon payment by Brickenden those mortgages will be assigned to him.
>
> At the discretion of the plaintiffs by counterclaim, there may be a sale under direction of the Master of the properties covered by these mortgages subject to the prior mortgages, and in the event of this course being adopted there will be judgment against Brickenden for the deficiency.[22]

Brickenden appealed successfully to the Ontario Supreme Court's Appellate Division.[23] The Ontario Weekly Notes do not provide a clear record of the Court's reasons,[24] but the Printed Case, prepared for the appeal to the Privy Council, contains Grant JA's full judgment, with which Mulock CJO and Riddell JA agreed. Grant JA rejected the evidence, and Raney J's conclusion, that the directors of London Loan & Savings had been unaware of Brickenden's interest in the transaction.[25] He also considered that the claim was premature, on the basis that no loss had yet been suffered because it was not clear that the mortgages would provide insufficient security for the debts.[26] And he also rejected the claim on the basis that

[19] Indeed, Brickenden had earlier extracted 'bonuses' totalling $1,420, in addition to his fees and disbursements of $73.85, from the Biggs for granting the loans that he had personally made. He had settled a claim brought against him for these commissions by repaying $1,000 to the Biggs: *London Loan* (n 9) 260–261; Record of Proceedings, *Privy Council Record: Brickenden v London Loan etc* (Lincoln's Inn Library, 1934/25), p 36.

[20] *Biggs* (n 8) 128.

[21] The report in the Ontario Weekly Notes mis-transcribes this word as 'mortgagees': see *Biggs v London Loan & Savings Co* (1930) 39 OWN 126, 129. The Privy Council understood it to be a reference to payments by the mortgagors: see *Brickenden* (n 1) 469.

[22] Record of Proceedings, *Privy Council Record: Brickenden v London Loan etc* (Lincoln's Inn Library, 1934/25), p 201. The report contained in the Ontario Weekly Notes is consistent with this, subject to the point made in the preceding footnote and some minor changes in punctuation: see *Biggs* (n 8) 129. For the formal orders, see Record of Proceedings, *Privy Council Record: Brickenden v London Loan etc* (Lincoln's Inn Library, 1934/25), pp 203–204.

[23] The Appellate Division also dismissed an appeal against Raney J's rejection of the claim against McCormick: see Record of Proceedings, *Privy Council Record: Brickenden v London Loan etc* (Lincoln's Inn Library, 1934/25), pp 212 & 223.

[24] See *Biggs v London Loan Co* (1932) 41 OWN 48.

[25] Record of Proceedings, *Privy Council Record: Brickenden v London Loan etc* (Lincoln's Inn Library, 1934/25), pp 214–216.

[26] ibid 218.

II. Interpreting *Brickenden*

Numerous courts have grappled with the meaning of Lord Thankerton's dictum in *Brickenden.* It is suggested that it is best understood as a statement of the relevant (or irrelevant) counterfactuals that fall for consideration when the court attempts to quantify the loss that a breach of fiduciary duty has been caused, but it is useful to consider the other possible interpretations that have developed in the subsequent case law as well.

A. Rescission

One possible interpretation of the *Brickenden* dictum is that Lord Thankerton was explaining that '[c]ausation is not a relevant concept in determining whether a contract between fiduciary and principal should be set aside'.[43] It is, of course, correct that the equity to a decree of rescission is generated immediately by the breach of fiduciary duty, without needing to consider any issues of causation.[44] The question, however, is whether this is what Lord Thankerton was saying in *Brickenden.*

This appears to be what Hobhouse LJ thought in *Swindle v Harrison.*[45] He treated *Brickenden* as involving a principle relating solely to rescission, and not to compensatory awards: when a principal elects to rescind a transaction entered into in breach of fiduciary duty, '[i]t is no answer for the fiduciary to say that the other party would still have entered into the transaction had he made full disclosure'.[46] Hobhouse LJ went on to say that 'this principle cannot be used to enable a claim to recover common law damages without establishing a causal connection between the relevant loss and the relevant wrong.'[47]

With respect, this is a very strained interpretation of what Lord Thankerton said in *Brickenden.* The remedy sought and awarded against Brickenden was a compensatory remedy (referred to as 'damages'), not rescission.[48] Brickenden was not himself a party to the $13,500 loan transaction, although he stood to benefit from it, and so rescission against him would not have made sense. It is also clear, from its resistance of the Biggs' initial claim, that the loan company wanted to enforce the loan against the Biggs rather than rescind it. The counterclaim was brought against Brickenden for the loss which the transaction caused the loan company, rather than

43 D O'Sullivan, S Elliott & R Zakrzewski, *The Law of Rescission*, 2nd edn (Oxford, Oxford University Press, 2014) [8.34].

44 *Maguire v Makaronis* (1997) 188 CLR 449, 467 ('*Maguire*').

45 [1997] 4 All ER 705 ('*Swindle*').

46 ibid 726.

47 ibid.

48 *Brickenden* (n 1) 466. Nor was the loan company seeking equitable compensation in lieu of rescission, as in *McKenzie v McDonald* [1927] VLR 134 (as to which, see R Nolan, 'Conflicts of Interest, Unjust Enrichment, and Wrongdoing' in W Cornish, R Nolan, J O'Sullivan & G Virgo (eds), *Restitution: Past, Present and Future* (Oxford, Hart Publishing, 1998) 87, 114–115).

merely for the benefit which he extracted from the transaction, which is all that he would have had to disgorge if rescission were somehow sought against him.

The Appellate Division's decision, exonerating Brickenden, was based partly on the fact that it considered the various counterclaim plaintiffs had failed to identify with sufficient precision the loss that each had suffered. In stating the dictum as he did, Lord Thankerton was at least in part rejecting that view, which undermines Hobhouse LJ's interpretation of what he said. Indeed, in *Maguire v Makaronis*, the majority in the High Court of Australia pointed out that *Brickenden* was not relevant to their deliberations as the case they had to decide concerned rescission rather than compensation.[49]

B. Breach

A second possibility considered in the cases is that Lord Thankerton's dictum was concerned with whether there had been a breach of fiduciary duty, rather than with how courts should approach causation of loss after a breach has been made out. In other words, Lord Thankerton may have meant that it is no defence to a claim alleging breach of fiduciary duty for the fiduciary to argue that disclosure of the relevant facts would not have altered the principal's decision to enter into the transaction: once the Court has concluded that the undisclosed facts were material, the fiduciary cannot avoid the finding of breach of fiduciary duty by arguing that their disclosure would have made no difference.

This was how Mummery LJ dealt with *Brickenden* in *Swindle v Harrison*: he considered that *Brickenden* established that it is no defence to a breach of fiduciary duty to show that the claimant would have acted in the same way,[50] but he did not treat it as relevant to causation or the extent of the fiduciary's liability. In other words, an interest can be material, and so must be disclosed by the fiduciary, even if the information would not necessarily have altered the claimant's course of conduct. Hence, failure to make that disclosure constitutes a breach of fiduciary duty irrespective of whether the claimant would have acted differently.

Somewhat confusingly, in the Court of Appeal's subsequent decision in *Johnson v EBS Pensioner Trustees Ltd*, Mummery LJ held that information was not material, and so *Brickenden* did not apply, if the plaintiff would have acted in the same way with the benefit of full disclosure.[51] This seems inconsistent with what he decided in

[49] *Maguire* (n 44) 471–472.

[50] *Swindle* (n 45) 733.

[51] *Johnson v EBS Pensioner Trustees Ltd* [2002] EWCA Civ 164 at [54]–[55], [2002] Lloyd's Rep PN 309. Somewhat similarly, Kirby J considered that facts are not material if the relevant loss would have happened if there had been no breach: *Maguire* (n 44) 492–493. Unlike Mummery LJ, however, Kirby J treated *Brickenden* as itself determinative of materiality. But this approach renders the *Brickenden* dictum meaningless. Lord Thankerton said that *once* non-disclosure of material facts has been made out, it is not relevant to speculate how disclosure might have altered the plaintiff's decision. If the materiality of the non-disclosed facts can only be determined once the court has concluded that the

Swindle v Harrison. In contrast, the other judges in *Johnson v EBS* considered that the information was material. Consistently with what Mummery LJ had said in *Swindle v Harrison*, Dyson LJ considered that *Brickenden* was relevant to the question of breach, in a negative sense: proof that the plaintiff would have acted in the same way does not establish that the information was immaterial, and thus does not provide a defence to an argument that the fiduciary has acted in breach of fiduciary duty.[52]

In the Court of Appeal's later decision, in *Gwembe Valley Development Co Ltd v Koshy (No 3)*,[53] Mummery LJ (delivering the judgment of the Court) again appeared to return to the approach that he had advocated in *Swindle v Harrison*. *Brickenden* was cited as authority for the proposition that causation was not relevant to the question whether there had been a breach of fiduciary duty: in other words, it is irrelevant to the question of breach whether the plaintiff would have acted differently if there had been full disclosure of all material facts.[54] However, if a breach was made out, and compensation was to be assessed, 'the court is not precluded by authority or by principle from considering what would have happened if the material facts had been disclosed.'[55] *Brickenden* was not cited in connection with this latter point, and appears to have been thought irrelevant to the causal inquiry. There is thus evidence of a developing view in England that the *Brickenden* dictum goes to the issue of breach rather than causation of loss.[56]

This approach has also found favour in some decisions in Canada and New Zealand, although it is not the current orthodoxy in either jurisdiction. In *Crighton v Roman*,[57] the Supreme Court of Canada found that a transaction amounted to a trustee purchasing from his beneficiary. The majority judgment invoked *Williams v Scott*[58] and the *Brickenden* dictum as showing the trustee bears the burden of establishing that there has been full disclosure of all material facts.[59] That was not shown, but the relief sought was not equitable compensation, so the *Brickenden* dictum appears to have been relied upon as showing that the trustee could not defend his breach by arguing that disclosure would not have made any difference.

Brickenden was also cited by Hardie Boys J in *Sims v Craig Bell & Bond*, for the proposition that:

> [w]hat the client subsequently does, or agrees to, is not relevant to whether the solicitor has earlier fulfilled his obligations towards the client. And as a consequence one who is

plaintiff would have acted differently, the prohibition in Lord Thankerton's dictum becomes nonsensical. See *Commerce Capital Trust Co v Berk* (1989) 68 OR (2d) 257, 262 (CA); *Short v Crawley (No 30)* [2007] NSWSC 1322 [426].

52 *Johnson v EBS Pensioner Trustees Ltd* [2002] EWCA Civ 164 at [72], [2002] Lloyd's Rep PN 309.

53 [2003] EWCA Civ 1048, [2004] 1 BCLC 131.

54 *Gwembe Valley Devt Co Ltd v Koshy (No 3)* [2003] EWCA Civ 1048 at [144]–[146], [2004] 1 BCLC 131.

55 ibid [147].

56 See also *Horn v Commercial Acceptances Ltd* [2011] EWHC 1757 (Ch) at [64].

57 [1960] SCR 858.

58 [1900] AC 499.

59 *Crighton v Roman* [1960] SCR 858, 869. See also *Krendel v Frontwell Investments Ltd* [1967] 2 OR 579.

in breach will not be heard to say that the client would not have acted differently had he discharged his duty.[60]

The Court of Appeal did not, however, decide what remedy was appropriate: the issue of remedy was sent back to the lower court for determination. Both in terms and in context, Hardie Boys J's invocation of *Brickenden* appears to have been in support of the view that it is no defence to an allegation of breach of fiduciary duty to argue that the principal would have acted in the same way.

Notwithstanding the support that this approach has in some of the case law, it is suggested that there are difficulties with treating this as the best explanation for what Lord Thankerton said in *Brickenden*. It is correct that a fact can be material, and so must be disclosed by the fiduciary in order that he be effectively insulated against a claim for breach of fiduciary duty, even if the information would not necessarily have altered the claimant's course of conduct.[61] However, this cannot explain why the *Brickenden* dictum appears in the Privy Council's advice *after* the court had already decided that Brickenden had acted in breach of duty *and after* it said that 'it remains to consider … whether any damage has been proved'.[62] If the *Brickenden* dictum were concerned only with the question whether there had been a breach of duty, and not with the calculation of the remedy for that breach, one would expect the advice to have been structured quite differently.

C. Trust Accounting

A third possible explanation for what Lord Thankerton said in *Brickenden* is that he may have had in mind the strictness of the trust accounting principles applied to a fiduciary steward of assets, and the fiduciary's inability to avoid liability for his stewardship by arguing that the assets would have been lost in any event. In addressing this possibility it is useful to consider first the similarities between trust accounting principles and what Lord Thankerton said, and then to consider whether those principles are an apposite reference point when dealing with non-stewardship situations such as the one in *Brickenden*.

[60] *Sims v Craig Bell & Bond* [1991] 3 NZLR 535, 545–546 (CA).

[61] *Demerara Bauxite Co Ltd v Hubbard* [1923] AC 673, 681 (PC); *Moody v Cox and Hatt* [1917] 2 Ch 71, 80 (CA); *Gray v New Augarita Porcupine Mines Ltd* [1952] 3 DLR 1, 14–15 (PC); *Commerce Capital Trust Co v Berk* (1989) 68 OR (2d) 257, 262 (CA); *Johnson v EBS Pensioner Trustees Ltd* [2002] EWCA Civ 164 at [55], [70]–[72] and [83] (although *cf* [54]), [2002] Lloyd's Rep PN 309. In other words, the materiality of information is determined not by whether it *would* have been decisive (although, if it would have been so, then it clearly was material: eg, *Imperial Mercantile Credit Association v Coleman* (1873) LR 6 HL 189, 200 and 205), but rather by whether it 'may have affected the consent given to the transaction': PD Finn, *Fiduciary Obligations* (Sydney, Law Book Co, 1977) [437].

[62] *Brickenden* (n 1) 469.

i. Similarities

There is a marked similarity between the phraseology of the *Brickenden* dictum and what Lord Halsbury LC said in *Magnus v Queensland National Bank*.[63] In *Magnus*, an executed transfer of stock held in trust by three trustees was accepted by a bank as security for a loan to one of the trustees, Goldsmid. The bank was aware that the shares were owned by the three trustees, not Goldsmid alone. The loan was subsequently repaid, but rather than transferring the shares back to the three trustees, without authority from the other two trustees the bank transferred the shares to purchasers from Goldsmid and the purchase money was received by Goldsmid alone. Goldsmid later absconded with the funds, and the bank was sued. The bank argued that it was not liable to account for the value of the shares because Goldsmid had such control over the other trustees that he would have defrauded the trust of its assets in some other way, even if the bank had acted properly. That argument was rejected, Lord Halsbury LC saying:

> once the fact is established that money belonging to this trust has got into the hands of one of the trustees without the consent of the others, and that by the default of the bank, *we are not at liberty to speculate* whether the same result might not have followed whether the bank had been guilty of that default or not. … I think that the loss to the trust happened when, instead of being re-invested in the names of the three trustees, it was placed in the hands of Goldsmid alone. … I have very little doubt that he might have defrauded the trust in some other way. But … *I am not entitled to speculate* whether he might have cheated his co-trustees in any other form.[64]

This raises the possibility that it may have been these trust accounting principles that Lord Thankerton had in mind when uttering the *Brickenden* dictum. The connection between the thinking in *Brickenden* and the strictness of trust accounting principles is also reflected in McHugh J's suggestion, in *Bennett v Minister of Community Welfare*,[65] that a novus actus interveniens argument might not succeed in a claim for equitable compensation. For that proposition, McHugh J cited *Brickenden* alongside *Caffrey v Darby*[66] and *Re Dawson*,[67] the latter two cases being well-known for their statements of the strictness of a trustee's obligation to account as steward of the trust property.[68]

There are other similarities between *Brickenden* and trust accounting. Raney J's decision required Brickenden to pay to London Loan & Savings the amounts outstanding on the mortgages, and then take an assignment of those mortgages,

[63] (1888) 37 ChD 466 (CA) ('*Magnus*'). This similarity is also noted in JD Heydon, M Leeming & PG Turner, *Meagher Gummow & Lehane's Equity: Doctrines & Remedies*, 5th edn (Sydney, LexisNexis Butterworths, 2015) [23–485].

[64] ibid 472–473 (emphasis added).

[65] (1992) 176 CLR 408, 426.

[66] (1801) 6 Ves 488 (31 ER 1159).

[67] [1966] 2 NSWR 211.

[68] For a brief modern re-statement of these principles, see *Libertarian Investments Ltd v Hall* [2013] HKCFA 93 at [166]–[172], (2013) 16 HKCFAR 681 per Lord Millett NPJ.

or alternatively the loan company could insist on the mortgaged properties being sold and Brickenden would pay compensation for any deficiency.[69] This mimics the remedy available in cases involving a breach of trust, particularly where the trustee has made an unauthorised investment of trust property. In such a case, the trustee is treated as if the investment had not been made, or had been made out of the trustee's own money for his or her own benefit,[70] and the trustee is required to pay the sum invested back into the trust. Raney J's remedy in *Brickenden* bears a distinct similarity to what was said in *Re Salmon*,[71] where a trustee made an improper investment in a mortgage. The trustee retired and transferred the mortgage to new trustees, who sold the properties under the mortgage and sought to recover the deficiency from the retired trustee. Fry LJ commented:

> the liability of the trustee in such a case is to make good the loss occasioned to the trust estate by the improper investment. The mode of enforcing this liability depends on the circumstances of the case. In some cases justice will be best done by realizing the security and making him pay the deficiency; but in some cases it may be right to make him pay at once the whole sum improperly invested, and let him take the benefit of the security.[72]

The properties had already been sold in *Re Salmon*, and so the order was for payment of the deficiency. In *Brickenden*, Raney J allowed the counter-plaintiff to elect between these two options. The similarities between Lord Halsbury LC's comments in *Magnus* and what Lord Thankerton said in *Brickenden*, and between Raney J's first instance decision and other cases applying traditional trust accounting principles, provide grounds for thinking that perhaps those trust principles were the inspiration for Lord Thankerton's dictum in *Brickenden*.

A further similarity between *Brickenden* and trust accounting principles lies in the approach which the Supreme Court of Canada took to the rate of interest in *Brickenden*. Rather than requiring Brickenden to compensate the loan company for the arrears due under the loan transaction, Smith J awarded $12,500 together with interest at the rate which the loan company could have achieved on a properly secured loan of that sum. This mirrors a surcharge of a trust account, in that the argument is that the investment ought not to have been made in the imprudent manner it was, and if the trustee had made a prudent investment it would have earned a different sum.[73] This similarity to trust accounting is, however, perhaps less obvious than the others, given similar considerations also arise in common law claims for damages.[74]

[69] See text accompanying n 22 above.

[70] *Knott v Cottee* (1852) 16 Beav 77, 79–80 (51 ER 705); *Re Salmon* (1889) 42 ChD 351, 357.

[71] ibid.

[72] *Re Salmon* (n 70) 371. See also *Knott v Cottee* (n 70); *Re Somerset* [1894] 1 Ch 231, 258; *Target Holdings Ltd v Redferns* [1996] AC 421, 437.

[73] Similarly in the case of an unauthorised investment of trust funds: where the trust account entry is falsified, the trustee is generally obliged to return the principal which was invested together with the interest which that sum would have earned if it had remained in the hands of the trustees.

[74] Either under *Hungerfords v Walker* (1989) 171 CLR 125, 143–144 and *Sempra Metals Ltd v Inland Revenue Commissioners* [2007] UKHL 34, [2008] AC 561, or under statutory interest awards: see A Kramer, *The Law of Contract Damages* (Oxford, Hart Publishing, 2014), 199 and 209.

It is also worth noting the slight irony in this aspect of Smith J's judgment, which Lord Thankerton affirmed. Smith J admitted that there was insufficient evidence to decide what interest rate the loan company would have achieved on $12,500 on proper security in 1924, and so he adopted the legal rate of 5%. This was done for reasons of cost and delay,[75] but it could also be read as Smith J in effect speculating as to the rate of interest that the loan company could have achieved on a proper loan.

There are, however, also differences between what was said in *Brickenden* and trust accounting principles, most obviously in the fact that both the Supreme Court of Canada and the Privy Council referred to the loan company having a right to 'damages'.[76] Indeed, Lord Thankerton even referred to Brickenden's breach as generating a right 'at least to nominal damages',[77] a remedy which is ordinarily associated with common law claims for torts actionable per se and with breaches of contract,[78] rather than with claims for equitable compensation. To talk of claims for damages, let alone nominal damages, in equity, tends to betray a lack of understanding of the equitable jurisdiction. As James LJ said in *Ex parte Adamson*, the 'Court of Chancery never entertained a suit for damages occasioned by fraudulent conduct or for breach of trust. The suit was always for an equitable debt or liability in the nature of debt.'[79] Indeed, only 15 years before *Brickenden* was decided, the Privy Council criticised a Manitoba Court of Appeal decision because it 'should have treated the claim as one for replacement of trust funds, and not for damages.'[80]

ii. Appropriateness of Exporting Trust Principles

It should come as no surprise that Raney J, Smith J and Lord Thankerton may have drawn on trust principles in formulating their thinking in their respective judgments in *Brickenden*, bearing in mind the role which the fiduciary concept has served, particularly historically, in exporting the incidents of the relationship between trustee and beneficiary to other similar relationships.[81] 'The archetype of a fiduciary is … the trustee'[82] and the 'fiduciary relationship has developed by

[75] See text accompanying n 36 above.

[76] *London Loan* (n 9) 258, 258; *Brickenden* (n 1) 466, 469 and 472.

[77] See text accompanying n 40 above.

[78] H McGregor, *McGregor on Damages*, 19th edn (London, Sweet & Maxwell, 2014) [12-002].

[79] *Ex parte Adamson* (1878) 8 ChD 807, 819 (CA). See also P Millett, 'Equity's Place in the Law of Commerce' (1998) 114 *LQR* 214, 225.

[80] *British America Elevator Co Ltd v Bank of British North America* [1919] AC 658, 666.

[81] LS Sealy, 'The Director as Trustee' [1967] *CLJ* 83, 85–86 & 91–103; LS Sealy, 'Fiduciary Relationships' [1962] *CLJ* 69, 71–73; PD Finn, *Fiduciary Obligations* (Sydney, Law Book Co, 1977) [7]; PD Finn, 'The Fiduciary Principle' in TG Youdan (ed), *Equity, Fiduciaries and Trusts* (Toronto, Carswell, 1989) 1, 34–35; PBH Birks, 'The Content of Fiduciary Obligation' (2000) 34 *Israel Law Review* 3, 3 & 8–9; M Conaglen, *Fiduciary Loyalty* (Oxford, Hart Publishing, 2010) 12–15.

[82] *Hospital Products Ltd v United States Surgical Corp* (1984) 156 CLR 41, 68.

analogy from the trust relationship.'[83] As Fry J said in *Re West of England & South Wales District Bank*:

> What is a fiduciary relationship? It is one in respect of which if a wrong arise, the same remedy exists against the wrong-doer on behalf of the principal as would exist against a trustee on behalf of the *cestui que trust*.[84]

The similarities between what Lord Thankerton said in *Brickenden* and basic principles of trust accounting provide reason for thinking that he may have had a form of those principles in mind when conveying the reasons for the Privy Council's advice in *Brickenden*. However, the differences suggest that he perhaps did not appreciate all of the nuances of trust accounting doctrine.[85]

Fiduciary doctrine's exporting function has been conducted in a way that is mindful of the differences between different types of fiduciary actor. Thus, for example, directors were held subject to duties of care, because the position they occupied was similar to that occupied by trustees,[86] but those duties of care took into account the more entrepreneurial role expected of directors when compared with trustees.[87] This emphasises the importance of considering the appropriateness of exporting trust accounting principles to non-stewardship fiduciary relationships like the one in *Brickenden*. It is suggested that this is inappropriate.

Notwithstanding his alignment of *Brickenden* with trust accounting cases in *Bennett*,[88] McHugh J subsequently observed, during argument in *Youyang v Minter Ellison*, that '[t]here is a difference between loss of trust property and breach of general fiduciary duty.'[89] The High Court of Australia also differentiated those two types of claim in its judgment in *Youyang*.[90] The key difference lies in the fundamental

[83] *Gwembe Valley Devt Co Ltd v Koshy (No 3)* [2003] EWCA Civ 1048 at [89], [2004] 1 BCLC 131. See also *Girardet v Crease & Co* (1987) 11 BCLC (2d) 361, 362 (BCSC); *Swindle* (n 45) 734.

[84] *Re West of England & South Wales District Bank, ex parte Dale & Co* (1879) 11 ChD 772, 778.

[85] Of the Lords who decided *Brickenden*, only Lord Russell had experience sitting in the Chancery Division. Lord Thankerton was appointed directly from his practice in Scotland to the House of Lords. Lord Alness became Lord Justice Clerk and President of the second division of the Scottish Court of Session in 1922, before his elevation in 1934. Lord Merrivale was appointed directly to the English Court of Appeal in 1918, and then made President of the Probate, Divorce and Admiralty Division of the High Court from 1919. Lord Wright began his judicial career in the King's Bench Division in 1925 before being appointed directly to the House of Lords in 1932. Lord Russell was appointed to the Chancery Division in 1919, to the Court of Appeal in 1928, and was appointed a Lord of Appeal in Ordinary in 1929.

[86] See, eg, *Charitable Corporation v Sutton* (1742) 2 Atk 400, 406 (26 ER 642); *Fraser v Whalley* (1864) 2 H & M 10, 28 (71 ER 361); *Land Credit Co of Ireland v Fermoy* (1870) LR 5 Ch App 763, 771; *Re Lands Allotment Co* [1894] 1 Ch 616, 631 & 638; *JJ Harrison (Properties) Ltd* v *Harrison* [2001] EWCA Civ 1467 at [26], [2002] 1 BCLC 162.

[87] *Lagunas Nitrate Co v Lagunas Syndicate* [1899] 2 Ch 392, 435 (CA); *Overend & Gurney Co v Gibb* (1872) LR 5 HL 480, 494–95; *Re Forest of Dean Coal Mining Co* (1878) 10 ChD 450, 451–53 (MR); *Re Faure Electric Accumulator Co* (1888) 40 ChD 141, 150–53; *Re City Equitable Fire Insurance Co Ltd* [1925] Ch 407, 426; *Daniels v Anderson* (1995) 37 NSWLR 438, 488–505 & 599–602 (CA); *Re Barings plc (No 5)* [1999] 1 BCLC 433, 488–89 (ChD) (approved on appeal: [2000] 1 BCLC 523, 535–36).

[88] See text accompanying nn 65–67 above.

[89] *Youyang Pty Ltd v Minter Ellison Morris Fletcher* [2003] HCA 15, (2003) 212 CLR 484, 489 ('*Youyang*').

[90] ibid [41]–[42].

duties of trustees to gather in the trust property, to hold on to that trust property, to manage it in compliance with applicable duties and powers, and to disburse it to the trust beneficiaries at the appropriate time. As Lindley LJ said, '[t]he duty of a trustee is properly to preserve the trust fund, and to pay the income and the corpus to those who are entitled to them respectively'.[91]

The fundamental importance of the trustee's duty to account for the trust property lies in his or her need to justify what has been done with that property.[92] Thus, for example, trustees must be able to point to a relevant power if they seek to justify a disposal of trust property:[93] the underlying default rule is that the trustees are expected to have the trust property in their control unless they have disposed of it in an authorised fashion and in accordance with any relevant duties. As has already been emphasised, in *Magnus* the bank was liable to account for its stewardship of the shares, and it was no defence to the bank that the trustees had negligently failed to call for them. As Cotton LJ said, the 'only defence they could set up would be that they paid the money to, or allowed it to be received by, a person authorized on behalf of the trustees'.[94] In the absence of that defence, it was not to the point to argue that the loss was caused by Goldsmid's absconding with the funds: in the absence of an authorised disposition, they 'must be held answerable to the trustees just as if the money was still in their hands.'[95] Bowen LJ addressed the question of causation in terms, and rejected that approach:

> in pressing home the argument that whatever the conduct of the bank may have been it did not cause the loss to the estate, [the bank's counsel] was using the term in a popular and non-legal sense, and one which is not sufficient to support his proposition. When was the property of the trust lost? At the time when it first passed into unauthorized hands. … The loss occurred as soon as the money which belonged to the trust was diverted into the hands of a person who had no right to represent the trust. The proposition presented to us by the Appellants, if divested of its popular and specious look, is this, that we ought not to visit those who lose trust property with the consequence of having to make it good, provided it can be shewn or surmised that, if they had made it good, somebody else would have lost it over again.[96]

The justification for this strict approach lies in the trustee's fundamental obligation to hold on to the trust assets unless they have been properly disposed of. As Brett LJ said in *Re Anglo-French Co-operative Society*, where directors had paid money out of the company in an ultra vires fashion:

> The moment you have paid away a person's money wrongfully he is damaged to the extent of that payment. Nothing can lessen the extent of that damage unless the money

[91] *Low v Bouverie* [1891] 3 Ch 82, 99.

[92] *Ultraframe (UK) Ltd v Fielding* [2005] EWHC 1638 (Ch) at [1513].

[93] *Pickering v Pickering* (1839) 4 My & Cr 289, 298–299 (41 ER 113).

[94] *Magnus* (n 63) 474.

[95] ibid 477.

[96] ibid 477 and 479–480. Similarly, see *Cocker v Quayle* (1830) 1 Russ & M 535 (39 ER 206); *Salway v Salway* (1831) 2 Russ & M 215 (39 ER 376) (aff'd, sub nom *White v Baugh* (1835) 3 Cl & Fin 44 (6 ER 1354)); *Re Dawson* [1966] 2 NSWR 211.

> has been, before the supposed action has been brought, paid back into the hands of the person from whom it was taken as free to him as it was before.[97]

These principles appear to have been modified in England, in a way which loosens the liability of trustees, by the House of Lords' decision in *Target Holdings Ltd v Redferns*,[98] although it remains unclear to what degree. Insofar as the reasoning in *Brickenden* was based on trust accounting principles, the modification of those principles for trusts may undermine any argument that *Brickenden* should continue to apply to non-stewardship fiduciary arrangements in England. Importantly, however, the traditional accounting principles applied to fiduciary stewardship of assets continue to remain in place in other jurisdictions, such as Australia,[99] as well as in other stewardship relationships in England, such as claims brought against directors for misapplication of company property.[100] The question remains, therefore, whether the *Brickenden* dictum is appropriate in non-stewardship fiduciary contexts.

The reason for emphasising the principles regarding fiduciary stewardship accounting is that the justification for those principles does not apply in non-stewardship cases. In particular, by definition, non-stewardship fiduciaries do not hold assets in their fiduciary capacity, and so there is no justification for requiring them to account for those assets 'just as if the money was still in their hands.'[101] This difference has been recognised in more recent case law. As Robert Walker LJ said in *Bairstow v Queens Moat Houses plc*, commenting on Lord Browne-Wilkinson's suggestion in *Target*[102] that a distinction should be drawn between traditional trusts and commercial trusts for accounting purposes:

> [i]t may be that a more satisfactory dividing line is [that] between a breach of fiduciary duty in the wrongful disbursement of funds of which the fiduciary has this sort of trustee-like stewardship and a breach of fiduciary duty of a different character (for instance a solicitor's failure to disclose a conflict of interest …).[103]

97 *Re Anglo-French Co-operative Society* (1882) 21 ChD 492, 506 (CA).

98 [1996] 1 AC 421. See also *AIB Group (UK) plc v Mark Redler & Co Solicitors* [2014] UKSC 58, [2015] AC 1503.

99 *Youyang* (n 89). The suggestion that *Youyang* changed the law in Australia (see JD Heydon, M Leeming & P Turner, *Meagher Gummow & Lehane's Equity: Doctrines & Remedies*, 5th edn (Sydney, LexisNexis Butterworths, 2015), [23-200]–[23-215]) overlooks the facts of the case and the orders made by the High Court.

100 *Bairstow v Queens Moat Houses plc* [2001] EWCA Civ 712; [2001] 2 BCLC 531. See also *Re Loquitur Ltd* [2003] EWHC 999 (Ch) at [135]–[137], [2003] 2 BCLC 442; *Re Paycheck Services 3 Ltd* [2009] EWCA Civ 625 at [96]–[98], [2009] 2 BCLC 309; *Revenue and Customs Commissioners v Holland* [2010] UKSC 51 at [49] & [56], [2010] 1 WLR 2973.

101 *Magnus* (n 63) 477.

102 *Target Holdings Ltd v Redferns* [1996] AC 421, 435.

103 *Bairstow v Queens Moat Houses plc* [2001] EWCA Civ 712 at [53], [2001] 2 BCLC 531. See also CEF Rickett, 'Equitable Compensation: Towards a Blueprint?' (2003) 25 *Sydney Law Review* 31.

In a similar vein, the Ontario Court of Appeal has said:

> [i]n breach of trust cases the object of the trust must be restored to the beneficiary, or, if that is not possible, the beneficiary must be compensated for the value of the object. In breach of fiduciary duty cases the court assesses the losses flowing from the breach.[104]

In *Maguire v Makaronis*, the majority of the High Court also recognised the differences between trusts and non-stewardship fiduciary arrangements, including the fact that breach of trust cases are generally concerned with restoration of the trust fund so that the reconstituted fund can be duly administered, rather than with recovering a specific sum as compensation for loss caused to particular beneficiaries.[105] The Court pointed out that nineteenth century cases like *Caffrey v Darby*[106] 'concerned failure to observe these rules for due administration rather than that disloyalty and conflict between interest and duty which was considered in *Nocton v Lord Ashburton*'.[107]

D. Counterfactuals

However, in the same case, the High Court went on to observe:

> Yet the policy of the law to hold the trustee up to the obligation to perform the trust is strongly manifested in cases where loss is occasioned upon breach arising from conflict between duty and interest. What one might call that heightened concern is manifested also, as we have sought to indicate earlier in these reasons, in the treatment of disloyalty by non-trustee fiduciaries. It may be that concern with respect to the apparent rigour of the reasoning in *Brickenden* reflects what has been seen as a tendency apparent in some recent decisions too readily to classify as fiduciary in nature relationships which might better be seen as purely contractual or as giving rise to tortious liability. Whilst that be so, it is not self-evident that the response should rest in a general denial of the applicability of the reasoning in *Brickenden* to delinquent fiduciaries, particularly solicitors and other professional advisers.[108]

The question this raises is whether, even if the apparent analogy with trust accounting principles does not justify the approach taken in *Brickenden*, the principles and policies of fiduciary doctrine might themselves justify that approach.

Where the remedy sought against a fiduciary involves rescission of a transaction, or the stripping of profits made by the fiduciary out of that transaction, it is irrelevant to consider what the fiduciary's principal would have done if there had been no breach of duty.[109] However, where the award sought is compensatory in

104 *Waxman v Waxman* (2004) 7 ITELR 162 at [657]. See also *O'Halloran v FT Thomas & Family Pty Ltd* (1998) 45 NSWLR 262, 277(CA) ('*O'Halloran*').

105 *Maguire* (n 44) 473.

106 (1801) 6 Ves 488 (31 ER 1159).

107 *Maguire* (n 44) 473.

108 ibid 474. See also *O'Halloran* (n 104) 281.

109 See n 4 above.

nature, the assessment of the principal's loss necessarily requires a counterfactual analysis of where the principal would have stood if there had been no breach. This creates difficulties where the claim is based on a breach of fiduciary duty, because a fiduciary who is faced with a situation where acting will involve a conflict or generate an unauthorised profit has two equally legitimate courses of conduct open: (1) the fiduciary can avoid the conflict, either by ceasing to act or by eschewing any personal interest in the transaction; or (2) the fiduciary can make full disclosure of all material facts to his or her principal and seek the consent of the principal to the fiduciary acting nonetheless.

Fiduciary doctrine does not mandate which of these options the fiduciary must pursue; the fiduciary can elect. Consequently, when a principal seeks equitable compensation for loss caused by a breach of fiduciary duty, it is not clear against which counterfactual the assessment of loss should be measured. One approach would be to insist on using the first counterfactual and ask what would have happened if the fiduciary had not acted with a conflict, ignoring what would have happened if full disclosure had been made. The other option is to permit the fiduciary to rely on the second counterfactual and prove what the principal would have done if the fiduciary had made full disclosure of all material facts.

Swindle v Harrison[110] is helpful in thinking about this choice, particularly as the facts are functionally equivalent to those in *Brickenden*. In *Swindle*, Mrs Harrison mortgaged her home in order to finance the purchase of a restaurant. She needed further finance, and her solicitor, Mr Swindle, arranged bridging finance for her. Unknown to Harrison, Swindle took a small commission on the bridging finance. When the restaurant business failed, Harrison's home was sold by the mortgagee, and she sued Swindle for equitable compensation for its loss. This is functionally equivalent to *Brickenden* in that it involves a transaction between the fiduciary's principal (here, Harrison; in *Brickenden*, the loan company) and a third party (here, the mortgagee; in *Brickenden*, the Biggs) in respect of which the fiduciary has acted in breach of fiduciary duty by reason of a conflict between his personal interest and the duties he owed to his principal. Swindle's personal interest was smaller than Brickenden's, but that should not affect the applicable principles.

In *Swindle v Harrison*, the English Court of Appeal rejected Harrison's claim because it was clear that, even if Swindle had made full disclosure of the existence and extent of his personal interest in the transaction, she would nonetheless have proceeded with it, and would thereby have lost her home in any event. As Mummery LJ said, in a passage subsequently cited with approval by the High Court of Australia,[111] '[t]here is no equitable by-pass of the need to establish causation.'[112] In contrast, a strict application of the *Brickenden* dictum would seem to prohibit the Court from inquiring into what Harrison would have done if Swindle

[110] n 45.
[111] *Youyang* (n 89) [44].
[112] *Swindle* (n 45) 733.

had disclosed his interest. As has been pointed out already, that does not entirely accurately reflect what the Supreme Court did in *Brickenden* itself, given Smith J effectively speculated as to what rate of interest the counter-plaintiff would have achieved on a proper loan.[113] But the point which matters for present purposes is the question whether it is legitimate for the Court to permit the fiduciary to argue about what the principal would have done with the benefit of full disclosure.

On one hand, there seems to be an element of penalty in requiring a fiduciary in a case like *Swindle* to compensate his principal for a loss-making transaction where it is shown that the principal would have acted in exactly the same way even if the fiduciary had acted perfectly properly by making full disclosure. Equity does not traditionally act in a penal fashion: even as regards fiduciaries, where its principles 'are often high and strict',[114] those principles have a deterrent effect but 'they are not penal or punitive in the sense of exacting any money sanction greater than that which is needed either to give full compensation for loss or full disgorgement of gain'.[115] The second counterfactual, against which the assessment of loss was measured in *Swindle*, was a legitimate course of conduct for the fiduciary to have taken, and it may be more penal than compensatory to allow the principal to recover for loss caused by the transaction where the fiduciary can prove (if such be the case) that the principal would have entered into it if the fiduciary had made full disclosure and obtained consent. If the fiduciary can show that the principal would have consented, albeit perhaps on different terms, if the fiduciary had made full disclosure of all material facts, it is legitimate to ask why the fiduciary should not be able to prove that and thereby avoid liability, at least pro tanto. It is not to the point, in answer to this question, to argue that counterfactuals are not considered where rescission or profit-stripping remedies are sought: counterfactuals are not considered in rescission and profit-stripping cases because they are not relevant to the exercise involved in such cases, whereas they are necessarily relevant in compensation cases.

Furthermore, the result in *Brickenden* itself can potentially also be justified on a counterfactual analysis of this sort. In *Brickenden*, the Court may have considered that the loan company, in contrast to Mrs Harrison, would not have made the $13,500 loan to the Biggs if it had known fully of Brickenden's interest in seeing the transaction proceed, particularly when it is borne in mind that the loan company had rejected an approach from the Biggs only a year earlier. Crocket J, in the Supreme Court, speculated that the loan company's managing director might not have agreed to the loan if he had known the full facts, but it was not possible to ascertain that given the managing director had died before trial.[116]

It is, however, not completely clear whether the loan company would have declined to make the $13,500 loan if it had been fully aware of Brickenden's

[113] See text accompanying n 75 above.
[114] *Harris v Digital Pulse Pty Ltd* [2003] NSWCA 10 at [406], (2003) 56 NSWLR 298 ('*Harris*').
[115] ibid [407]. See also *Cole v Manning* [2002] NSWCA 150 at [20].
[116] *London Loan* (n 9) 265.

interest in the transaction, as the loan company was clearly prepared to make the $13,500 loan at a time when it would have known, if it had checked the documentation, that there was no equity in the Biggs' properties. In this light, the *Brickenden* dictum might perhaps be a rejection of an argument Brickenden made in both the Privy Council and the Supreme Court of Canada that disclosure of his other mortgages would have made no difference, as the loan company would have proceeded nonetheless.[117] It is not entirely clear how these arguments were rebutted by the loan company, beyond it arguing that Brickenden had failed to disclose his interest.[118] The evidence in favour of Brickenden's argument appears to have been slender, particularly given a strong case was made for Brickenden having been the one who controlled the decision to make the $13,500 loan and the way in which the loan money would be used,[119] and so one can understand why it was rejected. But it does not follow automatically that such an argument should be rejected if it can be established, on the facts, what the fiduciary's principal would have done with the benefit of full disclosure of all material facts. It is, of course, a truism that judgments are not to be read as statutes, but rather in the light of the facts and circumstances with which they deal.[120]

However, against this position, it can be argued that it is more consistent with fiduciary doctrine's general policy of deterring fiduciaries from acting in breach of fiduciary duty to refuse to permit the fiduciary to rely on the second counterfactual, and to insist instead on the first counterfactual being used to determine the quantum of loss caused by the failure to abide by fiduciary doctrine's proscriptions on unauthorised conflicts and profits. By choosing to act in a way that involved a conflict, or the taking of an unauthorised profit, the fiduciary chose not to take the route of seeking consent, and it is legitimate for the law to take the position that, having chosen not to do so when the choice stood to be made, the fiduciary cannot now turn around and seek to use the second option as an 'escape route'[121] by which to avoid (or reduce) liability for having acted in breach of fiduciary doctrine's proscriptions.

In *Swindle v Harrison*, it seems likely on this approach that the transaction would still have proceeded, as Harrison was likely to have found bridging finance from somewhere (perhaps at a higher rate of interest) even if Swindle had not done that for her, or if he had chosen not to take the commission. Thus, her claim would fail. In a case like *Brickenden*, where at least a large part of the point of the $13,500

[117] Case for the Appellant, *Privy Council Record: Brickenden v London Loan etc* (Lincoln's Inn Library, 1934/25), p 5; Record of Proceedings, *Privy Council Record: Brickenden v London Loan etc* (Lincoln's Inn Library, 1934/25), p 257.

[118] Case for the Respondents, *Privy Council Record: Brickenden v London Loan etc* (Lincoln's Inn Library, 1934/25), p 4.

[119] Record of Proceedings, *Privy Council Record: Brickenden v London Loan etc* (Lincoln's Inn Library, 1934/25), pp 238–240.

[120] See, eg, *Quinn v Leathem* [1901] AC 495, 506; *Cassell & Co Ltd v Broome* [1972] AC 1027, 1085; *Scott v Davis* [2000] HCA 52 at [108]–[109], (2000) 204 CLR 333.

[121] *Bank of New Zealand v New Zealand Guardian Trust Co Ltd* [1999] 1 NZLR 664, 687 (CA); *Amaltal Corp Ltd v Maruha Corp* [2007] NZSC 40 at [30], [2007] 3 NZLR 192.

loan transaction was to ensure that Brickenden's loans were repaid, the transaction would not have proceeded if he had not been involved in a conflicted way, and so the award of compensation made in the case makes sense. This seems to be the approach which the High Court of Australia had in mind in *Maguire v Makaronis*.[122]

Ultimately, the choice between the two counterfactuals reduces to whether the law should permit a fiduciary to argue about what would have happened if the fiduciary had acted in a proper fashion by disclosing and seeking consent,[123] or should instead insist that the fiduciary has made his bed by not doing so and must now lie in it. That is an issue on which sensible minds may reasonably differ.

It is suggested that applying the first counterfactual would be more consistent with the strong deterrent approach which the law has taken towards fiduciary doctrine generally, in implementing its subsidiary and prophylactic form of protection for non-fiduciary duties. This helps to keep fiduciaries to their duty in the sense that they are not permitted to escape liability by arguing about how things might have turned out if the fiduciary had chosen to disclose and seek consent. It does not involve ignoring what would have happened but for the breach of fiduciary duty, as it still requires an assessment of what would have happened if the fiduciary had not acted with a conflict between duty and interest. Further, there are other contexts within private law where compensatory awards implement deterrent policies by focusing on wrongdoing as one cause of loss, and compensate for that loss without parsing out the degree to which the loss may have been foreseeable or to which other factors may have contributed to the loss.[124] As Lord Steyn said in *Smith New Court v Citibank*:

> imposing more stringent remedies on an intentional wrongdoer serves two purposes. First, it serves a deterrent purpose in discouraging fraud. Counsel for Citibank argued that the sole purpose of the law of tort generally, and the tort of deceit in particular, should be to compensate the victims of civil wrongs. That is far too narrow a view. Professor Glanville Williams identified four possible purposes of an action for damages in tort: appeasement, justice, deterrence and compensation.[125]

While a breach of fiduciary duty does not normally require any element of fraud or intention,[126] it is clear that fiduciary doctrine has a policy of seeking to deter fiduciaries from acting in ways which contravene its regulatory principles.[127]

122 See text accompanying n 108 above.

123 It is to be remembered that the principal might have refused consent if there had been full disclosure: see eg, *Jacks v Davis* (1982) 141 DLR (3d) 355, 360 (BCCA); *Cole v Manning* [2002] NSWCA 150 at [82].

124 See, eg, *Doyle v Olby (Ironmongers) Ltd* [1969] 2 QB 158, 167; *Smith New Court Securities Ltd v Citibank NA* [1997] AC 254, 262–265, 279–280 & 283; *Kuwait Airways Corp v Iraqi Airways Co (Nos 4 and 5)* [2002] UKHL 19 at [104], [2002] 2 AC 883.

125 *Smith New Court Securities Ltd v Citibank NA* [1997] AC 254, 279–280.

126 Breach of the inhibition principle is an unusual exception in this respect: see M Conaglen, 'Fiduciary Regulation of Conflicts Between Duties' (2009) 125 *LQR* 111, 127–133.

127 See, eg, *Docker v Somes* (1834) 2 My & K 655, 655 (39 ER 1095); *Guth v Loft Inc* 5 A 2d 503, 510 (1939); *Harris* (n 114) [161], [170], [407]and [414]; *Lindsley v Woodfull* [2004] EWCA Civ 165 at [30], [2004] 2 BCLC 131; *Murad v Al Saraj* [2005] EWCA Civ 959 at [74], [107] & [121], [2005] WTLR 1573; *Strother v 3464920 Canada Inc* [2007] SCC 24 at [70], [2007] 2 SCR 177.

As Mason P said in *Harris v Digital Pulse*, 'deterrence and vindication are universally accepted functions of these equitable remedies directed at defaulting fiduciaries.'[128] A comparable policy is not out of place in the fiduciary context.

III. Movements Away from *Brickenden*

In some jurisdictions, most notably Canada and New Zealand, rather than seeking to identify what the *Brickenden* dictum means, courts have instead consciously eschewed its perceived rigidity. This movement is less pronounced, as a matter of authority, in Australia, and the position remains rather unclear in England.

A. Canada

In *Howard v Cunliffe*,[129] which concerned a solicitor who owed conflicting duties to two clients and did not disclose relevant facts to the plaintiff, McFarlane JA said 'I do not think the Court should speculate or presume in favour of the defaulting solicitor … the onus lay upon him to show that his client's loss would have occurred in any event if he had performed his duty towards her.'[130] McFarlane JA did not refer to *Brickenden*, but subsequently in *Jacks v Davis*, the British Columbia Court of Appeal considered his approach to be 'in terms similar to those used by Lord Thankerton in the *Brickenden* case.'[131] While the first part of McFarlane JA's statement is similar to what appears on the face of *Brickenden* itself, the remainder of his proposition seems to be a departure from what Lord Thankerton said.

In *Jacks v Davis* itself, *Brickenden* did not need to be relied on, as the lower court had held that the plaintiff would not have completed the transaction if the secret profit had been disclosed. But in subsequent cases *Jacks v Davis*, apparently as a result of its reference to *Howard v Cunliffe*, has been treated as authority whereby:

> Once the … breach of fiduciary duty is shown, then the court assessing damages will not be exacting in requiring proof of the precise loss in circumstances where all reasonable efforts have been made by the plaintiff to establish the amount of the loss and the cause of the loss. The burden of leading the evidence to disprove the amount of the loss and the cause of the loss will then fall on the defendant who has been found to have been fraudulent or in breach of fiduciary duty.[132]

[128] *Harris* (n 114) [170].

[129] (1973) 36 DLR (3d) 212.

[130] ibid 221.

[131] *Jacks v Davis* (1982) 141 DLR (3d) 355, 360. See also *Tri-Crest Investment Corp v Davidson & Co* (1988) 50 DLR (4th) 81; *Wright v Bryant* (1988) 26 BCLR (2d) 359.

[132] *Huff v Price* (1990) 76 DLR (4th) 138, 149 (BCCA). See also *Ferris v Rusnak* (1983) 9 DLR (4th) 183, 195; *Ridge View Devt & Holding Co v Simper* (1989) 67 Alta LR (2d) 34; *Interstate Investments Ltd v Pacific International Securities Inc* (Unreported, BCSC, 4 April 1995); *Insurance Corp of British*

In *Commerce Capital Trust Co v Berk*,[133] the application of *Brickenden* was squarely before the Ontario Court of Appeal. Solicitors acting for different clients in the same transaction had failed to disclose relevant facts to the clients. At first instance, Steele J was not satisfied that the plaintiff would not have acted as it did if the relevant facts had been disclosed. The plaintiff appealed, relying on *Brickenden*. McKinley JA, speaking for the court, said:

> I interpret Lord Thankerton's statement to place the onus on the solicitors in a situation such as the one before us to prove that, despite the non-disclosure of material facts, the client would have proceeded with the transaction. However, proof in such a situation would undoubtedly be difficult, and 'speculation' would not suffice.[134]

This has been described as a modification of the traditional rule in *Brickenden* which has 'produced a more moderate rule.'[135]

Subsequently, in *Raso v Dionigi*,[136] a differently constituted bench of the Ontario Court of Appeal pointed out that McKinley JA's statement was obiter, and Dubin CJO (speaking for the Court) considered that McKinley JA had misinterpreted Lord Thankerton's dictum. In *Raso v Dionigi*, the court thought that *Brickenden* rendered irrelevant any speculation as to what would have happened if there had been proper disclosure. However, in *Raso* itself the claim was not for equitable compensation, and so the comments were also obiter.

The Canadian cases reflect an 'inherent distrust'[137] of *Brickenden* as it 'appears to [establish] an irrebuttable presumption as to causation'.[138] Notwithstanding the doubts raised by Dubin CJO in *Raso v Dionigi*, McKinley JA's re-interpretation of Lord Thankerton's dictum, which further reinforces the approach associated with *Jacks v Davis*, seems to have become adopted as the orthodoxy in Canada.[139] In *Hodgkinson v Simms*, for example, speaking for a majority of the Supreme Court of Canada, La Forest J cited *Brickenden*, *Huff v Price* and *Commerce Capital Trust Co v Berk* as authority for 'the long-standing equitable principle that where the plaintiff has made out a case of non-disclosure and the loss occasioned thereby is established, the onus is on the defendant to prove that the innocent victim would have suffered the same loss regardless of the breach'.[140]

Columbia v Eurosport Auto Co Ltd (2004) 8 CCLI (4th) 236; *Sable Mary Seismic Inc v Geophysical Services Inc* 2012 NSCA 33 at [136], (2012) 315 NSR (2d) 201.

133 (1989) 68 OR (2d) 257.

134 *Commerce Capital Trust Co v Berk* (1989) 68 OR (2d) 257, 261.

135 *Martin v Goldfarb* (1997) 31 BLR (2d) 265.

136 (1993) 12 OR (3d) 580.

137 *Ruxton v Kelly* [1985] 1 WWR 66, 76.

138 ibid.

139 In part, this may be because the disagreement with *Commerce Capital Trust Co v Berk*, expressed in *Raso v Dionigi*, has itself been misinterpreted as being consistent with the *Berk* approach: see, eg, *DiFlorio v Con Structural Steel Ltd* (2000) 6 BLR (3d) 253 at [107]–[108].

140 *Hodgkinson v Simms* [1994] 3 SCR 377, 441. See also *Hussey v Parsons* (1997) 152 Nfld & PEIR 1; *RWH Management & Investments Ltd v St Pierre* (1997) 55 Alta LR (3d) 68 (CA); *Prenor Trust Co of Canada v Nunn* (1998) 58 Alta LR (3d) 68 (QB); *DiFlorio v Con Structural Steel Ltd* (2000) 6 BLR (3d) 253; *Firemaster Oilfield Services Ltd v Safety Boss (Canada) (1993) Ltd* (2000) 87 Alta LR (3d) 366;

B. New Zealand

Brickenden was cited by the New Zealand Court of Appeal in *Farrington v Rowe McBride & Partners*,[141] in circumstances where solicitors had a conflict between duties. The case was ultimately remitted to the lower court to determine the appropriate remedy, as it had not considered the issue of compensation, but Richardson and McMullin JJ each cited the *Brickenden* dictum,[142] indicating that it ought to control the assessment of equitable compensation.

However, the authority of *Brickenden* began to erode in New Zealand with the same court's subsequent decision in *Witten-Hannah v Davis*.[143] A solicitor had acted for his client in a property transaction involving a conflict between duty and interest, without obtaining her fully informed consent. The transaction generated a loss, for which the client sued.[144] The solicitor argued that *Brickenden* dictated no more than a reversal of the onus of proof, so that he could prove that the client would have entered into the transaction even if he had made full disclosure of all material facts.[145] McKay J rejected that argument,[146] as any assessment of what the client might have done involved speculation and was thus rendered irrelevant by *Brickenden*. However, Richardson J appeared more drawn by the argument,[147] accepting that, if the inquiry is whether the loss would have happened but for the breach, that test may not be satisfied if it is shown that the client would have proceeded with the transaction even if she had the benefit of full disclosure.[148] Ultimately, he held it unnecessary to decide the point, as the solicitor had failed to show that the client would have proceeded. A few months later, delivering the court's judgment in *Haira v Burbery Mortgage Finance & Savings Ltd*,[149] Richardson J said, citing *Witten-Hannah v Davis*, that 'the Courts will not speculate on what might have happened if another course had been followed',[150] but went

Reid v Graybriar Industries Ltd (2006) 61 Alta LR (4th) 264; *Royal Lepage Team Realty Inc v Temple* (Unreported, Ontario Superior Court, 29 January 2008); *Procon Mining & Tunnelling Ltd v McNeil* 2010 BCSC 487 at [101], (2010) 81 CCEL (3d) 119; *Manitoba Métis Foundation Inc v Canada* 2010 MBCA 71 at [210]–[211], [2010] 12 WWR 599; *ICR Brokerage Inc v Crescent Restaurants Ltd* 2010 SKCA 92 at [76]–[78], (2010) 322 DLR (4th) 299; *Indutech Canada Ltd v Gibbs Pipe Distributors Ltd* 2011 ABQB 38 at [396], (2011) 508 AR 1; *Harris v Leikin Group Inc* 2011 ONSC 3556 at [330]; *Harris v Leikin Group Inc* 2013 ONSC 1525 at [406]; *First Majestic Silver Corp v Davila* 2013 BCSC 717 at [234]. *cf National Bank Financial Ltd v Potter* 2013 NSSC 248 at [685].

141 [1985] 1 NZLR 83.

142 *Farrington v Rowe McBride & Partners* [1985] 1 NZLR 83, 93 & 99.

143 [1995] 2 NZLR 141.

144 The client and solicitor had also had a sexual relationship, which ended badly: the client was convicted of counselling an undercover policeman to murder the solicitor and his wife (see 'Woman found guilty in hit man case', *New Zealand Herald*, 4 Aug 1993, Sec 1, p 2).

145 *Witten-Hannah v Davis* [1995] 2 NZLR 141, 147.

146 ibid 157.

147 ibid 148–149.

148 ibid 149.

149 [1995] 3 NZLR 396.

150 *Haira v Burbery Mortgage Finance & Savings Ltd (in rec)* [1995] 3 NZLR 396, 408.

on to comment that '[i]t is a matter of speculation, *rather than a conclusion from the evidence*, that Mrs Haira would or might have gone ahead'.[151] This confirmed that evidence could be led to establish what the plaintiff would have done, which had previously appeared to be barred by *Brickenden*. As Tipping J said in *Everist v McEvedy*,[152] '[p]ut figuratively, the pure *Brickenden* approach has the door entirely shut. *Haira* appears to have opened the door, not to admit speculation, but to admit a conclusion based on reasonable inference.'[153] This 'retreat from *Brickenden*'[154] is now well-established in New Zealand.[155] The Supreme Court has confirmed that the 'strict rule [in *Brickenden*] has been modified in this country by an approach which affords the fiduciary a limited opportunity of showing that all or some of the loss would have occurred even if disclosure had been made',[156] while emphasising that the fiduciary bears the onus of demonstrating that.

C. Australia and England

Some Australian courts have endorsed *Brickenden*, while others have suggested that it is now inaccurate as a statement of Australian law. The position in England is also unclear. Neither the High Court of Australia nor the United Kingdom's Supreme Court has ruled on the issue.

In *Commonwealth Bank of Australia v Smith*, a Full Court of the Federal Court upheld the trial judge's reliance on *Brickenden* as showing that common law concepts of foreseeability and remoteness do not necessarily limit equitable compensation awards,[157] but did not elaborate further on precisely what *Brickenden* stands for.[158] In doing so, the Court followed Richardson J's lead in *Farrington v Rowe McBride v Partners*.[159] Similarly, in *Gemstone Corp of Australia Ltd v Grasso*, Matheson J cited *Brickenden* in explaining that the lower court judge 'was wrongly

151 ibid (emphasis added).

152 [1996] 3 NZLR 348.

153 ibid 353.

154 *Gilbert v Shanahan* [1998] 3 NZLR 528, 536.

155 See also ibid 535; *Bank of New Zealand v New Zealand Guardian Trust Co Ltd* [1999] 1 NZLR 664, 687, CA; *Taylor v Schofield Peterson* [1999] 3 NZLR 434, 445–446, HC.

156 *Premium Real Estate Ltd v Stevens* [2009] NZSC 15 at [85], [2009] 2 NZLR 384. See also *Amaltal Corp Ltd v Maruha Corp* [2007] NZSC 40 at [30], [2007] 3 NZLR 192.

157 The court also relied on *Gray v New Augarita Porcupine Mines Ltd* [1952] 3 DLR 1, 15 (PC) to this effect, but that reliance was misplaced: in *Gray v New Augarita*, the Privy Council observed that it was 'an irrelevant speculation' to ask whether the plaintiff would have acted in the same way if his fiduciary had disclosed his interest in the transaction, but that case involved a claim to strip the fiduciary's profits rather than a claim to recover compensation for the principal's loss. The fact that the plaintiff would have acted in the same way is not relevant to quantification of the *profits* that the *defendant* made in breach of fiduciary duty, but that does not establish the irrelevance of that inquiry to an assessment of the *plaintiff's losses* from the transaction. (Burchett J was similarly misled in *Wan v McDonald* (1992) 33 FCR 491, 521, as was the Court in *Gemstone Corp of Australia Ltd v Grasso* (1994) 13 ACSR 695, 700 & 709.)

158 *Commonwealth Bank of Australia v Smith* (1991) 42 FCR 390, 394–396.

159 ibid 394, citing *Farrington* (n 142) 93. See also *Wan v McDonald* (1992) 33 FCR 491, 510–511.

influenced by his consideration of what the directors would have done if Grasso had made full disclosure … The authorities … make it clear that such considerations are irrelevant.'[160] Almost contemporaneously, Ipp J observed in obiter in *Permanent Building Society v Wheeler*, that *Brickenden* was an instance 'where the court does not inquire into aspects of causality'.[161]

Less stringently, in *Stewart v Layton*, Foster J held that *Brickenden* relieves the court of the 'tedious and painstaking task' of 'unravelling and exposing the strands of causation connecting breach with damage',[162] but that it 'does not mean, however, that the court must be otherwise blind to the reality of the situation.'[163] In that case, the claimant would have proceeded with the transaction but could have done so in a less disadvantageous way, and she was awarded compensation to place her in the position she would have occupied had she done so.[164]

More recently, however, the New South Wales Court of Appeal has repeatedly emphasised the need for 'a causal link between the breach and the loss'[165] where equitable compensation is sought for breach of fiduciary duty. In *Beach Petroleum NL v Abbott Tout Russell Kennedy*, the Court said that '*Brickenden* is not, in our opinion, authority for the general proposition that, in no case involving breach of fiduciary duty, may the court consider what would have happened if the duty had been performed.'[166] Leave to appeal to the High Court was refused, although in so doing Gleeson CJ, Gummow and Callinan JJ mentioned that they were 'not to be taken necessarily to be supporting all that was said by the Court of Appeal on the legal issues'.[167]

In an approach which differs from that taken in Canada and New Zealand, Hodgson JA said that in a case involving a conflict between duties, rather than between duty and interest, the plaintiff 'must prove that, but for the non-disclosure, he or she would not have entered into the transaction.'[168] Similarly, Powell JA considered that the plaintiff bore the onus of establishing that, if there

[160] *Gemstone Corp of Australia Ltd v Grasso* (1994) 13 ACSR 695, 700.

[161] *Permanent Building Society v Wheeler* (1994) 11 WAR 187, 245.

[162] *Stewart v Layton* (1992) 111 ALR 687, 713.

[163] ibid 713–714.

[164] ibid 714. An appeal was dismissed, Jenkinson J recording that no argument had been made that Foster J had misapplied *Brickenden*: *Layton v Stewart* [1993] FCA 532.

[165] *O'Halloran* (n 104) 274. See also *Beach* (n 32) [429]; *Cassis v Kalfus (No 2)* [2004] NSWCA 315 at [94]; *Short v Crawley (No 30)* [2007] NSWSC 1322 at [419]; *Hydrocool Pty Ltd v Hepburn (No 4)* [2011] FCA 495 at [442]–[466].

[166] *Beach* (n 32) [444]. See also *IMB Society Ltd v White* [2000] NSWSC 1085 at [141] (upheld on appeal: [2002] NSWCA 164); *ASIC v Adler* [2002] NSWSC 171 at [748]; *Fico v O'Leary* [2004] WASC 215 at [169]; *ASIC v Citigroup Global Markets Australia Pty Ltd (No 4)* [2007] FCA 963 at [366], (2007) 160 FCR 35; *Rigg v Sheridan* [2008] NSWCA 79 at [56]; *Mantonella Pty Ltd v Thompson* [2009] QCA 80 at [98]; *Menkens v Wintour* [2009] QSC 206 at [33]; *Hodgson v Amcor Ltd* [2012] VSC 94 at [1654].

[167] *Beach Petroleum NL v Abbott Tout Russell Kennedy* [2000] HCATrans 173, lines 476–477. See also *Youyang Pty Ltd v Minter Ellison Morris Fletcher* [2002] HCATrans 577, lines 3912–3914.

[168] *White v Illawarra Mutual Building Society Ltd* [2002] NSWCA 164 at [145]. See also *Dominic v Riz* [2009] NSWCA 216 at [113].

had been no breach of duty, she would not have entered into the transaction.[169] In *Watson v Ebsworth & Ebsworth*, the Court of Appeal of Victoria said that *Brickenden* 'does not negative the requirement for some proof of causation and does not, as the appellants verged on contending, reverse the onus of proof in relation to causation.'[170]

In the light of these decisions, lower courts have concluded that 'there is a conflict between the reasoning in *Brickenden* and the requirement that there be a causal relationship in a claim for equitable compensation between the breach of fiduciary duty and the loss for which compensation is sought'.[171] Pembroke J has said:

> Taken literally, [the *Brickenden* dictum] does not represent the law of New South Wales. But the essence of Lord Thankerton's dictum is an understandable reluctance to entertain submissions based on hypothesis and speculation when the fiduciary has taken positive steps to conceal his interest. In such a case, the inference of the relevant causal connection is obvious.[172]

In *BigTinCan Pty Ltd v Ramsay*,[173] Ball J hedged his bets as to the applicability of *Brickenden* when awarding compensation for a director's breach of fiduciary duty. Under *Brickenden*, 'the strict requirement of causation is not necessary',[174] but 'even if the approach in *Brickenden* is no longer good law',[175] in the circumstances the court could legitimately infer that the breach of duty had caused the company to lose an opportunity. The Court of Appeal affirmed, but on the basis of the second approach alone, thus finding it unnecessary to decide whether *Brickenden* applied.[176] The High Court refused leave to appeal.[177]

The meaning of *Brickenden* was addressed in England by the Court of Appeal in *Swindle v Harrison*.[178] Unfortunately, however, all three judges expressed differing views. As has already been mentioned, Hobhouse LJ treated *Brickenden* as relevant solely to rescission, and not to damages.[179] In contrast, Mummery LJ held that *Brickenden* related solely to the question of breach.[180] As has been discussed, neither view is a compelling interpretation of what Lord Thankerton said in *Brickenden*. The third member of the Court in *Swindle* adopted yet another approach.

169 *White v Illawarra Mutual Building Society Ltd* ibid [138]. See also *Simpson v Donnybrook Properties Pty Ltd* [2010] NSWCA 229 at [99]–[100].

170 *Watson v Ebsworth & Ebsworth* [2010] VSCA 335 at [165].

171 *Short v Crawley (No 30)* [2007] NSWSC 1322 at [427].

172 *Thomas v SMP International Pty Ltd (No 4)* [2010] NSWSC 984 at [75]. An appeal was allowed, but without contradicting these statements: *Willett v Thomas* [2012] NSWCA 97.

173 [2013] NSWSC 1248.

174 *BigTinCan Pty Ltd v Ramsay* [2013] NSWSC 1248 at [99].

175 ibid [100].

176 *Ramsay v BigTinCan Pty Ltd* [2014] NSWCA 324 at [58], (2014) 101 ACSR 415.

177 *Ramsay v BigTinCan Pty Ltd* [2015] HCATrans 59.

178 *Swindle* (n 45).

179 See text accompanying nn 45–47 above.

180 See text accompanying n 50 above.

Evans LJ considered that *Brickenden* created a 'stringent rule of causation' to be applied where the 'equitable equivalent of fraud' is proven.[181] It is unclear what he meant by this. It cannot mean the same thing as 'equitable fraud',[182] because the concept of 'equitable fraud' encompasses all breaches of equitable rules,[183] whereas Evans LJ clearly intended to differentiate some breaches of equitable rules from others: he considered there was a breach of fiduciary duty in *Swindle*, but that it was not the equitable equivalent of fraud and so the stringent rule of causation did not apply.[184] It seems Evans LJ meant his phrase to comprehend particularly egregious breaches of duty. In *Collins v Brebner*, Tuckey LJ emphasised that no other judge in *Swindle* adopted Evans LJ's distinction between fraudulent and non-fraudulent breaches of fiduciary duty.[185] Nor does it bear any relationship to what Lord Thankerton said in *Brickenden* itself.

While the individual judgments are regrettably opaque as to the continuing relevance of *Brickenden* in England, the Court of Appeal's decision in *Swindle v Harrison* nonetheless clearly indicates, consistently with some Australian authority,[186] that the plaintiff must establish causation in order to succeed with a claim for equitable compensation.[187]

IV. Conclusions

The meaning of Lord Thankerton's dictum in *Brickenden* is not easy to discern. Given it appears in a decision concerning a claim for compensation, it is not best understood as indicating the correct approach to rescission. Nor, given both the Supreme Court and the Privy Council were of the clear view that Brickenden had acted in breach of fiduciary duty, is it best explained as being relevant to the question whether a fiduciary has actually breached his or her duty. It is correct that what the plaintiff would have done is irrelevant both to whether the fiduciary has acted in breach, and to whether the plaintiff has an equity to rescind, but that is not an adequate explanation for what Lord Thankerton said in *Brickenden*.

[181] *Swindle* (n 45) 716–717.

[182] *cf* M Broderick, 'Equitable compensation—its place in the remedial sphere' (2005) 33 *Australian Business Law Review* 369, 383.

[183] *Nocton v Lord Ashburton* [1914] AC 932, 954; *SZFDE v Minister for Immigration and Citizenship* [2007] HCA 35 at [10], (2007) 232 CLR 189.

[184] *Swindle* (n 45) 718.

[185] *Collins v Brebner* [2000] Lloyd's Rep PN 587 at [57]; although see *Nationwide Building Society v Balmer Radmore (Introductory Sections)* [1999] Lloyd's Rep PN 241, 278 (ChD).

[186] See text accompanying nn 168–170 above.

[187] See also *Satnam Investments Ltd v Dunlop Heywood and Co Ltd* [1999] 3 All ER 652, 668, where the Court of Appeal was concerned with what the principal 'would probably have done' if the defendants had complied with their fiduciary duty. And see *Nationwide Building Society v Balmer Radmore (Introductory Sections)* [1999] Lloyd's Rep PN 241, 278–279 (ChD).

Instead, the *Brickenden* dictum is best understood as having been concerned with whether a fiduciary, who has been shown to have acted in breach of duty, is liable for the loss which his principal suffered in the transaction. The phraseology of the dictum suggests that it may have been based on comparisons with the accounting principles applied to fiduciary relationships involving the stewardship of assets. That was not what *Brickenden* itself involved, and it has been suggested here that there are reasons for not applying such considerations in non-stewardship fiduciary cases. Nonetheless, it is suggested that the approach in *Brickenden* does potentially have merit in non-stewardship fiduciary cases, in the sense that an award of equitable compensation following a breach of fiduciary duty requires a counterfactual analysis to determine the loss for which the defendant fiduciary will be held legally responsible. In a standard fiduciary breach case, there are two possible counterfactuals which could be considered to identify that loss, being the counterfactual where the fiduciary did not act with a conflict, and the counterfactual where the fiduciary made disclosure and obtained consent to that conflict. *Brickenden* can be read as prohibiting a fiduciary from resorting to the second counterfactual without necessarily ruling out the first kind of counterfactual analysis. That approach is consistent with other aspects of the approach taken towards remedies within fiduciary doctrine.

In part, the move away from *Brickenden* in New Zealand appears to rest on a misunderstanding of it. In *Everist v McEvedy*, for example, Tipping J said that '[p]ure *Brickenden* suggests that any consideration of what action the plaintiff would have taken had there been no breach of fiduciary duty by the defendant is irrelevant as speculation'.[188] But that is not what *Brickenden* prohibits.[189] *Brickenden* prohibits speculation as to what the principal would have done if there had been proper disclosure by the fiduciary, and it does so because there was no such disclosure. Contrary to what Tipping J said, the *Brickenden* dictum does not prohibit the court from considering what would have happened if the fiduciary had not acted with a conflict or not taken an unauthorised profit.

The approach which the Canadian courts have developed regarding *Brickenden* has arisen because they have focused on the fiduciary's failure to disclose information as the relevant breach of duty.[190] If that is the breach which the court identifies, then it is natural for the second counterfactual to be the relevant counterfactual when one assesses loss.[191] In Australia, on the other hand, the High Court has emphasised that the fiduciary's obligation is not to make full disclosure but rather to avoid conflicts: making full disclosure of all material facts and obtaining

188 [1996] 3 NZLR 348, 353.

189 A similar error is present in some of the Australian discussions of *Brickenden*: see, eg, text accompanying nn 161 & 171 above.

190 See, eg, *Howard v Cunliffe* (1973) 36 DLR (3d) 212, 219 (BCCA); *Jacks v Davis* (1982) 141 DLR (3d) 355, 359 (BCCA).

191 Note, however, that the Privy Council identified the breach in *Brickenden* as non-disclosure (see text accompanying n 39 above) and nonetheless seemed to rule out the relevance of the second counterfactual.

consent is simply a mechanism by which a fiduciary can avoid that liability.[192] In those terms, it is not so obvious that the second counterfactual is the appropriate one to use when it comes to assessing loss.[193] On the other hand, even if the breach is seen to lie in failing to avoid a conflict, rather than in non-disclosure, it is not necessarily illogical to assess compensation on the basis of the second counterfactual, given that would have been one legitimate course for the fiduciary to have followed and thereby to have acted in accordance with his or her duty.

In jurisdictions, like Australia and England, where the status of the *Brickenden* dictum remains unclear, what is needed is a decision as to whether a fiduciary, who has chosen not to disclose and seek consent, should nonetheless be able to escape liability by proving what would have happened if he or she had done so. It has been suggested that, while this is a possible position for the law to take, it would be more consistent with other aspects of fiduciary doctrine to refuse the fiduciary this 'escape route'.[194] However, it has been emphasised that this does not render a causal analysis irrelevant: the courts still need to determine what would have happened if the fiduciary had not acted with the conflict. One downside to this approach might be that the counterfactual analysis may be more difficult to conduct, as it may require the court to determine what would have happened if the defendant fiduciary had not acted, and another fiduciary had acted in his or her place.[195] That analysis may be more difficult than determining what would have happened if the defendant fiduciary, who did have a relationship with the plaintiff principal, had made full disclosure in the context of their relationship and sought consent. One potential way of tackling this problem, if it is found to be such in practice, may be, once the principal has established that a transaction was entered into in circumstances involving a breach of fiduciary duty by the fiduciary, for the fiduciary then to bear the onus of establishing what would have happened if the fiduciary had not acted. The law could legitimately take the prima facie position of assuming that the transaction would not have taken place,[196] and compensate accordingly unless the fiduciary can prove what would have happened.

[192] *Breen v Williams* (1996) 186 CLR 71, 125; *Maguire* (n 44) 467.

[193] *Blackmagic Design Pty Ltd v Overliese* [2011] FCAFC 24 at [105], (2011) 191 FCR 1.

[194] See text accompanying n 121 above.

[195] See, eg, M Conaglen, 'Remedial Ramifications of Conflicts between a Fiduciary's Duties' (2010) 126 *LQR* 72, 85–100.

[196] *Cole v Manning* [2002] NSWCA 150 at [80].

7

Falsifying the Trust Account and Compensatory Equitable Compensation

JAMES PENNER*

Whilst this chapter was prompted by the landmark (landmine?) decision of the United Kingdom Supreme Court in *AIB Group v Mark Redler & Co*,[1] I shall not undertake a close examination of that decision, which has been done elsewhere.[2] Here my purpose is twofold. First, I shall suggest an alternative analysis of the facts in *AIB Group* which indicates that the case was, plausibly, wrongly decided. Second, I shall press upon the uncertain ratio of the case to point out fact situations where the case should not be followed. Given the frailty of its reasoning, I doubt that the scope of the decision, ie how broad or narrow as a matter of precedent the ruling actually is, can easily be discerned, but this second part of the chapter is, I submit, a start on that project.

I. The Bank Adopted the Misapplication of Funds, so the Solicitors Ought Not to Have Been Liable at All

The facts in *AIB Group* were as follows: In 2006 the defendant solicitors were instructed by the claimant lender, AIB Group, who wished to lend £3.3m taking

* I owe thanks to Simone Degeling and Jason Varuhas for organising the 'Equitable Compensation and Disgorgement of Profit' symposium at UNSW Law in August 2015, and for helpful comments. Thanks also to Joe Campbell, Rob Chambers, Matthew Conaglen, Paul Davies, Jamie Edelman, Jamie Glister, Kelvin Low, Ben McFarlane, Charles Mitchell, Lionel Smith, and Sarah Worthington for responses to earlier versions of this chapter. All remaining deficiencies are mine alone.

1 [2014] UKSC 58, [2015] AC 1503 ('*AIB Group*').

2 In particular I would endorse the criticisms of the decision set out by J Edelman, 'An English misturning with equitable compensation', Ch 5 in this volume, Paul Davies, 'Remedies for Breach of Trust' (2015) 78 *MLR* 681, and Peter Watts, 'Agents' Disbursal of Funds in Breach of Instructions' [2015] *Lloyd's Maritime and Commercial Law Quarterly* 118. See also: JE Penner, 'Distinguishing Fiduciary, Trust, and Accounting Relationships' (2014) *Journal of Equity* 202, 223–26.

a first mortgage over land of the borrowers worth £4.25m. The land was already subject to a prior mortgage from Barclays Bank of about £1.5m, which secured two different loan accounts of the borrowers, one of about £1.23m and the other of about £270,000. Prior to the date when this transaction was to take place, the solicitors erroneously overlooked the second smaller loan account, and therefore paid Barclays only £1.23m, and paid the balance of the £3.3m, about £2.1m, to the borrowers. As Barclays' outstanding loan balance on the second loan account was not discharged, it did not release its security over the borrowers' land, although now it only secured an indebtedness of about £270,000. For about two years, nothing much further happened, but in 2008 AIB Group negotiated with Barclays to allow it to have a second mortgage on the land to secure the loan of £3.3m to the borrowers. The borrowers subsequently defaulted on the loan repayments, and the land was sold. The housing market had declined and the house only fetched about £1.2m, and so after paying the outstanding debt to Barclays, roughly £300,000, AIB Group recovered only £900,000.

In the Court of Appeal[3] it was held that, because of the solicitors' failure to discharge the prior mortgage, the entire outlay by the solicitors of AIB Group's £3.3m was a breach of trust, on the basis that obtaining a valid discharge of the prior mortgage (or obtaining a solicitor's undertaking from the prior mortgagee's solicitors that the mortgage would be discharged upon receipt of the payment) was a condition for paying out any funds at all. This finding was not appealed. Applying general principles of causation for loss as Lord Browne-Wilkinson did in *Target Holdings v Redferns*,[4] the Supreme Court, in concurring judgments by Lords Toulson and Reed, held the solicitors liable only for the £300,000 the lender paid to clear Barclays' prior mortgage; even if there had been no breach and both prior mortgages had been cleared, the house would still have sold for only £1.2m because of the decline in the housing market, so AIB Group's loss owing to the breach on this 'but for' test of causation was only the £300,000 odd needed to discharge the outstanding mortgage.

Unfortunately, neither Lord Toulson nor Lord Reed made it clear what the scope of the decision was, that is, it is not clear whether a beneficiary is now barred in all cases from falsifying the account so that the trustee's liability is to be determined on that basis, or whether only in certain cases. We shall consider this uncertainty in Part II.

But a better analysis, it is submitted, resolves the case without departing from traditional principles under which a beneficiary is prima facie entitled to falsify the trust account where the trustee, in breach of trust, misapplies trust property, in particular paying it away in contravention of the trust terms or his instructions where the trustee is acting under a mandate of agency. On the facts of the case, on the traditional analysis, AIB Group was entitled to falsify the account when

[3] [2013] EWCA Civ 45.
[4] [1996] AC 421 ('*Target Holdings*').

the solicitors advanced the funds in the wrong amounts to Barclays and to the borrowers because each disbursement was a misapplication of the trust money, not being in accord with the instructions the solicitors were given. However, it is also clear that AIB Group, when informed of the situation, proceeded to accept the disbursements of money, and proceeded on its own to negotiate with Barclays ultimately to acquire Barclays' consent to the second charge over the property in question to secure the full value of its loan to the borrowers. By pursuing off its own bat the second charge with Barclays, they proceeded on the basis that it was indeed their money that went to Barclays to pay off its prior mortgage; that is, they adopted the expenditure of the funds to Barclays as a disbursement on their behalf, and thus made it impossible for the solicitors to restore the account. If transferring the money to Barclays in this way was indeed an expenditure on behalf of AIB Group, there was no account to restore: the trust funds must be taken to have been properly disbursed at which time the trust is no more. AIB Group's actions were entirely reasonable, given their understanding of the situation at the time. AIB Group's rationale for proceeding in this way can be inferred quite straightforwardly; they reasoned (as it turned out, wrongly) that there was sufficient value in the property to serve as security for the borrowers' entire indebtedness, as well as for the £270,000 odd owed to Barclays. If this is right, then AIB Group adopted, or accepted, the result following their negotiations with Barclays, ie that the borrowers' loan would be secured by way of a second mortgage inferior to Barclays' first mortgage. On this analysis the solicitors should not have been liable at all, for the expenditure, though in breach, was effectively adopted or ratified after the fact.

It is important to notice that the adoption of a misapplication of trust property can only occur after the fact, whereas a consent to a breach of trust arises before or at the time of the breach.[5] As Lord Millett said:

> If the unauthorised investment has appreciated in value, then the beneficiary will be content with it. He is not obliged to falsify the account which the trustee renders; he can always accept it. … Where the beneficiary accepts the unauthorised investment, he is often said to affirm or adopt the transaction. That is not wholly accurate. The beneficiary has a right to elect, but it is really a right to decide whether to complain or not.[6]

It is trite law that a sui juris beneficiary who freely consents to, participates in, or ratifies a breach of trust may not sue the trustee to make good any loss caused by the breach,[7] and we shall consider that law below. But as to adoption per se, I am unaware of any cases which consider what test might be applied to determine whether a beneficiary has adopted a misapplication of trust assets. Some assistance on the question is provided by the recent Singapore Court of Appeal decision in *Chng Weng Wah v Goh Bak Heng*.[8] The facts of the case were simple. Chng held

5 I must thank Sean Chen and Isaac Tay for helping me to clarify my thoughts on this point.
6 PJ Millett, 'Equity's Place in the Law of Commerce' (1998) 114 *LQR* 217, 226.
7 See, eg: JE Penner, *The Law of Trusts*, 9th edn (Oxford, Oxford University Press, 2014) 11.55–58.
8 [2016] SGCA 9.

shares on trust for himself and Goh in equal shares. Sometime in 1999 or 2000 Goh asked Chng to sell the shares representing his beneficial interest, which Chng claimed he did, accounting to Goh for the money proceeds. Some 13 years later, Goh applied to the court for an account.[9] In considering this claim, Chao Hick Tin JA said:

> In our judgment, a distinction has to be drawn between the case of a trustee having to establish that he no longer owes a duty to account as a result of there being settled accounts between the parties and the case of a trustee having to give an *actual account* in the course of defending a claim for an account. … [T]he claim for a common account may be divided into three stages, namely: (a) whether the claimant has a right to an account; (b) the taking of the account; and (c) any consequential relief. While it is accepted that a trustee may, at the first stage of the claim, be able to prove that he or she no longer owes a duty to account *by providing an actual account* in the course of legal proceedings, that is only but one method by which the trustee is able to resist a claim for an account. For instance, if a trustee is able to produce a document evincing both parties' agreement that accounts have been settled conclusively, in the absence of any other evidence to the contrary, that should suffice and the trustee should not be made to go through the laborious, and if we may add, unnecessary, process of providing an actual account in the course of defending the action. … While it is acknowledged that, unlike the example given in the preceding paragraph, Chng has not managed to produce any documentary evidence to show that parties had agreed that accounts have been settled, that does not necessarily lead to the conclusion that Chng has to provide an actual account in the course of defending the present claim by Goh. Based on the evidence that has been led (such as the correspondence between the parties), the court may be able to draw an inference, on a balance of probabilities, that settled accounts *have already been provided* (ie, at some earlier point in time). In the circumstances, a trustee does not necessarily have to provide full accounts in order to defeat a claim for an account by a beneficiary.[10]

As applied to the facts in *AIB Group*, the question is whether, by its actions, it is right to infer that AIB Group adopted the transaction in the sense of taking the disbursements to be applications of its money, thus bringing the trust to an end. If so, then the trust accounts would be 'settled', that is, the solicitors liability to 'account' at any time in the future would be extinguished.

Although, as already pointed out, consent to a breach of trust is not equivalent to the adoption of a misapplication of trust assets after the fact, nevertheless some assistance on the test to be applied for determining whether a beneficiary adopts a misapplication of trust property can be derived from the law covering consent to a breach prior to or at the time of its commission. Of course, truly to consent to a breach, a beneficiary must be fully aware of the facts, although not necessarily of his legal rights. In *Re Pauling's Settlement Trusts*[11] Wilberforce J described the court's general approach to the question of consent or ratification as follows:

[9] Goh's claim was found by the court to be barred under the doctrine of laches. See [2016] SGCA 9, [44]–[60].

[10] [2016] SGCA 9 [38]–[39] [italics original].

[11] [1962] 1 WLR 86.

> [T]he court has to consider all the circumstances … with a view to seeing whether it is fair and equitable that, having given his concurrence, he should afterwards turn round and sue the trustees … it is not necessary that he should know that what he is concurring in is a breach of trust, provided that he fully understands what he is concurring in, and that it is not necessary that he should himself have directly benefited by the breach of trust.[12]

In a recent review of the authorities in *Barescape Pty Limited v Bacchus Holdings Pty Limited*[13] Black J said the following:

> In *Blackmagic Design Pty Ltd v Overliese* [2011] FCAFC 24; (2011) 191 FCR 1; 276 ALR 646 at 668 [110], Besanko J (with whom Finkelstein and Jacobson JJ agreed) observed that:
>
> > "There is no doubt that the disclosure required to avoid the consequences of a conflict is a full and frank disclosure of all material facts. The identification of the precise information which must be disclosed so that the fiduciary's principal is kept "fully informed of the real state of things" (Gray v New Augarita Porcupine Mines Ltd [1952] 3 DLR 1 at 14 per Lord Radcliffe) is likely to depend on the particular facts of the case before the court. It seems to me that the material facts in this case are the facts which give rise to the conflict …"

In that case his Honour noted that certain matters were, and others were not, necessary to be disclosed to obtain informed consent to the relevant conduct.

It is also important to recognise that consent is not an absolute defence to a breach of trust or breach of fiduciary duty. In *Spellson v George* (1992) 26 NSWLR 666 at 669 Handley JA noted that the authorities establish that:

> consent is only a prima facie defence and that the Court must consider in detail "all the circumstances" in order to determine whether it would be "fair and equitable" for that beneficiary to be permitted to complain of that breach.[14]

Applied to the facts of *AIB Group* it would appear that AIB Group was fully aware of all the circumstances when they began their negotiations with Barclays, and at no stage does it appear that they suggested that the solicitors should do anything further once AIB 'took charge' of the matter. Moreover, whilst early on the borrowers promised the solicitors that they would themselves would pay off the remaining amount on the prior Barclays mortgage, they never did so, and AIB seemed content with this when they pursued the matter with Barclays.

One final way of considering the matter is in terms of 'acquiescence'. In *Holder v Holder*[15] the plaintiff sued to set aside the purchase of trust property by his brother who had technically acquired the status of an executor, for breach of the 'self-dealing' rule. The plaintiff was held to have acquiesced in the sale although

[12] ibid 108.
[13] [2012] NSWSC 984. I thank Simone Degeling for bringing this case to my attention.
[14] ibid [160]–[161].
[15] [1968] Ch 353.

unaware at the time of the legal position. He had subsequently received part of the purchase price as a beneficiary under the will, and throughout had full knowledge of all the facts concerning the sale. Besides considering these facts that went to determining the plaintiff's acquiescence in the sale to his brother, the 'fair and equitable' requirement for allowing the beneficiary now to 'turn round and sue' was also applied, so it might be argued that more than acquiescence is necessary to bar a plaintiff from bringing a claim for relief. Even so, it must be just as much for an adoption case, where a beneficiary chooses not 'to complain' once in full possession of the facts, as AIB Group was when it set out to negotiate with Barclays, as for a consent case, that acquiescence should be seen as a factor weighing in favour of barring a later claim for breach of trust.

This analysis of *AIB Group*, subject to one point concerning whether AIB Group could falsify the account 'in part'—adopting the expenditure of the money to Barclays but falsifying the overpayment to the borrowers—which shall be discussed shortly, is fortified by the essentially identical analysis of the facts from the perspective of agency law. Peter Watts criticises the decision of the Supreme Court and argues that the case turns primarily on the application of the principles concerning the ratification of an agent's unauthorised acts. Watts says:

> [I]t seems…equally plain that once told of the delinquency the principal must take a stance on what has happened. It is not inconceivable that a legal system might place the burden on the agent expressly to require the principal to elect whether or not to adopt what has been done, albeit wrongly, in the principal's name. But it does seem inconceivable that a legal system would allow a principal, when pressed, to refuse an answer. We can put such speculation aside, since the common law does impose a duty on principals where fully informed, and it is simple enough to do so, to speak out or risk their silence being treated as a ratification of unauthorized action.
>
> [W]hilst the solicitors in *AIB Group* were initially not forthcoming about their having accidentally released the money without a first mortgage being in place, they were soon driven to reveal the facts, and indeed some negotiations then directly occurred between their client and the existing mortgagee. In those circumstances, an inference of ratification was almost irresistible.[16]

The only remaining question is whether AIB Group could have consented to the expenditure in part, say consenting to the payment of £1.23m to Barclays, but not to the £300k overpayment to the borrowers. On agency principles, Watts argues that the result in *AIB Group* can be justified on the basis that AIB Group's ratification of the transfer to Barclays need not encompass the overpayment to the borrowers. We shall return to that thought in a moment. On straight falsification principles, however, it would appear that AIB Group would have difficulty in making such a claim.

Where a trustee enters into two different unauthorised transactions, one of which causes a loss, but the other creates a gain for the trust, the beneficiary can, in principle, falsify only the loss-causing transaction, and adopt the successful one,

[16] Watts (n 2) 120–21 footnotes omitted.

if the transactions are distinct.[17] The trustee should not be exonerated of particular breaches because he can say, 'overall, the trust is in good shape'. However, where the losing and gaining unauthorised transactions form part of one composite transaction, the transactions must be falsified together or not at all.[18] For example, in *Bartlett v Barclays Bank Trust Co. Ltd*,[19] the court held that the disastrous investment in one property development project was part of a larger investment policy favouring land development. In taking the account, then, this decision required the beneficiary to 'falsify' both the winning and losing projects as one invalid investment, with a resulting reduction in the amount of compensation.[20]

The facts in *AIB Group* are, if anything, *a fortiori* to those in *Bartlett*. The payments to Barclays and to the borrowers were clearly part of a 'composite' transaction or, even, *one* transaction if we think of the payments being made in pursuance of AIB Group's contract of loan with the borrowers.

Does an analysis of the facts drawing on agency principles give a different result? Contrary to Watts, I think not. The gist of Watt's argument is found in the following two passages:

> A principal's decision to ratify *need not release the agent from all liability, particularly in respect of loss that has crystallised before any decision to adopt the agent's acts.* But loss that ensues from the transaction after its affirmation would ordinarily rest with the principal.

> In [the circumstances of AIB], an inference of ratification was almost irresistible. … *[R]atification would not necessarily have released the solicitors from indemnifying the lender from the increased exposure that the substitute transaction had created.*[21]

But, it is submitted, simply because the solicitors' actions exposed AIB Group to this loss, it does not follow that they are liable for it. Whilst there is no 'duty to mitigate' one's losses at common law, liability for damages both in contract and tort does not extend to losses which could reasonably have been avoided. In this case, AIB Group could easily have avoided the £300k loss. It had an immediate claim against the borrowers: the borrowers held the excess they received on trust, this amount being misapplied when transferred to them, and were in addition personally liable for that amount as knowing recipients. AIB Group could easily have got an order against the borrowers to transfer the requisite amount to Barclays to

[17] *Wiles v Gresham* (1854) 2 Drew 258, 61 ER 718 at 271, at 723.

[18] *Fletcher v Green* (1864) 33 Beav. 426, 55 ER 433, at 430–31, at 434–35

[19] [1980] Ch 515, at 538 C-E.

[20] '[F]alsify' here is placed in quotation marks as, strictly speaking, *Bartlett* was not a falsification case. The trustee in *Bartlett* was liable for not preventing the company in which the trust held shares from embarking on property developments. Thus the case was one of negligence, and the beneficiaries surcharged the account. But the principles of causation for loss in falsification cases were relevant because the transactions the company entered into were essentially ones that, had the company been the trustee, would have been misapplications of trust property, and so it was appropriate to analyse the facts in terms of falsification when assessing the loss to the trust.

[21] Watts (n 2)120, 21 (my italics in both passages).

discharge the remaining indebtedness to Barclays (at the borrowers' expense in costs) had the borrowers refused to do this themselves. On the facts, it is clear that AIB Group never concerned themselves with doing anything of the kind in keeping with the rationale for their actions following being informed of the solicitors' error, discussed above. On orthodox common law liability principles, then, the result would appear to be no different than on orthodox falsification principles, ie, that the solicitors ought not to have been liable for any amount.

II. The Scope of the Ratio Decidendi in *AIB Group*

The reasoning of Lords Toulson and Reed in *AIB Group* is far from crystalline, but the following two passages seem to be their respective statements of the principle of liability that arises from the decision.

> Lord Toulson: All agree that the basic right of a beneficiary is to have the trust duly administered in accordance with the provisions of the trust instrument, if any, and the general law. Where there has been a breach of that duty, the basic purpose of any remedy will be either *to put the beneficiary in the same position as if the breach had not occurred* or to vest in the beneficiary any profit which the trustee may have made by reason of the breach (and which ought therefore properly to be held on behalf of the beneficiary). Placing the beneficiary in the same position as he would have been in but for the breach may involve restoring the value of something lost by the breach or making good financial damage caused by the breach. But a monetary award which reflected neither loss caused nor profit gained by the wrongdoer would be penal.[22]

> Lord Reed: [T]he model of equitable compensation, where trust property has been misapplied, is to require the trustee to restore the trust fund to the position it would have been in if the trustee had performed his obligation.[23]

Now whilst these statements purport to be fully general, applying to any case of breach of trust, in keeping with Lord Browne-Wilkinson's preoccupation with 'commercial' reality in *Target*,[24] both Lords Reed and Toulson refer to the fact that the trust in question was one element of a commercial transaction,[25] which may be taken to narrow the ambit of the decision to 'commercial' rather than to 'traditional' trusts, ie family wealth management trusts. Such a consideration might explain in part the very first line of Lord Toulson's judgment:

> 140 years after the Judicature Act 1873, the stitching together of equity and the common law continues to cause problems at the seams.[26]

22 *AIB Group* (n 1) [64] (my italics).
23 *AIB Group* (n 1) [134].
24 See, eg: *Target Holdings* (n 4) 436.
25 *AIB Group* (n 1) [17], [34], [44], [67], [70–71], and [74] (Lord Toulson), [101–106] (Lord Reed).
26 *AIB Group* (n 1) [1].

The thought is that where a trust is a commercial one, both equity and the common law will have a role to play in analysing the facts, and any breach by the trustee, and thus common principles of liability ought to be found. But it is fair to say that there is no explicit statement by either of their Lordships qualifying the generality of the ratio, in particular narrowing it to trusts undertaken in 'commercial' circumstances, whatever they might be.[27] Nevertheless, it is submitted that the principle of liability endorsed by Lords Toulson and Reed cannot be general, and this can be shown by considering fact situations where its application would, intuitively at least, produce quite the wrong result.

Drawing upon these statements of their Lordships, we can restate the ratio decidendi of *AIB Group* as follows:

> Henceforward, where a trustee misapplies trust property, a beneficiary of a trust will be disentitled from falsifying the account. The unauthorised expenditure will be regarded as an expenditure of the beneficiary's funds for the beneficiary's purposes. However, the trustee's breach in expending the funds on an unauthorised asset will, on the other hand, amount to a wrong sufficient to support a claim to surcharge the account, so that if the expenditure as wrongly made causally gives rise to a lower value for the trust property than would have been obtained had the intended, authorised, asset been acquired, the trustee will be liable for the difference.

It is submitted that it cannot generally be the rule that a beneficiary is no longer entitled to falsify the account and has only a remedy for consequential loss, as the following examples demonstrate.

In the first place, if this were the general rule, then the House of Lords decision concerning the *Quistclose*[28] trust in *Twinsectra Ltd v Yardley*[29] was wrongly reasoned. The House of Lords found[30] that the lender, Twinsectra, advanced funds to the solicitor of the borrower, Mr Yardley, on trust for the purpose of purchasing 'property'. The funds were then transferred to a second solicitor of Mr. Yardley, who had some degree of notice or knowledge of the trust over the funds. The second solicitor released the funds to Mr Yardley, some of which funds were spent not in the acquisition of property.

It is worth pointing out first that the trust in *Twinsectra* was clearly a bare, commercial trust, identical in form to the trust in *AIB Group* itself, and yet the case proceeded on the basis that the trustee-borrower was liable for his wrongful expenditures of the trust money on falsification principles. As Mr. Yardley was insolvent by the time of the action, the lender sued Mr. Yardley's second solicitor for dishonest assistance, claiming that he was secondarily liable for the money wrongfully paid away. There would have been no claim against either the

27 For a persuasive criticism of the soundness of any distinction between 'commercial' and 'traditional' trusts, see Davies (n 2) 687–88.

28 *Barclays Bank Ltd v Quistclose Investments* [1970] AC 567.

29 [2002] AC 164.

30 On pretty flimsy facts, it must be said: see Penner (n 5) [7.28–29].

trustee-borrower or his solicitor if the claim was limited to one for consequential loss: had the trustee-borrower disbursed all the trust money *lawfully*—ie if the money was not disbursed in breach of trust—the lender would still have recovered little or nothing, for the borrower was insolvent. It was the borrower's insolvency that caused the loss, not the misapplications of the trust property, ie not the breach of trust. Indeed, on *AIB Group* principles no *Quistclose* trustee could ever personally be liable for the misapplication of the trust money, since on pure compensation for consequential loss principles the lender would always be in the position of an unsecured creditor whether the money is spent according to the trust terms or not.

Consider another example, which draws on the logic of *Clough v Bond*,[31] where Cottenham LC said:

> It will be found to be the result of all the best authorities on the subject, that, although a [trustee], acting strictly within the line of his duty, and exercising reasonable care and diligence, will not be responsible for the failure or depreciation of the fund…yet if that line of duty not be strictly pursued, and any part of the property be invested by such [trustee] in funds or upon securities not authorised, or be put within the control of persons who ought not to be instructed with it, and loss be thereby eventually sustained, such [trustee] will be liable to make it good, however unexpected the result, however little likely to arise from the course adopted, and however free such conduct may have been from any improper motive.[32]

Tom the trustee, in breach of trust, removes a gemstone from the trust collection held in a secure (ha!) vault in Hatton Garden in London, and sells it for £100,000. The gems, being in what is supposed to be secure safe-keeping, are uninsured. Later that week the secure vault is burgled, and all the gems are stolen. Tom must account for the £100,000 to the trust and cannot claim that had he complied with his duty all the gems, including the one he stole, would have been lost, so again, the claim that the beneficiaries undoubtedly have to the £100,000 cannot be founded as one for consequential loss. Rather, the beneficiaries in this case will elect not to falsify the account, but adopt the sale of the gem. This is the orthodox position, and it would seem that any claim by the trustee that he should not account for the funds because the beneficiaries suffered no consequential loss because of his breach (all the gems would have been lost in any case) would be rejected outright.

A similar set of facts presented itself in *Akai Holdings (in liquidation)*.[33] The case involved a fraudulent loan transaction, in which one Mr Ting purported to act with the authority of the Board of Directors of Akai Holdings. The transaction was a loan from the Farmer's Bank (the 'bank') of $30m US secured by the pledge of shares legal title to which belonged to Akai. The loan moneys were used to discharge a loan of the same amount that the bank held against Singer NV, a company

[31] (1838) 3 My & Cr 490, 40 ER 1016.
[32] ibid 496, 1018.
[33] [2011] 1 HKC 357.

more or less unrelated to Akai but one in which Mr. Ting was interested as a major shareholder. This was called a 'switch transaction' because the bank was able to switch a loan to Singer NV with negligible security for a loan to Akai with significant security in the form of the pledged shares. Later Akai defaulted on repayment of the loan, and the bank sold the pledged shares for about $20m, and sought to prove the outstanding loan amount in Akai's liquidation. The Court held that the bank should have realised that Mr. Ting had no actual authority to enter into the switch transaction on behalf of Akai, and thus it should have known that it was wrongfully pledged the shares. The Court found the bank liable for conversion of the shares when the bank sold them, but was also willing to hold that the bank, on some extension or application of the principles of 'knowing receipt', owed Akai equitable compensation in the amount of the money it received on the sale of the shares. But the court also found this:

> [I]t is clear on the balance of probabilities, indeed it is, in truth, clear beyond any real doubt, that, if the Bank had returned the share certificates to Akai, far from being sold earlier than the date upon which the Bank sold them, Akai would have kept the Shares until they had become worthless. The ironic fact is that Akai is substantially better off as a result of the Bank having received and sold the Shares. Of course, that does not mean that Akai has no right to equitable compensation, and the Bank is entitled to keep the proceeds of sale of the Shares: normal equitable principles entitle Akai to elect between receiving a sum equal to the proceeds of sale of the Shares or, unless it is impossible to obtain them, an equivalent number of Akai Electric shares.[34]

If Akai was to be placed in the position it would have been in had no breach occurred, in this case no switch transaction and no pledge of the shares to the bank, it would be entitled to no compensation at all. But that is not what the court held.

Take another example, where a trustee 'borrows' trust moneys. In personal financial difficulty, a trustee in breach of trust sells the trust's 20,000 shares in XYZ plc at $5 per share, thus for $100,000, and uses the money to discharge his debts. Later on, when the market price of XYZ shares has fallen to $1 per share, the trustee restores the trust by spending $20,000 to purchase 20,000 shares in XYZ.

The trustee makes a handsome profit from his breach of trust, viz $80,000, and the beneficiaries have not suffered in any way from his breach, ie they are in the same position they would have been in had the breach not occurred. They therefore have no personal claim against the trustee under the aegis of surcharging the account, ie making a claim for consequential loss. Only upon falsification/adoption principles does one get the right result: Upon the sale of the shares—in breach of trust—for $100,000, the beneficiaries can elect either to falsify the account or adopt the transaction. They will clearly adopt the sale. The trustee will be treated as holding the $100,000 on trust as a substitute asset acquired in

[34] ibid [154].

exchange for the shares. The beneficiaries will then go on to falsify each and every expenditure by the trustee of that money which was used to discharge his own personal debts. They can thus make a claim against the trustee for $100,000 plus interest, and it is neither here nor there that had the trustee not committed the breach of trust the trust fund would have declined in value by 80%.

It might be suggested that the same result, holding the trustee personally liable for $80,000, could be achieved by applying the no profit rule[35] governing fiduciaries. In my view, the suggestion is misguided. In the first place, the rule is not apt in these circumstances. The no profit rule is directed to receipts by a fiduciary from third parties acquired in conflict of interest; it is not directed to a trustee's misappropriation of the trust assets themselves. Moreover, the rule has no application where the trustee in question is not a fiduciary,[36] for example in the case of *Quistclose* trustees, so the rule would not cover all cases of concern, ie cases where trust assets are misappropriated. Finally, a misapplication of trust property is not per se 'a breach of fiduciary obligation' or, to put it better, is not per se an act attracting liability under fiduciary law. We can show this with a further example.

As we know from *Bristol and West Building Society v Motthew*,[37] fiduciary liability, including the 'no profit' rule, does not attach to a merely negligent breach of trust or contract. So consider this case: A trustee sells shares to meet her own indemnity or charging clause, and uses the money to pay her debts, expenses, etc. It turns out the indemnity was not available (say because she negligently failed to realise that she was not empowered to delegate, and pay, an agent under the trust terms, or had litigation costs not authorised by the trust and failed to get a Beddoe order, or the indemnity owing to her was not properly calculated, etc). There is no fiduciary liability here but there is also no way that the trustee can replace the shares at a lower price if the share price has fallen. Again, if there was a general decline in the market, there is no way she can replace the money she paid herself discounted by the percentage decline in the trust fund. The 'no profit' rule has no application to this fact situation. It's falsification/adoption principles or nothing.

We can consider another example, posed by Watts:

> Let us then assume that the lender [in *Target*] discovered the borrower's fraud and contacted the solicitors, conscious that it might have become too late to stop the transaction but hoping otherwise. The solicitors told it that the funds had been released [to a third party, not the intended payee] but that the mortgage was not yet in place. At least before *Target Holdings*, it was clear that in such circumstances the lender could disown the solicitors' conduct and withdraw its authority, thereby laying the loss of the funds at their door. It would not be open to the solicitors in the face of the client's protest to proceed to get in the mortgage, even assuming the fraudster remained content to sign the documents. In such circumstances, Lord Browne-Wilkinson's test for liability, namely

[35] This was suggested to me by Lionel Smith. For discussion of the 'no profit' rule, see Penner (n 2) 230–33; Penner (n 5) [12.48–59].

[36] For discussion of non-fiduciary trustees, see Penner (n 2) 219–23.

[37] [1998] Ch 1.

> that the loss would not have occurred but for the breach, would not be met. Rather than being a cause of the loss, the solicitors' default would, from the claimant's perspective, be a piece of good fortune. But that could not be an answer to the claimant's right to a return of its money.[38]

It is difficult to find a fault in this reasoning. Where a beneficiary/lender in such a case acts in time to withdraw its authority to lay out the funds, as a matter of principle it cannot be the case that the trustee can proceed anyway *without authority*, putting the risk of any loss on the beneficiary.

There is one further feature of understanding the beneficiaries' remedy for breach of trust as being a claim for consequential loss, which would lead to an *expansion* of the trustee's liability in certain cases. On orthodox principles concerning the trustee's liability to account, the only interest of the beneficiaries that the trustee's liability to account protects is their interest in the value of, or in the specific property in, the trust fund. It does not allow the beneficiaries any claim for consequential loss that they suffer which follows from the trust's being 'short of funds' owing to the breach.

Consider the following example: Because of the trustee's misapplication of the trust property, say making an unauthorised investment, Hazel, the income beneficiary, receives half the income in 2014 that she would have done if the authorised investment was retained. Let us also assume that Hazel can establish, on the standard 'but for' test of causation, that but for this reduction in her income she would have been able to make a profitable investment herself; instead, because of the reduced income, she could not afford it, and so can prove that the trustee's breach caused her a loss of profits. Has she any claim for this loss against the trustee?

Not by way of account. By falsifying the trust account her only claim is to have the trust restored, and this will include an amount of money to ensure that she receives the missing income for 2014, plus interest. But can she 'go outside the account' and claim her consequential loss on some broader notion of the trustee's liability for breach of trust? That would require founding a claim that would not be traditionally conceived of either as falsifying or surcharging the account, because the loss claimed is not a loss to the trust funds No such claim has ever been argued for in any decided case, although Jamie Glister has raised the possibility.[39] At first this might seem unjust, especially if our understanding of breach of trust is, by virtue of the kind of reasoning in *AIB Group*, shifted from principles of falsification and adoption to principles of compensation for 'but for' consequential losses. It is submitted that there is no injustice. Whilst a beneficiary is entitled to ensure that she receives all the distributions from the trust fund to which she is entitled, a trust fund which has all the property in it which it should (which rights the power to falsify and surcharge the account ensures), she should not be entitled to recover any losses she suffers in her own personal affairs because she relied upon receiving such and such a distribution on a timely basis.

38 Watts (n 2) 125.
39 Jamie Glister, 'Breach of Trust and Consequential Loss' (2014) 8 *Journal of Equity* 235.

The common law parallel in the law of torts is a wrongdoer's liability for consequential economic loss, or 'pure' economic loss as it is sometimes put. In general, tortfeasors are not liable to their victims for economic loss that does not directly follow from damage to the victim's person or to his tangible property. Why this is so, why a tortfeasor is not subjected to unlimited liability for all the economic losses his victim suffers that can be shown to flow from his wrong, is a controversial issue, but following Stevens,[40] the most satisfactory rationale for this position is this: the law does not protect your liberty to exploit economic opportunities for profit. It indirectly protects this liberty by prohibiting interferences to your person and property and, in the case of a beneficiary of a trust, by empowering the beneficiaries to claim distributions under a trust to which they are entitled. But the law does not make anyone, including wrongdoers, insurers of your economic well-being, even if their wrongful actions alter to your detriment the economic context in which you operate. So the question in this case is whether a trustee owes his beneficiaries a duty (presumably a duty of care) to ensure that he makes distributions of the right amounts on time under the terms of the trust such that he is liable to them for any consequential losses that might eventuate if he does not (beyond any amounts of interest the beneficiaries will receive for late distributions). There is, it is submitted, no good reason to impose such a duty, at least in the case of traditional trusts in which the benefits the beneficiary receives are by way of gift from the settlor; the trustee should not be liable for consequential losses you suffer because you receive the correct amount of a gift late. To hold otherwise would make the trustee liable for *foreseeable* losses occasioned by, say, the late distributions to Hazel in the example above. Which aspects of a beneficiary's financial wherewithal are supposed to be within the contemplation of the trustee? A trustee may have a duty to know something about the financial circumstances of different beneficiaries when exercising a discretion to invest the trust funds,[41] or in exercising a discretion to distribute property amongst a class of discretionary objects, but would this make it foreseeable that Hazel was unable, say, to borrow money to make the investment, the interest on which loan would be compensated more or less by the interest to which she would be entitled on the late distributions when they are later made to her? It is not clear what would justify placing this burden of investigation on the trustee. Moreover, it might be argued that a trustee should have no right, much less a duty, to know about any particular beneficiary's access to other funds.

Finally, there is a flip-side to this line of thinking. If a trustee is to be liable for consequential losses of this kind, should the trustee be relieved of liability if no consequential loss ensues? Consider this final example. Trudy the trustee has a duty to distribute the entirety of trust income to Ben the beneficiary which duty, however, is subject to a power to accumulate up to half the income which will

[40] Robert Stevens, *Torts and Rights* (Oxford, Oxford University Press, 2007), Chs 1–3.
[41] See *Nestle v National Westminster Bank plc* [1993] 1 WLR 1260, 1279C, D (Staughton LJ).

accrue to capital, held on trust for his wife and children. Ben is a notorious wastrel. Trudy, quite rightly, exercises her discretion to accumulate as much as she can with a view to distributing capital to his wife and children, when the former is released from Ben's affections by his death, and when the latter come of age. Trudy miscalculates. For the last five years she has accumulated 55% of the income, rather than 50%, such that Ben has received £250k less than he otherwise would have done. What if, during the period, Ben would, on the balance of probabilities, have lost the money gambling, or was a devoted collector of an artist whose work is junk? On orthodox accounting principles, neither of these facts would give Trudy any relief from her liability to make good the failure to pay Ben. But on pure 'compensation for consequential loss' principles, it would appear that they might do just that.

III. Conclusion

If *AIB Group* is not interpreted narrowly, or the decision comes to be understood by a future United Kingdom Supreme Court to have been based upon a faulty analysis of the facts as suggested in Part I above, then its scope, ie the extent to which it denies beneficiaries the power to falsify the account for misapplications of trust property, will need to be carefully examined. To the extent that *AIB Group* suggests that beneficiaries are generally disentitled from falsifying the account and may only make claims on the basis of their consequential loss, it is not the law in Australia[42] or Hong Kong[43] and your author would not recommend that judges there or elsewhere follow it.

[42] See, eg: Edelman (n 2); *Youyang Pty Ltd v Minter Ellison Morris Fletcher* (2003) 212 CLR 484; *Agricultural Land Management Ltd v Jackson (No 2)* [2014] WASC 102

[43] *Akai Holdings Ltd v Kasikornbank plc* [2011] 1 HKC 357; *Libertarian Investments Ltd v Hall* Hong Kong Final Appeal Nos 14 and 16 of 2012 (Civil) (2013) 16 HKCFAR 681.

8

Causation in the Restoration of a Misapplied Trust Fund: Fundamental Norm or Red Herring?

LUSINA HO*

I. Introduction

When a beneficiary seeks relief for misapplied trust assets, the emerging if not prevailing view amongst commentators is that he is but exercising his primary right to performance of the trust.[1] The beneficiary is not seeking compensation for the factual detriment caused by the breach. Thus, whether the claim assumes the form of taking a common account or equitable compensation (an unfortunate misnomer in this context), the substance of the ultimate monetary award is essentially one for an 'equitable debt',[2] for which issues of breach or causation—whether factual or legal—are irrelevant.

The United Kingdom Supreme Court in *AIB Group (UK) Plc v Mark Redler & Co*, however, was not swayed by these advocacies. The Court subsumed substitutive performance and reparative compensation under a unitary principle that it considered fundamental to all remedies, namely that: 'the basic purpose of any remedy [is] to put the beneficiary in the same position as if the breach had not

* The author is grateful to Simone Degeling and Jason Varuhas for organising the Symposium on Equitable Compensation and Disgorgement of Profits, and for beneficial comments received at the event. Thanks are also due to Nicholas McBride, Hon William Gummow, Rebecca Lee and Tom Ng for comments on an earlier draft of this chapter, and to Rosa Lee and Terrence Tai for their invaluable research assistance.

[1] C Mitchell, 'Stewardship of Property and Liability to Account' [2014] *Conveyancer and Property Lawyer* 215; C Mitchell and S Watterson, 'Remedies for Knowing Receipt' in C Mitchell (ed), *Constructive and Resulting Trusts* (Oxford, Hart Publishing, 2010) 115; P Millett, 'Equity's Place in the Law of Commerce' (1998) 114 *LQR* 214; *Agricultural Land Management Ltd v Jackson (No 2)* (2014) 48 WAR 1 ('*Agricultural Land*').

[2] *Ex parte Adamson* (1878) 8 Ch D 807, 819. In fact, Edelman J has advocated, extra-judicially, that the beneficiary should frame their claims in debt rather than equitable compensation: J Edelman, 'An English Misturning with Equitable Compensation', Ch 5 of this book.

occurred.'[3] It held that 'but for' causation applies to the accounting of misapplied trust funds. Lord Toulson dismissed arguments based on the orthodox accounting procedure as 'fairy tales'.[4] Lord Reed, in a more forward-looking approach, preferred to fashion remedies to reflect the characteristics of the particular obligation breached rather than its historical origin, albeit his Lordship did not explain how this was to be done.[5] The reasoning in *AIB Group* has drawn considerable criticism,[6] predictably from commentators who consider that the debt characterisation self-evidently demonstrates the irrelevance of but-for causation.[7]

Unfortunately, the impasse between the UK Supreme Court and its critics is due, in great part, to the failure to address the policy justification of the orthodox position. On the one hand, the switching of the label of the claim from account to equitable compensation has confusingly misled the Supreme Court into compensatory thinking. On the other hand, even if there is a grain of truth in analogising the traditional accounting remedy with debt and specific performance, it does not prohibit fashioning equitable compensation to ameliorate any potential hardship and injustice that may be brought by a strict adherence to the analogy.

The chapter seeks therefore to reinforce the underlying policy justifications of the orthodox position, and at the same time investigate possible situations where modification of the orthodox position is called for. To achieve this task, the chapter will, first, examine the historical approaches in common accounts, whereby it observes that amongst the plethora of earlier cases cited by critics of the compensation view, only a few expressly pronounce on the irrelevance of but-for causation; but, notwithstanding the dearth of direct authority on causation, it is well established that the nature of falsification is performance of the trustee's fundamental duty to account rather than compensation. Secondly, to bolster arguments based on the nature of the remedy as debt or specific performance, the chapter will take up Lord Reed's appeal to fashion remedies based on the justification of the duties breached; such a line of inquiry will show the orthodox position to be fully justified, at least as a default rule. The chapter will also explore situations where these underlying policies justify modifying the orthodox position. Lastly, the chapter examines how the decision in *AIB Group* may be reconciled with existing orthodox rules that permit beneficiaries to adopt or ratify the breaches of defaulting trustees, albeit it could also have provided the occasion for modifying the orthodox rules.

[3] [2015] AC 1503 ('*AIB Group*'), [64] (Lord Toulson). Except, of course, if the parties had agreed to a specific amount as remedy, such as in liquidated damages, or the apportionment of profits made by a fiduciary.

[4] ibid [69] (Lord Toulson).

[5] ibid [138] (Lord Reed).

[6] M Conaglen, 'Equitable Compensation for Breach of Trust: Off Target' (2016) 40 *Melbourne University Law Review* 1; P Davies, 'Remedies for Breach of Trust' (2015) 78 *MLR* 681; Hon W Gummow, 'Three Cases of Misapplication of a Solicitor's Trust Account' (2015) 41 *Australian Bar Review* 5; R Lee, 'Substitutive Compensation for Breach of Trust: An Irrelevant Fairy Tale?' (2015) 9 *Journal of Equity* 94; P Watts, 'Agents' Disbursal of Funds in Breach of Instructions' [2015] *Lloyd's Maritime and Commercial Law Quarterly* 118.

[7] Edelman (n 2).

II. Orthodoxy

A. Dearth of Direct Authority on But-for Causation

Shortly before *AIB Group*, Edelman J had provided judicial affirmation of the orthodox principle in *Agricultural Land Management Ltd v Jackson [No 2]*:[8]

> The "compensation" order following the common account required the defendant to perform his or her duty to maintain the trust fund in an authorised manner.[9] It was not a sufficient response to a disallowance, or falsification, that the disbursement would have been lost even if the trustee had acted properly.

In support of this statement, Edelman J cited *Knott v Cottee*[10] and *Magnus v Queensland National Bank*,[11] as well as a statement from the first edition of *Lewin on Trusts*,[12] which in turn cited *Dornford v Dornford*,[13] *Raphael v Boehm*,[14] and *Moons v De Bernales*.[15] A closer examination shows that only one of these authorities, *Magnus v Queensland National Bank*, is authority for the proposition that a court will not consider inevitable loss that would have been caused by a *wrongdoing third party*. But the case itself is not direct authority that inevitable loss arising outside of third party wrongdoing will also be irrelevant. Support for this wider proposition can be found in *Cocker v Quayle*,[16] which is not cited in *Agricultural Land*.[17]

The authorities cited by Edelman J may be divided into three groups.

The first group comprises authorities which held that for the purposes of making good the trust fund, the court would not take into account *profits* arising from the unauthorised investment. In *Knott v Cottee*, the executors made unauthorised

[8] *Agricultural Land* (n 1), 64–65 [338], generally at [333]–[359], applied in Dennis *Cassegrain v Gerard Cassegrain & Co Pty Ltd (in liq)* [2015] NSWSC 851, [23].

[9] His Lordship cited *Partington v Reynolds* (1858) 62 ER 98, 98–99 (Kindersley VC) to support this statement. In that case, the Vice Chancellor distinguished the common accounts from account on the basis of wilful default, in that the former 'is a decree compelling [the trustee] to account only for what he has received', whereas the latter 'is a decree compelling him to account, not only for what he has received, but also for what he might, without his wilful neglect or default, have received'. No comment was made as to whether the former decree excludes consideration as to whether the estate would not have lost the property in any event. The decision pertains to the procedural point that when a decree for common accounts was sought, the plaintiffs would not be allowed to vary or amend the decree to include account on the basis of wilful default.

[10] (1852) 51 ER 705, 706 (Romilly MR), citing 'had not been made or had been made for [the trustee's] own benefit out of his own monies'.

[11] (1888) 37 Ch 466, 474 (Cotton LJ).

[12] T Lewin, *A Practical Treatise on the Law of Trusts and Trustees* (London, A Maxwell, 1837) 634.

[13] (1806) 33 ER 49.

[14] (1805) 32 ER 1023 (Lord Eldon), affirmed in (1807) 33 ER 347.

[15] (1826) 38 ER 117. See also *Lord Montford v Lord Cadogan* (1810) 34 ER 188; *Scurfield v Howes* (1790) 29 ER 425; *Treves v Townsend* (1783) 28 ER 1191; *Forbes v Ross* (1788) 30 ER 52.

[16] (1830) 39 ER 206, discussed in Watts (n 6).

[17] (1838) 40 ER 1016.

investments in foreign—as opposed to British—stocks. They were ordered by the court to sell the unauthorised investments during a specified time, as a result of which loss was incurred on the investments, whereas if they had been retained until the date of the decree, a profit would have been made. Sir John Romilly MR stated the general approach, namely that the court would treat the unauthorised investments as not having been made, or as having been made out of the trustee's own monies, and that he had retained the monies of the trust. Under this approach, the proceeds obtained from the mandatory sale of the unauthorised investments were taken into account, but the court ignored the hypothetical gain these investments could have made if retained until the date of trial. In doing so, the court treated as irrelevant what would have happened to the trust fund had the breach continued, as opposed to the state it would have been in had the breach not been committed. This approach is sensible, for a trustee who has breached his primary duty and hence put the trust fund at risk should not be allowed to mitigate his liability by blaming the loss on the court's order to sell an investment which he had no authority to make in the first place. Importantly, however, such a ruling falls short of a clear statement rejecting the but-for test.

Likewise, the refusal in *Dornford v Dornford* to 'inquire into the particular benefit that has been made [by the trustee]'[18] is explicable on the basis that the profits made from the misapplication are irrelevant to the relief of surcharging granted in that case. Accordingly, *Dornford v Dornford* cannot provide authority for the proposition that for the purposes of falsification, the court would not take into account what would have happened to the trust fund had the trustee performed their duty.

The second group of cases include those in which the court charges the trustee for income or profits that the trust fund could have made but for the breach. These are best understood as examples of surcharging rather than falsification. Although *Lewin on Trusts* does reiterate the duty of a trustee to 'make good the situation of the *cestui que trust*',[19] the cases cited there, such as *Raphael v Boehm, Dornford v Dornford*, and *Moons v De Bernales*, are not cases of misapplication simpliciter. They involve the failure of executors to follow an express direction to accumulate the trust fund and invest in, for example, Government bonds. The trustees either retained the funds in their hands or invested them wrongfully. As the observation by Lord Erskine in the Court of Appeal of *Raphael v Boehm* shows, when a trustee who has failed to invest is charged with the notional profits that would have been made had he done so, namely 4 or 5% interest depending on the gravity of his misconduct, the court is concerned with surcharging rather than falsification:[20]

> A trustee, directed to do an act, from which the *cestui que trust* will derive a particular advantage, not performing that trust, shall be charged precisely in the same manner, as if

[18] (1806) 33 ER 49, 49.

[19] L Tucker, N Le Poidevin, J Brightwell and T Lewin, *Lewin on Trusts*, 19th edn (London, Sweet & Maxwell, 2015) 633–634.

[20] *Raphael* (1807) (n14) 348. If the trustee's mistake is negligent or excusable, interest would be 4% (*Bruere v Pemberton* (1806) 33 ER 146; if the assets are used for the trustee's personal profits or lost due to gross mismanagement, interest would be at 5% (*Raphael* (1805) (n 14)).

> he had performed it. Lord Eldon [at first instance] says, he shall not be permitted to go back, and account, as if he had invested the property according to his trust. Certainly a trustee cannot be permitted to speculate in that manner instead of performing his trust.

It is upon the same principle of surcharging that a trustee will be charged with interest on any sums misapplied. In *Norris v Wright*, where the trustees were supposed to invest in stock, but wrongfully invested in personal security, they were required not only to restore the misapplied amount, but the amount that the sum would have produced had it been invested in stock.[21] The focus here is upon what *income* could have been generated from the specific property that was misapplied—not whether part or all of the misapplied property would have been depleted in any event, as in *AIB Group*.

The third and most relevant group of cases are those where the trustee was required to replace the misapplied trust fund even though it would have been lost due to the wrongdoing of a third party or as a natural consequence of the strict performance of the trustee's duty. In *Magnus v Queensland National Bank*, a bank wrongfully placed funds with only one of the trustees who then absconded with the sum, and the bank argued that the trust fund would have been lost anyway due to the negligence of the co-trustees.[22] Bowen LJ did make a broad statement that if the lack of authority 'is made out, then the loss occurred at the moment of the unauthorized payment', and Lord Halsbury LC said the court is 'not at liberty to speculate whether the same result might not have followed whether the [defendant] had been guilty of that default'.[23] Nonetheless, the facts are more circumscribed, and involved the plea by a defaulting trustee to be exonerated from responsibility because a *third party* would have caused the loss to the trust fund anyway.

Inevitable loss arising from third party wrongdoing also arose in *Gibbins v Taylor*[24] and *Clough v Bond*,[25] where funds were wrongly placed in the control of a surviving trustee or co-administrator who misappropriated them. The respective courts found the defaulting parties liable notwithstanding their argument that the third party could have caused the same loss had the trust been properly performed.

However, none of these cases provides direct authority for the proposition that the court will not take into account defences that the disbursement would have been lost due to reasons *outside of* third party wrongdoing. This leaves *Cocker v Quayle*, which concerns loss that would have arisen as a natural consequence of the trustee's strict performance of his duty, as unequivocal authority for the irrelevance of causation.[26] In this case, the trustee wrongfully advanced a loan to the

[21] (1851) 51 ER 298, 305–306. See also *Holmes v Dring* (1788) 30 ER 1; *Perkins v Baynton* (1781) 28 ER 1022; *Adams v Clifton* (1826) 38 ER 115.

[22] (1888) 37 Ch D 466. The decision involves a defendant bank rather than trustee, but it can be assumed that the legal principle applies to trustees too.

[23] ibid 472, 478.

[24] (1856) 52 ER 1140.

[25] (1838) 40 ER 1016.

[26] Above (n 16).

life tenant's husband without taking any bond from him. The husband was subsequently declared bankrupt and the fund lost. In response to the trustee's argument that even if he had taken a bond, the same loss would have been sustained, Sir John Leach MR opined that a trustee could not be excused 'by reason of the subsequent event of the husband's bankruptcy'.[27]

But, as the following survey of the traditional account procedure will show, the lack of direct authority is due to the fact that redress secures actual performance of the trustee's primary duty, and not compensation for loss. Since causation is irrelevant to the former, equity has traditionally paid little attention to the issue.[28]

B. Performance of the Duty to Account as Opposed to Compensation for Breach

A brief survey of the traditional accounting procedure in relation to misapplication shows that it is concerned with replacing the misapplied asset and not compensating loss caused by the breach.[29] First, the trustee's duty to render account is not premised upon his breach, but his authorised control and possession of property belonging to another.[30] Hence, once the relation of trustee and beneficiary is established, the latter as the true owner of the property is entitled 'as of right' to call for an account, of which there are two forms: first, an account of the property subject to the trust received by the trustee; and second, an account of such property, or that which might but for the trustee's wilful default have been so received.[31]

Secondly, the basic principle underlying falsification is specific enforcement of the trustee's primary obligation to perform what he has promised to do, namely to account for the fund. In answer to the suit for account, the trustee may plead in bar that the parties have already in writing stated and adjusted the account and struck the balance. At this point, the beneficiary is at liberty to falsify or surcharge the account stated by showing mistakes and omissions.[32] These disputed issues will

[27] (1830) 39 ER 206, discussed in Watts (n 5).

[28] DWM Waters, *The Law of Trusts in Canada*, 2nd edn (Toronoto, Carswell, 1984) 710–715, 745–749.

[29] For detailed accounts, see WS Holdsworth, *A History of English Law* (London, Methuen, Sweet & Maxwell, 1922) vol 6, 651–658; J Story, *Commentaries on Equity Jurisprudence*, 6th edn (Boston, Little Brown & Co, 1853) 606–609; CC Langdell, 'A Brief Survey of Equity Jurisdiction' (1889) 2 *Harvard Law Review* 241; EO Belsheim, 'The Old Action of Account' (1932) 45 *Harvard Law Review* 466. For recent literature, see SB Elliott 'Remoteness Criteria in Equity' (2002) 65 *MLR* 588; C Mitchell and Watterson (n 1) 115; Millett (n 1); J Edelman and S Elliott, 'Money Remedies Against Trustees' (2004) 18 *Trust Law International* 116; *Agricultural Land* (n 1); L Ho, 'An Account of Accounts' (2016) 28 *Singapore Academy of Law Journal* 849.

[30] *Wynne v Humberstone* (1858) 54 ER 165; JW Perry, *A Treatise of the Law of Trusts and Trustees*, 2nd edn (Boston, Little Brown & Co, 1929) vol 2, [822]; Langdell (n 29) 244–249.

[31] A Birrell, *The Duties and Liabilities of Trustees: Six Lectures* (London, MacMillan, 1920) 147.

[32] *Vernon v Vawdry* (1740) 26 ER 474; *Pit v Cholmondeley* (1754) 38 ER 360, 360–361 (Lord Hardwicke). Story (n 27) 605–607; PT Van Zile, *A Treatise on Equity Pleading and Practice* (Chicago, Callaghan & Co, 1904) 210–212. If there has been fraud instead of mere mistakes and omissions, the whole account shall be opened.

be referred to the Master, but significantly his investigation focuses on whether the charge is authorised, and not whether loss has resulted from the misapplication. If the Master finds that the charge is not authorised, it will be disallowed and the balance of the account will be struck on the basis that the disposed amount is still held by the trustee. In this process, disallowance (or falsification) is but an intermediate legal step to compel the trustee's performance of his primary duty to account for the trust funds.

The same basis of replacement rather than compensation applies where the trustee wrongly sells trust property. Here, the beneficiary has the right to elect to have the property restored (if it has risen in value)[33] or be paid the proceeds (if it has depreciated),[34] as 'the trustee shall never make the advantage when he could replace the stock at a less price than at which he sold it.'[35] It is irrelevant that the beneficiary has not suffered any actual loss as the court is not concerned with compensating losses. In *Re Massingberd's Settlement*, trustees sold stocks and reinvested the proceeds without authorisation, but the reinvestment did not cause any loss to the trust fund. In response to the beneficiaries' argument that they were entitled to replacement of the original stock (which had gone up in value) or its monetary equivalent, the Court reluctantly granted the beneficiaries' claim and required the trustee to replenish the specific stock that had been wrongfully sold.[36] Clearly, these rules are calibrated to compel the trustee's performance of his primary duty to maintain the trust assets. Where there is room to choose between different ways to replace the trust assets, the court is also motivated by the concern to deprive the trustee of any chance of profiting from his wrongdoing. The fact that the beneficiary may obtain a windfall as a result or has not suffered any actual loss is irrelevant.

Thirdly, the language of equitable debt in the early cases is not merely a label, but an appropriate characterisation of the award.[37] This is because traditionally,

33 *Mansell v Mansell* (1732) 24 ER 913; *Pye v Gorges* (1710) 24 ER 323, affirmed sub nom *Gorges v Pye* (1712) 3 ER 144. Restoration of the property may take the following forms: (a) restoration of the property *in specie*; (b) paying the value of the property at the date of the wrongful sale with interest; (c) paying the value of the property at the time of the decree, with the income that would have accrued from the property had it not been sold: *Vyse v Foster* (1872) LR 8 Ch 309, 337; see generally SM Wright, 'The Measure of the Trustee's Liability for Improper Investments' (1932) 80 *University of Pennsylvania Law Review* 1105, 1108.

34 *Pocock v Reddington* (1801) 31 ER 862, 865–866; *Bostock v Blakeney* (1789) 29 ER 362; *Bate v Scales* (1802) 33 ER 152.

35 *Bostock* (n 34). The same point was made in *Pocock* (n 34) 865: the trustee must 'answer for [his unauthorised act], with what he may be supposed reasonably to have made; and if he made more, he must answer for that too.' For a critique of the draconian nature of this rule and the suggestion that a damages-like compensatory award should be treated as sufficient satisfaction, see W Strachan, 'Compensation for Breach of Trust' (1918) 34 *LQR* 168.

36 (1890) 63 LT 296, 298 (Cotton LJ), 299 (Fry LJ). Similarly, in *Phillipson v Gatty* (1848) 67 ER 1067, where stock was sold (without breach) with a view to making an unauthorised reinvestment, the court insisted that the trustee not only restore the moneys obtained from the sale, but restore the stock sold.

37 *Ex parte Adamson* (n 2).

the accounting would be followed up by a decree for the payment of the debt.[38] The award could not be analogised to an unliquidated damages claim, which in any event does not lie even in relation to an accounting party at common law, let alone in equity and against a trustee.[39] It is unfortunate, therefore, that Lord Reed inferred from the switch to the unsatisfactory label of equitable compensation that the remedy necessarily involves assessing loss. His Lordship assumed that 'equitable compensation is to compensate' 'what has been lost as a result of a breach of duty', and 'the concept of loss necessarily involves the concept of causation'.[40]

The idea of 'equitable compensation' is of very recent vintage. It was used in the seminal decision of *Nocton v Lord Ashburton* in 1914[41] to denote the monetary award granted in equity for breach by a fiduciary, just as the word 'damages' is used to refer to the monetary award at common law. The concept of equitable compensation had only been employed in the context of *fiduciary* breaches (most famously in *Canson Enterprises Ltd v Boughton & Co*)[42] until the House of Lords in *Target Holdings v Redferns*, departing from the two lower courts, used the term in to the context of a breach of *trust*.[43] Since then, both litigants and courts have switched to the new label.[44] Yet just as common law damages can be gain-based, substitutive or even 'penal', equitable compensation is not necessarily reparative. The remedial approach should be consistent whether the beneficiary claims equitable compensation or takes account, for, as Lord Reed himself recognized, it would be odd if a litigant could improve his remedy for the same misconduct by switching to a different label.[45]

III. The Basis and Justification of the Duty Breached

Needless to say, knowing how the remedy was conceptualised in the past does not dictate how it should conceptualised in the future. Receptiveness to the orthodox

38 Langdell (n 29) 259; *Ex parte Blencowe* (1865–1866) LR 1 Ch App 393; *Vernon* (n 32). This should be distinguished from an unliquidated damages claim, which would not of itself be sufficient to support a petition for the trustee's bankruptcy: I thank Gummow NPJ for this point.

39 *Spurraway v Rogers* (1706) 88 ER 1489. The court has also warned against confusing the reconstitution of trust fund with the damages claim in *British America Elevator Co Ltd v Bank of British North America* [1919] AC 658.

40 *AIB Group* (n 3) [136].

41 [1914] AC 932.

42 [1991] 3 SCR 534.

43 [1996] AC 421, 439.

44 *Youyang Pty Ltd v Minter Ellison Morris Fletcher* (2003) 212 CLR 484; *Libertarian Investments Ltd v Hall* (2013) 16 HKCFAR 681; *AIB Group* (n 3); *Bank of New Zealand v New Zealand Guardian Trust Co Ltd* [1999] 1 NZLR 664 (CA). As observed by Davies, after *Target Holdings v Redferns*, a long line of decisions have continued to use common accounts to make good misapplied trust funds: *Knight v Haynes Duffell Kentish & Co* [2003] EWCA Civ 223; *DB UK Bank Ltd v Edmunds & Co* [2014] PNLR 12; *Madoff Securities International Ltd (In Liquidation) v Raven* [2013] EWHC 3147, cited in Davies (n 6) 683, fn 13.

45 *AIB Group* (n 3) [90]–[91] (Lord Reed).

position will ultimately depend on identifying sound policy justifications for it. This part of the chapter takes up Lord Reed's challenge to develop remedies based on the characteristics of the particular obligation at issue rather than its historical origin,[46] and examines the basis of the duty breached and policies justifying the orthodox approach. In particular, it seeks to show that precisely this line of inquiry reinforces the irrelevance of 'but for' causation in misapplication cases, at least as a default rule—but that there are circumstances where modifications are justified.

The duty at issue here is the trustee's fundamental duty to protect and augment the trust fund. A trustee who misapplies the trust fund exposes it to the risk of depletion, which is the very harm that he has undertaken as his primary duty to avoid. As Sir R P Arden MR stated aptly in *Pocock v Reddington*,[47] a trustee's misapplication of the trust fund:

> is a transaction that it is impossible to permit to pass without animadversion and without reprobating in the strongest manner… Trustee had no right to put the trust fund in that hazard. No man is justified in putting the property, of which he is trustee, in jeopardy.

By requiring the trustee to replenish the trust fund, equity is specifically enforcing the trustee's fundamental duty and providing the innocent beneficiary with the ideal remedy that fulfils his rights and expectation as, unlike compensation for loss, it does not transform his right into an alternative, second-best right. It is the same remedial policy that justifies the contractual remedies of specific performance and action for an agreed sum, namely that this is simply a logical extension of the innocent party's entitlement to performance.

Recognising this remedial goal allows one to see that the statement of Street J in *Re Dawson*—that the aim of taking account is to put the parties in the position they would have been in had the trust been properly performed—need not be interpreted as requiring but-for causation in misapplication cases.[48] This is because the meaning of the word 'position' in these judicial statements is ambiguous: it can mean the financial position of the beneficiary, or his legal position. The former requires ascertaining the detrimental consequence of the breach on the overall financial position of the plaintiff, which is often hard to establish without the aid of causal enquiries. The latter refers to his legal entitlement to the trustee's performance of his duty, which is readily discernible as it is what the trustee has promised to perform. Hence, the remedial goal can easily be satisfied without any causal enquiry: compelling the defendant to perform his primary duty logically entails that the plaintiff will be put into the *legal* position he would have been in had the trust been properly performed.[49] Lord Toulson may have overlooked

[46] ibid [138].

[47] *Pocock* (n 34) 865.

[48] *Re Dawson* (1966) 2 NSWLR 211, 216 (Street J); J Hill, *Practical Treatise on the Law Relating to Trustees*, 2nd edn (Philadelphia, T & J W Johnson, 1854) 522–524.

[49] The same ambiguity can be found in the recantation of this principle in the context of common law claims. It has led to the assumption that it only encompasses the compensatory principle, and not actions for an agreed sum and specific performance: D Winterton, *Money Awards in Contract Law* (Oxford, Hart Publishing, 2015) ch 1.

this important distinction when he assumed that the compensatory principle is dictated by the statement that 'the basic purpose of any remedy [is] to put the beneficiary in the same position as if the breach had not occurred'.[50]

The primary goal of specific enforcement renders irrelevant issues of causation. The subsidiary rationale of deterrence also reinforces equity's refusal to consider arguments made by the trustee based on intervening[51] or concurrent sufficient causes.[52] In relation to intervening causes, it is the misapplication or breach itself which puts the fund at the risk of being affected by the intervening cause. In relation to concurrent sufficient causes, such as the wrongdoing of third parties that would have led to the same consequence in any event, it is difficult to see why a trustee who fails to observe his fundamental duty should have the benefit of moral luck. As a matter of policy, allowing such arguments may also tempt the trustee to try his chances and resort to such arguments as an excuse to exonerate himself from liability. Considerations of deterrence also explain the beneficiaries' right to elect between restoration or payment of money, so the trustee will not be able to restore the property should it depreciate in value, nor keep it should it appreciate in value.[53]

The effect of these rules is to turn a trustee who commits a breach into an insurer of the trust fund. The rules can operate harshly, especially if the trustee has acted in good faith. For example, consider the case where a trustee who is supposed to deposit the trust fund into a designated trust account opened in a bank deposits the same into his own personal account at the same bank, which fails one day later. He will be liable to replenish the full amount deposited, even though he acted in good faith, and the same amount would have been lost had he performed the trust properly. If his personal account had an empty balance and did not have set-off facility, so that the funds were not exposed to any real risk, the rule operates very harshly. In a similar vein, suppose a trustee who was instructed to invest $10 million in a particular stock made a good faith mistake and invested $11 million ($1 million in excess) in a single transaction in the same stock, which plummeted to half of its original value. Since the whole disbursement of $11 million is unauthorised, the trustee will be compelled to replenish it in full, even though he only exposed $1 million to risk that would not otherwise have been exposed to risk.[54]

[50] *AIB Group* (n 3) [64].

[51] Such as in *Caffrey v Darby* (1801) 31 ER 1159; *Fyler v Fyler* (1841) 49 ER 216, 223 ('but being unauthorized and a subsequent loss (which could not have occurred but for the first deviation from the trust) having happened, the principals may be liable'), 224 ('became responsible for any future loss traceable to that first error'); *Kellaway v Johnson* (1842) 49 ER 601, 603 (trustees are 'answerable for any future loss, the root and cause of such loss being the original [misapplication]').

[52] That is, but-for causation, see *Cocker* (n 16); AW Scott, WF Fratcher, ML Ascher, *Scott and Ascher on Trusts*, 5th edn (Wolters Kluwer, 2015) vol 3, [205.1].

[53] Above (n 34).

[54] *Fry v Tapson* (1884) 28 Ch D 268. In the UK, s 9 of the Trustee Act 1925 used to limit the trustee's liability to the excess, but it was repealed in Trustee Act 2000.

In both cases, where the trustee acted in good faith, the investment was of a type authorised by the trust deed, his conduct did not expose the trust fund to any sensible possibility of jeopardy or any additional hazard, and he did not put himself in a position where he might be able to make a retroactive allocation of loss to the trust fund, it would be harsh to hold him liable for the full amount. It is submitted that the fact patterns of *Target Holdings v Redferns* and *AIB Group* are very close to these situations. In such cases where the sole and absolute beneficiary has already determined how the trust fund is to be invested, and gives instructions to the trustee from time to time, it is responsible for the causal structure that has made the depletion inevitable. The beneficiary should not be allowed to deny its at least equally responsibility in bringing about the depletion. In claiming that the trustee is, through its misconduct, responsible for the depletion, the beneficiary is seeking to shift its own responsibility to the trustee. Such a situation can be distinguished from one where the alternative cause is a third party's wrongdoing, where it is the trustee who attempts to shift his responsibility to the third party, and the beneficiary is not directly responsible for the acts of the third party. In theory the court has discretion to invoke statutory relief to reduce part or all of the trustee liability,[55] but if the inequity stems from the absolutist nature of the remedial rule, the better solution is to modify those rules and spell out the (narrow) parameters of an exception rather than to leave the matter to judicial discretion.

IV. Justifying the *AIB Group* Decision

AIB Group presented the UK Supreme Court with an opportunity to examine the underlying policies discussed above, and perhaps also to consider ways to address the potentially harsh effects of the orthodox rules. In this case, a conveyancing solicitor who held around £3.3 million loan monies on trust in a remortgage transaction was instructed to obtain a first legal charge by disbursing the necessary portion to redeem an existing mortgage before releasing the balance to the borrower. However, it mistakenly transferred around £0.3 million in short to the first mortgagee (Barclays Bank) and the same amount in excess to the lender, with the result that the lending bank's security was subject to the first mortgage to the extent of the shortfall. When the borrowers defaulted and the property was sold for about £1.2 million, the bank needed to pay off £0.31 million to Barclays Bank, pocketing only £0.88 million. The solicitor admitted liability and was willing to make good the shortfall, which would be the amount recoverable in a claim for negligence at common law. However, the bank claimed equitable compensation or

[55] See, eg, UK Trustee Act 2000, s 61. The extent to which s 61 can help a defaulting trust also seems more limited after *Santander UK Plc v RA Legal Solicitors* [2014] EWCA Civ 183, where Briggs LJ rejected the but-for test as excluding from the court's consideration unreasonable conduct that led to the loss.

reconstitution of the full amount of the trust fund disbursed, taking into account the offsetting benefit of the amount recovered from the sale. This would give the bank an award of £2.5 million, making it much better off than it would have been had there been no breach.

The Supreme Court rightly rejected the bank's claim, and both Law Lords who delivered judgments expressly declined to employ the traditional accounting procedure of falsification. Lord Toulson considered falsification an erroneous approach that made it 'necessary to create fairy tales',[56] whereas Lord Reed held it inapplicable to a bare trust created as part of the machinery of a commercial transaction that had been completed, such as the one in the present case.[57] Lord Reed also warned against 'clinging atavistically to differences which are explicable only in terms of the historical origin of the relevant rules'.[58]

Significantly, while their Lordships denied that specialist *rules* apply to commercial trusts, they emphasised the relevance of the commercial context in the *application* of such rules.[59] For Lord Toulson, the contractual background 'defines the parameters of the trust',[60] and may be a 'highly relevant' fact 'in looking at what loss the bank suffered by reason of the breach, because it would be artificial and unreal to look at the trust in isolation from the obligations for which it was brought into being.'[61] Lord Reed expressly agreed with Lord Toulson on this point,[62] adding that the assessment of equitable compensation should reflect the characteristics of the particular obligation breached.[63] And the particular trust obligation in the present case arose from a contract. Yet their Lordships were adamant that as a matter of law, the beneficiary should not be allowed to recover loss that would have been suffered in any event.[64] Lord Toulson went further, saying that in the circumstances of such commercial trusts, 'the extent of equitable compensation should be the same as if damages for breach of contract were sought at common law.'[65] These exhortations fly in the face of their Lordships' insistence that there are no specialist rules for commercial trusts. Moreover, their Lordships interpreted the fundamental principle of putting the beneficiary in the same position as he would have been in but for the breach as requiring the application of the but-for test,[66] holding that the same basis of assessment applies to the accounting procedure as well as to the claim for equitable compensation.[67] These observations

[56] *AIB Group* (n 3) [69].
[57] *AIB Group* (n 3) [91] (Lord Toulson), [134] (Lord Reed).
[58] *AIB Group* (n 3) [138].
[59] *AIB Group* (n 3) [70]–[71](Lord Toulson), [102], [137] (Lord Reed).
[60] *AIB Group* (n 3) [70].
[61] *AIB Group* (n 3) [71].
[62] *AIB Group* (n 3) [137].
[63] *AIB Group* (n 3) [138].
[64] *AIB Group* (n 3) [62], [64], [71] (Lord Toulson), [107]–[108], [139] (Lord Reed).
[65] *AIB Group* (n 3) [71].
[66] *AIB Group* (n 3) [64], [70] (Lord Toulson), [134], [140] (Lord Reed).
[67] *AIB Group* (n 3) [134] (Lord Reed).

depart dramatically from the orthodox view of the accounting rules laid down by earlier authorities.[68]

Adherents to the orthodox view have sought to justify the *AIB Group* decision without resort to but-for causation. They argue that when the claimant-bank was informed of the breach of trust, it had the option to falsify the wrongful disbursement and claim restoration of the full amount of disbursement, or adopt it and claim any shortfall between the benefits obtained from it and the wrongfully disbursed amount. On the facts, since the bank accepted a deed of postponement with Barclays, it could be treated as having affirmed the unauthorised acquisition of the second mortgage, so that it was no longer possible for the bank to claim the full amount.[69] This is certainly tenable as a matter of principle, and if it works, would obviate the need to resort to statutory relief or modify the traditional rules to avoid harsh outcomes. A beneficiary may give prior consent to, subsequent release from, or affirmation of an unauthorised misapplication if he is *sui juris*, has knowledge of all relevant facts that the trustee knew or should have known, and also of his legal rights, and the consent, release, or affirmation was not induced by improper conduct on the part of the trustee.[70]

The underlying principle is one of election of remedies in much the same way as a defrauded purchaser may affirm the sale or set it aside. The innocent beneficiary may also affirm the unauthorised transaction or falsify the disbursement.[71] But as with the defrauded purchaser he is expected to act with reasonable promptness once he knows all of the relevant facts, and is not permitted to acquiesce opportunistically, so as to affirm the transaction if the property purchased upon breach appreciates and set it aside if it depreciates.[72] In *AIB Group*, the defaulting solicitor owed a continuing obligation to replenish the trust fund. The procurement of the second mortgage would not have amounted to a replenishment unless it was affirmed by the bank.[73] AIB's acceptance of the deed of postponement with Barclays can fairly be treated as affirmation, hence precluding it from denying that the trust fund has been replenished at least to the extent of the benefits obtained from the second mortgage.

[68] Mitchell (n 1); Millett (n 1); *Agricultural Land* (n 1).

[69] See the suggestion of Lee (n 6) 100; Watts (n 6); J Penner, 'Falsifying the Trust Account and Compensatory Equitable Compensation', Ch 7 of this book; Davies (n 6) 682 (taking into account the conduct of the plaintiff). See also Millett J in 'Equity's Place in the Law of Commerce' (n 1) 226 mentioning the option to 'affirm or adopt' the disputed transaction or to falsify it. While adoption is the well accepted terminology in the agency context, it is a misnomer in the context of a breach of trust. The more appropriate legal doctrine is affirmation.

[70] *Re Patten* (1883) 52 LJ Ch 787; *In re Jenkins and HE Randall & Co's Contract* [1903] 2 Ch 362, citing *Power v Banks* [1901] 2 Ch 487, 496. See, in relation to a similar principle of consent prior to the breach, *Re Pauling's Settlement Trust* [1964] Ch 303, and a recent discussion of the doctrines of consent, ratification and waiver in *Barescape Pty Ltd v Bacchus Holdings Pty Ltd* [2012] NSWSC 984, [152] *et seq*.

[71] See *Long v Lloyd* [1958] 1 WLR 753.

[72] Scott, Fratcher and Ascher (n 52) [218].

[73] A sui juris beneficiary has the right to elect to take the replaced property: *Power v Banks* (n 70) 496.

Nonetheless, whether such affirmation can lead to the same result as that reached by the Supreme Court in the *AIB Group* is another matter, for much depends on the terms of the affirmation. The first hurdle, is whether the beneficiary is allowed to affirm the investment, which is worth much less than the amount misapplied, as *partial* satisfaction of the misapplication and also demand for the shortfall. In the context of *AIB Group*, if the bank were treated as having affirmed the second mortgage, would it be allowed to make any further personal claim for reconstitution? On this point there are conflicting authorities in equity. In *Thornton v Stokill*, when the trustee wrongfully invested the trust funds in real estate without the consent of the beneficiaries, the court held that the beneficiaries had the option to take the houses in satisfaction of the full trust amount wrongfully laid out, or have the houses sold for their benefit and claim for the shortfall if any deficiency arises on sale, but not both.[74] The contrary approach was taken in *re Lake*, where trustees who were held to have 'adopted' an unauthorised investment of £5,500 by entering into a compromise agreement for a lesser sum were allowed to claim for the difference between the two amounts.[75] *Thornton v Stokill* has been favoured by commentators who also happen to support the orthodox view of falsification,[76] on the ground that the beneficiary must elect between either adoption or falsification. Underhill and Hayton have sought to reconcile the two approaches by suggesting that if the beneficiary has made clear that he is only taking the substituted asset in part satisfaction of his claim for reconstitution of the trust fund, he should be allowed to claim the shortfall.[77] It is doubtful that the bank in *AIB Group* made this clear. In any event, the better view, put forward by Fox, is to treat the beneficiary as affirming the transaction only for the limited purpose of claiming part satisfaction of the amount misapplied, such that he is at liberty to recover the shortfall.[78] This will not render the trustee worse off than he already is in so far as the misapplied amount serves as a cap of the total amount recovered, but at the same time bolsters the protection of the beneficiary in giving him access to the assets purchased in satisfaction of his claim.

Assuming that the beneficiary is allowed to recover the shortfall in the misapplied amount after affirmation, the second hurdle is whether the shortfall is assessed to be £0.3million as decided in the *AIB Group* or £2.5 million as claimed by the bank. It was held in *Re Lake* that the measure of recovery will be 'the difference between the [amount misapplied] and the assessed value of the document of

[74] (1855) 1 Jur (NS) 751.

[75] [1903] 1 KB 439.

[76] J Penner, 'Duty and Liability in Respect of Trust Funds' in J Lowry and L Mistelis (eds), *Commercial Law: Perspectives and Practice* (London, Butterworths, 2006) 219. See also Mitchell and Watterson (n 1) 58, fn 58.

[77] C Mitchell, DJ Hayton and P Matthews, *Underhill and Hayton Law of Trusts and Trustees*, 19th edn (London, LexisNexis, 2016) p 1152.

[78] D Fox, 'Overreaching' in P Birks and A Pretto (eds), *Breach of Trust* (Oxford, Hart Publishing, 2002) 108, fn 38.

compromise'.[79] It was not necessary for the court in *Re Lake* to clarify upon which date the value of the compromise should be assessed, but this was relevant on the facts of *AIB Group*, where the second mortgage had only yielded about a third of the loan it secured. It is submitted that as a general principle, the affirmed investment should be assessed at the date of the affirmation, for this is the date at which the beneficiary treated it as partial substitution of the misapplied amount. In *AIB Group* this would be the difference between the £3.3 million misapplied and the (higher) value of the second mortgage at the time of affirmation, as opposed to the time of sale. Since these issues were not explored in the litigation, there is no information as to the value of the second mortgage at the date of affirmation. Nonetheless, the shortfall of £0.3 million is a good starting point, as it represented the additional value needed to redeem the first mortgage.

In the final analysis, justice could have been served in *AIB Group* by applying the traditional doctrines of falsification, albeit not for the full amount wrongfully disbursed, but only for the shortfall between this amount and the offsetting benefits of the second mortgage adopted by the claimant-bank. It would not have been necessary to abandon the debt characterisation of the claim, let alone assert confusingly that the well established principle, of putting the beneficiary in the position it would have been in but for the breach, requires a causal link between the wrongful disbursement and the loss.

V. Conclusion

Writing in 1889, Christopher Langdell remarked that 'the obligation to account has never been well understood by equity lawyers'.[80] More than a century has now passed; although equity lawyers have acquired a better understanding of the remedy, it remains shrouded in mystery. This chapter has sought to show, by a historical survey of the early cases and examination of the characteristics of the trustee's obligation, that both tradition on the one hand and the policies of protecting the beneficiary's expectation and deterrence on the other justify redressing misapplication by specific enforcement of the very promise that the trustee has undertaken. Such specific enforcement can be encompassed within the categorical principle laid down by Lord Toulson, that 'the basic purpose of any remedy [is] to put the beneficiary in the same position as if the breach had not occurred',[81] as the principle does not necessarily compel compensation of but-for losses.

The chapter also recognises that there may be situations where the remedy operates harshly on the trustee, and postulates qualifications where the trustee acted

[79] [1903] 1 KB 439, 443.
[80] Langdell (n 29) 242.
[81] *AIB Group* (n 3) [64].

in good faith, his conduct did not expose the trust fund to any sensible possibility of jeopardy or any additional hazard, and deterrence concerns are insignificant so that the balance of justice between the parties does not compel specific enforcement. In these situations it may be said that compensation of loss is sufficient satisfaction. While it was not necessary to deal with the need for such a new exception in *Target Holdings v Redferns* and *AIB Group*, which can arguably be explained on traditional grounds, the occasion may arise at some point in the future.

9

Accounts of Profits and Third Parties

JAMIE GLISTER

I. Introduction*

It is axiomatic that a trustee or other fiduciary can be required to disgorge profits made in breach of his or her fiduciary duties. That proposition is 'integral to the formulation of the fiduciary principle itself'.[1] But the position of third parties who are somehow involved in a breach of fiduciary duty, and who make a profit as a result of that involvement, is more complicated.

Sometimes, the third party and the wrongdoing fiduciary are treated as relevantly the same actor.[2] This can happen when the third party is a company that is controlled by the fiduciary. The company may be seen as the wrongdoing fiduciary's alter ego, with both the company and the fiduciary made jointly and severally liable for the whole profit made by both of them. In such cases the issue of accounting for profits is straightforward: the company will be liable to disgorge its own profits as well as those of its controller. But these are not orthodox cases of third party liability: the company is being treated as the mere creature or vehicle of the wrongdoing fiduciary; it is not being treated as a third party liable on its own account.[3]

This chapter is concerned with the position of third parties who are treated as conventional third parties; that is, who are made liable on their own account for

* I would like to thank Matthew Conaglen and Simone Degeling for comments on a draft, and Tatiana Cutts for discussion of many of the issues raised below. I am also very grateful to Newcastle Law School, UK, where I wrote part of this chapter as a visiting fellow.

[1] *Grimaldi v Chameleon Mining NL (No 2)* [2012] FCAFC 6 ('*Grimaldi*') [513].

[2] See, eg: *Gencor ACP Ltd v Dalby* [2000] EWHC 1560, [2000] 2 BCLC 734; *Trustor AB v Smallbone (No 2)* [2001] 1 WLR 1177; *CMS Dolphin Ltd v Simonet* [2001] EWHC 415 (Ch). *Cook v Deeks* [1916] 1 AC 554 may also be an example, but this was doubted in *Ultraframe (UK) Ltd v Fielding* [2005] EWHC 1638 (Ch) ('*Ultraframe*') [1574]. In Australia, see *Green & Clara Pty Ltd v Bestobell Industries Pty Ltd (No 2)* [1984] WAR 32; *Grimaldi* (n 1) [243]; but cf *Cornerstone Property & Development Pty Ltd v Suellen Properties Pty Ltd* [2014] QSC 265 [97]–[103].

[3] The correctness of this alter ego model of liability was doubted in *Prest v Petrodel Resources Ltd* [2013] UKSC 34, [2013] 2 AC 415 [31]–[33]; [68]. For discussion, see J Glister, 'Equitable Liability of Corporate Accessories' in P Davies and J Penner (eds), *Equity, Trusts and Commerce* (Hart Publishing, forthcoming).

their involvement in a breach of trust or fiduciary duty. Such third party liability is commonly referred to as liability in knowing receipt or in knowing/dishonest assistance. The central argument made is that accounts of profits should not always be available in response to knowing receipt: I suggest that the nature of the 'profit' being accounted for here is important, and it should not be assumed that a knowing recipient will be liable to disgorge discrete profits. This can be contrasted with liability based on assistance, inducement or procurement, where it can be argued that the ingredients of the wrong automatically justify disgorgement. In the final sections I also make some comments on the assessment of accounts awarded against third parties.

II. Proprietary Claims and Personal Remedies

There is an immediate difficulty with terminology when discussing gain-based relief and knowing recipients. The difficulty lies in distinguishing accounts of profits from claims to property held by the defendant in which the plaintiff asserts an equitable interest. The latter can be seen as 'proprietary' claims, whereas accounts of profits are 'personal' in nature; but the two are not always easy to separate.

In the discussion below I make two linked points. First, I show that the term 'profits' is used in this context to mean different things. Sometimes it simply describes a situation where goods acquired by a defendant from a wrongdoing trustee or fiduciary have risen in value since the defendant's receipt of them. More precisely, the term identifies discrete assets that a defendant has acquired because of a breach of trust or fiduciary duty, but which are not subject to a proprietary claim by the beneficiary or principal because they are not the traceable substitutes of assets lost to the beneficiary or principal. I suggest that the type of profits in question is important, but that the distinction is not at all clear in cases of knowing receipt.[4]

Second, even where the 'profits' are simply increases in value of assets that can be subject to a proprietary claim, the remedy granted by a court may be a personal award of an amount of money. These awards are simply judicial substitutes for proprietary relief, and the situations in which they may be awarded are considered in more detail below. But the essential point is as follows. If the traceable

[4] A further complication exists because, when used in a strict accounting sense, 'profit' cannot necessarily be equated with 'gain' or 'benefit' and still less with 'receipts' used as a noun. See *Ultraframe* (n 2) [1471]: 'the concept of a profit is an accounting concept; it is not itself an identifiable asset, although it may be represented by an identifiable asset'. This chapter is concerned with initial liability to account in respect of discrete gains/benefits/receipts acquired as a result of the receipt of trust property. It is not concerned with the allowances that may be brought into the account to reduce the net disgorgeable profit.

assets have risen in value since receipt, and a personal award is made calculated on the current value, then that award may be called an account of profits. However, we should recognise that this account of profits is not necessarily a remedy for a wrong. It may even be that such awards can be made when the recipient is not subject to any personal liability at all. These awards do not tell us much about when awards of discrete profits can be made against people who *are* wrongdoers.

A. Traceable Profits and Discrete Profits

Money or other assets misdirected to a third party in breach of trust or fiduciary duty may, of course, be put to gainful use by the recipient. A plaintiff may be able to make a proprietary claim over those goods. Generally speaking, a wronged beneficiary can assert a proportionate ownership share in substitute goods bought with money held on trust for him or her, and this is true regardless of whether the value of those substitutes has risen, fallen or remained steady.

It is not always easy to distinguish between (i) an existing asset rising in value; (ii) accretions to existing assets; and (iii) discrete profits made as a result of the existence of an asset. Clearly, houses or shares can rise (or fall) in value. These situations are examples of type (i). The owners of houses may also receive rent payments, or the owners of shares may receive dividends. These might be seen as examples of type (ii), because once received they will be seen for tracing purposes as an accretion to the house or shares. On the other hand, the right to receive a dividend might be seen as simply an incident of the chose in action represented by the share. It may therefore be likened to interest 'added' to a bank account; although we know that in the case of bank accounts the chose in action against the bank remains the same throughout.

While it can be difficult to distinguish between type (i) and type (ii) situations, at least it is clear that tracing can apply to both, and a proprietary claim may be available in respect of the asset and its accretions.[5] That claim may not be available if certain facts cannot be proved, and it may be that an award is limited for discretionary reasons.[6] But the point is that tracing is possible and a claim might then be brought. At least on an orthodox approach to tracing, this means that the plaintiff is asserting a proprietary interest in the relevant asset. The plaintiff is saying that the relevant asset is *not* a profit genuinely made by the defendant for himself or herself.

The profits in type (iii) situations, however, are not traceable. These are discrete, independent profits that can factually be tied to a breach of trust or fiduciary duty,

[5] I am here eliding claims based on breach of trust, where there is an extant equitable interest, and claims based on breach of fiduciary duty, where there is not. I return to this point below, text associated with n 11.

[6] See below, text associated with n 24.

in that they would not otherwise have been made, but where the profit is not subject to a proprietary claim by the beneficiary. Consider this example:

> A trustee pays money to a third party in breach of trust. The recipient is a little suspicious of the gift, so places the money in a separate interest-bearing account and does not make any withdrawals. Because of the presence of those funds, the recipient's bank lends money to the recipient at a more advantageous interest rate than would otherwise have been offered. This enables the recipient to buy a nicer house, which appreciates more rapidly. Throughout, the trust money is still sitting in the separate account, earning interest.

The interest that is earned on the bank account is clearly traceable, but the recipient has benefited through the mere presence of the trust money. Assuming liability in knowing receipt,[7] is the recipient liable to account for the gain made by borrowing money from the bank at the lower rate? Is she liable for the increased gain made by buying a house that has appreciated more rapidly than others she could have bought? Is she liable for the entire increase in value of her newly-bought house?

Again, I do not suggest that the distinction between traceable and discrete profits is always easy to draw. Professor Smith gave the following example:

> Assume that a thief steals a car and uses it to run a taxi service, earning a large profit. There might be some way to claim that profit, perhaps by suing for the wrongful taking of the car and seeking a legal response measured not by the plaintiff's loss but rather by the defendant's gain. That, however, is an issue of the remedies available for that particular wrong, and nothing to do with tracing.[8]

But can it not be argued that the thief is exchanging the engine wear on the car for the fares given by the passengers? On that basis the fares would be traceable. It is true that the car itself would still exist, but then so does the chose in action against the bank when money is withdrawn from a bank account. When money is withdrawn from a bank account, the chose in action remains the same although its value has diminished. The money withdrawn from the account can be traced, as can property later bought with that money. Isn't that what is happening with the car, too?

At all events, the purpose of this discussion is simply to show that the word 'profit' can mean different things. I will argue later that, while the ingredients of liability mean that profits made by assisters, inducers and procurers must always be disgorged, the same is not necessarily true in respect of knowing recipients. In other words, it is not inherent in a finding of liability for knowing receipt that the recipient should be liable to disgorge discrete profits.

[7] See below, text following n 37.

[8] L Smith, *The Law of Tracing* (Oxford, Oxford University Press, 1997) 156; cited with approval in *Ultraframe* (n 2) [1472].

B. Personal Awards to Quell Controversies

At least in Australia, personal relief can be granted in preference to proprietary relief if a personal award is the appropriate way to 'quell the controversy'.[9] A personal award might therefore be made even though a tracing exercise had successfully identified assets in respect of which a proprietary claim could lie. The point made in this section is that such personal awards should not unthinkingly be called accounts of profits. This is because proprietary claims can be made in respect of assets in a defendant's hands without alleging fault on the part of that defendant. Of course, the defendant in a proprietary claim will often be personally at fault (and so, in this context, will be liable for knowing receipt). Indeed, the cases that discuss awarding personal relief in preference to proprietary relief have so far all involved wrongdoing defendants.[10] But this wrongdoing is not necessary for a proprietary claim to lie, and it is not clear that wrongdoing must be present before the court's ability to award personal relief is enlivened. If anything, it could be argued that the court should be *more* readily able to award personal relief as an alternative when the defendant is an innocent volunteer.

At this point it is necessary to distinguish between claims based on breach of trust and those based on breach of fiduciary duty. In cases of breach of trust, the beneficiary has a prior equitable interest in the trust property that is not overreached by a valid transfer or extinguished by sale to a bona fide purchaser for value without notice. By tracing or following, the beneficiary may be able to assert that interest against goods in the hands of an innocent defendant.

The position in respect of breaches of fiduciary duty (most obviously, corporate property cases) is more complicated. Here, it used to be said that an entitlement to trace was provided by the property being held subject to fiduciary duties. It now appears common to say that the requisite 'proprietary base' is provided by the recipient's knowledge of the wrongful transfer.[11] This knowledge creates an equitable interest in the principal. Under this approach, however, it is easy to conflate the points of entitlement to trace with entitlement to remedy. If a director misdirects company money to her husband, who is aware of the provenance of the funds, it can straightforwardly be said that he will be liable for knowing receipt. If the money is still traceable, he may be liable to a proprietary claim. But what if he subsequently gives the money to their wholly innocent daughter? If the money had come from a breach of trust, it would be traceable and claimable in her hands. Is it traceable and claimable against the daughter because it has been through the

[9] *Bathurst City Council v PWC Properties Pty Ltd* (1998) 195 CLR 566 [42]; *Farah Constructions Pty Ltd v Say-Dee Pty Ltd* [2007] HCA 22, (2007) 230 CLR 89 ('*Farah Constructions*') [200]; *John Alexander's Clubs Pty Ltd v White City Tennis Club Ltd* [2010] HCA 19, (2010) 241 CLR 1 [128]–[129].

[10] See the discussion in *Grimaldi* (n 1) [504]–[512].

[11] Eg *Clark v Cutland* [2004] 1 WLR 783; *Grimaldi* (n 1) [564]–[567]; *Credit Agricole Corporation and Investment Bank v Papadimitriou (Gibraltar)* [2015] UKPC 13 (although it seems the right to trace there was conceded).

hands of the father, and his knowledge created an interest in the company? Does the ability to trace and claim against the daughter depend solely on the daughter's own knowledge?

These questions do tend to answer themselves in large extent. In corporate property cases there is often no question of any traceable substitutes remaining, so the question simply turns on the recipient's state of mind. If the property has been dissipated, but the recipient was sufficiently knowledgeable before that dissipation,[12] the personal liability in knowing receipt remains. That said, there may still be differences between trust and fiduciary cases. In *Grimaldi*, the Full Court of the Federal Court of Australia said:

> So far as the recipient is concerned, it is its knowledge of the directors' misapplication of the company's funds, ie their breach of fiduciary duty, that can turn it into a constructive trustee and thus give the company its proprietary base justifying both following its property into the recipient's hand and tracing into its substitutes. ... The constructive trusteeship envisaged here is what Lord Selborne in *Barnes v Addy* described as that of a person who receives and becomes chargeable with the 'trust property'. ... If, then, a proprietary base sufficient to justify following and tracing corporate property turns critically on the court imposing a constructive trust on the property received (the company having no antecedent interest in it in the recipient's hands), the fundamental question becomes whether the court has any discretion not to do so. ... It may be conceded that a court would ordinarily as of course award proprietary relief against a knowing recipient where the property received (or its proceeds) was still extant. ... Nonetheless, consistent with what we have said earlier in relation to discretion and the constructive trust as a remedy—and it is being used as such in this context—we consider that, both as a matter of binding authority and of proper principle, the court is not obliged to do so. The circumstances may be such as to make it appropriate to leave the company to its personal remedies of an account of profits or compensation in equity.[13]

The Full Court was saying that, even in cases where traceable substitutes exist, and where the requisite knowledge exists (both to create the tracing proprietary base, and to ground personal liability in knowing receipt), the court may decide not to award proprietary relief. The comment was made in a breach of fiduciary duty case. The question is whether the analysis also applies to breach of trust cases where the proprietary relief sought is based on the assertion of a continuing equitable interest, and where that interest does not depend for its existence on the knowledge of the recipient. In other words, does the ability to refuse proprietary relief extend to institutional as well as remedial constructive trusts? This point was recently left open by the NSW Court of Appeal in *Sze Tu v Lowe*,[14] although it

[12] Knowledge is normally present at the time of receipt, but can be given later to someone who is not already an innocent purchaser and who still holds the relevant property: see *Agip (Africa) Ltd v Jackson* [1990] Ch 265, 291 (appeal dismissed [1991] Ch 547).

[13] *Grimaldi* (n 1) [564]–[567] (references omitted).

[14] [2014] NSWCA 462 [157]–[158]. See also K Mason, 'Deconstructing constructive trusts in Australia' (2010) 4 *Journal of Equity* 98, 109–111; M Bryan, 'Constructive Trusts: Understanding Remedialism' in J Glister & P Ridge (eds), *Fault Lines in Equity* (Oxford, Hart Publishing, 2012) 215, 235;

seems that the Court doubted an ability to refuse proprietary relief. If that ability to refuse proprietary relief does exist in cases of continuing equitable interests, it is interesting as a matter of principle because it effectively involves a forced judicial sale of the plaintiff's property. On the other hand, if the ability does not exist, there is a potentially stark difference in treatment between cases where property is initially held on trust and where it is initially held subject to fiduciary duties.

A further comment may be made about the *Grimaldi* passage quoted above. The Full Court referred to the plaintiff being left to its personal remedies of account of profits or equitable compensation. It is clear that those remedies are indeed available in response to knowing receipt (although I argue that there is more to be said on the availability of accounts of profits). But, as remedies for wrongs, it is not clear that they are available in the absence of fault-based liability. So far we have been discussing cases where there are traceable substitutes *and* personal fault. The question raised was whether the court can refuse proprietary relief in breach of trust cases as well as in breach of fiduciary duty cases. But, at least in breach of trust cases, it is possible to make a proprietary claim against a recipient *without* alleging fault on his or her part. This is because the beneficiary's initial equitable interest still binds the traceable substitute asset, regardless of fault. Is the court able to substitute a personal remedy for a proprietary one even here?

One answer to this question is that proprietary liability cannot exist in the absence of personal liability, since the defendant is given knowledge of the plaintiff's interest when the plaintiff brings his or her claim. If the relevant property is still traceable in the defendant's hands, which it must be for proprietary liability to exist, then the knowledge fixes the defendant with accompanying personal liability.[15] That may indeed be the solution, but it simply shifts the problem further down the line. What is the extent of that personal liability? If the recipient made discrete profits *before* receiving knowledge of the plaintiff's claim, it would seem very harsh indeed to require disgorgement of those profits. Allsop P addressed exactly this point in *Heperu v Belle*:

> To call the volunteer recipient a constructive trustee and to call upon him or her to account as a constructive trustee (because he or she upon discovery of the fund or asset belonging to another has become one) does not mean the volunteer comes under personal liabilities, independently of, or beyond, the obligation to restore the fund or asset and any attendant obligation.[16]

RP Austin, 'Constructive Trusts' in PD Finn (ed), *Essays in Equity* (Sydney, Lawbook Co, 1985) 196, 240: 'a proprietary remedy should not ever be regarded as mandatory'.

15 It might be better to say that the recipient can thenceforth only deal with the property in a manner consistent with the trust, *on pain of* personal liability: see *Karak Rubber Co Ltd v Burden (No 2)* [1972] 1 WLR 602, 632.

16 [2009] NSWCA 252 [154], and see also [163]. At [145] the Court also found a concurrent personal liability to exist at law, which again reflected 'the measure of the value surviving in the hands of an innocent voluntary recipient when notice of the claim is received, rather than the measure of value received'.

In conclusion; it may be the case that Australian courts can always award a personal remedy in these situations, either because personal liability will always exist, or because of a general ability to award less-invasive remedies even in cases that involve continuing equitable interests. Where the value of assets has risen since the defendant's acquisition of them, it is also likely that such awards will be called accounts of profits. But attention should be paid to the meaning of 'profit' here. We are dealing with personal awards that are essentially substitutes for proprietary awards. To the extent that an 'account of profits' describes a personal remedy calculated on the increased value of traceable property in a defendant's hands, it can be distinguished from *discrete* profits that are made by the defendant but not traceable by the plaintiff. It should not be assumed that discrete profits are recoverable just because traceable ones are.

III. Accounts of Profits and Knowing Receipt

If traceable property is still in the hands of a knowing recipient, a remedy will lie in respect of those assets. That remedy might be proprietary or it might be personal, as discussed above. If it is personal, it may be called an account of profits even though it is awarded in respect of traceable property and not discrete profits. The question addressed in this section is whether accounts of discrete, non-traceable profits ought to be available against knowing recipients.

While it is easy to find authority for the proposition that an account of profits may be awarded against a knowing recipient, it is harder to work out whether such an account would include discrete as well as traceable profits. In *Grimaldi*, the Full Court said that 'the recipient can be required to pay compensation for loss arising from the misapplication of the trust property, or to account for gains made from it'.[17] However, it seems that the profits in that case were traceable:

> We have, for discretionary reasons, refused to give Chameleon full proprietary relief by way of a proportionate interest in the tenements themselves. Nonetheless, Chameleon is entitled by way of a personal remedy to the benefit they provided to the extent that those benefits were referable to Chameleon's proportionate contribution to their acquisition and to the rights they gave to ownership of, and to take, remove and dispose of, minerals mined from the leased land.[18]

[17] *Grimaldi* (n 1) [253], [555]. See also *Super 1000 Pty Ltd v Pacific General Securities Ltd* [2008] NSWSC 1222 [133]–[134].

[18] *Grimaldi* (n 1) [727], re the award made against Murchison. Also see [740], re the award made against Winterfall: 'the benefit/profit to which Chameleon was entitled was its proportionate share in the net profits (providing the proportion itself was identifiable) from ore found, extracted, transported and marketed and sold which had been, *or would be*, extracted over the life of the Project less the costs of finding, etc that ore and, arguably, less any such allowance as Winterfall would be allowed for its skills and risk taking and for its exertion in finding, etc, the ore' (original emphasis). The Full Court did not actually award any accounts of profits, and instead remitted the point to the trial judge. But

A different approach was taken in the English case of *Ultraframe (UK) Ltd v Fielding*.[19] There, Lewison J held that business profits could not be the subject of a proprietary claim: 'a proprietary remedy is not available in the case of an alleged misappropriation of a business (as opposed to a proprietary claim to shares in a company or to a specific business asset, including an intangible but proprietary asset)'.[20] But although it was not possible to *trace* into business profits, those profits could still be disgorged through the mechanism of an account of profits:

> In addition to the proprietary remedy (if it is still available) the claimant has a personal remedy for an account against the knowing recipient. Obviously, the personal remedy depends on establishing knowing receipt, but it does not depend on retention. Indeed it is needed precisely where the recipient has not retained the property. In addition, the personal remedy requires the knowing recipient to account for any benefit he has received or acquired as a result of the knowing receipt.[21]

I mentioned above that the dividing line between traceable and discrete profits is not easy to draw. Here, we see the additional complication that the same type of profit may be seen as traceable in Australia and discrete in England. The English approach is to take a 'hard-nosed'[22] view of property rights, and therefore a narrow approach to tracing. In *Ultraframe*, Lewison J thought it paradoxical to, on one hand, permit the claimant to trace and make a proprietary claim, and, on the other, allow the fiduciary an allowance for care and skill.[23] In Australia, by contrast, *Grimaldi* suggests that a wider approach to tracing can be permitted while still recognising that the court can prevent inequitable results. In Australia, the tracing question in this context is 'Are these assets in the defendant's hands sufficiently linked to the plaintiff's original assets that a remedial constructive trust could be declared over them?'[24] In *Grimaldi*, the answer to that question was 'yes', but a trust was still refused. The English courts would view that result as internally inconsistent, since they would see any substitute assets as held on institutional constructive trust. Putting aside the remedial/institutional language,[25] we might simply say that the English courts are more reluctant to recognise an ability to refuse proprietary claims made over traceable property.[26] For this reason the

there is no doubt that the personal remedy in play was an account of profits, even though those profits were traceable.

[19] *Ultraframe* (n 2).

[20] ibid [1547].

[21] ibid [1577].

[22] *Foskett v McKeown* [2001] 1 AC 102, 109.

[23] *Ultraframe* (n 2) [1542].

[24] cf P Ridge, 'Constructive Trusts, Accessorial Liability and Judicial Discretion' in E Bant and M Bryan (eds), *Principles of Proprietary Remedies* (Sydney, LawBook Co, 2013) 73, 87.

[25] See Lord Neuberger, 'The Remedial Constructive Trust—Fact or Fiction' (speech delivered to BSFLA conference, 10 August 2014) [22], questioning whether at least some Australian remedial constructive trusts are really institutional; cf *Wambo Coal Pty Ltd v Ariff* [2007] NSWSC 589 [42].

[26] See *Foskett v McKeown* [2001] 1 AC 102, 109: 'There is no discretion vested in the court'; Neuberger (n 25) [26]: 'property rights are a matter of strict law'.

limiting work on these claims is done at the tracing stage in England, whereas in Australia it can be done at the remedy stage.

None of this difference in treatment is problematic in itself, but it does provide a further reason for taking care when discussing the availability of accounts of profits against knowing recipients. Indeed, if it is true that a wider approach to tracing is taken in Australia, with the limiting work being done at the remedy stage, then Australian profits that are discrete and non-traceable will probably be quite remote from the initial money or goods. This provides a reason for not assuming that those profits will be recoverable simply by dint of them having been made by a knowing recipient.

A. Levels of Fault and Types of Conduct

A person can be liable for knowing receipt while exhibiting only a relatively low level of fault: in Australia, the requisite level of knowledge on the recipient's part is probably level (iv) of the *Baden* scale.[27] However, while a low level of fault may be appropriate when the question is whether or not to make the recipient liable for the value of the received assets, it is suggested that it does not automatically follow that the same threshold should apply when the question involves the disgorgement of discrete gains.

In an essay published in 1998, Lord Nicholls made this point in the context of advocating strict liability for receipt.[28] He argued that receipt-based liability ought to be strict, but that fault, by which he meant conduct which an honest person would regard as dishonest behaviour,[29] ought to be the basis for anything beyond restitution of the initial value. There might be little point in Australia in arguing for the former proposition, given the *Farah Constructions* case.[30] However, it is still worth discussing the latter.

[27] See *Grimaldi* (n 1) [263]–[270]; See also *Horsman v MG Kailis Pty Ltd* [2009] WASC 166 [112]; *Westpac Banking Corporation v The Bell Group Ltd (in liq) (No 3)* [2012] WASCA 157 [2127]–[2130]; M Bryan, 'Notice and knowledge in private law claims' (2009) 3 J Eq 204.

[28] D Nicholls, 'Knowing Receipt: The Need for a New Landmark' in W Cornish et al (eds), *Restitution Past, Present and Future* (Oxford, Hart Publishing, 1998) 231. See also P Birks, *Unjust Enrichment*, 2nd edn (Oxford, Clarendon Press, 2005) 156–58; R Walker, 'Dishonesty and Unconscionable Conduct in Commercial Life—Some Reflections on Accessory Liability and Knowing Receipt' (2005) 27 *Syd LR* 187, 202; J Dietrich and P Ridge, '"The Receipt of What?": Questions Concerning Third party Recipient Liability in Equity and Unjust Enrichment' (2007) 21 *MULR* 47, 66; E Bant, 'Statute and Common Law: Interaction and Influence in Light of the Principle of Coherence' (2015) 38 *UNSWLJ* 367, 382–85.

[29] Nicholls (n 28) 243, citing *Royal Brunei Airlines Sdn Bhd v Tan* [1995] 2 AC 378 (and writing before *Twinsectra Ltd v Yardley* [2002] 2 AC 164 and *Barlow Clowes International Ltd v Eurotrust International Ltd* [2006] 1 All ER 333).

[30] But see Bant (n 28) 384, and the sources discussed. A strict liability claim is seen as a possibility in England in DJ Hayton, P Matthews and C Mitchell, *Underhill and Hayton Law of Trusts and Trustees* 18th edn (London?, LexisNexis, 2010) 98.37–98.39 Also, and since this chapter was written, see *Great Investments Ltd v Warner* [2016] FCAFC 85.

B. Assistance, Inducement and Procurement

It is useful to compare knowing receipt with the other forms of *Barnes v Addy* liability.[31] It will be argued that the very ingredients of the offence justify the award of an account of discrete profits in respect of these other forms of liability, but that this is not so in the case of knowing receipt.

The correct classification of these other forms of *Barnes v Addy*-type liability is a matter of some debate, but the current fashion in the cases is to recognise heads based on assistance, inducement and procurement (in addition to receipt). It can immediately be noted that inducing or procuring a breach requires active conduct on the part of the third party. While knowing assistance can be committed fairly passively, the law ensures in two ways that only the more blameworthy defendants are caught. First, there will be no liability, regardless of knowledge, if the assistance given is so passive that it is not 'of a nature sufficient to make her an accessory'.[32] Second, the assistant's knowledge must include an element of dishonesty.

That last sentence may have raised some Australian eyebrows. Clearly, dishonesty is required of the assistant in England. In Australia, on the other hand, it is emphatically said that the trustee's design must be dishonest, whereas the fault requirement of the assistant is based on knowledge. But it is suggested that the point is more subtle, because it is not just that the assistant must have knowledge of the trustee's dishonest design; it is that the assistant must have knowledge *of the dishonest nature* of the trustee's dishonest design.

This point, admittedly, is far from certain and I have not found a case that expressly deals with it. The issue would only arise if the assistant knew only some of the facts surrounding a trustee's dishonest design, and those facts told of a breach of trust but not of a dishonest breach. Judicial comments that appear to support the point must therefore be treated with caution.[33] One principled reason to think that the assistant's knowledge must include knowledge of the dishonest nature of the trustee's breach is the requirement that the trustee's dishonesty be distinctly pleaded and particularised, even when the trustee is not being joined to the action.[34] Of course the dishonest nature of the trustee's design must always be *proved* before assistance liability can be grounded upon it, but the point here is that it must be specifically *pleaded* against the assistant. It must be accepted, however, that the line between objective dishonesty (not required in Australia)

[31] *Barnes v Addy* (1873–4) LR 9 Ch App 244.

[32] *Brink's Ltd v Abu-Saleh* [1999] CLC 133, 147; *Brown v Bennett* [1999] 1 BCLC 649, 659.

[33] See *Baden v Société Générale pour Favoriser le Développement du Commerce et de l'Industrie en France SA* [1993] 1 WLR 509, 575 (decided when English law still required a dishonest and fraudulent design, although perhaps not involving the same level of fault as the modern Australian law); *Hasler v Singtel Optus Pty Ltd* [2014] NSWCA 266 ('*Hasler*') [129], [136]; *Nicholson v Morgan (No 3)* [2013] WASC 110 [80]; *Andrews Advertising Pty Ltd v Andrews* [2014] NSWSC 318 [128].

[34] *Hasler* (n 33) [110]. See also *Farah Constructions* (n 9) [170]. The *assistant's* dishonesty need not be pleaded, because it is not a necessary ingredient of the wrong in Australia: *Ramsay v BigTinCan Pty Ltd* [2014] NSWCA 324 [55].

and objective knowledge of another's dishonesty (which I am arguing is required) may be rather thin.

In contrast to these other heads, knowing receipt can be committed wholly passively and does not depend on the recipient's knowledge including an element of dishonesty.[35] We should not be misled by the fact that in Australia level (iv) *Baden* knowledge is required to ground liability in assistance, inducement, procurement and receipt cases.[36] The conduct elements in those categories, and exactly *of what* the mental elements require knowledge, are important too.

C. When Recipient Liability Arises

At this point it is necessary to address the question of when exactly a knowing recipient will become personally liable in respect of the assets received. This is because it might be argued that a knowing recipient who, for example, merely deposits money in a bank account and does not make any withdrawals, like the example of the house purchase given earlier in this chapter,[37] has not actually done anything wrong.

In *Robb Evans of Robb Evans & Associates v European Bank Ltd*,[38] Mr Taves acquired $47.5m through credit card fraud. Of that sum, $7.5m was paid to an account at European Bank in the name of Benford Ltd. At the same time, European Bank paid an equivalent amount of money to Citibank to hold in an account in European Bank's name. Robb Evans, who had been appointed as Benford's receiver, argued that European Bank held its deposit at Citibank on constructive trust for Benford.

The New South Wales Court of Appeal held that European Bank was not a constructive trustee of the debt owed to it by Citibank. The Court decided that Benford held the initial $7.5m on trust for the defrauded credit card holders, but the deposit of those funds with European Bank did not involve a breach of that trust. This was because Benford was under a duty to properly invest the fund, and an interest-bearing account at a bank was an appropriate way to do this. It followed that the deposit with European Bank did not involve a misapplication of funds, so receipt of those funds by European Bank could not ground liability in knowing receipt.[39] Neither could the funds received by European Bank be further traced to Citibank.

[35] As it can be committed passively, Davies does not treat knowing receipt as a form of accessory liability at all: PS Davies, *Accessory Liability* (Oxford, Hart Publishing, 2015) 91–93, 104–08.

[36] Assistance: *Farah Constructions* (n 9) [177]. Inducement and procurement: *Australian Super Developments Pty Ltd v Marriner* [2014] VSC 464 [302]–[305]. Receipt: *Grimaldi* (n 1) [263]–[270].

[37] See above, text to n 7. I thank James Penner for raising this point.

[38] (2004) 61 NSWLR 75.

[39] Even if the deposit had involved a misapplication, the fact of receipt would still have been absent since the bank received only as a depository. Also, the requisite degree of knowledge may not have been present: see ibid, [152]–[162]. The final claim was for inconsistent dealing, the argument being that

As we have seen, Benford was a trustee and it was not a breach for Benford to deposit the trust funds with European Bank. But Benford was not an orthodox trustee; it was essentially a *Black v Freedman* trustee of stolen property.[40] The relevant question for the current discussion is whether the analysis that applied to Benford can also apply to knowing recipients; that is, can a knowing recipient be called a constructive trustee of the property received, and will it then follow that depositing the money in a bank account is not a breach of that trust? If so, it might be that simply accepting and depositing tainted funds is not enough to ground personal liability in knowing receipt (although those funds would be traceable and susceptible to a proprietary claim). The question of personal liability for discrete profits would not then arise.

Although this is a conceivable analysis, the preferable view is that liability in knowing receipt is grounded by the mere fact of accepting with knowledge assets transferred in breach of trust or fiduciary duty. Were it otherwise, a positively dishonest recipient who had simply banked the funds would escape liability in the event that the bank failed. This is because depositing the funds would not be a breach of trust, and a trustee who has taken reasonable care in selecting a bank is not liable if that bank fails. It is more appropriate to see the liability as being established when the funds are received with knowledge. This receipt with knowledge may be contemporaneous with the deposit, of course, because the funds might not be received until the credit appears in the recipient's bank account. But the recipient should owe a personal liability at *that* point, not at some later point of misapplication or dissipation.[41] This analysis is consistent with the comments of Lord Sumption, with whom Lord Neuberger and Lord Hughes agreed, in the UK Supreme Court case of *Williams v Central Bank of Nigeria*:

> The essence of a liability to account on the footing of knowing receipt is that the defendant has accepted trust assets knowing that they were transferred to him in breach of trust and that he had no right to receive them. His possession is therefore at all times wrongful and adverse to the rights of both the true trustees and the beneficiaries. No trust has been reposed in him. He does not have the powers or duties of a trustee, for example with regard to investment or management. His sole obligation of any practical significance is to restore the assets immediately.[42]

European Bank had dealt inconsistently with the money by moving it to Citibank. This failed because while informal reference might be made to the 'money being moved', in fact European Bank still owed Benford a straightforward debt in the amount of the initial deposit. This was 'full acknowledgement of the bank's obligation': [180].

[40] See *Black v S Freedman & Co* (1910) 12 CLR 105. In the *Robb Evans* case, Spigelman CJ described Benford as 'the Vanuatu emanation of the fraudsters': (2004) 61 NSWLR 75 [111].

[41] The situation is different when an innocent volunteer is given knowledge *after* receipt: see above, n 15.

[42] [2014] UKSC 10, [2014] AC 1189 ('*Williams*') [31]. See also C Mitchell and S Watterson, 'Remedies for Knowing Receipt' in C Mitchell (ed), *Constructive and Resulting Trusts* (Oxford, Hart Publishing, 2010) 115; *Arthur v Attorney General of the Turks and Caicos Islands* [2012] UKPC 30 [37]; *Agip (Africa) Ltd v Jackson* [1990] Ch 265, 291–92.

The *Robb Evans* case itself is not inconsistent with this position because the personal liability of Benford was not in issue, and in any event was obvious. The question was whether a deposit with European Bank was a breach of trust for the purposes of tracing into that bank and possibly remoter recipients. The question in *Robb Evans* was not whether Benford owed personal liability in respect of the deposited funds. *Williams* and *Robb Evans* may be inconsistent on the point of knowing recipients owing duties to invest, but that is an issue that goes to the measure of liability owed by an initial knowing recipient and to the grounding of liability in a subsequent recipient. It does not affect the point of *when* the knowing recipient's personal liability is established.

As a final point, it may be thought surprising to argue that a recipient with a relatively low level of knowledge will be liable if he or she deposits the money and the bank then fails. However, this seems more palatable than a dishonest recipient with actual knowledge *not* being liable in the same circumstances. In addition, it may be remembered that the knowledge formulation in England can take this into account, since it requires a level of knowledge sufficient to make it unconscionable for the recipient to retain the benefit of the receipt.[43] Finally, this point can only strengthen the argument that not all knowing recipients ought to be treated in the same way in respect of liability for gains.

D. Duties of Recipients

The innocent recipient of an asset transferred in breach of trust or fiduciary duty owes no duties in respect of that asset for so long as he or she is unaware of its provenance. Even if an innocent recipient is liable to make restitution of value received,[44] that still does not imply a duty in respect of the transferred asset itself. So, although an innocent recipient is susceptible to a plaintiff making a proprietary claim, he or she can dissipate with impunity until that happens. As Lloyd LJ said in *Independent Trustee Services Ltd v G P Noble Trustees*:

> The beneficial title of the beneficiaries under the pension schemes would still have subsisted in the money after the payment to [the recipient]. Therefore, she would not have had a defence to a proprietary claim by the trustee for the recovery of the money. Being innocent, she would not, on the other hand, be liable to a personal claim.[45]

A knowing recipient, on the other hand, is subject to duties in respect of the received money or goods. He or she must not disburse it,[46] and it may even be that

[43] *BCCI (Overseas) Ltd v Akindele* [2001] Ch 437.

[44] See above, n 30.

[45] [2012] EWCA Civ 195; [2013] Ch 91 at [75]. Note again the difference between breaches of trust, where there is a dormant equitable interest that binds the assets, and breaches of fiduciary duty, where there is not (unless, perhaps, those assets have already been through the hands of someone who was aware of the breach: see above, text following n 11).

[46] cf *Robb Evans of Robb Evans & Associates v European Bank Ltd* (2004) 61 NSWLR 75.

the recipient owes a positive duty to reconvey.[47] But the question in our context is whether the recipient also owes a duty not to make a discrete profit. We have seen that Lord Nicholls thought that the 'extended' liability of a knowing recipient—ie, beyond strict liability to make restitution of the value at receipt—should depend on objective dishonesty. It is hard to dissent from that view, in that intuitively a dishonest recipient ought not to retain any benefit—traceable or otherwise—that was made as a result of the dishonest receipt.

In a chapter published in 2010, Professor Mitchell and Dr Watterson approach the point from another angle and ask on what basis the law generally imposes fiduciary obligations.[48] Subsequent cases suggest that accessories to breaches of trust and fiduciary duty are not to be treated as fiduciaries in England: *Williams v Central Bank of Nigeria* decided this point for limitation purposes,[49] and *Novoship (UK) Ltd v Mikhaylyuk* did so in the context of accountability for gains.[50] Importantly, the court in *Novoship* held that even in the case of a *dishonest* assistant the calculation of an account of profits would be different from an award made against a first-party fiduciary. A true fiduciary must not make a profit out of the fiduciary position, and it is no defence to show that the profit could have been properly made. To put it another way, the making of the profit *is* the primary wrong. In contrast, the third party must account for his or her profit as a remedy for committing the wrong of dishonest assistance. A profit will not be disgorgeable if it would have been made notwithstanding the assistance or receipt. This is discussed further in part IV below.

E. Conclusion

None of this is to say that the conduct of a recipient cannot justify the award of an account of discrete profits. However, two points can be made. First, a recipient is not precluded by the fact of receipt from also being an inducer, procurer or assistant, and liability under those heads has been argued to justify disgorgement. Indeed, there may even be an advantage to pursuing a claim in knowing assistance in preference to one in knowing receipt if both are available. This is because, in England at least, an assistant can be made liable for all losses suffered as a result of the breach and 'it is not necessary to show a precise causal link between the assistance and the loss'.[51] But the same rules do not apply to those knowing recipients

47 *Arthur v Attorney-General of the Turks & Caicos Islands* [2012] UKPC 30 [37]; *Williams* (n 42) [31]; Mitchell and Watterson (n 42). One problem is that it is not always clear to whom the goods should be reconveyed.

48 Mitchell and Watterson (n 42) 144.

49 *Williams* (n 42).

50 [2014] EWCA Civ 908; [2015] 1 QB 499 ('*Novoship*').

51 *Casio Computer Co Ltd v Sayo* [2001] EWCA Civ 661 [15]; *Grupo Torras SA v Al-Sabah (No 5)* [1999] CLC 1469, 1667; [2001] CLC 221 [119]; *Madoff Securities International Ltd v Raven* [2013] EWHC 3147 (Comm) [339]. The position in Australia is unclear. It might be thought that *Michael Wilson & Partners Ltd v Nicholls* (2011) 244 CLR 427 [106] excludes this rule, and this view was taken

who cannot also be characterised as assistants: to use the old language, recipients are made constructive trustees of what they have received, whereas assistants are made constructive trustees of the original trust. The point is important because a wrongful disbursement of funds may cause loss far in excess of the value of the disbursement, and indeed in excess of the amount received by any given recipient. This could make an election for equitable compensation against the defendant as knowing assistant more attractive than an election for an account of profits against the defendant as knowing recipient. Second, the fact that some recipients may justly be required to disgorge discrete profits does not mean that all can be.

Putting these two points together, it is tempting to conclude that an account of profits ought not to be available as a response to knowing receipt. The degree of fault that justified a recipient being liable to disgorge discrete profits would, if it existed in a given case, render that recipient liable as a knowing assistant or even a de facto trustee. Writing about recipient liability in 1993, Professor Finn said:

> [An account of profits] should only be imposed on a third party who properly can be said to be a wrongdoer either because that person knowingly participated in the fiduciary's wrong or because, after the receipt, and not being a bona fide purchaser, he became so appraised of the fiduciary's wrong as would make him an accessory in that wrong if he continued to retain the property as his own.[52]

Although that position would perhaps be desirable, it is clearly not the law. Indeed, liability to account for profits for knowing receipt (albeit traceable profits) was found in *Grimaldi*.[53] But it may be that a more tentative position can be defended: it is suggested that the liability to account for profits should not automatically attend a finding of knowing receipt.

Before leaving the point, it is worth noting that this analysis will apply mainly to cases involving voluntary recipients. This is because, in the case of recipients who give value, it is likely that the recipient will only be liable at all in knowing receipt if he or she exhibits such a level of fault as would justify the award of an account of profits. Commercial actors do not need to make inquiries at all if the transaction appears to be a proper one, and, in the event that some inquiries are required, the answers are presumed to be honest.[54] For this reason, it has recently been said

in the *Hasler* trial decision: *Singtel Optus v Almad* [2013] NSWSC 1427 [280] (point not discussed on appeal, but note *Hasler* (n 33) [118]). But the point was not truly in issue in the *Michael Wilson* case, and *Almad* can be explained on the grounds that the third party did not relevantly assist in many of the breaches in respect of which compensation was sought. See J Glister, 'Knowing Assistance and Equitable Compensation' (2016) 42 *Aust Bar Rev* 152.

[52] PD Finn, 'The Liability of Third Parties for Knowing Receipt or Assistance' in DWM Waters (ed), *Equity Fiduciaries and Trusts 1993* (Carswell, 1993) 195, 211.

[53] See *Grimaldi* (n 1) [729]; and at trial: *Chameleon Mining NL v Murchison Metals Ltd* [2010] FCA 1129 [1036]–[1037].

[54] *Selangor United Rubber Estates Ltd v Cradock (No 3)* [1968] 1 WLR 1555, 1590; cited with approval in *Consul Development Pty Ltd v DPC Estates Pty Ltd* (1975) 132 CLR 373, 396.

that the proprietary defence of bona fide purchase and the personal liability in knowing receipt are likely to stand or fall together.[55] It is possible that a purchasing recipient could have sufficient knowledge to disentitle him or her from using the bona fide purchase defence, and to ground liability in knowing receipt, yet not be sufficiently dishonest to justify the award of an account of discrete profits. But it does seem likely that all three would go together. In the English context, Snell even suggests that 'where there is no [practice of making inquiries into title] and where transactions need to be concluded promptly, the defendant may need to be subjectively aware that he is receiving tainted property before his receipt could be stigmatised as unconscionable'.[56] If that is correct, then in England the basic liability and the liability to disgorge discrete profits would indeed go together.

IV. Accounts of Profits and Knowing Assistance

For completeness it is worth mentioning the position in respect of accounts of profits and knowing assistance. It has already been noted that genuine third party recipients, as opposed to alter egos, are liable for their own profits but not for the profits made by the fiduciary. The position is probably the same in respect of knowing assistants, but a little more can be said.

First, there is an argument that a knowing assistant ought to be liable for the fiduciary's profit. This proposition, which derives support from a line of Canadian cases,[57] has been examined and rejected in recent years by courts in Australia[58] and England.[59] It should be noted, however, that the Full Court in *Grimaldi* did suggest that for reasons of legal policy a fiduciary and a third party may be jointly and

[55] *Otkritie International Investment Management Ltd v Urumov* [2014] EWHC 191 (Comm) [83]. To the same effect *Armstrong DLW GmbH v Winnington Networks Ltd* [2013] Ch 156 [122]–[132]; *Credit Agricole Corporation and Investment Bank v Papadimitriou (Gibraltar)* [2015] UKPC 13 [33]. It is too much to say they are the same thing, as Lord Sumption appears to suggest. One is a defence to be raised by the defendant and the other is an ingredient of liability to be proved by the plaintiff. But it seems right to say that they will often stand and fall together. cf *Grimaldi* (n 1) [251]–[252].

[56] J McGhee (gen ed), *Snell's Equity* (33rd edn, Sweet & Maxwell, 2015) 30–072, referring to the knowledge test in *BCCI (Overseas) Ltd v Akindele* [2001] Ch 437.

[57] *Canada Safety Ltd v Thompson* [1951] 3 DLR 295, 323; *D'Amore v MacDonald* (1973) 32 DLR (3d) 543, 549; *Abbey Glen Property Corp v Stumborg* (1976) 65 DLR (3d) 235, 282; *MacDonald v Hauer* (1976) 72 DLR (3d) 110, 130; *Hanson v Clifford* 1994 CanLII 2982 (BCSC). See SB Elliott and C Mitchell, 'Remedies for Dishonest Assistance' (2004) 67 MLR 16, 40–41.

[58] *Glandon v Tilmunda* [2008] NSWSC 218 [108]; *Grimaldi* (n 1) [557]; cf *Hodgson v Amcor Ltd* [2012] VSC 94 [1718]–[1721]. See also *Agricultural Land Management Ltd v Jackson (No 2)* [2014] WASC 102 [480]; JD Heydon, MJ Leeming and PG Turner, *Meagher Gummow & Lehane's Equity: Doctrines & Remedies*, 5th edn (Sydney, LexisNexis, 2015) [5.270].

[59] *Ultraframe* (n 2) [1595]–[1601]; *Electrosteel Castings (UK) Ltd v Metalpol Ltd* [2014] EWHC 2017 (Ch) [50]–[51].

severally liable for their profits if they acted in concert to secure a mutual benefit.[60] An example of this may be *Andrews Advertising Pty Ltd v Andrews*,[61] where a wrongdoing fiduciary and his knowing assistant wife were jointly liable for what was treated as a joint profit. It may also be noted that the occasional tendency of English courts to speak of equitable compensation being awarded pursuant to a liability to disgorge profits may confuse things here.[62] In England at least, it appears that an assistant is jointly and severally liable with the fiduciary for the principal's loss.[63] But, if the fiduciary's liability to account for profits is referred to as a liability to pay equitable compensation calculated according to the amount of the profit, there is a risk that the assistant may be held jointly and severally liable for that amount.

Second, there may be several parties who have assisted in any given breach. Each will be liable for their own profit, but—as discussed above—will probably not be liable for the fiduciary's profit. I have not found direct authority on the slightly separate point of whether assistants can be liable for profits made by each other, but it would seem that again each party is only liable to disgorge their own profit (subject again to the plaintiff not being required to disentangle profits made by two parties acting in concert with one another).

In *Warman International Ltd v Dwyer*,[64] two companies that Dwyer created and controlled (ETA and BTA) were held liable for knowingly participating in Dwyer's breach of fiduciary duty. Those companies made profits through exploiting a business opportunity that Dwyer had secured in breach of his fiduciary duty to Warman International. While ETA might properly have been seen as Dwyer's alter ego, BTA was not, and Dwyer and the two companies were treated as independent actors. Nonetheless, the trial judge made a single order, against all three of Dwyer, ETA and BTA, of the combined amount of the profits made by ETA and BTA. The structure of this order was not challenged in the High Court, although the Court did make the following comment:

> It is arguable that any order, such as that made by the trial judge, for payment of a sum determined by an account of BTA's and ETA's profits should be divided into two orders, one against BTA alone for the amount determined by reference to its profits and the other against ETA alone for the amount determined by reference to its profits.[65]

This suggests that each assistant will be liable only for its own profits. Liability will be several among assistants, as well as between assistants and fiduciaries.

[60] *Grimaldi* (n 1) [558].

[61] [2014] NSWSC 318 [135]. In fact the 'profits' were funnelled through a company controlled by Mrs Andrews. Mrs Andrews' act of assistance consisted in making her company available for that purpose. Mr and Mrs Andrews were liable to disgorge the 'benefit' they received.

[62] Eg, *FHR European Ventures LLP v Cedar Capital Partners LLC* [2014] UKSC 45, [2015] AC 250 [6].

[63] See n 51 above.

[64] (1995) 182 CLR 544.

[65] ibid 569.

V. Causation and Gains

The assessment of accounts of profits ordered against fiduciaries and third parties may differ. This is shown by two bribes cases: *Fyffes Group Ltd v Templeman*,[66] and *Novoship (UK) Ltd v Mikhaylyuk*.[67] These two cases both involved dishonest assistants, but it is suggested that courts will view the principles discussed below as relevant to accounts of profits awarded against all third party wrongdoers.

In both *Fyffes* and *Novoship*, third parties bribed fiduciaries into setting up deals between the third parties and the fiduciaries' principals. In this way the third parties dishonestly assisted the fiduciaries to breach their fiduciary duties. The third parties made substantial profits on those deals, but in neither case was the third party liable to disgorge those profits. This was because the profits had not relevantly been caused by the acts of dishonest assistance, or by the breaches of fiduciary duty that those acts assisted.[68]

In the case of first party fiduciaries, it is the making of the profit itself that is the wrong: 'A fiduciary's liability to account for a secret profit does not depend on any notion of causation. It is sufficient that the profit falls within the scope of his duty of loyalty to the beneficiary'.[69] But third parties who assist in a breach of trust or fiduciary duty are not themselves fiduciaries. In *Novoship*, ship charterers paid bribes to Mikhaylyuk, the manager of a ship-owning company, who was responsible for negotiating charters on behalf of ship owners. The charterers made huge profits on those charters when the market moved in their favour and they sub-chartered the ships. But the Court of Appeal concluded:

> Mr Nikitin [one of the charterers] was not a fiduciary either as regards NOUK or the ship owning companies. He is not sued for a breach of fiduciary duty. He is sued because he has committed an equitable wrong. Where a claim based on equitable wrongdoing is made against one who is not a fiduciary, we consider that, as in the case of a fiduciary sued for breach of an equitable (but non-fiduciary) obligation, there is no reason why the common law rules of causation, remoteness and measure of damages should not be applied by analogy. We recognise that these rules do not apply to the case of a fiduciary sued for breach of a fiduciary duty; but that is because the two cases are different.
>
> We would therefore hold that there was an insufficient direct causal connection between entry into the Henriot charters and the resulting profits. We must stress, however, that had Mr Nikitin been a true fiduciary, and had entry into the Henriot charters been a breach of fiduciary duty, then the causation test we have adopted would not have applied.[70]

[66] [2000] 2 Lloyd's Rep 643 ('*Fyffes*').

[67] *Novoship* (n 50).

[68] ibid [114]: 'what Mr Nikitin acquired as a result of his dishonest assistance (and also as a result of Mr Mikhaylyuk's breach of fiduciary duty)…'. cf the position in respect of loss, where at least in England the relevant breach is the trustee's and we ask what loss flowed from the trustee's *breach*, not from the third party's *assistance*: see n 51 above.

[69] ibid [98].

[70] ibid [107], [115].

A question of onus arises in the context of a 'sufficiently direct causal connection'. Usually, a plaintiff at common law has to establish causation and loss. Applying this to the *Novoship* scenario, it seems that the plaintiffs would have to prove that the breach of duty was not only a 'but for' cause of the third party's profit but was also the 'real and effective cause' of it. That would involve the plaintiffs having to prove that the defendants would not have done something—after all, the point here is not that the principal has suffered loss; it is that the third party has made a gain. A more appropriate position might therefore be that the third party is required to prove that he or she would have made the same profit.[71] The arguments that justify gain-based relief being available at all against a third party[72] suggest that the third party ought to carry the burden of proving that the 'but for' measure of loss is inappropriate. The mere fact the third party is allowed to prove that point, and so reduce or eliminate the disgorgeable profit, is generous enough.

It will be interesting to see how this area develops, because one view of *Novoship* and *Fyffes* is that accounts of profits will be difficult to secure in cases where the plaintiff did not suffer a loss or in cases where the defendant would have made a similar profit in another way. The fact that the plaintiff did not suffer a loss can, oddly, indicate that an account ought not to be ordered.

The reason for refusing an account in *Fyffes* was that the relevant contract would have been entered into regardless of the bribe, and so the profits made under that contract were not legally caused by the breach or the assistance. To the extent that the contract price would have been different, that could be remedied by an award of damages.[73] No loss was suffered in *Novoship* because the ships were chartered at market rate notwithstanding the bribe, and in any case they would have been chartered to someone else if not the defendants. Again, this was a reason why an account would not be ordered: the profits made by the defendants were not profits lost to the plaintiffs:

> [T]he profits that Mr Nikitin in fact made were the kind of profits that the ship owning companies deliberately decided to forgo. In our judgment they cannot be described as profits which ought to have been made for the beneficiary, and therefore they fall outside the rationale for the ordering of an account.[74]

But if an account of profits will only be ordered in a situation where the defendant's profits would otherwise have been made by the plaintiff, this does not seem very different from a compensatory award. If the plaintiff would have made certain profits, but has not done so because of the third party's actions, then the

[71] Christopher Clarke J held that, even if that fact could be established, it was irrelevant: [2012] EWHC 3586 (Comm) at [530]. On appeal, it was apparently assumed that the charterers would have made the same profit.

[72] On which see P Ridge, 'Justifying the Remedies for Dishonest Assistance' (2008) 124 *LQR* 445, 452–455; T Ng (2015) 21 T & T 571, 576.

[73] *Fyffes* (n 66) 672.

[74] *Novoship* (n 50) [117].

plaintiff has suffered a loss. The only profits that would be disgorgeable would then be second-order profits, whereby a third party took an asset that should have been directed to the beneficiary (for which the beneficiary can seek a compensatory award), and then used that asset in a more fruitful way than the beneficiary or his properly-performing fiduciary would have done.[75] Even then the profits may not be disgorgeable. First, there would be a causation point. The breach of fiduciary duty may not be the real and effective cause of the gain, because the third party could show that he or she would have made it anyway (or the beneficiary could not show that this would not have happened). Second, the Court in *Novoship* also reiterated that an account of profits will not be awarded as of right in a non-fiduciary case: it may be refused if it 'would be disproportionate in relation to the particular form and extent of wrongdoing'.[76]

All this is rather speculative, of course, as the area is still very new. There will surely be cases where the plaintiff has suffered no or little loss and yet the defendant could not have made the gain without the breach of duty.[77] It will also be interesting to see how the English courts will balance these principles with their view of 'hard-nosed' property rights in a case involving receipt and traceable profits, but where the traceable profits could have been made in another way. In the usual English law of tracing, this does not prevent the beneficiary asserting ownership. Finally, it is worth highlighting that equity is here allowing counterfactuals to come in to the question of profit disgorgement.[78] Allowing the third party to raise a counterfactual here is not the same as allowing someone to prove, as a matter of fact, that certain profits *actually were* made from an untainted source.[79]

As far as Australia is concerned, it may be that courts do not take the view that third parties should be treated differently from fiduciaries. In the *Consul Development* case, Gibbs J famously said:

> The strict rule of equity that forbids a person in a fiduciary position to profit from his position appears to be designed to deter persons holding such a position from being swayed by interest rather than by duty; it is 'a rule to protect directors, trustees, and others against the fallibility of human nature'. If the maintenance of a very high standard of conduct on the part of fiduciaries is the purpose of the rule it would seem equally necessary to deter other persons from knowingly assisting those in a fiduciary position to violate their duty. If, on the other hand, the rule is to be explained simply because it would be contrary to equitable principles to allow a person to retain a benefit that he had gained from a breach of his fiduciary duty, *it would appear equally inequitable* that one

[75] By this I do not mean that a plaintiff could seek compensatory and gain-based awards against the same party; I mean that an account would only be available in cases where a compensatory award was also available. The smart plaintiff would bring both under the umbrella of gain-based relief.

[76] *Novoship* (n 50) [119].

[77] Perhaps the position of BTA in *Warman International Ltd v Dwyer* (1995) 182 CLR 544.

[78] cf the position of fiduciaries: *Murad v Al-Saraj* [2005] EWCA Civ 959. Counterfactuals are employed in fiduciary cases when the focus is on recovery of loss: see Matthew Conaglen's chapter 6 in this volume.

[79] See *Warman International Ltd v Dwyer* (1995) 182 CLR 544.

> who knowingly took part in the breach should retain a benefit that resulted therefrom. I therefore conclude, on principle, that a person who knowingly participates in a breach of fiduciary duty is liable to account to the person to whom the duty was owed for any benefit he has received as a result of such participation.[80]

More recently, however, Jackson J expressed a different view in *Cornerstone Property & Development Pty Ltd v Suellen Properties Pty Ltd*:

> In the context of liability for breach of fiduciary duty, whether by a trustee or another fiduciary such as a company director, it is rightly emphasised that the strictness of fiduciary obligations and the sometimes heavy burden of the relief which is granted to remedy a breach are warranted by the object or purpose of maintaining the high standards required of a trustee or other fiduciary, including a company director. But the liability of a stranger to the trust or fiduciary office to personally account under first limb *Barnes v Addy* liability is not as directly attended by that purpose or object. In my view, there is no reason, per se, why their position should be equated to the position of the trustee or fiduciary. I acknowledge, however, the existence of statements that tend in the opposite direction.[81]

VI. Conclusion

The central argument made here is simply that knowing recipients should not automatically be liable to disgorge discrete profits. This is because liability in knowing receipt can exist in a situation where disgorgement of discrete profits is not warranted, unlike liability under what might be called the other *Barnes v Addy* heads or liability as a de facto trustee. Several factors complicate the issue: the difficulty of distinguishing between traceable and discrete profits; the availability of personal awards as judicial substitutes for proprietary relief; and the fact that recipients may also be liable under other heads. But, for the reasons given in this chapter, it can still be argued that in the core case of a knowing recipient whose conduct cannot be characterised as anything other than mere receipt, and who has a relatively low level of knowledge, liability to account for discrete profits should not be assumed.

[80] *Consul Development Pty Ltd v DPC Estates Pty Ltd* (1975) 132 CLR 373, 397 (references omitted; emphasis added). See WMC Gummow, 'Dishonest Assistance and Account of Profits' [2015] *CLJ* 405, 408, approving this passage in a note critical of *Novoship* (n 50).

[81] [2014] QSC 265 [79], referring in the final sentence to *Consul Development Pty Ltd v DPC Estates Pty Ltd* (1975) 132 CLR 373 and *Zhu v Treasurer (NSW)* (2004) 218 CLR 530, 572. In the subsequent *Sino Iron Pty Ltd v Palmer (No 3)* [2015] QSC 94, Jackson J would have awarded an account of profits against a knowing recipient if the claim had not failed because the property was not initially held on trust. But that case has odd features and the defendants conceded the plaintiffs' sought remedies in the event that liability was established.

10

Monetary Remedies for Equitable Participatory Liability: General Principles and Current Questions

PAULINE RIDGE

I. Introduction

Participatory liability concerns personal, fault-based liability that is contingent upon the commission of another's equitable wrongdoing. It includes accessory liability (for procuring, assisting or otherwise facilitating an equitable wrong) and recipient liability (for knowing receipt of trust property for personal benefit in breach of trust or fiduciary duty).[1] A distinguishing feature of participatory liability is that, although the culpable accessory or recipient is liable because of his or her own wrongdoing, that liability is ancillary, or secondary, in that it depends upon wrongdoing by another (the primary wrong).

Until relatively recently, the remedies available for participatory liability have escaped scrutiny.[2] In the most commonly litigated scenarios—those concerning participation in a breach of trust or fiduciary duty—the remedy for participatory liability has usually been dealt with in a few lines towards the end of judgments that focus upon the remedies available against the defaulting trustee or fiduciary. The most that could be said was that the culpable participant was liable as a constructive trustee or, more broadly speaking, 'accountable in equity'.[3] Generally this

[1] In Australia, see *Farah Constructions Pty Limited v Say-Dee Pty Limited* [2007] HCA 22, (2007) 230 CLR 89 ('*Farah Constructions*'); *Grimaldi v Chameleon Mining NL (No 2)* [2012] FCAFC 6, (2012) 200 FCR 296 ('*Grimaldi*'). In England, see in relation to accessory liability: *Twinsectra Ltd v Yardley* [2002] UKHL 12, [2002] 2 AC 164 (adopting *Royal Brunei Airlines Sdn Bhd v Tan* [1995] 2 AC 378 (PC) ('*Royal Brunei Airlines*')); *Abou-Rahmah v Abacha* [2006] EWCA Civ 1492, [2007] Bus LR 220 (adopting subsequent clarification by the Privy Council in *Barlow Clowes International Ltd (in liquidation) v Eurotrust International Ltd* [2005] UKPC 37, [2006] 1 WLR 1476); and in relation to recipient liability: *Bank of Credit and Commerce International (Overseas) Ltd v Akindele* [2001] Ch 437 (CA) ('*Akindele*'). This chapter draws upon Joachim Dietrich and Pauline Ridge, *Accessories in Private Law* (Cambridge, Cambridge University Press, 2015).

[2] *Cf Lewis v Nortex Pty Ltd (In Liq)* [2005] NSWSC 482 [30] (Hamilton J).

[3] *Dubai Aluminium Co Ltd v Salaam* [2002] UKHL 48, [2003] 2 AC 366 [142] ('*Dubai Aluminium*').

meant that the participant was liable for the same remedy as that ordered against the trustee or fiduciary. In the last ten years or so, however, this has changed as the remedies available for various forms of equitable participatory liability have been relied upon to support competing theories as to the rationale/s for liability.[4] As well as academic commentary, there have been important judgments explicitly addressing the question of remedy.[5]

The purpose of this chapter is to address three questions concerning the monetary remedies for equitable participatory liability that have crystallised as a result of the recent commentary and case law. It is difficult to resolve such questions by resort to consistent case law that is directly on point because the principles concerning both participatory liability and its remedies are still evolving. Accordingly, the approach taken here is first to identify general principles that are of particular relevance to the remedies for participatory liability (Part II) and then, after a brief outline of accounting and compensatory remedies for breach of trust and fiduciary duty (Part III), to discuss the three questions with reference to the general principles (Part IV).

By 'general principles' I mean informing and fundamental principles that are consistently stated or implicit in the case law over time. 'Monetary remedies' refers to the court orders that result in a personal liability to pay a monetary sum and that flow from either:

(i) the procedure available against an accounting party for an account in relation to property;
(ii) a loss-based claim for equitable compensation in response to equitable wrongdoing; or,
(iii) a claim for an account of profits in response to equitable wrongdoing.[6]

These remedies are explained in more depth in Parts III and IV.

'Participatory liability' is used in this chapter as a generic label because of its usage in recent Australian cases[7] and because it captures the essential common denominator in accessory liability and recipient liability of culpable association with the primary wrong.[8] Jurisdictional differences concerning the formulation

[4] See, eg Steven B Elliott and Charles Mitchell, 'Remedies for Dishonest Assistance' (2004) 67 *MLR* 16; Charles Mitchell and Stephen Watterson, 'Remedies for Knowing Receipt' in Charles Mitchell (ed), *Constructive and Resulting Trusts* (Oxford, Hart Publishing, 2009) 115.

[5] See, eg, in Australia, *Michael Wilson & Partners Ltd v Nicholls* [2011] HCA 48, (2011) 244 CLR 427 [106] ('*Michael Wilson*'); *Grimaldi* (n 1) and in England, *Novoship (UK) Limited v Mikhaylyuk* [2014] EWCA Civ 908, [2014] QB 499 ('*Novoship*').

[6] Monetary orders accompanying an order for rescission of a transaction between the claimant and the third party defendant as a consequence of the defendant's participatory liability are not discussed in this chapter.

[7] See, eg, *Grimaldi* (n 1).

[8] Alternative labels that could be used are 'ancillary liability': *Williams v Central Bank of Nigeria* [2014] UKSC 10, [2014] 2 WLR 355 [9] ('*Williams*'); *Hasler v Singtel Optus Pty Ltd* [2014] NSWCA 266, (2014) 87 NSWLR 609 [72] ('*Hasler*') or 'secondary liability'. Each has its own limitations and the potential to cause confusion.

of participatory causes of action (for example, a requirement of knowledge in Australia and dishonesty in England, for accessory liability) do not affect the remedial focus of this chapter and are not commented upon. A distinction between accessory liability and recipient liability that should be noted, however, is that, in the case of recipient liability, the third party's 'participation' is not restricted to the time of commission of the primary wrong, whereas the concept of accessory liability requires involvement by the accessory before or during the commission of the primary wrong.[9] But for the purposes of this chapter, it will be assumed that it is appropriate to conceptually group recipient liability with accessory liability in this way. This grouping reflects the current Australian law;[10] the English courts also appear to be reverting to such a conceptual grouping by emphasising the similarities between accessory liability and recipient liability.[11] But in any event the conclusions reached here in relation to remedy are equally justified even if accessory and recipient liabilities are not conceptually grouped in this way.

From now on, the participant defendant will be referred to as 'D', the party who commits the primary wrong as the 'primary wrongdoer' or 'PW', and the victim of that wrongdoing as the claimant, 'C'. Whilst the law to be discussed here concerns the primary wrongs of breach of trust and breach of fiduciary duty, the same principles apply where participatory liability attaches to other equitable wrongs such as, for example, breach of confidence. The chapter's focus is upon Australian and English law, although jurisdictional differences and the nature of the subject matter make it dangerous to generalise. Consequently, the chapter's conclusions may have more or less weight depending on the supporting cases in each jurisdiction.

II. General Principles of Relevance to the Remedies for Equitable Participatory Liability

A. The Rationale and Purposes of Participatory Liability Determine which Remedies may be Considered

The rationale and purpose, or purposes, of a cause of action determine which remedies are available in principle, how they are to be selected and how they are

9 See also, Dietrich and Ridge, *Accessories* (n 1) ch 7.

10 *Farah Constructions* (n 1); *Grimaldi* (n 1). But see *Hasler* (n 8) [75]–[76].

11 See *Williams* (n 8) [9] (Lord Sumption); *Novoship* (n 5) [67]–[68]. See also *Dubai Aluminium* (n 3) [87] (Lord Millet); Lord Nicholls, 'Knowing Receipt: the Need for A New Landmark' in WR Cornish, R Nolan, J O'Sullivan and G Virgo (eds), *Restitution: Past Present and Future* (Oxford, Hart Publishing, 1998) 231, 243. But see Paul S Davies, *Accessory Liability* (Oxford, Hart Publishing, 2015) 92.

to be calculated where calculation is necessary.[12] Furthermore, an inquiry into the purpose of a cause of action necessitates judicial consideration of policy matters.[13] This fundamental principle is not confined to equity, of course.[14]

Often such an inquiry is unnecessary because the law is settled as to the cause of action and associated remedies.[15] But even then there will be instances where, although a remedy is clearly available, its mode of calculation in relation to a particular cause of action is uncertain. The remedy of equitable compensation is a case in point. An award of equitable compensation must reflect the character of the obligation that is breached[16] but, as current controversy surrounding its availability and calculation in relation to breaches of trust shows, it is not yet settled as to what this entails.[17] Hence, it may still be necessary to consider the purpose and rationale of the cause of action in order to finesse a remedy that is clearly available.

What, then, are the rationale and purpose/s of equitable participatory liability?[18] The rationale is simple: equity intervenes because of D's culpable (unconscionable) association with the primary wrong. The combination of D's conduct and D's mental state (generally, knowledge of the primary wrong) renders D's conduct culpable and creates a link to the primary wrong that justifies making D legally responsible for that primary wrong. The most pervasive formulation of this rationale across different forms of equitable participatory liability refers to interference for personal gain: it is unconscionable for D knowingly to interfere for personal gain with a relationship between C and PW that is governed by equity.[19] So, for example, in *Fyffes Group Ltd v Templeman*, it was said:

> although [D] owes no personal obligation of loyalty to [C], it is unconscionable for him dishonestly to suborn the loyalty of the agent [PW] and equally unconscionable for him to keep benefits which he has obtained by dishonestly abusing to his own advantage the position of [PW] whose duty was to [C].[20]

This gain-based, exploitation, rationale resonates particularly with recipient liability: the knowing recipient of trust property has taken advantage of a breach of trust for personal gain. In relation to the accessory form of participatory liability, however, the rationale for D's liability is sometimes phrased more broadly and without the emphasis upon personal gain.[21] For example, in relation to the English

[12] It could be said that 'purposes' and 'rationales' are the same thing. The meaning I intend to convey by 'purpose' is a rationale that has a pragmatic objective. *Cf* Pauline Ridge, 'Justifying the Remedies for Dishonest Assistance' (2008) 124 *LQR* 445, 447.

[13] *Canson Enterprises Ltd v Boughton & Co* [1991] 3 SCR 534, 85 DLR (4th) 129, 155 ('*Canson*').

[14] *AIB Group (UK) plc v Mark Redler & Co* [2014] UKSC 58, [2014] 3 WLR 1367 [92] (Lord Reed JSC) ('*AIB*').

[15] *Grimaldi* (n 1) [503].

[16] *AIB* (n 14) [138].

[17] See below, Part III.

[18] See generally, Dietrich and Ridge, *Accessories* (n 1) [8.1.3].

[19] See, eg, *Consul Development Pty Ltd v DPC Estates Pty Ltd* (1975) 132 CLR 373 (HCA) 397 ('*Consul Development*'); *Zhu v Treasurer (NSW)* [2004] HCA 56, (2004) 218 CLR 530 [121] ('*Zhu*').

[20] *Fyffes Group Ltd v Templeman* [2000] 2 Lloyd's Rep 643 (QB) 669 ('*Fyffes Group*').

[21] This is not to suggest, however, that the gain-based rationale does not also apply.

form of equitable accessory liability (dishonest procurement or assistance), it has been said that trust beneficiaries 'are entitled to expect that third parties will refrain from intentionally intruding in the trustee-beneficiary relationship…'.[22] Here, the gravamen of D's participatory liability concerns the knowing interference with, or disruption of, the trust or fiduciary relationship between C and PW that is protected in equity, regardless of whether this was for gain.

The purposes of participatory liability are reflected in its fault-based rationale and demonstrate the importance attached by equity to relationships of trust and confidence, particularly trust and fiduciary relationships. Thus, one purpose of participatory liability is to deter third parties from culpable participation and hence to make it more difficult for trustees and fiduciaries to commit equitable wrongs.[23] Another is to increase the chances of a successful claim for C by increasing the number of possible defendants.[24] Another is to encourage de facto regulation of trustee and fiduciary conduct by professional agents who may be able to detect and expose equitable wrongdoing.[25] Thus, by various means, participatory liability protects the integrity of trust and fiduciary relationships. Policy concerns are important here and may militate for, or against, the imposition of liability. For example, the courts may be concerned not unduly to restrict legitimate commercial dealings, not overly to burden professional agents, or not to outflank concurrent statutory regulatory regimes.

The current law concerning remedies for participatory liability accords with the rationale and purposes of the liability: D is potentially liable to the complete range of equitable remedies. This is what is meant by saying that D is 'accountable in equity' or a 'constructive trustee'.[26] Gain-based remedies are clearly consistent with the most pervasive formulation of the rationale for participatory liability, and their availability is supported by the case law.[27] This is discussed further in Part IV C. Loss based remedies are also clearly available and readily justified given the rationale and purposes of participatory liability. They are also coherent with the common law's most common remedial response to culpable interference with legal relationships.[28] But it should not be forgotten that a loss-based remedy may be extremely onerous—more so than a gain-based remedy—because D is made jointly and severally liable with PW for *all* of C's losses that result from the primary wrong.[29] That is, as discussed below in Part IV B, D assumes the same

22 *Royal Brunei Airlines* (n 1) 386–387.

23 See, eg, *Consul Development* (n 19) 397; *Zhu* (n 19) [121].

24 See, eg, *Royal Brunei Airlines* (n 1) 386–387.

25 ibid.

26 See, eg, *Dubai Aluminium* (n 3) [142].

27 *Consul Development* (n 19) 397; *Michael Wilson* (n 5) [106]; *Novoship* (n 5). See also, Ridge, 'Justifying the Remedies' (n 12) 451–457. The extent to which gain-based *proprietary* remedies are allowed depends upon the jurisdiction in question and is beyond this chapter's scope.

28 See generally, Dietrich and Ridge, *Accessories* (n 1) [5.7] (Torts).

29 *Blyth v Fladgate* [1891] 1 Ch 337; *Cowper v Stoneham* (1893) 68 LT 18; *Trustor AB v Smallbone (No 3)* (CA, 9 May 2000) [97]; *Ultraframe (UK) v Fielding* [2005] EWHC 1638, [2006] FSR 17 [600] ('*Ultraframe*'). In Australia, see *Grimaldi* (n 1) [558].

compensatory liability as PW. This fact must surely temper a court's readiness to impose liability.

B. The Rationale and Purpose/s of the Primary Wrong are Also Relevant

What is clear from the foregoing discussion of the rationale and purposes of participatory liability is that their ascertainment also requires an inquiry into the rationale and purposes of the primary wrong with which D is culpably associated. The ancillary nature of participatory liability makes this inevitable. The inquiry with respect to the primary wrong, however, has an indirect, more nuanced, relevance to the remedies available against D, as will now be explained.

Most obviously, D is *not* the primary wrongdoer: he or she is not a trustee or fiduciary and hence the rationale and purposes underpinning PW's liability cannot automatically apply to D.[30] Furthermore, whilst D's liability is *derivative* in the sense that the primary wrong is a precondition for D's liability, D's liability does not necessarily *duplicate* that of PW.[31] D is liable for D's own wrongdoing. Thus, it is not necessarily the case that the full range of remedies available against a trustee or fiduciary must be available against PW, nor that they should necessarily be measured in the same way.

Nonetheless, whilst D's wrongdoing is of a different nature to that of PW, this does not mean that it cannot be equally egregious. Although the rationale and purposes of the two wrongs are clearly different, it does not follow that a *lesser* range of remedies must apply to D. The remedies available against PW and D may differ because they are liable in relation to different wrongs and because different consequences may ensue in relation to each, not because the nature of D's wrongdoing is of lesser consequence in the eyes of equity.

Because D is not a trustee or fiduciary, policy considerations that influence the claimant-friendly determination of remedy in relation to a trustee or fiduciary do not automatically apply to D;[32] however, this cannot be a hard and fast rule. One way in which the rationale and purposes of fiduciary law do influence participatory liability is in relation to the former's well-established prophylactic character. The purposes of participatory liability ensure, in pragmatic ways, that the particular trust or fiduciary relationship between C and PW is vindicated and that other such relationships are also protected. Accordingly, a prophylactic spirit infuses participatory liability as well as trust and fiduciary law.

The rationale and purposes of fiduciary law may also be applicable to PW directly where the nature of the relationship between PW and D renders their wrongdoing

30 *Novoship* (n 5).
31 *Michael Wilson* (n 5) [106]. See also, Dietrich and Ridge, *Accessories* (n 1) [8.1.5].
32 *Novoship* (n 5). See also, Part IV C below.

virtually indistinguishable. This appears to be what is happening in those cases where the court refers to D having a 'transmitted fiduciary obligation'.[33] Such reasoning has most weight where D and PW are closely related, most obviously where one is the corporate alter ego of the other, or where D and PW are in an intimate relationship.[34] But even when D and PW are not closely related, if they are nonetheless essentially of one mind and purpose in their commission of the primary wrong, a court might exceptionally find that they should be jointly and severally liable for each other's gains.[35] In such a case, it would seem, the mode of calculation and imposition of the remedy should be the same, regardless of whether D or PW's liability is in question, and the rationale and purposes of fiduciary law would apply directly.

Similarly, equitable remedies may have vindicatory and deterrence functions. This is most clearly seen in relation to trustee and fiduciary wrongdoing:

> [t]he fiduciary relationship has trust, not self-interest, at its core, and when breach occurs, the balance favours the person wronged... [E]quity is concerned, not only to compensate the plaintiff, but to enforce the trust which is at its heart.[36]

The goals of vindication and deterrence can also be pursued against D, but generally this would only be where a close relationship between D and PW warrants the transmission of the fiduciary relationship. It is clear that the jurisdiction is not penal.[37] Hence, the courts have warned against automatically rendering D liable for PW's profits.[38] Similarly, 'a third party participant, is not to be punished for misconduct by making him or her account for more than what was actually received by him or her as a result of [the participation].'[39]

C. Equitable Remedies are Discretionary

A third general principle governing the remedies for participatory liability is that equitable remedies are not available as of right, but are subject to the court's discretion which is exercised according to 'settled principles'.[40] These principles

33 See, eg, *Bli Bli No 1 Pty Ltd v Kimlin Investments Pty Ltd* [2008] QSC 289 [48]. See also, *Club of the Clubs Pty Ltd v King Network Group Pty Ltd (No 2)* [2007] NSWSC 574 [58] (Bergin J citing *Queensland Mines Ltd v Hudson* (1975–76) CLC 40–266 (NSWSC) 28,709; *Timber Engineering Co Pty Ltd v Anderson* [1980] 2 NSWLR 488 (NSWSC) 495; *Natural Extracts Pty Ltd v Stotter* (1997) 24 ACSR 110 (FCA) 138).

34 See, eg, *Warman International Ltd v Dwyer* (1995) 182 CLR 544 ('*Warman*').

35 *Grimaldi* (n 1) [558] citing *inter alia CMS Dolphin Ltd v Simonet* [2001] 2 BCLC 704 (Ch) ('*CMS Dolphin*'); *Green & Clara Pty Ltd v Bestobell Industries Pty Ltd (No 2)* [1984] WAR 32 (WASC) ('*Green & Clara*').

36 *Canson* (n 13) 154. Quoted with approval in *Youyang Pty Ltd v Minter Ellison Morris Fletcher* [2003] HCA 15, (2003) 212 CLR 484 [40] ('*Youyang*').

37 See, eg, *Grimaldi* (n 1) [680].

38 See *Ultraframe* (n 29) [1600].

39 *Grimaldi* (n 1) [748] (citations omitted).

40 *Warman* (n 34) 559 (in the context of an account of profits for breach of fiduciary duty).

include recognised defences 'such as estoppel, laches, acquiescence and delay', but also allow a court to refuse a remedy 'where it would be unconscientious [for C] to assert it'[41] or if it would be 'disproportionate in relation to the particular form and extent of wrongdoing'.[42]

This feature of equity's remedial jurisdiction is extremely valuable because it allows a greater range of remedies to be potentially available, whilst precluding or moderating outcomes that do not accord with the rationale and purpose of the liability. Necessarily, the exercise of remedial discretion may require that painstaking attention be paid to the particular facts of a case.[43] A recent example of the value of remedial discretion is the Federal Court's decision in *Grimaldi v Chameleon Mining NL (No 2)*.[44] In this case an inquiry was conducted into whether the sought-after remedy of remedial constructive trust was commensurate with the rationale and purposes of participatory liability on the specific facts in question. The Court refused, as a matter of discretion, to impose a constructive trust over certain assets of D Company, as a remedy for recipient liability; instead, an account of profits was ordered. The Court considered that the rationale and purposes of recipient liability did not warrant the imposition of an onerous proprietary remedy upon D on these facts. The arms-length relationship of PW and D meant that the rationale and purposes of fiduciary duty were not directly applicable; the egregiousness of D's wrongdoing and significant changes in the composition of D's investors over time, as well as pragmatic concerns as to the feasibility of such remedy, were additional factors in the Court's exercise of discretion.[45]

D. The Remedy Will Be Moulded to the Particular Facts

In *Warman International Ltd v Dwyer*, a case involving the calculation of an account of profits against a fiduciary and his corporate alter egos, the High Court of Australia referred to the 'cardinal principle of equity' that 'the remedy must be fashioned to fit the nature of the case and the particular facts.'[46] This means, for example, that equitable remedies against D may be awarded on terms or otherwise limited so as to prevent unjust enrichment by either party.[47] As with the previous

[41] ibid citing *Chan v Zacharia* (1984) 154 CLR 178 (HCA) 204–205.

[42] *Novoship* (n 5) [119]. See also, *Grimaldi* (n 1) [674].

[43] See *The 'Juliana'* (1822) 2 Dods 504, 521; 165 ER 1560, 167 (Lord Stowell): 'A Court of law works its way to short issues, and confines its views to them. A Court of Equity takes a more comprehensive view, and looks to every connected circumstance that ought to influence its determination upon the real justice of the case.'

[44] *Grimaldi* (n 1).

[45] See generally, Pauline Ridge, 'Constructive Trusts, Accessorial Liability and Judicial Discretion' in Elise Bant and Michael Bryan (eds), *Principles of Proprietary Remedies* (Sydney, LawBook Co, 2013) 73.

[46] *Warman v Dwyer* (n 34) 559.

[47] See, eg, *Ninety Five Pty Ltd (in liq) v Banque Nationale de Paris* [1988] WAR 132 (WASC).

general principle, this principle emphasises the fact-centred nature of the court's remedial inquiry.

In summary, the rationale and purposes of participatory liability justify the full range of remedies available against trustees being available in principle against D. The basis of D's liability is not the same as that of PW and so the principles governing the award of remedies against a defaulting trustee or fiduciary do not *automatically* apply. Nevertheless, they must always be indirectly relevant given that the purposes of participatory liability are to protect the trust or fiduciary relationship. Furthermore, their relevance may increase according to the nature of the relationship between D and PW such that, in some instances, the remedial objectives become indistinguishable. The court has a discretion both to withhold a remedy on general equitable principles or because the remedy is not commensurate with the rationale and purposes of liability. The court may also mould a remedy to suit the specific facts.

A brief digression is now necessary in order to explain the remedial context in which questions concerning monetary remedies for participatory liability arise.

III. The Current State of the Law Concerning Monetary Remedies for Breach of Trust and Fiduciary Duty

As will be evident from a perusal of other chapters in this book, there are many questions concerning the characterisation and assessment of monetary remedies for breach of trust and fiduciary duty. The answers to these questions are relevant to the choice and measure of the monetary remedies available against D. This is because, first, D is said to be liable to the full range of equitable remedies—those available against a trustee—and secondly, as discussed above, the remedial objectives of the two forms of liability—primary and participatory—are closely related and may be indistinguishable in some scenarios. A third reason is that, in relation to accessory liability, D will be jointly and severally liable with the trustee or fiduciary PW for whatever monetary order is awarded against PW excluding, generally, gain-based orders. Hence, it is necessary to give a brief outline of the monetary remedies for breach of trust and fiduciary duty before exploring, in greater depth, their application to D. In doing so, it must be acknowledged that there are conflicting authorities and inconsistent uses of terminology: the law is in a state of flux.

There are at least three sources of law that inform the modern remedial jurisdiction concerning personal monetary remedies for breach of trust and fiduciary duty and that consequently inform the remedies available against D:

(i) the jurisdiction concerning the monetary orders and procedures that accompany a trustee or other custodial fiduciary's duty to account by way of an account of administration in common form or an account of administration on the basis of wilful default;

(ii) the compensatory jurisdiction for breach of fiduciary duty recognised by the House of Lords in *Nocton v Lord Ashburton* and as subsequently developed by the courts;[48] and,

(iii) the jurisdiction informing a trustee or fiduciary's liability to account for profits made through a breach of duty (whether or not a misapplication of property was involved).

The term 'equitable compensation' is often used indiscriminately to describe the remedy awarded pursuant to (i) and (ii) regardless of the particular source of the principles applied. It does not have a consistent and reliable meaning. In general terms, equitable compensation is a remedy that is available wherever a defendant has acted 'against the dictates of conscience as defined by the Court.'[49] But the term can be used in a narrower sense to refer to the loss-based personal remedy that is available for a claim grounded in breach of an equitable duty. The term sometimes is used more broadly to refer to the money order that follows an account in common form or for wilful default taken against a trustee in relation to his or her stewardship of the trust property (category (i) above),[50] and to the money orders accompanying or substituting for equitable rescission. Those orders may be distinguished from equitable compensation in the narrower sense because—although this is not wholly accepted—they are not necessarily loss-based even though they may have the effect of compensating for losses suffered by C.

A helpful way of describing equitable compensation is to say that it is available for wrongs that either do not depend upon there being a misapplication of property in a fiduciary's custody (non-custodial equitable wrongdoing) and hence that do not attract restitution or accounting orders or for custodial equitable wrongdoing where those remedies are no longer appropriate. In other words, equitable compensation is the appropriate monetary remedy when there is *no* fund to be accounted for at all or the fund is no longer subsisting.[51]

The jurisdiction governing equitable compensation for non-custodial fiduciary breaches is relatively young.[52] Conversely, although the accounts jurisdiction is older, much of its operation has occurred 'off-stage', as it were, being undertaken by court officers following judgment and not detailed in the law reports. Hence, substantive discussion of the jurisdiction is rare.[53] Moreover, nowadays courts often refer in general terms to a trustee or fiduciary's obligation 'to account'

48 *Nocton v Lord Ashburton* [1914] AC 932 (HL) ('*Nocton*').

49 ibid 952.

50 See, eg, *Libertarian Investments Limited v Hall* [2013] HKCU 2562 [167]–[170] ('*Libertarian Investments*').

51 *Canson* (n 13) 163. See also, *Youyang* (n 36) [37] citing *Maguire v Makaronis* (1997) 188 CLR 449 (HCA) 473.

52 *Nocton* (n 48) is generally regarded as the seminal decision.

53 But see *Glazier Holdings Pty Ltd v Australian Men's Health Pty Ltd (No 2)* [2001] NSWSC 6 ('*Glazier Holdings*'); *Libertarian Investments* (n 50); *Agricultural Land Management Ltd v Jackson [No 2]* [2014] WASC 102.

without necessarily invoking the technical account procedures and sometimes as a way of calculating an award of equitable compensation. Thus, questions arise as to the modern application and reach of the accounts jurisdiction. Other unresolved questions include the extent to which the approach of the accounts jurisdiction, which is procedurally-driven, applies, either directly or indirectly, to the calculation of equitable compensation for equitable wrongs not involving misapplication of property.[54] The precise relationship of equitable compensation to the money orders following an account is unclear. A further question is how a monetary order made for an equitable wrong that *does* involve a misapplication of property is to be assessed, whether or not following an account. Clearly a 'one size fits all' approach is not to be taken. Indeed, speaking of the 'money remedy for breach of an express trust', the High Court of Australia has said that the 'nature of that remedy may vary to reflect the terms of the trust, and the breach of which complaint is made. Generalisations may mislead.'[55] It also unclear how much weight, if any, should be given to common law principles for calculating compensatory damages awards.

This chapter does not attempt to resolve these questions. In particular, it does not consider the calculation of an account or the calculation of equitable compensation for breach of trust or fiduciary duty. Instead, with this context by way of background, Part IV now discusses three particular questions relating to the account, compensatory and gain-based jurisdictions as they apply to a culpable participant in trust or fiduciary wrongdoing.

IV. Three Questions Concerning the Monetary Remedies for Participatory Liability

A. When and How Do Equity's Account Procedures and Consequent Monetary Remedies Apply to Participatory Liability for Breach of Trust or Fiduciary Duty?

There are two ways in which account-related remedies may be available for participatory liability. The first is where an account is taken directly against D in relation to D's own control and use of custodial property that is the subject of PW's trust or fiduciary duties.[56] This may occur in relation to both recipient

[54] See, eg, Charles Mitchell, 'Equitable Compensation for Breach of Fiduciary Duty' (2013) *Current Legal Problems* 1.

[55] *Youyang* (n 36) [36]. See generally, the Hon William Gummow AC, 'Three Cases of Misapplication of a Solicitor's Trust Account' (2015) 41 *Australian Bar Review* 5.

[56] An accounting party need not be a trustee. See generally, James Penner, 'Distinguishing fiduciary, trust, and accounting parties' (2014) 8 *Journal of Equity* 202.

and accessorial forms of participatory liability,[57] but appears to be uncommon. The second arises only in relation to accessory liability and is indirect: D is jointly and severally liable for the 'compensation' awarded against PW for PW's equitable wrong and, as explained above, such label may refer to the monetary order consequent upon an accounting taken against PW. Whether an account is available directly or indirectly, it can only be an account by wilful default—or, expressed more generally, an account based upon wrongdoing by D or PW—as will now be explained.

The account in common form is available against a custodial fiduciary. If a deficiency in the trust fund is thereby revealed, the resulting order is that the trustee or fiduciary make good the deficiency by restoring the fund. Logically, the account in common form procedure cannot apply to participatory liability because the procedure is not premised upon wrongdoing by the accounting party. Hence it cannot apply directly to D (for D's liability is fault-based) or indirectly to D (for there is no primary wrong pleaded, to which a participatory liability claim can attach).[58] The account in common form can be put to one side for present purposes, whilst noting that it is possible that its informing principles may nevertheless have an indirect influence on the direct claim for equitable compensation that is available against a *defaulting* trustee or fiduciary (a primary wrongdoer) and hence upon D's liability.[59]

The account by wilful default that is available against a custodial fiduciary in relation to a misapplication of property, conversely, does require a primary wrong to be pleaded, namely, the wilful default by trustee or custodial fiduciary: a breach of duty which has caused something to be lost to the fund or not received by the fund when it should have been received.[60] Accordingly *accessory* liability can attach to a claim for an account by wilful default, although it appears unusual for accessory liability claims to be pleaded in this fashion.[61]

Recipient liability is the clearest instance of where an account can be taken directly against D in relation to D's own control and use of custodial property that is the subject of PW's trust or fiduciary duties. Recipient liability, as opposed to accessory liability, has a more obvious affinity with the account procedures and orders given that, at some point, D must have held the trust property for personal benefit. The determination of C's remedy for recipient liability focuses squarely upon D's wrong: the culpable receipt of misappropriated trust property for

[57] *British America Elevator Co Ltd v Bank of British North America* [1919] AC 650 ('*British America*').

[58] Contra Mitchell and Watterson, 'Remedies for Knowing Receipt' (n 4).

[59] For the view that it is relevant, see *Canson* (n 13). Contra Mitchell, 'Equitable Compensation' (n 54) 19.

[60] As to the meaning of 'wilful default' see *Meehan v Glazier Holdings Pty Ltd* [2002] NSWCA 22, (2002) 54 NSWLR 146 [65]–[66] (Giles JA) ('*Meehan*'); cited with approval in *Byrnes v Kendle* [2011] HCA 26, (2011) 243 CLR 253 [43]. See also, *Bartlett v Barclays Trust Co Ltd (No 2)* [1980] 1 Ch 515 (Ch) 546 as discussed in *Glazier Holdings* (n 53) [49]-[56].

[61] But see *Glazier Holdings* (n 53) [8]; *Meehan* (n 60) [11].

personal benefit. The cases use the language of 'account' in the sense that A is liable for the value of the property at receipt, plus interest, and for an account of profits made with the trust property.[62] Where the remedy is more broadly described as 'compensation', the measure of such compensation is still the amount necessary to restore the trust fund; that is the label is being used to describe an account, debt-like liability, rather than a loss-based remedy, although the cases, on the whole, appear not to have explicitly recognised that distinction.[63] Thus, in *Grimaldi* the Federal Court of Australia stated that 'the knowing recipient is obliged (no less than the wrongdoing trustee) to restore the trust fund by way of monetary compensation for the assets which have been lost…'.[64] In other words, the objective of the remedy for recipient liability is to provide a substitute for the trust fund received by D, even though D is only treated as a trustee of the trust fund for remedial purposes and although D's liability, unlike that of a true trustee, can only be wrong-based.[65] This suggests that the account-based remedies available against an express trustee and those available against a knowing recipient will not necessarily be identical. It is also doubtful whether a further loss-based compensation remedy in relation to consequential losses should be available given the rationale and purposes of the liability.[66]

An account may also be taken directly against an accessory D in relation to D's own control and use of custodial property that is the subject of PW's trust or fiduciary duties. Viscount Haldane's judgment for the Privy Council in 1919 in an appeal from the Court of Appeal of Manitoba, *British America Elevator Co Ltd v Bank of British North America*, is an authority for this proposition.[67] The case involved both assistance in breach of a custodial fiduciary duty by PW and receipt for personal benefit, yet the remedial approach taken was the same: an account for the trust money that passed through D's hands irrespective of whether there was any receipt for personal benefit.

The case concerned the liability of D Bank for knowingly participating in breaches of fiduciary duty by C's agent, PW (who was not a party to the proceedings). The breaches by PW concerned the misapplication of C's funds. D's

62 See, eg, *Akindele* (n 1) where this was assumed to be the appropriate remedy if liability was found. See also, *Williams* (n 8) [31] (Lord Sumption JSC).

63 See, eg, *Farrow Finance Co Ltd (in liq) v Farrow Properties Pty Ltd (in liq)* [1999] 1 VR 584 (VSC) 636–637.

64 *Grimaldi* (n 1) [559]. See also, *Arthur v Attorney General of the Turks & Caicos Islands* [2012] UKPC 30, [2012] All ER (D) 164 [37]: '[t]he recipient's personal liability to account as a constructive trustee by virtue of knowing receipt means that the recipient is subject to custodial duties which are the same as those voluntarily assumed by express trustees…The recipient's core duty is to restore the misapplied trust property.'

65 See Dietrich and Ridge, *Accessories* (n 1) [7.6.3].

66 But see recent academic speculation upon the import of the reasoning in *Novoship* (n 5) [107]: Jamie Glister, 'Breach of Trust and Consequential Loss' (2014) 8 *Journal of Equity* 235, 255 (suggesting that the way has been left open for recipient liability for compensation in relation to consequential loss).

67 *British America* (n 57). See generally, JD Heydon, MJ Leeming, PG Turner, *Meagher, Gummow and Lehane's Equity: Doctrines and Remedies*, 5th edn (Sydney, LexisNexis Butterworths, 2015) [23-060].

culpable participation encompassed both knowing assistance and knowing receipt for personal benefit,[68] although the Privy Council did not use that terminology. The Privy Council instead described the Bank, through its manager, as 'being party to a misapplication of trust funds, which they must restore to [C].'[69] The proper procedure, according to Viscount Haldane, was for C to claim:

> on the ground of breach of trust, and for an account to be taken of all the sums so received, in which case the result of the account, after any proper deductions had been claimed and established on the initiative of the [Bank], would have been followed by a judgment on further consideration for the balance found due…'.[70]

Instead, in the lower courts, C had claimed for specific amounts. Accordingly, the Privy Council intimated that additional proceedings might be taken by D against C to recoup some of the money that had in fact been paid out by D on C's account and that had not been properly accounted for.

More commonly, a claim for equitable compensation for breach of trust or breach of fiduciary duty is made against PW with an ancillary claim for accessory liability in the same measure against D; that is, D's account-based liability is indirect. D is jointly and severally liable with PW for the same sum.[71] The form of the order against D where the primary wrong involves misapplication of property controlled in a fiduciary capacity, depends upon whether there is an ongoing trust or not, that is, the order is fashioned to the particular facts:

> in some circumstances the remedy to be granted [against D] will be an order for the restitution of the trust fund in respect of an amount abstracted, whereas in other circumstances it will be an award of equitable compensation to the beneficiary in respect of the beneficiary's personal loss.[72]

In principle, the amount ordered to be paid by D on either approach should be the same.[73]

[68] A proportion of the funds were paid into overdrawn accounts with the Bank.

[69] *British America* (n 57) 663.

[70] ibid 664.

[71] See above, (n 29). Contra Heydon, Leeming and Turner, *Meagher, Gummow & Lehane's Equity* (n 67) [23-555] fn 419: '[i]n Australia, the liability of a knowing participant for loss suffered by the principal is now several only'. The authors cite *Michael Wilson* (n 5) [106], but the case does not support their position. See also on this point, Jamie Glister, 'Knowing assistance and equitable compensation' (2016) 42 *Australian Bar Review* 154.

[72] *Lewis v Nortex* (n 2) [30] (Hamilton J). As to the various remedies given in this case, see at [42] in relation to accessory liability: 'appropriate orders need to be made against [D], who has been found to have accessorial liability for these breaches of trust, in order to remedy the situation. But, as the trust is subsisting, the order should not be in favour of [C] for payment to it of its 40% share, but should be, at its suit, an order for the reconstitution of the unit trust fund by the payment of the above sums by [D] to that fund. See also, at [39] 'In the circumstances, there is no point in reconstituting the long disbursed bare trust fund. [C] is therefore entitled to an order for compensation in its favour, provided there can now be regarded as being a loss which [C] has suffered by reason of this breach of trust.' The facts are given in *Lewis v Nortex Pty Ltd (in liq)* [2004] NSWSC 1143.

[73] *AIB* (n 14) [90]–[91]. For an example of an Australian judge referring to an account on the basis of wilful default to confirm his assessment in relation to PW and D's liability for equitable compensation for breach of fiduciary duty by a non-custodial PW, see *Hasler* (n 8) [152] (Leeming JA).

B. Why Is an Accessory Liable for Losses Resulting From the Primary Wrong, Rather than from the Accessory's Own Wrong?

As already noted, where D is an accessory to a breach of trust or fiduciary duty, D is jointly and severally liable with PW for all losses flowing from *the primary wrong*.[74] As discussed above, such liability is generally described as equitable compensation, whether it results from a direct claim for such remedy or is ordered following an account against either PW or D.[75] This is consistent with accessory liability under Anglo-Australian tort law: joint tortfeasors are liable for damages for the full losses caused to C by a joint endeavour, even where distinct torts were committed as a part of that joint endeavour.[76] D's loss-based accessory liability is assessed in relation to the primary wrong, rather than in relation to D's own, accessorial, wrongdoing. Furthermore, the measure of C's loss is calculated according to the (possibly stricter) rules governing the loss-based liability of the trustee or fiduciary, PW.

We can quickly dismiss one suggested explanation for this situation, namely, that secondary liabilities, such as equitable accessory liability, must necessarily duplicate the primary liability. That explanation is conceptually flawed, inconsistent with the availability of gain-based relief in relation to D's gains, and not accepted by the courts.[77] D is clearly liable because of D's own wrongdoing.[78] But one might assume from this that D should only be liable for the losses caused by that wrongdoing:

> [u]nder [both common law and equity] liability is fault-based: the defendant is only liable for the consequences of the legal wrong he has done to the plaintiff and to make good the damage caused by such wrong. He is not responsible for damage not caused by his wrong or to pay way of compensation more than the loss suffered from such wrong.[79]

This raises the question whether an accessory must *necessarily* be liable in the same measure as PW for a loss-related remedy. Paul Davies has proposed, for example, that consistently with the rationale for participatory liability, an accessory D 'should only be liable for losses suffered as a result of the accessory's participation in the breach of trust or fiduciary duty.'[80] It is difficult to see how the cases

74 See above, n 29. See generally, Dietrich and Ridge, *Accessories* (n 1) [8.8.1].

75 Part IVA.

76 See, eg, *Smithson v Garth* (1691) 3 Lev 323, 324; 83 ER 711, 712. See further Dietrich and Ridge, *Accessories* (n 8) [5.7.1].

77 See, eg, *Michael Wilson* (n 5) [106]. See generally, Ridge, 'Justifying the Remedies', (n 12).

78 See Part IIA.

79 *Target Holdings Ltd v Redferns* [1996] 1 AC 421 (HL) 432 (Lord Browne-Wilkinson).

80 Davies, *Accessory Liability* (n 11) 257. See also, Graham Virgo, *The Principles of Equity & Trusts* (Oxford, Oxford University Press, 2012) 710–711; Glister, 'Breach of Trust and Consequential Loss' (n 66) 256–257.

cited by Davies support that proposition. The first case cited by Davies, *Aerostar Maintenance International Ltd v Wilson*, is a straightforward example of compensation for C's lost opportunity to secure a contract that was instead secured by one of the accessory defendants pursuant to a breach of fiduciary duty by PW (the director of C).[81] There is no suggestion by Morgan J that the award of compensation was calculated in relation to D's wrongdoing, rather than the primary wrong and it is implicit that PW and the two defendants were made liable for the same amount.[82] The second case cited by Davies is *Goldtrail Travel Ltd v Aydin*.[83] In that case the two defendants were made liable only in relation to the specific fiduciary breaches that they had facilitated. PW's liability was discussed only briefly as he was impecunious: he was 'liable to account' to C for the sums he received that should have gone to C.[84] But there is no suggestion that the equitable compensation awarded against the two accessories was assessed upon a different basis, nor was this a case of breach of trust where the language of 'account' might have had a more specific meaning that could not apply to the accessories.

Putting concerns about the cases used by Davies to support his proposition to one side, however, does the current law reflect only its nascent state (and hence is amenable to further development) or is it consistent with general principle? How can this apparent anomaly be explained and is there a case for change?

D's joint and several liability with PW is consistent with the fundamental rationale of accessory liability, namely, that D has culpably interfered with C's rights through D's involvement in the breach of PW's duties to C. The combination of the requisite elements of accessory liability (the primary wrong, involvement through conduct by D in that wrong and a requisite mental state) create a 'participation' link between D and the primary wrong, the purpose of which is to justify making D liable for the primary wrong. 'When such a link exists, the risk of wrongdoing is enhanced and [D] ought not to be able to hide behind the fact that he did not himself, *commit* the primary wrong.'[85] In other words, the nature and degree of D's wrongdoing justifies D's liability for the primary wrong.

For this reason, all jurisdictions set a high culpability threshold for D's accessory liability. In Australia, D must have had actual knowledge or have been morally obtuse in relation to the primary wrong. In England, D must have actual knowledge and be dishonest in all the circumstances. That is, the degree of D's culpability—the combination of the requisite conduct and mental elements that creates a participation link to the primary wrong—indeed warrant D becoming fully liable for losses resulting from the primary wrong. It is precisely because D's loss-based liability will mirror that of PW that the culpability threshold is set high. Where D's accessorial involvement is through procurement of the primary wrong, making

[81] *Aerostar Maintenance International Ltd v Wilson* [2010] EWHC 2032 (Ch) [209]–[216].

[82] *Cf Colour Control Centre Pty Ltd v Ty* (NSWSC, July 24 1995).

[83] *Goldtrail Travel Ltd v Aydin* [2014] EWHC 1587 (Ch) [174]–[178] (on appeal at the time of writing).

[84] ibid [158].

[85] Dietrich and Ridge, *Accessories* (n 1) [2.4.2].

D liable for the primary wrong itself is even more justified, given the extremely strong participation link to the primary wrong and D rightly is made responsible in relation to losses flowing from that wrong.[86]

The purposes of equitable participatory liability discussed in Part II are also relevant here. The pragmatic objectives of deterrence, increasing C's chance of recourse, encouraging de facto regulation of trustee and fiduciary behaviour by third parties and vindication of relationships of trust and confidence, all support the imposition upon a culpable accessory of joint and several liability for the primary wrong.[87] A further pragmatic consideration is that it may be extremely difficult to determine the relative responsibility of D and PW where D has assisted, rather than procured, the primary wrong. It is appropriate that the risks inherent in such an evidential task are shifted from C to the wrongdoers via the rules of contribution:

> One can readily understand why, when wrongdoers so entangle their affairs, that the law as a matter of legal policy might wish to make it their responsibility—and not [C's]—to untangle them for accountability purposes.[88]

Thus, it is only in relation to C, that D and PW's relative responsibility for the primary wrong is ignored. D may claim contribution from PW and the preferred view is that such contribution may be ordered on a proportionate basis that reflects each party's responsibility for the loss.[89] Of course, this is of small comfort to D where PW has absconded or is impecunious, but this is precisely why D is made liable and such outcomes accord with the purposes of the liability.[90]

Thus, the current law makes most sense where D has procured the primary wrong, but is still justified in relation to liability for assistance by the pragmatic purposes of participatory liability and—assuming the culpability threshold is set at an appropriate level—is also supported by the principled rationale for liability. The case for change is not yet made out.

C. When Is an Account of Profits Available Against an Accessory and How Is It Assessed?

Two questions have recently come to the fore in England in relation to equitable accessory liability, but have caused little or no angst in Australia: is an account

86 It could be argued here, however, that even if D were to be made liable in relation to his or own wrong of procurement, the relevant losses would still be those resulting from the (procured) primary wrong.

87 See generally, Dietrich and Ridge, *Accessories* (n 1) [2.4], [8.1.3].

88 *Grimaldi* (n 1) [558] (citing *inter alia CMS Dolphin* (n 35); *Green & Clara* (n 35)).

89 See *George v Webb* [2011] NSWSC 1608 [339]–[354] (Ward J). See also, Alison Gurr, 'Accessory Liability and Contribution, Release and Apportionment' (2010) 34 *Melbourne University Law Review* 481, 497, 499.

90 See *Royal Brunei Airlines* (n 1) 386–387. The application of proportionate liability legislative schemes to participatory liability is unclear: see Gurr, 'Accessory Liability' (n 89) 511–517.

of profits an available remedy against an accessory and, if it is, when should it be awarded?[91]

I will not dwell on the first question here.[92] Gain-based relief is clearly consistent with, indeed, is a perfect match for, the most pervasive formulation of the rationale for all forms of equitable participatory liability.[93] Gain-based relief is the most easily justified: to require D to disgorge personal gains obtained through exploitative interference with a trust or fiduciary relationship is surely less contentious than requiring D to compensate C for all losses flowing from the primary wrong, irrespective of D's causal contribution to that wrong, and yet, as just discussed, the latter relief is well-established.[94] Furthermore, there is ample and highly respectable authority to support the availability of gain-based relief for equitable accessory liability.[95] Those who argue against gain-based relief for equitable accessory liability on the grounds that it is not available for common law forms of accessory liability appear to overlook the quite different nature of the equitable wrongs that equitable accessory liability protects, as well as the discretionary nature of the relief and the well-established equitable jurisdiction to award gain-based relief.[96] As discussed above, an important proviso is that equitable remedies are not available as of right.[97] An account of profits may be awarded, but need not be.[98]

This brings us to the second, more difficult, question: when is an account of profits an available remedy? That is, what is the requisite causal connection between a gain made by D and the breach of trust or fiduciary duty by PW for which D is accessorily liable such that D can be required to account for that gain to C? The causal question has been addressed with respect to a fiduciary's gains: the court must 'determine as accurately as possible the true measure of the profit or benefit obtained by the fiduciary in breach of his duty.'[99] The question is

[91] There appear to be no such concerns regarding the availability of an account of profits for recipient liability. See *Charter plc v City Index Ltd* [2007] EWCA 1382, [2008] Ch 313 [64]–[71]; *Williams* (n 8) [31]; *Grimaldi* (n 1) [555]. But see further, Jamie Glister's chapter in this book.

[92] See Ridge, 'Justifying the Remedies' (n 12).

[93] See Part II A.

[94] See Part II A.

[95] The remedy is more established in Australia than England: see, eg, *Consul Development* (n 19) 397; *Michael Wilson* [106] (n 5); *Grimaldi* (n 1). It has been reasserted by the English Court of Appeal: *Novoship* (n 5). See also, *Cook v Deeks* [1916] AC 554 (PC); *Fyffes* (n 20); *Ultraframe* (n 29) [1589]–[1601].

[96] See, eg, Peter Devonshire, 'Account of Profits for Dishonest Assistance' (2015) *CLJ* 1 who argues that gain based relief should only be available for dishonest procurement and not dishonest assistance. He argues further (fn 1) that the latter 'should be recast as a common law wrong and governed by existing forms of liability in tort.' These arguments are fundamentally at odds with the current law, would require legislation to implement and, in my view, cannot be supported on principled grounds. Contrast to Devonshire, the Hon William Gummow, 'Dishonest Assistance and Account of Profits' (2015) 74 *CLJ* 405.

[97] Part II C.

[98] See, eg, *Grimaldi* (n 1).

[99] *Hospital Products Limited v United States Surgical Corporation* (1984) 156 CLR 41 (HCA) 110 (Mason J). See also *Warman* (n 34) 558.

whether the profits were 'within the scope and ambit of [the fiduciary's] duty.'[100] But, of course, D is not a fiduciary and does not owe fiduciary duties so the same approach does not necessarily apply. Just as the causation test for fiduciary profits must 'express the policy of the law in holding fiduciaries to their duty',[101] so must the causation test that applies to D's gains express the policy underpinnings of participatory liability. But what appears to have happened so far is that the assessment of D's gain-based liability is bundled indiscriminately with the assessment of PW's gain-based liability; either by choice[102] or by oversight, different bases for gain-based relief have not been contemplated.

A recent decision of the English Court of Appeal, *Novoship (UK) Limited v Mikhaylyuk (Novoship)*, has now considered this question.[103] *Novoship* concerned a claim for dishonest assistance in breach of fiduciary duty. In simplified terms, the fiduciary PW was a director and the general manager of C. The relevant breach of fiduciary duty was in 'negotiating new and different contracts with [D] with whom he was contemporaneously sharing bribes' in relation to the chartering of vessels owned by companies in C's corporate group.[104] D dishonestly participated in the bribery (thereby satisfying the elements of the dishonest assistance claim) and received some of the bribe monies. D went on to negotiate shipping charters, through PW, with C. The charters turned out to be lucrative due to unexpected changes in the state of the market. An issue for the Court of Appeal was whether the profits made by D from the charters were referable to D's dishonest assistance in PW's breaches of fiduciary duty such that D should be liable to account for those profits.

The Court held, consistently with the general principles discussed in Part II above, that a dishonest accessory's equitable wrongdoing is distinct from, and different in nature to, PW's breach of fiduciary duty. There are two forms of equitable wrongdoing at play. Therefore, it was held, the rules pertaining to an account of profits against a fiduciary should not apply to the dishonest assistant. This, perhaps, does not accurately reflect the flexibility of the principles discussed in Part II above. Consistently with those principles, it would be more accurate to say that the rules pertaining to an account of profits against a fiduciary may have more or less relevance depending upon the nature of the relationship between D and PW. On the facts of *Novoship*, however, D was not the alter ego of PW, nor closely related; the parties were independent actors pursuing independent ends and there was no reason to take the approach adopted with respect to fiduciary profits.

100 *Phipps v Boardman* [1967] 2 AC 46 (HL) 127 (Lord Upjohn). See also *Warman* (n 34) 558–559; Gummow, 'Dishonest Assistance' (n 96) 407.

101 *Maguire v Makaronis* (n 51) 468.

102 See, eg, *Warman* (n 34): the parties agreed that the accessories' liability would be determined on the same basis as PW's liability.

103 *Novoship* (n 5).

104 ibid [54].

The next step in the Court's reasoning in *Novoship* was as follows:

> Where a claim based on equitable wrongdoing is made against one who is not a fiduciary, we consider that, as in the case of a fiduciary sued for breach of an equitable (but non-fiduciary) obligation, there is no reason why the common law rules of causation, remoteness and measure of damages should not be applied by analogy.[105]

There can be no argument with the need to ensure coherence and consistency across the common law, including equity, but this proposition in its more specific formulation is problematic. Why are the principles governing *loss*-based remedies at common law assumed to apply to equity's *gain*-based remedies? If analogies are to be drawn with the common law, then it should be with the assessment at common law of gain-based relief. A difficulty that then arises is that gain-based relief is largely an equitable phenomenon for which there is no obvious common law analogy.[106] Hence, with respect, the Court's reasoning in *Novoship* is flawed on this point.[107] A further difficulty, at least from an Australian perspective, is that the High Court has not accepted that analogies should be drawn with the assessment of common law damages even in relation to loss-based remedies for breach of non-fiduciary equitable duties.[108] Hence the reasoning does not accord with Australian law.

The Court in *Novoship* then extrapolated, from common law principles concerning causation of loss, a distinction between 'a breach which is the effective cause of a loss and one which is merely the occasion for the loss'.[109] That distinction was to be made 'by the application of common sense.'[110] Applying this test to the facts, rather than the 'but for' test that applies to a fiduciary's liability for equitable compensation, the Court found that 'the effective cause' of D's profits was an 'unexpected change in the market'; the dishonest assistance merely providing 'the occasion for [D] to make a profit'.[111] Therefore, there was an 'insufficient direct causal connection' between the dishonest assistance which led to D's use of C's vessels and the resulting profits made by D.[112]

This step in the Court's reasoning also provokes questions. The determination of legal causation as a normative matter, rather than simply establishing a factual causative link between a legal wrong and resulting loss or gain, is bedevilled by

105 ibid [107].

106 *Cf* the judgments of Lord Nicholls and Lord Hobhouse in *Attorney-General v Blake* [2001] 1 AC 268.

107 See also Andrew Stafford and Stuart Richie, *Fiduciary Duties: Directors and Employees*, 2nd edn (Bristol, Jordan Publishing, 2015) [9.329].

108 *Youyang* (n 36) [39]. See also, *Pilmer v Duke Group Ltd (in liq)* [2001] HCA 31, (2001) 207 CLR 165 [85].

109 *Novoship* (n 5) [108].

110 ibid [108] (citing *Galoo Ltd v Bright Graham Murray* [1994] 1 WLR 1360).

111 *Novoship* (n 5) [114].

112 ibid [115].

complexity and (at least from the perspective of this non-specialist) confusion. The references to 'common sense' and 'effective causes' pertain originally to the determination of causation questions by juries.[113] They do not boost confidence that the importation of the common law rules on causation will bring clarity to the question whether D should account to C for D's profits.

The Court in *Novoship* went on (under the heading of 'Discretion') to find, in addition, that the sought-after account of D's profits fell outside the rationale for ordering an account of profits. This, according to the Court, was to ensure that 'profits which ought to have been made for [C]' were restored to C.[114] But this rationale for awarding an account of profits was taken from *fiduciary* law; it does not necessarily apply to D's accessory liability.[115] In the normal course of events D would never be expected to make profits for C. It is also contrary to Australian law which requires a fiduciary to account for *all* gains made within the scope of the fiduciary duty, whether or not they 'ought to have been made for [C]': 'it is no defence that the plaintiff was unwilling, unlikely or unable to make the profits for which an account is taken…'.[116] Leaving those concerns to one side, however, it is the rationale and purposes of *participatory* liability that should determine whether an account of profits is an available remedy. The rationale and purposes of fiduciary law are relevant to the inquiry, but only indirectly. As discussed above,[117] the awarding of an account of profits for participatory liability addresses both the principled rationale for liability (it is unconscionable for D to knowingly interfere for personal gain with the fiduciary relationship between C and PW)[118] as well as the pragmatic purposes of the liability.

Finally, the Court held that, unlike the 'automatic' ordering of an account of profits against a fiduciary,[119] the remedy here was discretionary and should be withheld on the facts because it 'would be disproportionate in relation to the particular form and extent of wrongdoing'.[120] This is consistent with the general principle that the Court may withhold an equitable remedy in its discretion upon settled principles.[121] Yet, in *Novoship* this discretionary exercise appears to

[113] See *Amaca Pty Ltd v Booth* [2011] HCA 53, (2011) 246 CLR 36 [65]. See also, Gummow, 'Dishonest Assistance' (n 96) 408.

[114] *Novoship* (n 5) [116]–[117].

[115] Nor does it appear consistent with the UK Supreme Court's decision in *FHR European Ventures LLP v Cedar Capital Partners LLC* [2014] UKSC 45 [47]; [2015] AC 250 which requires a fiduciary to account for bribes that, by their nature, should not have been taken at all. But see Lusina Ho, 'Equitable Compensation on the Road to Damascus?' (2015) 131 *LQR* 213, 217–218.

[116] *Warman* (n 34) 558 citing *Birtchnell v Equity Trustees, Executors & Agency Co Ltd* (1929), 42 CLR 384, 409; *Furs Ltd v Tomkies* (1936) 54 CLR 583, 592; *Consul Development* (n 19). Quoted with approval in *Grimaldi* (n 1) [509] (see also at [514] (ii)).

[117] Part II A.

[118] *Fyffes Group* (n 20) 669.

[119] Strictly speaking, the award of equitable remedies is always in the court's discretion. See above, Part II C.

[120] *Novoship* (n 5) [119] citing *Fyffes Group* (n 20); *Satnam Investments Ltd v Dunlop Heywood & Co Ltd* [1999] 3 All ER 652, 672b-c; and *Walsh v Shanahan* [2013] EWCA Civ 411.

[121] See Part II C.

be surplus, given the Court's prior finding that D's dishonest assistance was not a legally relevant cause of D's profits.

If these criticisms of the reasoning in *Novoship* are valid, what is the preferable approach? I would suggest that a normative inquiry into causation based upon common law principles is an obfuscatory exercise in this context. Instead, once D's participatory conduct is found to be a factual ('but for') cause of D's gains (that is, that the gains were 'received as a result of such participation')[122] the normative inquiry into whether D *should* account to C for those gains is better conducted by reference to the general principles outlined above in Part II. In particular, the question in *Novoship* could have been more simply framed as whether an account of profits on the particular facts was consistent with the rationale and purposes of dishonest accessory liability and, if so, whether the Court should exercise its discretion to award that remedy.[123] In fact, this approach *was* taken in *Novoship*, but the clarity of the reasoning was muddied by the additional reliance upon common law principles concerning a normative, rather than a factual, causative link.

V. Conclusion

It is trite, but nonetheless important, to say that the remedies for equitable participatory liability must be consistent with the rationale and purposes of that liability. Because participatory liability is ancillary to a primary wrong, this in turn requires examination of the rationale and purposes of trust and fiduciary law. Current questions concerning the monetary remedies for equitable participatory liability are inextricably linked to those concerning the remedies for breach of trust and fiduciary duty. The latter questions must be resolved before the former can be fully addressed. A potential error for courts addressing the remedies for breach of trust and fiduciary duties, however, is to assume that the same answers will necessarily apply to the liability of a third party participant. The participant's remedial liability must still be addressed in relation to his or her own wrongdoing and in a way that is consistent with the rationale and purposes of that form of liability. In doing so, it remains the case that the equitable nature of that liability fundamentally shapes the availability and determination of the appropriate remedy.

122 *Consul Development* (n 19) 397.
123 *Cf Grimaldi* (n 1).

11

Equitable Compensation for Equitable Estoppels

JESSICA HUDSON*

I. Introduction

This chapter interrogates the role of equitable compensation as a response to equitable estoppels. Broadly speaking, an equitable estoppel arises in B's favour where A, by her representation, acquiescence or promise has induced an expectation on the part of B, upon which B reasonably relied in changing her position such that B will suffer detriment should A be allowed to depart her promise. Once the elements of an equitable estoppel are made out, an equity arises in B's favour that entitles her to equitable relief, subject to the application of equitable discretionary factors. One of the possible remedial responses to an equitable estoppel is a monetary award, which particularly in Australia has been characterised as equitable compensation. A review of the cases in which equitable compensation is awarded or considered as a response to an equitable estoppel reveals some disparity as to the function and measure of equitable compensation. Sometimes equitable compensation is measured by reference to the level of detriment that B has suffered in reliance upon B's expectation as induced by A's promise. On other occasions, equitable compensation effectively vindicates B's expectation. There are also differing approaches towards causation, remoteness and foreseeability.

This chapter argues that equitable compensation has two distinct remedial functions in the area of equitable estoppels. One is to provide a remedial substitute or alternative to specific relief, where specific relief has been identified as the remedy that satisfies the equity raised by an equitable estoppel, but which is not available on account of equitable discretionary factors. The other is to compensate for B's detriment where it has been decided that the extent of the equity raised by an equitable estoppel requires B's detriment to be compensated. The significance of distinguishing between these two remedial functions is that each demands a

* I am grateful to Simone Degeling for helpful comments on an earlier draft. All errors are my own.

different measure of equitable compensation. Further, it is the existence of two discrete remedial functions that accounts for the apparent disparity in the case law as to the measure of equitable compensation within equitable estoppels. The arguments in this chapter also have significance beyond equitable estoppels, and contribute to the broader debate concerning the extent to which the remedial purpose of equitable compensation extends beyond compensation for loss. At least within equitable estoppels, equitable compensation does more than compensate for loss or detriment, and in some circumstances provides a monetary substitute for specific relief.

II. The Different Types of Equitable Estoppels

The availability and measure of equitable compensation as a response to an equitable estoppel depends upon the type of estoppel raised, the extent of the equity created and the type of relief considered necessary to satisfy that equity. Thus, before asking whether and how much equitable compensation is available, it is first necessary to identify the type of equitable estoppel raised, then to assess the extent of the equity, and finally to determine the type and measure of relief that satisfies that equity. The first of these questions is considered in this part, that is, how the availability and role of equitable compensation might vary depending on which type of equitable estoppel is raised. It is important to distinguish between the discrete types of equitable estoppels on account of their having different elements and modes of operation.[1] The significance for the analysis here is that the availability and measure of equitable compensation may be different depending on which equitable estoppel is raised.

Proprietary estoppel is 'a category of equitable estoppel'[2] that can be raised where A has made a promise to B which has induced an assumption or a belief on the part of B, that B has or will acquire an interest in A's property, upon which B has reasonably relied in changing her position such that B will suffer detriment if A were allowed to contradict the assumption.[3] This assumption might be that

[1] *DHJPM Pty Ltd v Blackthorn Resources Ltd* (2011) 83 NSWLR 728 [43]–[44] (Meagher JA, with whom Macfarlan JA agreed); *Ashton v Pratt* [2015] NSWCA 12 [137]–[138] (Bathurst CJ, with whom McColl JA agreed) ('*Ashton*'), *cf Waltons Stores (Interstate) Ltd v Maher* (1988) 164 CLR 387 404 (Mason CJ and Wilson J) ('*Waltons Stores*'); *Commonwealth v Verwayen* (1990) 70 CLR 394 409–410 (Mason CJ) ('*Verwayen*'); E Cooke, *The Modern Law of Estoppel* (Oxford, Oxford University Press, 2000); E Bant and M Bryan, 'Fact, Future and Fiction: Risk and Reasonable Reliance in Estoppel' (2015) *OLJS* 1. See generally *Thorner v Major* [2009] UKHL 18, [2009] WLR 776 [67] (Lord Walker) ('*Thorner*').

[2] *Giumelli v Giumelli* (1999) 196 CLR 101 [6] (Gleeson CJ, McHugh, Gummow and Callinan JJ) ('*Giumelli*'); *Sidhu v Van Dyke* (2014) 251 CLR 505 [2] (French CJ, Kiefel, Bell and Keane JJ) ('*Sidhu*').

[3] See, eg, *Thorner* (n 1) [29] (Lord Walker); *Sidhu* ibid [2] (French CJ, Kiefel, Bell and Keane JJ); K Handley, *Estoppel by Conduct and Election, 2nd ed* (London, Sweet & Maxwell, 2016) Chapter 11; B McFarlane, *The Law of Proprietary Estoppel* (Oxford, Oxford University Press, 2014) Chs 1–2; JD Heydon, M Leeming and P Turner, *Meagher, Gummow and Lehane's, Equity, Doctrines and Remedies*, 5th ed (Sydney, LexisNexis, 2015) ('*Meagher, Gummow and Lehane's, Equity*') [17-065]–[17-130].

B has or will acquire a right in relation to A's property, and could be created by A's acquiescence, representation or A's promise. Within the category of proprietary estoppel, there are multiple sub-species which reveal further nuances in the elements and operation of these estoppels.[4] Proprietary estoppel is distinct from promissory estoppel, which is also equitable in nature. Broadly speaking, a promissory estoppel can be raised where A has made a promise or assurance to B upon which B reasonably relied in forming an expectation, and which induced B to change her position such that B will suffer detriment should A depart A's promise.[5]

Where a proprietary estoppel is raised, B has a positive right enforceable against A. The equity raised may require A to do something, such as hold property on constructive trust or to pay a sum of money. Hence proprietary estoppel has been described as a sword,[6] in distinction to a promissory estoppel which is often described as a shield.[7] The scope of promissory estoppel, in England and New South Wales at least, is confined to assurances given in relation to an existing legal relationship, or one that is about to come into existence.[8] As such, the equity raised by a promissory estoppel is confined to a negative right in B's favour to restrain A from enforcing A's right against B. To this limited extent, a promissory estoppel *does* provide B with a cause of action, for example to seek an injunction that restrains the enforcement by A of A's legal rights.[9] But accepting that promissory estoppel operates as a shield and not a sword, promissory estoppel does not create positive rights that B can enforce against A to require A to do something. For example, where A promises to do something in the future, such as enter into a contract, pay a sum of money, or give notice, a promissory estoppel cannot create an equity in B's favour that requires A to perform that promise or do something else in the event of non-performance, such as pay equitable compensation to compensate for loss.

The issue of whether a promissory estoppel can only ever create a negative right in B's favour remains unresolved.[10] There is some support for the view that promissory

[4] See generally: McFarlane, *Proprietary Estoppel* ibid.

[5] See, eg, *Central London Property Trust Ltd v High Trees House Ltd* [1947] KB 130 (KB); *Baird Textile Holdings Ltd v Marks and Spencer plc* [2001] EWCA Civ 274 [83]–[89] (Mance LJ); *Waltons Stores* (n1) 404–406 (Mason CJ and Wilson J), 428–429 (Brennan J); *Ashton* (n 1) [140]–[141] (Bathurst CJ, with whom McColl JA agreed); Handley (n 3) Ch 13.

[6] *Crabb v Arun District Council* [1976] Ch 179 (CA) 187 (Denning MR) ('*Crabb*'); J Edelman 'Remedial Certainty or Remedial Discretion in Estoppel after Giumelli?' (1999) 15 *Journal of Contract Law* 179 186–187.

[7] *Combe v Combe* [1951] 2 KB 215 (CA) 220 (Denning LJ); *Waltons Stores* (n 1) 444–445 (Deane J), 459 (Gaudron J).

[8] *Bank Negara Indonesia v Hoalim* [1973] 2 MLJ 3 (PC) 5 (Lord Wilberforce); *Baird Textile Holdings Ltd v Marks and Spencer plc* [2001] EWCA Civ 274 [38]–[39] (Sir Andrew Morritt V-C); *Saleh v Romanous* (2010) 79 NSWLR 453 [62]–[79] (Handley AJA, with whom Giles JA and Sackville AJA agreed).

[9] Handley (n 3) [13-006]–[13-007].

[10] A controversy acknowledged in *Construction Technologies Australia Pty Ltd v Doueihi* [2014] NSWSC 1717 [130] (White J); *Ashton* (n 1) [138] (Bathurst CJ, with whom McColl JA agreed); *Mineralogy Pty Ltd v Sino Iron Pty Ltd (No 6)* [2015] FCA 825 [769] (Edelman J).

estoppel can operate as a source of positive rights.[11] This debate is further complicated by whether, irrespective the scope of promissory estoppel, there exists a distinct and broader type of estoppel, labelled generally as 'equitable estoppel' that confers on B a positive right to enforce an obligation against A to do what is necessary to meet the equity raised by the estoppel.[12] This type of equitable estoppel has supported the award of specific relief requiring performance by A of her promise, such as to re-new a contract,[13] grant a sub-lease,[14] or pay equitable compensation in the event of non-performance of the promise.[15] Resolution of this issue is outside the scope of this chapter, save to note that it is important to distinguish between the different types of equitable estoppels to the extent they generate different equities which in turn might demand different roles and measures for equitable compensation.

III. Expectation, Detriment and Causation

Unlike other equitable causes of action, which do not require the identification and cause of the claimant's loss to be established, to make out any type of equitable estoppel it is necessary for B to establish her expectation and detriment, and that B's expectation and detriment were induced or caused by A's conduct.[16] As such, the existence and cause of detriment do not directly impact on the measure of equitable compensation for equitable estoppels as these elements have already been established prior to the remedial stage of inquiry. Irrespective which equitable estoppel is in view, it is important to bear in mind that B's expectation and detriment, and the link with A's conduct, all have an indirect effect on the availability

[11] *Waltons Stores* (n 1) 400–407 (Mason CJ and Wilson J); *Metropolitan Transit Authority v Waverley Transit Pty Ltd* [1991] 1 VR 181 205 (the Court) ('*Metropolitan v Waverley*'). See also, A Robertson, 'Three Models of Promissory Estoppel' (2013) 7 *Journal of Equity* 226.

[12] *Waltons Stores* (n 1) 416 428–429 (Brennan J); *Silovi Pty Ltd v Barbaro* (1988) 13 NSWLR 466 472 (Priestley JA, with whom Hope and McHugh JJA agreed); *Austotel Pty Ltd v Franklins Selfserve Pty Ltd* (1989) 16 NSWLR 582 615–616 (Priestley JA); *Verwayen* (n 1) 413 (Mason CJ), 428–429 (Brennan J); *Metropolitan v Waverley* (n 11) 205–207 (the Court); *S&E Promotions Pty Ltd v Tobin Brothers Pty Ltd* (1994) 122 ALR 637 651–654 (the Court); *EK Nominees Pty Ltd v Woolworths Ltd* [2006] NSWSC 1172 [219]–[223], [278] (White J); *Tipperary Developments Pty Ltd v Western Australia* (2009) 38 WAR 488 [128]–[147] (McLure JA, with whom Newnes JA agreed); *Vosnakis v Arfaras* [2015] NSWSC 625 [165] (Robb J); M Spence *Protecting Reliance* (Oxford, Hart Publishing 1999) Chapter 2; B McFarlane and P Sales, 'Promises, Detriment and Liability' (2015) 131 *LQR* 610.

[13] *Metropolitan v Waverley* (n 11).

[14] *S&E Promotions Pty Ltd v Tobin Brothers Pty Ltd* (1994) 122 ALR 637.

[15] *EK Nominees Pty Ltd v Woolworths Ltd* [2006] NSWSC 1172.

[16] *Eves v Eves* [1975] 1 WLR 1338 (CA) 1345 (Brightman J); *Gillett v Holt* [2000] EWCA Civ J0308-3, [2001] Ch 210 226–227, 230 (Robert Walker LJ, with whom Beldam and Waller LJJ agreed) ('*Gillett*').

and measure of equitable compensation. The elements of expectation, detriment and causation are key variables in the assessment of the extent of the equity raised by an equitable estoppel, which in turn will affect the amount of any equitable compensation payable by A. As will be discussed further below, these variables arguably also negate equity's need to turn to other conceptual apparatus such as causation, remoteness and foreseeability, in order to confine the scope of A's liability at the remedial stage of inquiry.

In relation to the element of expectation which is necessary to make out an equitable estoppel, B's expectation could include an expectation of acquisition of an interest in specific property, or that an existing contractual right would not be enforced. But equitable estoppels are not concerned with any expectation that B might have. It is only those expectations that are reasonably or fairly induced by A's conduct and upon which B reasonably relied in changing her position, that are relevant to raising and assessing the extent of the equity.[17] B's expectation must be reasonable in light of A's promise,[18] although it is not necessary for A to have subjectively intended for B to have formed that belief.[19] *Jennings v Rice*,[20] provides a good example of the scope of the inquiry as to B's expectation. A's promise of 'this will all be yours' caused B to expect that he would receive A's house and furniture. As B did not know what else A owned, B could not have held an expectation as to a greater interest, irrespective of the scope of A's promise and what expectation could have been objectively drawn. Nonetheless, B's actual expectation of receipt of A's house and furniture, was not 'fairly derived' from reasonable reliance upon A's promise in the circumstances of the case, and B's expectation was confined to something less.[21] The equity raised required vindication of B's expectation, but B's expectation had been confined so that the extent of the equity raised and relief necessary to satisfy that equity were confined as well.

B must also show detriment and that detriment is linked to A's promise. The relevant type of detriment is that which B would suffer as a result of her original change of position, if the assumption which induced B's change, was repudiated by A.[22] What counts as detriment is any material disadvantage that is substantial,

[17] *Jennings v Rice* [2002] EWCA Civ 159, [2003] 1 P&CR 8 [47] (Robert Walker LJ, with whom Aldous and Mantell LJJ agreed) ('*Jennings*').

[18] *Milling v Hardie* [2014] NSWCA 163 [70] (Macfarlan JA, with whom Beazley P agreed); *Doueihi v Construction Technologies Australia Pty Ltd* [2016] NSWCA 105 [138], [187] (Gleeson JA, with whom Beazley P and Leeming JA agreed).

[19] *Thorner* (n 1) [2]–[6] (Lord Hoffman), [78], [85] (Lord Neuberger).

[20] *Jennings* (n 17).

[21] ibid [17], [45]–[47] (Robert Walker LJ).

[22] *Gillett* (n 16) 233 (Robert Walker LJ, with whom Beldam and Waller LJJ agreed); *Grundt v Great Boulder Pty Gold Mines Ltd* (1937) 59 CLR 641 674–675 (Dixon J) ('*Grundt*'); *Delaforce v Simpson-Cook* (2010) 78 NSWLR 483 [42] (Handley AJA, with whom Allsop P and Giles JA agreed); *Sidhu* (n 2) [81] (French CJ, Kiefel, Bell and Keane JJ); *Ashton* (n 1) [141] (Bathurst CJ, with whom McColl JA agreed); Handley (n 3) [5–016].

but need not be quantifiable in pecuniary terms.[23] Detriment can include life changing decisions with irreversible consequences.[24] A decision to forego an opportunity or chance may constitute detriment sufficient to raise an estoppel.[25] For example B might decide to forego education or employment, pursue some other business venture or acquisition, or forego a claim against a third party.[26] B's change of position need not amount to actual detriment at the time the change was made; rather it is at the time A seeks to resile from her promise that detriment must be demonstrated.[27] Detriment thus includes detriment that B *has been suffered* in reliance upon A's promise, and detriment which *would be suffered* from B's change of position in reliance upon A's promise.[28] For example, in *Sidhu v Van Dyke*,[29] B had spent time and money on the promised property. Prior to A reneging on his promise, B's improvements to a property of which B expected to be the owner would not constitute detriment in the relevant sense. B's actions only constituted detriment once A reneged on his promise to transfer the property to B.

It is possible for the level of B's detriment to be reduced to take account of benefits which have accrued to B as a result of B's reliance upon A.[30] For example, where B has had the benefit of free or cheap occupation of A's land, this might be taken account of to reduce the level of B's detriment.[31]

Just as B's expectation formed in reliance on A's promise must be reasonable, so too is it necessary for B's actions to be reasonable having regard to the nature of her expectation.[32] For example, if A made a promise which induced B to expect to acquire an interest in property worth $100, B's subsequent improvements worth $10,000 would be unreasonable in relation to the expectation induced by A's promise. B's detriment must be distinguished from the detriment which flows from the disappointment of B's expectations.[33] Loss of a bargain or expectation

[23] *Donis v Donis* (2007) 19 VR 577 [30] (Nettle JA, with whom Maxwell ACJ and Ashley JA agreed) ('*Donis*'); *Australian Financial Services and Leasing Pty Ltd v Hills Industries Ltd* (2014) 253 CLR 560 [150] (Gageler J); *Ashton* (n 1) [147] (Bathurst CJ, with whom McColl JA agreed).

[24] *Gillett* (n 16) 233 (Robert Walker LJ, with whom Beldam and Waller LJJ agreed); *Donis* ibid [34] (Nettle JA, with whom Maxwell ACJ and Ashley JA agreed); *Sidhu* (n 2) [84] (French CJ, Kiefel, Bell and Keane JJ).

[25] *Austral Standard Cabels Pty Ltd v Walker Nominees Pty Ltd* (1992) 26 NSWLR 524 540 (Handley JA); *S&E Promotions Pty Ltd v Tobin Brothers Pty Ltd* (1994) 122 ALR 637 654 (the Court).

[26] See, eg: *Gillett* (n 16); *Thorner* (n 1); *Williams v Wardley* (1997) 7 Tas R 35; *Giumelli* (n 2); *Waddell v Waddell* [2012] NSWCA 214; *Delaforce v Simpson-Cook* (2010) 78 NSWLR 483 [5] (Allsop P), [48]–[50] (Handley AJA); *Sidhu* (n 2).

[27] *Grundt* (n 22) 674–675 (Dixon J); *Verwayen* (n 1) 415 (Mason CJ); *Sidhu* (n 2) [80]–[81] (French CJ, Kiefel, Bell and Keane JJ).

[28] *Verwayen* (n 1) 415 (Mason CJ); J Campbell 'Waltons v Maher: History, Unconscientiousness and Remedy—The Minimum Equity' (2013) 7 Journal of Equity 171, 192–193.

[29] *Sidhu* (n 2).

[30] See generally: McFarlane, *Proprietary Estoppel* (n 3) [4.113]–[4.180].

[31] *Milling v Hardie* [2014] NSWCA 163 [55], [69] (Macfarlan JA, with whom Beazley P agreed); *Henry v Henry* [2010] UKPC 3, [2010] 1 All ER 988 [51] (the Board).

[32] *Thorner* (n 1) [29] (Lord Walker); McFarlane, *Proprietary Estoppel* (n 3) [2.93].

[33] *Verwayen* (n 1) 429–430 (Brennan J).

profits do not constitute detriment in the relevant sense.[34] The relevant types of detriment must flow from B's own change of position. As will be discussed further below, the extent of the equity raised by an equitable estoppel may often require that B's expectation be made good so that this type of detriment would be avoided. But nonetheless the detriment resulting from the disappointment of B's expectations is not sufficient to make out the requirement for detriment sufficient to raise the estoppel.

The processes of characterising and defining each of B's expectation and detriment must be undertaken by reference to the extent to which each were caused by A's conduct. It is only B's expectation *that was induced by A's promise*, and only B's detriment *incurred on the faith of B's expectation* that are relevant to raising an equitable estoppel and defining the extent of the equity raised. The existence of two causal links between three anchors must be shown: that A's conduct induced B's expectation, and that B's change of position was made on the faith of her expectation.[35] As to the quality of the causal links between A's promise, B's expectation and B's detriment, it is necessary to show that B's reliance upon A's promise, would 'in the natural chain of causation' result 'in actual and temporal damage'.[36] There have been multiple causal tests expressed in relation to this inquiry.[37] In *Sidhu v Van Dyke*, Gageler J favoured use of the 'but for' test because 'there can be no real detriment if the party asserting the estoppel would have been in the same position in any event.'[38] However, the tenor of the formulations approved by the plurality in *Sidhu v Van Dyke*,[39] suggest that it is possible for causation to be established where A's promise contributed to or played a part in B's decision. According to the approach of the plurality in *Sidhu v Van Dyke*, it is not necessary for B to show that A's promise was the sole inducement of B's decision to change her position and it is possible for other factors to have played a part in B's decision.[40] This raises the possibility for an equitable estoppel to be raised even where B's detriment might have been suffered in any event.[41] This possibility was not expressly considered by the plurality in *Sidhu v Van Dyke* and it seemed to be accepted that 'but for' causation would have been satisfied in the circumstances of the case.[42] Thus the door

34 *Grundt* (n 22) 674–675 (Dixon J); *ACN 074 971 109 (as trustee for the Argot Unit Trust) v The National Mutual Life Association of Australasia Limited* (2008) 21 VR 351 [158]–[159] (the Court).

35 See also: E Bant, *The Change of Position Defence* (Oxford, Hart Publishing, 2009) 30–31.

36 *Osborne Park Co-operative Society Ltd v Wilden Pty Ltd* (1989) 2 WAR 77 101–102 (Franklyn J); *Williams v Wardley* (1997) 7 Tas R 35 47–48 (Crawford J).

37 As discussed in *Mineralogy Pty Ltd v Sino Iron Pty Ltd (No 6)* [2015] FCA 825 [770]–[779] (Edelman J); McFarlane, *Proprietary Estoppel* (n 3) [3.104].

38 *Sidhu* (n 2) [91]–[95] (Gageler J).

39 ibid [66]–[69], referring to *Amalgamated Investment & Property Co Ltd (In Liquidation) v Texas Commerce International Bank* [1982] QB 84 (CA) 104–105 (Robert Goff J); *Gillett* (n 16) 226–227 (Robert Walker LJ, with whom Beldam and Waller LJJ agreed); *Steria Ltd v Hutchison* [2006] EWCA Civ 1551 [117] (Neuberger LJ).

40 *Sidhu* (n 2) [72]–[73] (French CJ, Kiefel, Bell and Keane JJ).

41 See also: McFarlane, *Proprietary Estoppel* (n 3) [3.107].

42 *Sidhu* (n 2) [77]–[78] (French CJ, Kiefel, Bell and Keane JJ).

appears to be open as to whether B will be able to establish the requisite causal link in circumstances where B would have nonetheless taken the same course of conduct had A's promises not been made. Nonetheless, the existence of other causes for B's expectation and detriment is a factor which will be relevant at the next stage of inquiry, as to the extent of the equity raised by the estoppel. An equitable estoppel may well have been made out, but the extent of the equity raised by that estoppel reflects, and thus may be limited to the extent to which A's conduct is actually induced by B's expectation and detriment.

IV. How Does Equitable Compensation Satisfy the Equity Raised?

Once the elements to an equitable estoppel have been made out, an equity arises in favour of B that binds A[43] and the following questions arise: what is the extent of the equity raised by the equitable estoppel, and what type of relief will satisfy that equity? The significance of the answers to these questions is to reveal the two distinct functions of equitable compensation as a response to equitable estoppels. The inquiry as to the extent of the equity is conceptually distinct from the inquiry into the type of relief that will satisfy the equity.[44] Whilst these inquiries are not always kept separate,[45] it is nonetheless important to distinguish between them because they each take account of different considerations.[46] The inquiry into the extent of the equity raised by an equitable estoppel depends upon what is considered sufficient to remedy A's unconscionable conduct.[47] Unconscionability speaks to B's unfulfilled expectation, detriment, *and* the extent to which A's conduct caused B's expectation and detriment.[48] The inquiry as to what type of relief

[43] *Plimmer v Mayor & Council of Wellington* (1884) 9 App Cas 699 (PC) 714 (the Board); *Crabb* (n 6) 187–188 (Denning MR) 192–193 (Scarman LJ); *Thorner* (n 1) [12] (Lord Scott); *Waltons Stores* (n 1) 404 (Mason CJ and Wilson J), 416, 430 (Brennan J); *Giumelli* (n 2) [2]–[6] (Gleeson CJ, McHugh, Gummow and Callinan JJ). See also, J Campbell, 'When and Why a Bribe is Held on Constructive Trust: The Method of Reasoning Towards an Equitable Remedy' (2015) 39 *Australian Bar Review* 320, 325–327.

[44] *Crabb* (n 6) 193 (Scarman LJ); *Griffiths v Williams* [1978] 2 EGLR 121 (CA) 122 (Goff LJ).

[45] See, eg: *Campbell v Griffin* [2001] EWCA Civ 990 [34]–[36] (Robert Walker LJ).

[46] *Van Dyke v Sidhu* [2013] NSWCA 198 [138]–[140] (Barrett JA, with whom Basten JA and Tobias AJA agreed).

[47] *Crabb* (n 6) 192–193, 195 (Scarman LJ); *Gillett* (n 16) 225 (Robert Walker LJ, with whom Beldam and Waller LJJ agreed); *Austotel Pty Ltd v Franklins Selfserve Pty Ltd* (1989) 16 NSWLR 582 606 (Priestley JA); *Australian Securities Commission v Marlborough Gold Mines Ltd* (1993) 177 CLR 485 506 (the Court); *DHJPM Pty Ltd v Blackthorn Resources Ltd* (2011) 83 NSWLR 728 [75] (Meagher JA, with whom Macfarlan JA agreed); Campbell 'Waltons v Maher: History, Unconscientiousness and Remedy' (n 28) 187–188.

[48] *Olsson v Dyson* (1967) 170 CLR 394 464, 478 (Kitto J); *Riches v Hogben* [1985] 2 Qd R 292 300–301 (McPherson J); *Giumelli* (n 2) [35] (Gleeson CJ, McHugh, Gummow and Callinan JJ); *Sidhu* (n 2) [58], [77] (French CJ, Kiefel, Bell and Keane JJ).

is necessary to satisfy the equity, involves the exercise by the court of its remedial discretion, which takes account of a broader range of considerations beyond those relevant to A's unconscionable conduct, and include for example, the interests of third parties.

As to the extent of the equity raised by an equitable estoppel, there has been some divergence between assessing the equity as requiring vindication of B's expectation or the prevention of B's detriment. Outside of proprietary estoppel, there has been support for the view that the equity raised is confined to prevention of detriment.[49] According to this view, the extent of the equity might still be assessed as requiring B's expectations to be made good, but only where this is the best means of avoiding detriment, for example where detriment is difficult to quantify.[50]

There is however a growing trend in favour of the view that the starting point for assessing the extent of the equity raised by all equitable estoppels, is that B's expectation should be made good.[51] On this approach, the relief to an equitable estoppel is not always confined to what is required to prevent detriment. In *Ashton v Pratt*,[52] Bathurst CJ stated:

> What now appears clear is that there is no need to mould any remedy in the case of equitable estoppel to reflect the minimum relief necessary to remove the detriment. Prima facie the courts should enforce a reasonable expectation which [A] created or encouraged.

However, vindication of B's expectations is only the starting point of the inquiry, and is not necessarily the endpoint. The overriding requirement is that the extent of the equity cannot go beyond what is needed to prevent unconscionable

49 See, eg: *Crabb* (n 6) 193 (Scarman LJ); *Sledmore v Dalby* [1996] 74 P & CR 196 (CA) 208 (Hobhouse LJ); *Waltons Stores* (n 1) 401 (Mason CJ and Wilson J) 418–419, 421–423 (Brennan J); *Silovi Pty Ltd v Barbaro* (1988) 13 NSWLR 466 472 (Priestley JA); *Verwayen* (n 1) 417, (Mason CJ), 429–430 (Brennan J), 454 (Dawson J), 476 (Toohey J), 487 (Gaudron J), 501, 504 (McHugh J); *IOOF Building Society Pty Ltd v Foxeden Pty Ltd* [2009] VSCA 138 [135]–[136] (Maxwell P, Ashley JA and Hansen AJA); *ACN 074 971 109 (as trustee for the Argot Unit Trust) & Anor v The National Mutual Life Association of Australasia Limited* (2008) 21 VR 351 [167] (the Court); McFarlane, *Proprietary Estoppel*, (n 3) Ch 7; B McFarlane and P Sales, 'Promises, Detriment and Liability' (2015) 131 *LQR* 610.

50 *Verwayen* (n 1) 429–430 (Brennan J), 454 (Dawson J), 501 (McHugh J); A Robertson, 'The Reliance Basis of Proprietary Estoppel Remedies' (2008) 72 Conveyancer and Property Lawyer 295.

51 See, eg: *Gillett* (n 16); *Jennings* (n 17); *Thorner* (n 1); *Sullivan v Sullivan* [2006] NSWCA 312 [18]–[19] (Handley JA); *Donis* (n 23) [19] (Nettle JA, with whom Maxwell ACJ and Ashley JA agreed); *Delaforce v Simpson-Cook* (2010) 78 NSWLR 483 [54]–[93] (Handley AJA); *DHJPM Pty Ltd v Blackthorn Resources Ltd* (2011) 83 NSWLR 728 [56]–[57], [80]–[82] (Meagher JA, with whom Macfarlan JA agreed); *Sidhu* (n 2) [58], [75]–[78], [85] (French CJ, Kiefel, Bell and Keane JJ); *Ashton* (n 1) [142] (Bathurst CJ, with whom McColl JA agreed); S Barkehall Thomas, 'Proprietary Estoppel: Enforcing Expectations (Most of the Time)' (2014) 31 *Journal of Contract Law* 234; *Meagher, Gummow & Lehane's, Equity* [17-285].

52 *Ashton* (n 1) [142] (Bathurst CJ, with whom McColl JA agreed).

conduct. Recall, unconscionability is a function of expectation and detriment, and the extent to which each have been caused by A's conduct. The equity will not require fulfilment of B's expectation where B's expectation would be out of all proportion to the detriment. So, where B has been induced to make a relatively small outlay on the faith of A's promise, then it might not be unconscionable for A to resile from her promise on the condition that A reimburse B for the outlay.[53] The extent of the equity would be assessed as requiring prevention of B's detriment, not fulfilment of her expectations.

The debate as to the extent of the equity raised by an equitable estoppel ultimately reflects a deeper uncertainty as to the type of unconscionability with which estoppel is concerned to prevent. Specifically whether unconscionability relates solely to A's leaving B to suffer a detriment or whether unconscionability is also concerned with the existence of B's unfulfilled expectation.[54] Resolution of this debate is beyond the scope of inquiry for this chapter and does not change the thesis presented here. That is because irrespective how this debate is resolved, on either approach, the extent of the equity in a given case might be assessed as requiring either the prevention of detriment, or the fulfilment of B's expectations.

In relation to promissory estoppel, a further qualification to the extent of the equity raised is its limitation in some common law jurisdictions, as a source of negative rights.[55] The result being that where a promissory estoppel is so confined, then the equity raised can only ever operate as a restraint against the enforcement by A of her rights against B. A promissory estoppel of this nature for example would not confer upon B a positive right to equitable compensation in the event of A's non-performance.

After the extent of the equity raised by an equitable estoppel has been ascertained, the next stage of inquiry considers *the type of relief* that satisfies the equity raised. The type of remedy must be that which is the 'minimum equity to do justice'.[56] Albeit the reference to 'minimum' does not mean that the court must be 'constitutionally parsimonious',[57] but requires the type of relief to be fashioned to satisfy the equity raised in an individual case and not go beyond what is required to prevent unconscientiousness.[58]

[53] *Sidhu* (n 2) [84] (French CJ, Kiefel, Bell and Keane JJ).

[54] See for example, *Riches v Hogben* [1985] 2 Qd R 292 300–302 (McPherson J); *Giumelli* (n 2) [35] (Gleeson CJ, McHugh, Gummow and Callinan JJ); Robertson (n 50); Campbell 'Waltons v Maher: History, Unconscientiousness and Remedy' (n 28); McFarlane and Sales, 'Promises, Detriment and Liability' (n 49).

[55] See text accompanying notes 6–15.

[56] *Crabb* (n 6).

[57] *Jennings* (n 17) [48] (Robert Walker LJ, with whom Aldous and Mantell LJJ agreed).

[58] *Giumelli* (n 2) [50] (Gleeson CJ, McHugh, Gummow and Callinan JJ); *Donis* (n 23) [20] (Nettle JA, with whom Maxwell ACJ and Ashley JA agreed); *John Alexander's Clubs Pty Ltd v White City Tennis Club Ltd* (2010) 241 CLR 1 [128] (French CJ, Gummow, Hayne, Heydon and Kiefel JJ).

Some preliminary finding will be made as to the type of remedy that meets the equity raised and this inquiry will take into account the extent of the equity and the particular equitable estoppel raised. Where the extent of the equity raised requires prevention of B's detriment, equitable compensation is in view as a possible remedial response. Here, equitable compensation is the direct response to the equity raised, and the function of equitable compensation is to compensate for B's detriment. Considered in the next part is the measure of equitable compensation when it has this function. It is important to note that equitable compensation is not the only available remedy where the equity raised requires prevention of detriment. It is possible for the equity to require other types of relief, and could include, an injunction restraining the exercise by A of her rights against B. Further the extent of the equity may not require permanent relief, and the period of time for which A is restrained might be temporary if that is all that is necessary to prevent B's detriment in a given case.[59]

Where the extent of the equity is assessed as requiring fulfilment of B's expectations, the relief that might initially be considered appropriate to meet the equity raised by an equitable estoppel, or the 'prime facie' relief,[60] includes a constructive trust, or an order requiring performance by A of her promise, such as to re-new a contract,[61] grant a sub-lease,[62] or an injunction restraining A from doing something, such as exercising her rights under an existing contract.[63]

Identification of one or multiple forms of relief which satisfy the equity raised is not the end of the inquiry. Like any other entitlement to equitable relief, B's equitable rights are not absolute and are subject to the court exercising its discretion whether to award equitable relief at all, and as to the type of relief.[64] Identification of the appropriate type of relief takes account of factors beyond those which are relevant to assessment of the extent of the equity. These factors might arise after the events giving rise to the estoppel, and can include the defendant's unexpected financial hardship, the interests of third parties, what has happened to specific property, and the parties' need for a clean break.[65] These discretionary factors may well mean that the type of relief ultimately awarded is different to the type of relief which prime facie, is considered necessary to satisfy the equity raised

[59] *Tool Metal Manufacturing Co Ltd v Tungsten Electric Co Ltd* [1955] 2 All ER 657, [1955] 1 WLR 761 (HL) 785 (Lord Tucker); P Feltham, D Hochberg and T Leech (eds), *Spencer Bower: The Law Relating to Estoppel by Representation*, 4th edn, (London, Tottel Publishing, 2004), para [XIV.3.1]; Handley (n 3) [13–007].

[60] *Giumelli* (n 2) [50] (Gleeson CJ, McHugh, Gummow and Callinan JJ).

[61] *Metropolitan v Waverley* (n 11) 205–207 (the Court).

[62] *S&E Promotions Pty Ltd v Tobin Brothers Pty Ltd* (1994) 122 ALR 637.

[63] *Legione v Hateley* (1983) 152 CLR 406.

[64] *Giumelli* (n 2) [9] (Gleeson CJ, McHugh, Gummow and Callinan JJ).

[65] See, eg, *Gillett* (n 16) 237–238 (Robert Walker LJ, with whom Beldam and Waller LJJ agreed); *Jennings* (n 17) [52] (Robert Walker LJ, with whom Aldous and Mantell LJJ agreed); *Giumelli* (n 2) [49]–[50] (Gleeson CJ, McHugh, Gummow and Callinan JJ); *Milling v Hardie* [2014] NSWCA 163 [55] (Macfarlan JA, with whom Beazley P agreed).

by an equitable estoppel. For example in *Giumelli v Giumelli*,[66] the prime facie relief that satisfied the equity raised by a proprietary estoppel was a constructive trust in favour of B over land owned by A. However, due to the effect that such an order would have on the interests of third parties, equitable compensation was ordered as the alternative remedy, secured by an equitable charge over the specific property. *Giumelli* thus demonstrates the other function of equitable compensation: which is to provide a remedial alternative or substitute to the specific relief which prime facie meets the equity raised but is not available in the circumstances of the case.[67]

V. The Two Functions of Equitable Compensation for Equitable Estoppels

It has been argued above that equitable compensation has two distinct functions within equitable estoppels; compensation and substitution. Whether equitable compensation is required and which function it pursues, depend on the extent of the equity raised by an equitable estoppel, and what form of relief is considered appropriate in the circumstances of the case. The following parts examine archetype cases which evidence the two functions of equitable compensation within equitable estoppels. An examination of these archetypes reveals that different measures of equitable compensation and different principles are employed depending on which function equitable compensation pursues.

A. Equitable Compensation as a Substitute for Specific Relief

In *Sidhu v Van Dyke* a proprietary estoppel was found where A had made promises to B to the effect that A would transfer to B ownership of a cottage and the parcel of land upon which the cottage stood. The cottage stood on a block of land owned by A and A's wife. A's promise was conditional upon council approval for subdivision of the block of land and consent from A's wife. As events transpired, the cottage burnt down, the conditions to council approval for the subdivision were not satisfied and A refused to convey to B the land. In reliance on A's promises, B chose to forgo an opportunity to obtain a more favourable property settlement with her ex-husband, forego extra employment and B also expended her own money and time in making improvements to the cottage and land owned by A in reliance on A's promise.[68]

[66] *Giumelli* (n 2).
[67] See also: McFarlane, *Proprietary Estoppel* (n3) [9.08].
[68] *Sidhu* (n 2)[10]–[12] (French CJ, Kiefel, Bell and Keane JJ).

The High Court found that the causal links between A's promise, B's expectation and B's detriment were satisfied, and that B's reliance was reasonable.[69] The extent of the equity raised in B's favour was assessed as requiring A to be held to his promise to transfer to B both the cottage and land.[70] The prime facie remedy was specific relief in the form of a constructive trust.[71] However, other factors came into play which rendered the contemplated specific relief unavailable, such as A's wife's interest in the property.[72] Thus it was necessary to turn to equitable compensation as an alternative remedy to satisfy B's equity.[73] The case was one 'for the fixing of a monetary sum to represent the value of the equitable claim of [B] to the promised lot.'[74] In the Court of Appeal, Barrett JA distinguished between the two functions of equitable compensation within equitable estoppels referring to equitable compensation where its function is to compensate for B's detriment suffered through reliance upon A's promise, and equitable compensation where it operates as '[t]he monetary substitute for preclusion of [A] from disappointing the expectation that his promises engendered in [B] (that is that the … [c]ottage would be given to her)'.[75] The measure of equitable compensation involved an inquiry into the value of the contemplated specific relief considered necessary to satisfy the equity raised. Barrett JA described the measure of equitable compensation as the sum 'equal to the value [B] would now have had the promises been fulfilled.'[76] Equitable compensation was ultimately calculated according to the value of the property which had been promised to be conveyed, which included the non-existent cottage.[77]

The significance of characterising the role of equitable compensation as a substitute to specific relief is that the measure of equitable compensation is not tied to loss or detriment, and principles such as causation, foreseeability and remoteness do not have roles to play. The measure of equitable compensation is the value of the specific relief for which equitable compensation is the remedial alternative. In *Sidhu v Van Dyke*, the inquiry into the value of the specific relief B should have received, did not take account of factors relevant to the different question of the value of the hypothetical position lost by B which B expected to be in upon performance by A. The fact that the subdivision required for the transfer of the property

[69] ibid [78], [86].

[70] ibid [86].

[71] *Van Dyke v Sidhu* [2013] NSWCA 198 [137], [140] (Barrett JA, with whom Basten JA and Tobias AJA agreed), approved in *Sidhu* (n 2) [87] (French CJ, Kiefel, Bell and Keane JJ).

[72] *Van Dyke v Sidhu* [2012] NSWSC 118 [249] (Ward J); *Van Dyke v Sidhu* [2013] NSWCA 198 [138] (Barrett JA, with whom Basten JA and Tobias AJA agreed), approved in *Sidhu* (n 2) [87] (French CJ, Kiefel, Bell and Keane JJ).

[73] *Van Dyke v Sidhu* [2013] NSWCA 198 [139], approved in *Sidhu* (n 2) [87] (French CJ, Kiefel, Bell and Keane JJ).

[74] ibid [139] quoting *Giumelli* (n 2) [5] (Gleeson CJ, McHugh, Gummow and Callinan JJ) .

[75] *Van Dyke v Sidhu* [2013] NSWCA 198 [140] (Barrett JA, with whom Basten JA and Tobias AJA agreed), approved in *Sidhu* (n 2) [87] (French CJ, Kiefel, Bell and Keane JJ).

[76] ibid.

[77] ibid [142] (Barrett JA, with whom Basten JA and Tobias AJA agreed).

never occurred, and that the cottage no longer existed, did not reduce the sum awarded to B. Had the function of equitable compensation been to compensate for expectation loss, then the measure adopted and the process for calculation may have been very different. Rather than asking what is the value of specific relief, the inquiry focuses on the value of the difference between the position B is in and the hypothetical position she would have been in had A performed their promise, which may take account of factors such as intervening events.

Causation does not have a direct role to play in calculation of equitable compensation where it is a remedial substitute because the inquiry into the value of the contemplated specific relief does not require a causal link to be established and in any event causation has already been established in order to raise the estoppel. As discussed above, the extent to which B's expectation and detriment are causally linked to A's conduct will be a factor that defines the extent of the equity raised in B's favour. Of course, causation may have the effect of confining the extent of the equity raised by an estoppel and thus have an indirect effect on the level of equitable compensation awarded.

Concepts such as remoteness and foreseeability have no role to play either. Leaving aside the broader debate about whether such concepts can ever have a role to play within equitable compensation,[78] they have no function in the assessment of equitable compensation as a substitute to specific relief for estoppel because there is no assessment of loss. That is not to say that there are no other factors which might be relevant to assessing the value of equitable compensation when it is a substitute for specific relief. For example, if an estoppel is enforced prior to when performance of A's promise is required, then an allowance might have to be made for the acceleration of B's expectation.[79]

In addition to cases which expressly award equitable compensation as a remedial alternative to specific relief,[80] there are cases which award a monetary sum in lieu of specific relief, without reference to the label of equitable compensation.[81] It might be suggested that the monetary sum awarded in these latter cases is best characterised as equitable damages. For example, in *Waltons Stores (Interstate) Ltd v Maher*[82] an award of equitable damages under the NSW equivalent s 2 of *Lord Cairns' Act* (1858), awarded at first instance[83] and upheld on appeal,[84] was upheld

[78] See n 97 below.

[79] *Gillett* (n 16) 237–238 (Robert Walker LJ, with whom Beldam and Waller LJJ agreed); *Quinn v Bryant* [2012] NSWCA 377 [40] (Sackville AJA, with whom Allsop P and Barrett JA agreed); *Rodda v Ian Rodda Pty Ltd; Ian Rodda Pty Ltd v Rodda* [2015] SASC 95 [304] (Nicholson J).

[80] *Ronowska v Kus* [2012] NSWSC 280; *Rodda v Ian Rodda Pty Ltd* [2015] SASC 95.

[81] *Baker v Baker* [1993] 2 FLR 247 (CA); *Wayling v Jones* (1993) 69 P&CR 170 (CA); *Campbell v Griffin* [2001] EWCA Civ 990; *Gillett* (n 16); *Giumelli* (n 2); *Donis*(n 23).

[82] *Waltons Stores* (n 1).

[83] *Maher v Waltons Stores (Interstate) Ltd* (1984) 1 BCL 187 199 (Kearney J), *Supreme Court Act* 1970 (NSW), s 68.

[84] *Waltons Stores Limited v Maher* (1986) 5 NSWLR 407 421–424 (Priestley JA, with whom Glass and Samuels JJA agreed).

by the High Court in response to a promissory estoppel.[85] However, it is submitted that *Waltons Stores (Interstate) Ltd v Maher* provides little support for the availability of equitable damages for an equitable estoppel because the basis upon which the award of equitable damages was made at first instance was very different to that in the High Court. Kearney J's decision at first instance was based on a finding that a binding agreement existed between the parties which was capable of specific performance. The High Court decision turned on the basis that there was no actual contract in existence between the parties and rather a promissory estoppel existed. The implications for the form of relief given the different findings made in the High Court were not directly addressed in the High Court judgments. But according to the findings made in the High Court, there was no contract capable of specific performance and which could trigger the jurisdiction to award equitable damages. To the extent that the jurisdiction to award equitable damages is conditioned upon the existence of common law rights,[86] then in principle, equitable damages were not available as a response to an equitable estoppel in *Waltons Stores (Interstate) Ltd v Maher* and for the same reason would not generally be available as a response to an equitable estoppel.

Whether equitable compensation might be available in its substitutive form in response to other equitable estoppels, depends on the extent of the equity raised by the equitable estoppel in question. For example, where a promissory estoppel or an equitable estoppel is established and the extent of the equity raised requires vindication of B's expectations, specific relief may be available.[87] In the event that specific relief is not possible due to other considerations, then equitable compensation might be available as the remedial alternative. But whether equitable compensation can ever have such a role to play in response to promissory estoppel or equitable estoppel, depends upon the resolution of the broader debates as to the nature and scope of these estoppels and whether the extent of the equity generated by a promissory estoppel or equitable estoppel can ever be such to require vindication of B's expectations.

Finally, mention should be made of proprietary awards. Sometimes the award of equitable compensation will be secured by an equitable lien or charge over A's property, particularly in the context of proprietary estoppel claims.[88] The question of when an award of equitable compensation should be secured over property is beyond the scope of this chapter, but will ultimately be a function of the extent of the equity raised and what form of relief is considered necessary to satisfy all the circumstances of the case.

85 *Waltons Stores* (n 1) 408 (Mason CJ and Wilson J), 430–433 (Brennan J).

86 *Meagher, Gummow and Lehane's, Equity* [24-090]; cf ICF Spry, *Equitable Remedies*, 2nd edn (London, Sweet & Maxwell, 1980) 552–555.

87 See, eg, *Waltons Stores* (n 1) 407–408 (Mason CJ and Wilson J), 430, 432–433 (Brennan J); *Vosnakis v Arfaras* [2015] NSWSC 625.

88 See, eg, *Giumelli* (n 2), cf *Sidhu* (n 2) where equitable compensation was not secured against the promised property.

B. Compensating for Detriment

The compensatory function of equitable compensation comes into view when the extent of the equity raised demands that B's detriment be compensated for by A. Equitable compensation may be an appropriate form of relief to satisfy that equity and in this instance, operates as a compensatory response rather than a substitute for specific relief. The measure of equitable compensation is the monetary value of B's detriment. The assessment of equitable compensation is simply a matter of assigning a monetary figure to B's detriment as previously identified in order to establish the estoppel. This assessment does not encompass the question of causation, or proof of the existence of detriment. B's detriment has already been identified, and the causal links between A's promise, B's expectation and B's detriment have already been established in order to make out the elements to the estoppel. If B's detriment is not sufficiently proven or not sufficiently connected to A's promise and B's expectation, then the estoppel will not be made out in the first place.

A useful case example is *E K Nominees Pty Ltd v Woolworths Ltd.*[89] The prospective landlord (B) and tenant (A) had been in negotiations for an agreement for lease, which, among other things required council approval for development of the site in accordance with A's site specifications. B incurred expenditure in obtaining development approval, satisfying the conditions for development and preparing the development site in anticipation of entering into a formal agreement for lease with A. A had encouraged B's expenditure, and held out to B that A would enter into an agreement for lease with B. However, A decided not to enter into an agreement for lease when another opportunity arose. B successfully raised an equitable estoppel and White J found that the extent of the equity required A to compensate B for its detriment.[90] The measure of equitable compensation reflected the value of B's expenditure incurred in reliance upon A's promise. Expenses incurred *after* A's promise was made, but not before, were recoverable.[91]

A distinction can be made between a claim for equitable compensation for detriment incurred in reliance upon A's promise and a claim in *quantum meruit* for reasonable remuneration for work done.[92] For example, where A promises B an interest in land in return for B's services, it is possible for B to raise either an equitable

[89] *E K Nominees Pty Ltd v Woolworths Ltd* [2006] NSWSC 1172. See also, *Williams v Wardley* [1997] 7 Tas LR 35; *Petronijevic v Milojkovic* [2014] NSWSC 1337; *Nguyen v Condo* [2014] QSC 239.

[90] *E K Nominees Pty Ltd v Woolworths Ltd* [2006] NSWSC 1172 [278], [281], [291] (White J).

[91] ibid [279]–[290].

[92] See, eg: C Mitchell, P Mitchell and S Watterson, *Goff & Jones, The Law of Unjust Enrichment*, 8th edn (London, Sweet & Maxwell, 2011) [16–21]; HW Tang, 'An Unjust Enrichment Claim For the Mistaken Improver of Land' [2011] *Conveyancer & Property Lawyer* 8, cf S Degeling and B Edgeworth, 'Improvements to Land Belonging to Another' in L Bennett Moses, B Edgeworth and C Sherry (eds), *Property and Security: Selected Essays* (Sydney, Lawbook Co, 2010) 277.

estoppel or a claim in *quantum meruit*. In the latter type of claim, the measure of the monetary award is the value of the benefit of B's services *to A*,[93] not the value of the detriment incurred by B, for example B's opportunity cost. These values may not always coincide and it is important to distinguish between the two different types of claim and measures that follow. For example, the market rate of services conferred upon A by B might represent the appropriate measure of the sum payable by A in a claim in *quantum meruit*, but is not *always* the appropriate measure for equitable compensation for equitable estoppel.[94] The market rate of B's services represents A's gain, and does not necessarily represent B's detriment.[95] The appropriate measure of B's detriment is B's lost opportunity to engage in paid employment. Of course where the services conferred on A by B represents B's usual employment, then market value will measure both A's gain and B's detriment. The value of the forgone employment (B's detriment) would correspond with the value of the services conferred on A (A's gain). However where the services conferred on A are not B's usual course of employment and B's earning potential is greater than the value of the services rendered to A then there may be a difference between A's gain and B's detriment. In these circumstances, an award of equitable compensation calculated by reference to the value of B's services conferred on A (rather than B's lost opportunity) does not compensate for B's detriment and would leave the equity raised by an equitable estoppel unsatisfied.

As discussed above, the process of identifying B's detriment and establishing causation are part of the inquiry as to the existence of the cause of action and the extent of the equity raised. The measure of equitable compensation when it compensates for B's detriment is simply a function of valuing B's (in)actions which have already been identified as detriment. One might ask whether there are nonetheless other principles which might apply to limit the value of equitable compensation, or to frame the question another way, is A to be left responsible for any and all of B's detriment? In answer to this question, it has been suggested that A is responsible for B's detriment to the extent B's detriment was reasonably foreseeable.[96]

Leaving aside the issue of whether foreseeability, remoteness and mitigation may or may not have a role to play within equitable compensation more broadly,[97]

93 *Benedetti v Sawiris* [2013] UKSC 50, [2014] AC 938 [13]–[17] (Lord Clarke), [100]–[101] (Lord Reed), [180]–[185] (President Neuberger).

94 See also, *Jennings* (n 17) [54] (Robert Walker LJ, with whom Aldous and Mantell LJJ agreed); *Williams v Wardley* (1997) 7 Tas R 35 37 (Crawford J).

95 *Williams v Wardley* (1997) 7 Tas R 35 37 (Crawford J).

96 *Ciavarella v Polimeni* [2008] NSWSC 234 [176]–[184] (Young CJ in Eq); McFarlane, *Proprietary Estoppel* (n 3) [4.69]–[4.76].

97 See, eg: *Re Dawson; Union Fidelity Trustee Co Ltd v Perpetual Trustee Co Ltd* [1966] 2 NSWR 211 215 (Street J); *O'Halloran v R T Thomas & Family Pty Ltd* (1998) 45 NSWLR 262 273 (Spigelman CJ); *Youyang Pty Ltd v Minter Ellison Morris Fletcher* (2003) 212 CLR 484 [77] (the Court); *Pilmer v Duke Group Ltd (In Liq)* 207 CLR 165 [85]–[87] (McHugh, Gummow, Hayne and Callinan JJ); WMC Gummow, 'Compensation for Breach of Fiduciary Duty' in TG Youdan (ed), *Equity, Fiduciaries and Trusts*

it is submitted here that these principles are not relevant to the measure of equitable compensation for equitable estoppels. Concepts such as remoteness, foreseeability and mitigation are rendered functionally redundant within equitable estoppels because there are already objective limits to A's responsibility which are built into the elements for equitable estoppels. Recall that the expectation and detriment which count to raise an estoppel and according to which the extent of the equity will be defined are not simply B's actual expectation and detriment causally linked to A's promise. It is also necessary for B's expectation and B's detriment to be reasonable in light of A's promise. These reasonableness requirements are objective benchmarks that limit the extent of the equity raised in favour of B and ultimately the measure of equitable compensation payable by A. Further, the requirement that B's expectation and detriment be reasonably foreseeable by A has not been imposed in other cases. In *Thorner v Major*, for example, there was no evidence to the effect that A knew, or could have known of the opportunities foregone by B in reliance upon A's promise.[98] This did not render B's detriment irrelevant and a different objective limit was imposed, that B's expectation and detriment were both reasonable in light of A's conduct and in the context of the relationship between A and B.[99]

VI. Conclusion

This chapter has argued that within the realm of equitable estoppels, equitable compensation has two different functions. One function is as a remedial substitute to specific relief, where specific relief has already been identified as the optimal remedy to satisfy the equity raised by an estoppel, but for other reasons is not available. The other function of equitable compensation is to compensate for B's detriment in the situation where it has been decided that the extent of the equity raised by an equitable estoppel requires B's detriment to be compensated. It is important to distinguish between these two remedial functions because each demands a different measure for equitable compensation.

The arguments presented in this chapter have significance outside of equitable estoppels, and speak to the ongoing debate regarding the remedial role and measure of equitable compensation. It has been argued that the function of equitable

(Toronto, Carswell, 1989) 57–92; JD Heydon, 'Causal Relationships Between a Fiduciary's Default and the Principal's Loss' (1994) 110 *LQR* 328; S Elliott, 'Remoteness Criteria in Equity' (2002) 65 *MLR* 588; J Allsop, 'Causation in Commercial Law' in S Degeling, J Edelman and J Goudkamp (eds), *Torts in Commercial Law* (Sydney, Thomson Reuters, 2011) 269–330.

98 *Thorner* (n 1) [40] (Lord Walker), [78] (Lord Neuberger).

99 ibid, [3]–[4] (Lord Hoffman), [15]–[17] (Lord Scott), [79]–[80] (Lord Neuberger).

compensation in some instances is to provide a monetary substitute for performance rather than compensate for loss.[100] However it has also been argued that equitable compensation is confined to compensating for loss[101] and as a result of this divergence, there is uncertainty regarding the role and standard of causation and other limiting concepts within equitable compensation. So far, this debate has largely focused upon equitable compensation as a response to misapplication of trust property and breach of fiduciary duty. This chapter contributes to this debate by providing clear evidence that equitable compensation can and does have multiple remedial functions. At least within equitable estoppels, equitable compensation is not always concerned with loss, and in some instances provides a substitute for specific relief.

100 See, eg, *Agricultural Land Management v Jackson (No 2)* [2014] WASC 102 [334]–[349] (Edelman J); *Libertarian Investments Ltd v Hall* (2013) 16 HKCFAR 681 [167]–[169] (Millett LJ); S Elliott, 'Compensation Claims against Trustees' DPhil thesis, University of Oxford (2002); S Elliott, 'Remoteness Criteria in Equity' (2002) 65 *MLR* 588; S Elliott and C Mitchell, 'Remedies for Dishonest Assistance' (2004) 67 *MLR* 16; C Mitchell, 'Equitable Compensation for Breach of Fiduciary Duty' (2013) 66 *Current Legal Problems* 307; C Mitchell, 'Stewardship of Property and Liability to Account' [2014] *Conveyancer and Property Lawyer* 215; S Elliott, 'Personal Monetary Claims' in McGhee J (ed) *Snell's Equity* (Sweet & Maxwell, 2015) Ch 20; P Davis, 'Remedies for Breach of Trust' (2015) 78(4) *MLR* 672; J Edelman, Ch 5 in this volume.

101 *Target Holdings Ltd v Redferns* [1995] UKHL 10, [1996] 1 AC 421; *AIB Group (UK) plc v Mark Redler & Co Solicitors* [2014] UKSC 58, [2014] 3 WLR 1367 [64]–[77] (Lord Toulson JSC), [136]–[141] (Lord Reed); P Turner, 'Measuring Equitable Compensation for Breach of Fiduciary Duty' (2014) 73 CLJ 257; *Meagher, Gummow and Lehane's, Equity*, Ch 23.

12

Rudiments of the Equitable Remedy of Compensation for Breach of Confidence

PG TURNER*

I. Introduction

Materials relating to the equitable remedy of compensation for breach of confidence are insufficient to afford a complete view of the nature and incidence of the remedy in the four jurisdictions to be studied in this chapter: Australia, Canada, England and Wales[1] and New Zealand. From England, Arnold J laments that:

> It is very difficult to find a clear, accurate and comprehensive statement of the principles applicable to the assessment of damages or equitable compensation for breach of confidence. The case law is very confused, and none of the existing commentaries deal[s] entirely satisfactorily with it.[2]

The contributing causes are several. Only as recently as 1978,[3] 1984,[4] 1988[5] and 1999[6] was it definitively settled, respectively, in New Zealand, Australia, England

* The author is grateful for the comments of Mr Astron Douglas, the Hon. Justice Mark Leeming, Professor Richard Nolan and Dr Jason Varuhas. The normal disclaimers apply.

1 For brevity, England and Wales will hereinafter be referred to as 'England'.

2 *Force India Formula One Team Ltd v 1 Malaysia Racing Team Sdn Bhd* [2012] EWHC 616 (Ch), [374]. Similarly, *Flogas Britain Ltd v Calor Gas Ltd* [2013] EWHC 3060 (Ch), [40].

3 *AB Consolidated Ltd v Europe Strength Food Co Pty Ltd* [1978] 2 NZLR 515, 520–521 (CA) (obligations of confidence 'are founded in equity and arise quite independently of contract—or of tort').

4 *Moorgate Tobacco Co Ltd v Philip Morris Ltd (No 2)* (1984) 156 CLR 414, 437–438 (HCA) ('equitable jurisdiction to grant relief against an actual or threatened abuse of confidential information not involving any tort or any breach of some express or implied contractual provision, some wider fiduciary duty or some copyright or trade mark right').

5 *A-G v Observer Ltd* [1990] 1 AC 109, 255 (HL) ('an independent equitable principle of confidence' apart from contract), 268 ('not dependent on contract and exists as an equitable remedy'), 281 ('a duty of confidence may arise in equity independently of' contract), 293.

6 *Cadbury Schweppes Inc v FBI Foods Ltd* [1999] 1 SCR 142, [19]–[28] (SCC) ('The equitable doctrine … potentially runs alongside a number of other causes of action for unauthorized use or disclosure of confidential information, including actions sounding in contract, tort and property law [sic]').

and Canada that non-contractual obligations of confidence are in nature equitable and arise in equity's exclusive jurisdiction—rather than in aid of common law rights. Only later again was it definitively settled in Australia,[7] Canada[8] and New Zealand[9] that equitable compensation is available for breach of such an equitable obligation; even now, as Arnold J has observed, the remedy's availability in England is not settled. Further, the novel genus of 'equitable compensation', of which equitable compensation for breach of confidence is but one species, is yet to be well understood.

This chapter seeks to identify the rudiments of the equitable remedy of compensation for breach of confidence. It particularly seeks those rudiments capable of combining together to form the clear and accurate statement of principle for which there is desire. Those rudiments, it will be argued, include the following. Contract and statute aside, obligations of confidence are equitable. A compensatory remedy for breach of such an equitable obligation should be equitable also. The character and features of that remedy should stem from the root of the equitable obligation of confidence, which lies in conscience. Just as compensatory relief at common law differs according to the principles and policies served by each common law cause of action, so the equitable remedy of compensation for breach of confidence should differ from awards of compensation that satisfy liabilities arising from obligations with roots in different principles and policies, such as the enforcement of promises.

In order to show the force of those propositions, however, a further argument must also be pursued. Though the situation lamented by Arnold J can be attributed to the recency of developments both in the nature of non-contractual obligations of confidence and the field of equitable compensation generally, the current obscurity of the remedy of equitable compensation for breach of confidence is mainly the result of category errors. Non-contractual obligations of confidence have been recognised as equitable. But the attributes of obligations in that category have been confused with the attributes of other categories. Liability for breach of the equitable obligation has been confused with liability for breaches of obligations in tort and contract. Principles of compensation that are properly adapted to the equitable liability have remained obscure. Instead, priority has wrongly been given to principles adapted to liability in tort and in contract, or the development of settled principles has been abandoned in favour of newly found broad judicial discretion. Confusion amongst categories at times places the possibility of an equitable remedy of compensation for breach of confidence wholly in doubt.

[7] *Smith Kline & French Laboratories (Aust) Ltd v Department of Community Services and Health* (1990) 22 FCR 73, 83 (*semble*) (FCA). This was foreshadowed in *Concept Television Productions Pty Ltd v Australian Broadcasting Corp* (1988) 12 IPR 129, 136 (FCA).

[8] *Cadbury Schweppes* (n 6) [59]–[61].

[9] *Aquaculture Corporation v New Zealand Green Mussel Co Ltd* [1990] 3 NZLR 299, 301 (CA).

A comprehensive examination of those problems ought to allow the rudiments of an equitable remedy of compensation for breach of confidence to be distinguished from erroneous and unsafe ideas. That is the task attempted in what follows. The chapter will begin by considering the most basic of doubts: those concerning the very status of the equitable remedy. Though the equitable nature of obligations of confidence has been clearly affirmed, confusion over equitable and other types of liabilities still undermines the remedy's status. Assuming that the remedy commands a secure status, the chapter will then consider less fundamental but nevertheless important areas of confusion. Problems relating to concurrent liabilities, concurrently available remedies, equitable discretion and quantification will in turn be addressed. A succinct statement of the principles of equitable compensation for breach of confidence will then be offered in conclusion.

II. Status of the Remedy

Doubts over the status of the remedy of equitable compensation for breach of confidence are the most fundamental of doubts to affect current legal understanding thereof. When these doubts have arisen, they have been coupled to doubts over other questions. Four 'constitutional' doubts over the remedy will be discussed. In order, these arise from related doubts over 'the cause of action' for breach of confidence; obligations of confidence as a *sui generis* type of obligation; the legal policy of protecting confidences; and the practical distinctness of equitable compensation for breach of confidence. Upon consideration, these doubts over the status of the remedy can each be dismissed.

A. Causes of Action and Forms of Action

Until an 'action' for breach of confidence apart from contract became recognised in the twentieth century, confidences had been protected in law with no unity of legal concept.[10] For centuries the means of protection were sundry: the reliance on civil procedure, the law of master and servant, conditional bonds and actions of covenant in order to protect confidences has recently been documented.[11] Principles began to coalesce in Chancery around nineteenth century decisions in which an equity to injunctive relief was established.[12] However, a unitary doctrine of confidence

[10] T Aplin, L Bently, P Johnson and S Malynicz, *Gurry on Breach of Confidence: The Protection of Confidential Information*, 2nd edn (Oxford, Oxford University Press, 2012) Chs 2 and 4.

[11] Aplin et al (n 10) Ch 2.

[12] Especially *Abernethy v Hutchinson* (1825) 1 H & Tw 28; *Prince Albert v Strange* (1849) 2 DeG & Sm 652 (V-C); 1 Mac & G 25; 1 H & Tw 1302 (LC); *Morison v Moat* (1851) 9 Hare 241; (1852) 21 LJ Ch 248 (Ch App).

and, thus, an 'action' for breach of confidence only developed during the twentieth century. The key-note was struck in *Saltman Engineering Co Ltd v Campbell Engineering Co Ltd*,[13] where Lord Greene MR accepted a principle that:

> If a defendant is proved to have used confidential information, directly or indirectly obtained from a plaintiff, without the consent, express or implied, of the plaintiff, he will be guilty of an infringement of the plaintiff's rights.[14]

From the late 1960s onwards, the language of 'the action' for breach of confidence became frequent in the reported decisions of the courts.[15] The new idiom represented a change of understanding of the nature of non-contractual obligations of confidence. Whereas confidences were once protected only by sundry means, they were now protected through a unitary equitable obligation and cause of action for breach thereof.

The new idiom in which judges spoke of 'an action' and a 'cause of action' for breach of confidence was also significant in what it said of the relationship between liability for breach of confidence in equity and liabilities elsewhere in civil law. The idiom ought to have had little significance. As Diplock LJ explained in *Letang v Cooper*,[16] a cause of action 'is simply a factual situation the existence of which entitles one person to obtain from the court a remedy against another person'.[17] 'Action' and 'cause of action' are words without magic. In particular, a cause of action is distinct from the old forms of action which, until they were progressively abolished in England during the nineteenth century,[18] divided causes of action into categories according to the facts required to be shown in order to obtain a particular court remedy.[19] The cause of action for breach of confidence was established over 70 years after the forms' extinction in 1875. In 1941, soon before *Saltman*, and in the 1960s, when the new equitable cause of action increased in prominence, judges no less than Lord Atkin,[20] Lord Denning MR[21] and Diplock LJ[22] declared that the old forms of action were irrelevant to the work of a twentieth century judge. Indeed, how could the forms of action—which all lay at common

[13] *Saltman Engineering Co Ltd v Campbell Engineering Co Ltd* (1948) 65 RPC 203 (CA). See *Hubbard v Vosper* [1972] 2 QB 84, 88 (CA) (counsel asserting that a 'modern resuscitation of the [purely equitable] doctrine of confidentiality' occurred in *Saltman*).

[14] *Saltman* (n 13) 213. See the mention by counsel for the plaintiff of 'an action for breach of confidence' (at 210), and of the alternative pleaded 'courses of action', one of which was for a breach of confidence, and see the similar language of Somervell LJ: 216–217.

[15] Below (nn 25–27).

[16] *Letang v Cooper* [1965] 1 QB 232 (CA).

[17] ibid 242–243.

[18] See Uniformity of Process Act (2 Wm IV c 39) 1832 s 21; Common Law Procedure Act (15 & 16 Vict c 76) 1852 ss 2–3; Judicature Act (36 & 37 Vict c 66) 1873 sch, paras 1–3.

[19] *Letang* (n 16) 243.

[20] *United Australia Ltd v Barclays Bank Ltd* [1941] AC 1, 29 (HL).

[21] *Letang* (n 16) 239.

[22] ibid 243.

law—be significant to a cause of action that was not only established some seven decades after the forms' extinction, but that was also founded in what Lord Greene MR saw as an equitable obligation of conscience?[23]

However, the developments following *Saltman* support Maitland's view that '[t]he forms of action we have buried, but they still rule us from their graves'.[24] To recognise a cause of action for breach of confidence is only to indicate that a breach of confidence is a factual situation that entitles one person to obtain from a court some remedy against another person. It would be no less a cause of action were the relief limited to injunction and orders for delivery up, and it would be no more a cause of action if the relief included monetary relief for loss. It is striking, therefore, that once judges and lawyers began speaking of a 'cause of action' for breach of confidence, they soon also spoke of a cause of action for breach of confidence for which 'damages' were an available remedy. They were encouraged by the Court of Appeal's unexplained award of 'damages' in *Saltman.* The terminology of a 'cause of action' for breach of action sounding in 'damages' subsequently became more frequent in legal usage,[25] was well established in England by 1980,[26] and is current in England today.[27] The action for breach of confidence was thus assimilated to the old personal forms of action abolished in 1832 and 1852; more specifically, the *ostensurus quare* writs for the recovery of damages—trespass, case, trover and assumpsit—rather than the *praecipe* writs of debt, detinue, covenant and account.[28] The ruling influence of the old forms of action seems undeniable. In declaring a cause of action for misuse of private information in English law to lie at common law, not in equity, the Court of Appeal[29] laid great weight on loose descriptions of breach of confidence as a 'tort'.[30] The lingering question of whether a confider must show 'detriment'[31] before an action will lie for breach of confidence has all the appearance of a discussion of whether the confider must,

23 *Saltman* (n 13) 213.

24 FW Maitland, in AH Chaytor and WJ Whittaker (eds), *The Forms of Action at Common Law* (Cambridge, Cambridge University Press, 1965) 2.

25 *Seager v Copydex Ltd* [1967] 1 WLR 923, 930A, 932A, 939H-940A (CA); *Coco v AN Clark (Engineers) Ltd* [1969] RPC 41 (headnote, holding (1); similar language is not used in the judgment, but see at 50 on the relationship between the equitable duty and liability to pay 'damages'); *Fraser v Evans* [1969] 1 QB 349, 353 (report), 355 (submissions), 357–358 (submissions and argument) (CA); *Hubbard* (n 13) 97; *Beloff v Pressdram Ltd* [1973] FSR 33, 56 (ChD). For references to 'the cause of action' that do not obviously link it to the possibility of recovering 'damages' for loss, see *A-G v Jonathan Cape Ltd* [1976] QB 752, 769 (QBD); *Yates Circuit Foil Co v Electrofoils Ltd* [1976] FSR 345, 384 (ChD); *British Steel Corp v Granada Television* [1981] AC 1096, 1148 (argument) (HL).

26 See *British Steel* (n 25) 1153–1154 (argument).

27 See, eg, *ReachLocal UK Ltd v Bennett* [2014] EWHC 3405 (QB), [10]; *Breitenfeld UK Ltd v Harrison* [2015] EWHC 399 (Ch), [10].

28 Maitland (n 24) 7, 61.

29 *Vidal-Hall v Google Inc* [2015] 3 WLR 409, [17]–[43]; *Gulati v MGN Ltd* [2015] EWCA Civ 1291, [88].

30 *Campbell v MGN Ltd* [2004] 2 AC 457, [12]–[15]. See also *HRH Prince of Wales v Associated Newspapers Ltd* [2008] Ch 57, [64]; D Ibbetson, *A Historical Introduction to the Law of Obligations* (Oxford, Oxford University Press, 1999) 187.

31 Originally mooted, though without the tortious connotation, by Megarry J in *Coco* (n 25) 48.

in the old pleading idiom, plead an action in case—damage being the gist of that action.[32]

Treating the 'cause of action' for breach of confidence as sharing in the characteristics of one or another of the old forms of action puts the status of the equitable remedy of compensation for breach of confidence in doubt. If the action for breach of confidence is assimilated to a common law form of action, such as in tort, then equity can only protect confidences through relief granted in aid of common law rights. But equitable compensation is not a remedy in aid of common law rights. It is not a remedy on a cause of action in tort. It is a remedy available on a cause of action in equity's exclusive jurisdiction in aid of wholly equitable rights.[33] Doubts over the 'cause of action' for breach of an equitable obligation of confidence have arisen through confusion and do not truly undermine the status of compensation in equity.

B. Provenance and Pedigree

Doubts over the status of equitable compensation for breach of confidence have been attributed to 'the "sui generis" nature of the action' for breach of confidence.[34] In the leading Canadian case of *Cadbury Schweppes Inc v FBI Foods Ltd*,[35] Binnie J said that referring to laws as *sui generis* 'tends to create a *frisson* of apprehension or uncertainty amongst lawyers'.[36] However, the doubts over equitable compensation rather arise from the description's liberating effect on legal thought. That liberation has yielded the notion that liability for breach of confidence is not, or not 'purely', equitable in provenance. If that impure provenance controls the modern pedigree of actions for breach of confidence, then a remedy of equitable compensation is in doubt since the action is not as such equitable.

The English Law Commission was the first to assert the *sui generis* provenance of the action in a working paper of 1974,[37] following which the idea was taken up

[32] See *Smith Kline* (n 7) 111–112; *G(HR) v L(MS)* (2007) 75 BCLR (4th) 141, [46] ('Breach of confidence has not historically been actionable *per se* (ie without proof of damage)'); *Doe 464533 v NB* 2016 ONSC 541, [24]; W Cornish, D Llewellyn and T Aplin, *Intellectual Property: Patents, Copyright, Trade Marks and Allied Rights*, 8th edn (London, Sweet & Maxwell, 2013) [8–39]; R Dean, *The Law of Trade Secrets and Personal Secrets*, 2nd edn (Sydney, Lawbook Co, 2002) [3.315]; JD Heydon, MJ Leeming and PG Turner, *Meagher, Gummow and Lehane's Equity: Doctrines and Remedies*, 5th edn (Sydney, LexisNexis, 2015) [42–095].

[33] Above (nn 3–6).

[34] J Stuckey-Clarke, '"Damages" for Breaches of Purely Equitable Rights: the Breach of Confidence Example' in PD Finn (ed), *Essays on Damages* (Sydney, LawBook Co, 1992) 73.

[35] Above (n 6).

[36] *Cadbury Schweppes* (n 6) [28].

[37] Law Commission, *Breach of Confidence* (Working Paper No 58, 1974) [16]. The idea, however, was mentioned elsewhere around that time: PM North, 'Breach of Confidence: Is there a New Tort?' (1972–3) 12 *Journal of the Society of Public Teachers of Law* 149, 149.

in the leading monograph on breach of confidence[38] and in the courts of Canada and New Zealand. An equitable remedy of compensation was firmly in doubt according to that understanding of the action at each of these four stages but, as will be argued below, is not in fact doubtful.

At the first stage, when the Law Commission wrote in 1974, the basis of the jurisdiction to protect confidences had been persistently uncertain: the courts had drawn variously on concepts of property, contract, bailment, trust, fiduciary relationship, good faith and unjust enrichment. More recently, English cases had founded the action on equitable principles. The Law Commission was unmoved by that equitable development:

> The cases show, however, that the courts do not confine themselves to purely equitable principles in solving the problems which arise in breach of confidence cases and it would seem more realistic to regard the modern action simply as being sui generis.[39]

The provenance and therefore the pedigree of the modern action were therefore not purely equitable.

Secondly, in a bold chapter of only four pages, entitled 'A *Sui Generis* Action', Gurry developed that description in his monograph of 1984. He wrote:

> While the jurisdictional basis is fundamental to the breach of confidence action, considerable uncertainty still surrounds it. For this reason, any conclusions drawn about it must necessarily be tentative and devoid of dogmatism. The view offered here is that the courts have relied on principles freely drawn from the fields of contract, equity, and property, and that the liberal use of these principles points to the existence of a *sui generis* action which has, in terms of conventional categories, a composite jurisdictional basis.[40]

Thirdly, thence the idea was received by the Canadian Supreme Court. In *Lac Minerals Ltd v International Corona Resources Ltd*,[41] McIntyre and Sopinka JJ cited Gurry's work and said:

> The foundation of action for breach of confidence does not rest solely on one of the traditional jurisdictional bases for action of contract, equity or property. The action is *sui generis* relying on all three to enforce the policy of the law that confidences be respected ... This multi-faceted jurisdictional basis for the action provides the Court with considerable flexibility in fashioning a remedy. The jurisdictional basis supporting the particular claim is relevant in determining the appropriate remedy.[42]

38 F Gurry, *Breach of Confidence* (Oxford, Oxford University Press, 1984). Other works of the time were J Kearney, *The Action for Breach of Confidence in Australia* (Sydney, Legal Books, 1985) and BC Reid, *Confidentiality and the Law* (London, Waterlow, 1986).

39 Law Commission (n 37) [16] (emphasis in original); see also [40].

40 Gurry (n 38) 58.

41 [1989] 2 SCR 574 (SCC).

42 ibid 615. McIntyre J, Lamer J, Sopinka J and La Forest J held that there was no relevant fiduciary relationship but that there was an equitable obligation of confidence. That majority divided over the proper remedy. McIntyre and Sopinka JJ held that equitable compensation was the proper remedy. La Forest J held that a constructive trust was the proper remedy. A different majority gathered around La

Wilson J and La Forest J were influenced by the same aspect of Gurry's exposition.[43]

Fourthly, soon afterwards the New Zealand Court of Appeal in *Aquaculture Corp v New Zealand Green Mussel Co Ltd*[44] assumed an approach to remedies 'broadly similar' to that taken in *Lac Minerals*. According to this, it was 'debatable' whether a non-contractual obligation of confidence 'should be classified as purely an equitable one'. It was also 'immaterial', since 'monetary compensation (which can be labelled damages) may be awarded for breach of a duty of confidence or other duty deriving historically from equity'.[45] Cooke P added that, for breach of the obligation of confidence, 'a full range of remedies should be available as appropriate, no matter whether they originated in common law, equity or statute'.[46]

According to those understandings, equitable compensation can have little or no place in remedying breaches of confidence. However, while the influence of the *sui generis* characterisation of the action for breach of confidence cannot be gainsaid, that character does not invalidate an equitable remedy of compensation for breach of confidence. An important distinction should be drawn between legal provenance and legal pedigree. The provenance of the action for breach of confidence features concepts of property, contract, bailment, trust, good faith and so on; but the action's pedigree is now equitable. The judges have founded or re-founded the action on an equitable ground in all of Australia, Canada, England and New Zealand. The action no longer has a 'mixed jurisdictional basis'—assuming it ever did, from the time at which *Saltman* established the unitary action and thereafter.

The equitable re-founding of the action was of special importance in Canada. Following *Lac Minerals*, the British Columbia Court of Appeal held in *Cadbury Schweppes Inc v FBI Foods Ltd*[47] that '[t]here can be no argument' that the primary judge had correctly proceeded from 'the fact' that the action for breach of confidence 'does not rest solely on one of the traditional jurisdictional bases for action of contract, equity or property'[48] and that it 'is *sui generis* and combines aspects of contract law, equity and property'.[49] However, on a further appeal, the Supreme Court—through Binnie J—stridently dismissed that idea. Contrary to the fact, Binnie J said the primary judge and Court of Appeal had decided the case, not as depending on a synthetic cause of action comprising legal and equitable elements,

Forest J in support of his proposed relief: Lamer J on the basis of a breach of an equitable obligation of confidence; Wilson J on the basis that the breach of confidence amounted to a breach of fiduciary and 'a breach of confidence at common law' and a breach of an equitable obligation of confidence. Sopinka J also cited Lord Goff of Chieveley and G Jones, *The Law of Restitution*, 3rd edn (London, Sweet & Maxwell, 1986) 664–667, but the treatment is materially different to that of Gurry.

[43] *Lac Minerals* (n 41) 630–632 (Wilson J), 657–658 (La Forest J).

[44] *Aquaculture* (n 9).

[45] ibid 301.

[46] ibid.

[47] (1996) 23 BCLR (3d) 326 (CA).

[48] *Cadbury Schweppes* (n 47) [16].

[49] ibid [32]. The relevant passage of the primary judge's reasoning appears to be *Cadbury Schweppes Inc v FBI Foods Ltd* (1994) 93 BCLR (2d) 318, [5].

but an equitable obligation only.[50] He then re-founded the action wholly in equity. Characterising the action as *sui generis*, Binnie J said, merely indicates that (*a*) monetary relief for loss is available in equity's inherent jurisdiction to compensate, rather than depending on common law or statutory grounds including the doubtful ground of 'Lord Cairns' Act';[51] and (*b*) thereapart, a 'full range' of equitable remedies is also available in Canada as appropriate to the particular facts.[52] The equitable remedy of compensation could in Canada be fashioned by analogy to common law concepts. The action and the remedy are nevertheless equitable.[53]

The mixed provenance of the action for breach of confidence has no logical bearing on the status of equitable compensation for breach of confidence now that non-contractual obligations of confidence are founded in equity. Gurry's views of 1984, in particular, nevertheless continue to hold influence.[54] Mention of a contradiction at the heart of Gurry's treatment is therefore required. Gurry wished to explain how the courts had drawn on the concepts of property, contract, good faith and so on when deciding past cases. He saw that as the best way of predicting how future cases might in turn be decided, and—recalling Holmes[55]—of stating the law. Once Gurry committed to that method, it was inevitable that he should describe the action as *sui generis*. Yet while he described his conclusions as tentative and undogmatic[56]—since predictions must change as their factual bases change—Gurry was resolute that 'attempts to confine [the action] within one conventional jurisdictional category'—such as equity—'should be resisted'.[57] That reasoning was, and remains, false.

The course of authority requires the principles by which relief is granted for non-contractual breaches of confidence to be expressed in terms consistent with the equitable ground of the action for breach of confidence. The cause of action is not heterogeneous in including common law elements that attract relief in the form of damages in tort or in contract. The action's nature is equitable alone. The only suitable compensatory relief is equitable compensation.

50 *Cadbury Schweppes* (n 6) [20] ('The equitable doctrine … is the basis on which the courts below granted relief …'). Compare also *Cadbury Schweppes Inc v FBI Foods Ltd* (1994) 93 BCLR (2d) 318, [77]–[84]; *Terrien Bros Construction Ltd v Delaurier* 2006 BCSC 1645, [61]; *Aram Systems Ltd v Novatel Inc* (2008) 98 Alta LR (4th) 1, [133] ('An action for breach of confidence is an action in equity'); *No Limits Sportswear Inc v 0912139 BC Ltd* 2015 BCSC 1698, [11], [21].

51 *Cadbury Schweppes* (n 6) [60], referring to the Chancery Amendment Act 1858 (21 & 22 Vict c 27) s 2 and its statutory descendants. The import of *Cadbury Schweppes* may not yet be understood: see PD Maddaugh and JD McCamus, *The Law of Restitution*, looseleaf (Canada Law Book) [28:100] (December 2014 supplement).

52 *Cadbury Schweppes* (n 6) [26]. Unlike in New Zealand, it appears that legal and statutory remedies are not as such available for breach of the equitable obligation: at [26], [61].

53 ibid [76].

54 Aplin et al (n 10) Chs 2, 4, 19.

55 OW Holmes, 'The Path of the Law' (1897) 10 *Harvard Law Review* 457, 461 ('The prophecies of what the courts will do in fact, and nothing more pretentious, are what I mean by the law.').

56 Above (n 40).

57 Gurry (n 38) 26.

C. Policy and Realism

There is a 'long history of damages being awarded in confidence cases by the courts without any express indication of the basis upon which the award was made'.[58] As already seen, an equitable remedy of compensation for breach of confidence is not truly placed in doubt by the deficit of reasoning and analysis in such cases. However, the remedy's status is placed in doubt if, in cases of breach of confidence, judges are free to disregard legal analysis and, in a 'realist' manner, award whatever relief they believe will advance the 'policy' of protecting confidences.

In Canada, policy has been assigned precedence over precedents and legal analysis. In *Lac Minerals*,[59] McIntyre and Sopinka JJ approved Gurry's judgment that the diverse approaches of the courts in past cases in which 'damages' had been awarded did not result from confusion. To Gurry, the cases showed:

> ... that it is the *policy* of the law which is 'the basis of the courts' jurisdiction'. This policy ... is to enforce confidences created by the communication limits of confidential information. Underlying all of the cases in which the courts have granted relief is a broad notion of confidence reposed by one party in another which the courts will enforce. Once this policy is brought to mind, it is possible to regard the jurisdictional sources on which the courts rely as merely secondary mechanisms which provide the means by which the courts can enforce a confidence.[60]

A remedy of equitable compensation might be employed to enforce a confidence, but would have no claim to respected status. Instead of equitable compensation being reliably available wherever a confider suffers loss through breach of a non-contractual obligation of confidence, the courts would pragmatically grant whatever relief might advance the policy of protecting confidences, be that equitable compensation or not. McIntyre and Sopinka JJ said that courts therefore enjoy 'considerable flexibility in fashioning a remedy':[61] '[r]emedies available from both law and equity are available'.[62]

These views give cause for substantial concern.[63] Policy cannot substitute for law.[64] A law may express a policy. However, to give the policy priority over the law expressing it is erroneous. Whereas a policy may admit of pure expression, a law rarely expresses only one policy, allowing nought for competing policies or practical considerations. In the same way as it is only legitimate to pursue the purpose of a statute in accordance with the statute's terms,[65] where several laws advance the

[58] Aplin et al (n 10) [19.08].
[59] Above (n 41).
[60] Gurry (n 38) 25–26 (original emphasis).
[61] *Lac Minerals* (n 41) 615.
[62] ibid 657–658.
[63] For another account, see P Birks, 'Three Kinds of Objection to Discretionary Remedialism' (2000) 29 *University of Western Australia Law Review* 1.
[64] *Wainwright v Home Office* [2004] 2 AC 406, [31].
[65] *Carr v Western Australia* (2007) 232 CLR 138, [5]–[7]; *Milne v The Queen* (2014) 252 CLR 149, [38].

one policy it is normally legitimate only to pursue that policy by applying those laws.[66] In terms of realism, the non sequitur is to perceive a policy beneath a body of decided cases and from thence to conclude that the legal reasoning by which that policy was advanced can be discarded as a mere instrument by which courts strove for the outcomes they desired. In recognition of the fact that such views of policy and of legal realism diminish the authority of law, when the Supreme Court of Canada elevated the policy of protecting confidences as Gurry suggested, it had to assign Canadian courts a wide discretion over relief.[67]

The 'realism' of that discretionary approach depends on a misleading portrayal of the courts' activities. Gurry said, numerous times, that the courts' principal concern had been to 'use' existing categories as instruments to achieve the end of protecting confidences.[68] The courts' attitudes had been so 'eclectic' that, in predicting the results of future cases, it was safest to examine when each basis of relief was 'likely to be used' by the courts.[69] Litigants were peripheral. When a basis for the grant of relief was required, it was 'provided' by the court. When the *sui generis* action did not govern the result of a case, that was due not to pleadings or argument but to the jurisdiction on which '*the court* relie[d]'.[70] In one case, Gurry said, the English Court of Appeal 'changed the basis of the defendant's obligation [from equity] to contract': an adroit construction or reconstruction of liability, according to Gurry.[71] However, whatever fumbling might be found in the reasoning of cases, the courts decided them on the basis of arguments put to them. They were not free to do otherwise. If the grounds of liability have ever been 'constructed' or 'reconstructed' merely as a judge wished, then that has happened through legal error and should be eschewed.

The status of equitable compensation as a remedy for breach of confidence should not be thought to be undermined by the want of explanatory reasoning for compensatory awards in some cases, nor by the occasional elevation of policy above law. Those features have in fact confused the remedy, but only by practically and normatively invalid means.

[66] See, eg, *Wainwright* (n 64) [18]–[35]; *Australian Broadcasting Corp v Lenah Game Meats Pty Ltd* (2001) 208 CLR 199, [80]; *Friend v Brooker* (2009) 239 CLR 129, [7]; *Bofinger v Kingsway Group Ltd* (2009) 239 CLR 269, [85]–[98]. See C Conte, 'From Only the "Bottom-up"? Legitimate Forms of Judicial Reasoning in Private Law' (2014) 35 *Oxford Journal of Legal Studies* 1, 15–18; M Leeming, 'Subrogation, Equity and Unjust Enrichment' in J Glister and P Ridge (eds), *Fault Lines in Equity* (Oxford, Hart Publishing, 2012) Ch 2; K Mason, 'Do Top-down and Bottom-up Reasoning Ever Meet?' in E Bant and M Harding (eds), *Exploring Private Law* (Cambridge, Cambridge University Press, 2010) Ch 1.

[67] *Lac Minerals* (n 41) 615, 657–658.

[68] Gurry (n 38) esp Part II of the work at 26, 27, 35, 36, 37 (heading), 42, 43 (heading), 45, 46, 58, 60.

[69] ibid 28.

[70] ibid 26, 27 (emphasis added).

[71] ibid 29, 29 fn 30. See also at 43, 45.

D. Indistinct Relief

The status of equitable compensation for breach of confidence would be undermined if it were indistinct from the relief available, say, for breach of contract or the commission of a tort. As will later be seen, the question has arisen in a different form where equitable relief may, in a court's discretion, be moulded on analogies with common law (Canada) or common law and statutory (New Zealand) relief. In Australia and England the question has not squarely arisen.

However, it squarely arises from leading English commentaries. Lord Toulson and Mr Phipps effectively argue that awards of equitable compensation would in England be indistinct from other relief. While noting 'considerable historical authority on the difference between compensation in equity and damages at law', they stress that 'the principles underlying the both are the same, the fundamental object being to compensate the innocent party for the loss caused by the wrong'.[72] Equitable compensation would be distinct only in being termed 'equitable' and in being subject to an equitable requirement that the claimant not unduly delay in suing once the breach of confidence is known.[73] The second edition of *Gurry* proceeds similarly: '[t]he basic approach to any monetary award, whether assessed under common law damages, Lord Cairns' Act, or as equitable compensation (despite some apparent distinctions), is likely to be more or less the same.'[74]

While these accounts assert that equitable compensation is an indistinct remedy, the assertion is wanting. Damages under 'Lord Cairns' Act' are only available where an injunction would otherwise have gone to restrain the breach of confidence, and—properly understood—where the confidence is protected by contractual rights.[75] Equitable compensation is not so confined. Further, assuming that damages and equitable compensation have 'the same' purpose of compensating for loss, the principles pursued by grants of damages vary considerably at common law between, for example, trespass, deceit and breach of contract. Distinct rules of quantification have been adapted to each. When it is recommended that equitable compensation be assimilated to 'common law damages', resort is made to a category of meaningless reference.[76] The real determinant of the recommendation must lie elsewhere.

Constitutional doubts over the remedy of equitable compensation for breach of confidence may be dismissed. The remedy exists, in some form, in Australia,

[72] RG Toulson and CM Phipps, *Confidentiality*, 3rd edn (London, Sweet & Maxwell, 2012) [2–083]. Similarly [9–039].

[73] ibid [9–060].

[74] Aplin et al (n 10) [19.25]. See also A Burrows, 'Limits on Compensation' in A Burrows and E Peel (eds), *Commercial Remedies: Current Issues and Problems* (Oxford, Oxford University Press, 2003) 46.

[75] Toulson and Phipps (n 72) [2-074]–[2-075].

[76] J Stone, *Legal System and Lawyers' Reasonings* (London, Stevens & Sons, 1964) 241. See also *AIB Group (UK) plc v Mark Redler & Co Solicitors* [2015] AC 1503, [92] (Lord Reed JSC); W Gummow, 'Dishonest Assistance and Account of Profits' [2015] *Cambridge Law Journal* 405.

Canada and New Zealand—and it probably exists in England as, it is suggested, it ought to. What considerations bear on the award of this equitable remedy? The chapter now turns to that question.

III. Concurrence

To date, the considerations of most force in the award of the remedy have been notions of concurrence: concurrent liabilities and concurrently available remedies. In view of the settled principles as to concurrent liabilities and concurrently available remedies, this is surprising. Fallacies have been employed generously.

A. Concurrent Liabilities in Contract and Equity

Several points are straightforward. First, the possibility of suing for breach of contract, where a contractual obligation of confidence was broken, has never been seriously challenged.[77] The advent of 'the action' for breach of confidence in and since *Saltman* has not reduced the operation of the law of contract. Secondly, misuse of the one piece of confidential information can found both a contractual liability in a party who is bound by contract not to use the information, and an equitable liability in a third party to whom that contract party imparts the information in circumstances importing confidentiality. Thirdly, where a confider imparts one confidence to a confidant pursuant to a contractual obligation of confidence, and imparts a different confidence to that confidant outside of contract, the confidant will be liable in contract and in equity for misuse of the two pieces of confidential information.

So much is elementary. Problems arise for equitable compensation where contractual and equitable obligations are alleged between the same parties in respect of the same secret. If a confidant cannot be concurrently liable in contract and in equity to the one confider in that situation—and if the confidant can only be

[77] Even in Canada: *L(MS) v G(HR)* (2005) 42 BCLR (4th) 136, [56]; *Scott & Associates Engineering Ltd v Finavera Renewables Ltd* (2013) 79 Alta LR (5th), 172 [68] ('[T]he suggestion by Sopinka J, dissenting in *International Corona Resources Ltd v LAC Minerals Ltd* … that the foundation for an action of breach of confidence is a *sui generis* hybrid of contract, equity and property theories has not been widely followed by Canadian courts. Thus, the prevalent modern view in Anglo-Canadian jurisprudence is that a claim for breach of confidential business information is based in either contract or equity'); *No Limits Sportswear* (n 50) [11], [21]. The crucial passage in Gurry's analysis is ambiguous: (n 38) 26–27. On the one hand, by accepting that the ordinary remedies for breach of contract would still lie if a court decided a given breach of confidence claim 'on contract', he assumed that a contractual action would still lie. On the other hand, by asserting that 'the action' was a composite of contract, property and equity that should not be confined to existing 'jurisprudential categories' known by those names, he suggested the absorption of contractual claims into the putative *sui generis* action.

liable in contract—then equitable compensation will be unavailable. How, then, do contract and equity interact in this matter?

One theory is that an equitable obligation of confidence cannot lie alongside a contractual obligation of confidence in respect of the same secret unless the contract and contract law would inadequately protect the confidence. According to this theory, the remedy of equitable compensation lies in aid of common law rights where the common law provides inadequate relief.[78] Moreover, according to this theory the equitable *obligation* is a kind of 'remedy'[79] and is supplied by equity only where the contractual obligation is inadequate to protect the confidence. This theory, which was suggested in *Streetscape Projects (Australia) Pty Ltd v City of Sydney*[80] by the New South Wales Court of Appeal, is, with respect, mistaken. Equitable obligations of confidence are not conditioned on the inadequacy of common law protection. Nor are awards of equitable compensation for breach of confidence conditioned on the inadequacy of common law relief, especially common law damages for breach of a contractual obligation to keep a confidence. Equitable obligations and the equitable remedy of compensation for breach of confidence lie in equity's exclusive jurisdiction.[81]

Whether an equitable and a contractual obligation of confidence can co-exist in respect of the one secret is determined not by a concept of inadequacy, but a concept of inconsistency. The cases for and the cases against such co-existence of liabilities are divided only by different understandings of that concept of inconsistency. For instance, the gist of Lord Greene MR's opinion—'you cannot as result of a contract of employment have two quite separate obligations: one arising from the contract and the other disconnected with the contract and arising not by virtue of the contract, but by virtue of some equitable doctrine'[82]—is that a contractual obligation of confidence is *ipso facto* inconsistent with a coextensive equitable obligation. No further enquiry is necessary, according to Lord Greene MR's view. No investigation is made into how wide or narrow or exhaustive or non-exhaustive of the contractual obligation.

[78] On auxiliary equitable jurisdiction in aid of common law rights, see J Story, *Commentaries on Equity Jurisprudence*, 1st English edn by WE Grigsby (London, Stevens & Haynes, 1884) § 33; D Yale, 'A Trichotomy of Equity' (1985) 6 *Journal of Legal History* 194.

[79] Compare *Campbell* (n 30) [44].

[80] *Streetscape Projects (Australia) Pty Ltd v City of Sydney* (2013) 85 NSWLR 196, [123], [150]–[151] (*obiter dicta*). The origin of the theory is evidently *Coles Supermarkets Australia Pty Ltd v FKP Ltd* [2008] FCA 1915, [63], in which *Deta Nominees Pty Ltd v Viscount Plastic Products Pty Ltd* [1979] VR 167 (SC) was incorrectly understood as relating to an equitable obligation of confidence. In *Deta Nominees*, the court was addressing the adequacy of common law relief when deciding what equitable relief to grant in aid of the successful plaintiff's contractual rights of confidentiality: at 195–196. See also Aplin et al (n 10) [4.53]–[4.55]. Compare *Hunt v A* [2008] 1 NZLR 368, [74].

[81] Above (nn 3–6). See also P Finn, 'Fiduciary Reflections' (2014) 88 *Australian Law Journal* 127, 143–144.

[82] *British Celanese Ltd v Moncrieff* [1948] Ch 564, 578 (CA). See also *Faccenda Chicken Ltd v Fowler* [1987] Ch 117, 135–136 (CA).

Such an approach to inconsistency is unsatisfactory. Equitable obligations of confidence are imposed by law in that they arise other than from the terms of a contract. As obligations imposed by law, equitable obligations of confidence arise whenever the requirements of their creation are fulfilled. The conditions of the creation of an equitable obligation of confidence may be fulfilled where no contract exists. The conditions of the creation of an equitable obligation of confidence may equally be fulfilled where a contract exists. The presence of a contract precludes neither a finding that there is information of the requisite quality of confidence nor a finding that the information was imparted in circumstances importing an obligation of confidence.[83]

If equitable and contractual obligations of confidence in respect of the one secret cannot coexist, then that must be because the party otherwise entitled to its benefit—the confidant—forsook that benefit by consent. Such consent may be expressed in a bilateral contract with the confidant. Or the benefit of the equitable obligation may be forsaken by consent expressed other than by the terms, express or implied, of a contract. A contract is neither necessary nor sufficient to forsake an equitable obligation of confidence. Consent is both necessary and sufficient. Subject to statute,[84] this approach to inconsistency corresponds to the approach to inconsistency between contract, on the one hand, and express trusts,[85] fiduciary obligations[86] and duties of care in tort,[87] on the other hand. That approach was applied in *Optus Networks Pty Ltd v Telstra Corp Ltd*,[88] which held that a contractual stipulation against the use of confidential information (which was elaborately defined) did not, on the facts, preclude concurrent liability in equity to keep the same information in confidence.[89]

Assuming that concurrent liabilities in contract and equity exist in respect of the one confidence, the availability of equitable compensation has been said to be affected by the concurrence of contractual and equitable liabilities. Toulson and Phipps say that the measure of available compensation is affected. They invoke the reasoning of Lord Browne-Wilkinson in *Henderson v Merrett Syndicates Ltd*,[90] in which the House of Lords held that the duty of professional persons to exercise care in performing their professional tasks for their clients arises in tort and,

[83] See *Coco* (n 25) 47–48.

[84] See, eg, Unfair Contract Terms Act 1977 s 2.

[85] See *Barclays Bank Ltd v Quistclose Investments Ltd* [1970] AC 567, 581–582 (HL); compare *Quistclose Investments Ltd v Rolls Razor Ltd* [1967] Ch 910, 930D (ChD).

[86] *Hospital Products Ltd v United States Surgical Corp* (1984) 156 CLR 41, 97; *Bristol & West Building Society v Mothew* [1998] Ch 1, 18 (CA).

[87] *Chapelton v Barry Urban District Council* [1940] 1 KB 532, 537–538 (CA).

[88] *Optus Networks Pty Ltd v Telstra Corp Ltd* (2010) 265 ALR 281 (FCAFC).

[89] ibid [29], [38]; *Vercoe v Rutland Fund Management Ltd* [2010] EWHC 424 (Ch), [329] (more readily inferring inconsistency). See M Leeming, 'The Scope of Fiduciary Obligations: How Contract Informs, but Does Not Determine, the Scope of Fiduciary Obligations' (2009) 3 *Journal of Equity* 181, 194–196.

[90] [1995] 2 AC 145 (HL).

absent an express term, is replicated in the contract by a term implied by law. The House of Lords held that a client may choose whether to sue a negligent professional in contract or tort or both.[91] Toulson and Phipps write:

> In *Henderson v Merrett Syndicates Ltd*,[92] Lord Browne-Wilkinson, dealing with the relationship of law and equity in a different context, warned of the need to ensure that the law did not 'become again manacled by "clanking chains" this time represented by causes, rather than forms[,] of action'. Similarly the court's power to award monetary compensation for breach of confidence should not differ according to whether the cause of action lies in contract or in an equitable obligation of confidence.[93]

Hence their view that the sums of compensation granted for a given breach of confidence should not differ according to whether the cause of action is legal or equitable.[94] Quantification will be discussed more fully later in this chapter.

It is clear that the concurrence of contractual and equitable obligations of confidence does not support Toulson and Phipps' conclusion. Indeed, Toulson and Phipps invert Lord Browne-Wilkinson's reasoning. Lord Browne-Wilkinson did not maintain that a client should be unable to choose whether to sue a negligent professional in contract or in the tort of negligence: he thought the client should be able to 'choose that remedy which appears to him to be the most advantageous'.[95] It was 'important not to exclude concepts of concurrent liability which the courts of equity have over the years handled without difficulty', he said.[96] This tells strongly against Toulson and Phipps' view of the effects of concurrent contractual and equitable liabilities on the recovery of equitable compensation for breach of confidence. Their reasoning would restore the thinking of the abolished forms of action to its former prominence,[97] at the expense of modern legal attitudes towards concurrent liability.

[91] ibid 188–194. Similarly, Canada: *Central Trust Co v Rafuse* [1986] 2 SCR 147, 206 (SCC); Australia: *Astley v Austrust Ltd* (1999) 197 CLR 1, [44]–[48]. The position in New Zealand is described as 'vexed': *Body Corporate 202254 v Taylor* [2009] 2 NZLR 17, [122]; see also [16] and S Todd (ed), *The Law of Torts in New Zealand*, 6th edn (Wellington, Thomson Reuters, 2013) 5–7.

[92] *Henderson* (n 90) 206.

[93] Toulson and Phipps (n 72) [9–041].

[94] ibid [9–041] (citing *Force India* (n 2) [424]), [9–042] ('the measure of compensation for breach of the equitable obligation of confidence was the same as for tort').

[95] *Henderson* (n 90) 194D. Compare *Wellesley Partners LLP v Withers LLP* [2016] 2 WLR 1351, [66], [68] (purporting to hold, surprisingly, that 'where … contractual and tortious duties to take care in carrying out instructions exist side by side, the test for recoverability of damage for economic loss *should* be the same, and should be the contractual one' (emphasis added)); see the criticisms made by M Balen, 'Concurrent Liability and Remoteness in Long-term Relationships' [2016] *Lloyd's Maritime and Commercial Law Quarterly* 186.

[96] *Henderson* (n 90) 206F. Compare *Mouat v Clarke Boyce* [1992] 2 NZLR 559, 565 (CA). The reliance by Toulson and Phipps (n 72) [9–040]) on Lord Diplock's theory of the 'fusion' of law and equity is erroneous for reasons stated elsewhere: PV Baker, 'The Future of Equity' (1977) 93 *Law Quarterly Review* 529; *Bank of Boston Connecticut v European Grain and Shipping Ltd* [1989] AC 1056, 1109 (HL); Heydon et al (n 32) ch 2.

[97] See JA Jolowicz, 'Forms of Action—Causes of Action—Trespass and Negligence' [1964] *Cambridge Law Journal* 200, 202.

In *Lac Minerals*, Wilson J thought differently of the effects of concurrent contractual and equitable obligations of confidence on the remedy of equitable compensation. She said:

> It seems to me that when the same conduct gives rise to alternate causes of action, one at common law and the other in equity, *and the available remedies are different*, the Court should consider which will provide the more appropriate remedy to the innocent party and give the innocent party the benefit of that remedy.[98]

Her Ladyship thus thought that a discretionary power to consider 'the more appropriate remedy' of those available at law and in equity vests in a judge where three cumulative conditions exist:

(i) the breach of confidence founds 'alternate causes of action' (not cumulative causes of action); and
(ii) of the alternate causes of action, one is legal, the other equitable (concurrent causes of action at common law will not suffice); and
(iii) the available legal and equitable remedies are 'different'.

Wilson J possibly laid the most weight on the third of these conditions, which will be considered below. But to concentrate for now on concurrent liability, it is difficult to see how conditions (i) and (ii) are probative of a discretionary power to decide what is 'appropriate' relief, especially with respect to common law relief otherwise available as of right.[99] The reasoning and conclusion are suspect.

In sum, concurrent obligations of confidence can exist in contract and equity except where a contrary intention is shown. Where such concurrent obligations exist, it is inconsistent with the principles of concurrent liability recognised in Australia, Canada and England[100] that the availability or measure of equitable compensation should be affected by the coexistence of the contractual and equitable obligations.

B. Concurrently Available Remedies

Apart from the weight they place on concurrent liabilities, the legal materials place weight on the concurrent availability of two or more remedies for breach of confidence, where one of the available remedies is equitable compensation. The Supreme Court of Canada and the New Zealand Court of Appeal have held that the existence of concurrently available remedies engages a judicial discretion

[98] *Lac Minerals* (n 41) 631 (emphasis in original). Wilson J did not share in the view that causes of action for breach of confidence are a *sui generis* cause of action made up of elements of all of contract, equity and property law.

[99] See *Legal & General Life of Australia Ltd v A Hudson Pty Ltd* (1985) 1 NSWLR 314, 331–336 (CA) (McHugh JA).

[100] As to New Zealand, see (n 91).

to grant 'appropriate' relief, of which equitable compensation is only one form. Is the reasoning sound?

Until the decisions in *Lac Minerals* and *Aquaculture*, the relief available in Australia, Canada, England and New Zealand for a breach of confidence differed according to whether the claim lay in contract or in equity; and the available relief differed according to whether the breach was of a simple equitable obligation of confidence or amounted to a breach of fiduciary duty. For instance, it was doubted that compensation was available for breach of an equitable obligation of confidence, but undoubted that damages could be recovered for breach of a contractual obligation of confidence. Proprietary relief was available for breach of fiduciary duty but not for breach of an equitable obligation of confidence *simpliciter*. Except for the fact that equitable compensation for breach of confidence is now available in Australia, Canada and New Zealand—and, probably, in England—those differences remain in Australia and England;[101] they are diminished in Canada and New Zealand.

It was seen above that, in *Lac Minerals*, Wilson J thought a discretionary power to select 'the more appropriate remedy' vests in a court where the alternative legal and equitable causes of action give rise to different 'available remedies'.[102] This presents difficulties. Just as it is difficult to appreciate how the concurrence of contractual and equitable liabilities for breach of confidence rationally supports such a discretionary power, it is difficult to appreciate how the existence of concurrent claims to relief—some legal, some equitable—supports such a power.[103] But the criticism extends to the other judges' reasoning in *Lac Minerals*. Whereas Wilson J saw breach of confidence as an equitable action, the other Justices saw the action as a *sui generis* amalgam: because the contractual, proprietary and equitable elements of the amalgam would attract various potential remedies, their Lordships likewise thought that a discretionary power to award the 'appropriate' remedy was invested in the court.[104] In *Aquaculture*, the New Zealand Court of Appeal adopted that reasoning and a theory that law and equity had become 'mingled or merged'.[105] Neither case as such denied that equitable compensation was available. The Canadian court thought that 'damages'—whose legal nature they did not explore—were available; and the New Zealand court's central holding was that 'monetary compensation (which can be labelled damages) may be awarded for breach of a duty of confidence ... historically deriving from equity'.[106] However, the effect of the discretionary power adopted in the two cases is that the grant and refusal of equitable

[101] See, eg, above (n 93); below (n 128); M Conaglen, 'Thinking about Proprietary Remedies for Breach of Confidence' [2008] *Intellectual Property Quarterly* 82.

[102] *Lac Minerals* (n 41) 631.

[103] ibid 631.

[104] ibid 615, 630, 657–658, 671–672.

[105] *Aquaculture* (n 9) 301.

[106] ibid.

compensation lies in a court's discretion. How that power finds rational support in the existence of concurrent claims to relief is, again, obscure.

The Canadian Supreme Court has since narrowed and broadened the discretionary power. The power is narrowed in that the discretion now only relates to equitable relief; it affords no power to award common law or statutory relief 'as appropriate' where an equitable obligation of confidence is breached, nor to award relief 'as appropriate' where the cause of action lies at common law.[107] The power is broadened in that it is now engaged wherever concurrent common law and equitable liabilities and claims are found, not only in cases of breach of confidence.[108] Where damages could have been recovered for breach of a contractual obligation of confidence but the suit is for breach of a coextensive equitable obligation, an award of equitable compensation may be reduced by analogy to the rules of quantification of damages for breach of contract where that assists the court in 'matching the remedy to underlying policy objectives'.[109]

The discretionary powers announced in *Lac Minerals*, *Aquaculture* and *Cadbury Schweppes* have motivations—and difficulties—beyond those discussed here. So far as they affect equitable compensation for breach of confidence, it is false to reason that the actual or potential availability of more than one remedy for a breach of confidence shows that judges have a power either (*i*) to award a remedy of the judges' own choosing or (*ii*) to cut down equitable relief to some other form of relief that might have been, but was not, ultimately claimed.

Any appeal those discretions may have is merely superficial. Pursuing underlying policy objectives unhampered by putative hindrances and diversions may sound attractive. But how are the underlying policy objectives to be identified? According to Binnie J's explanation in *Cadbury Schweppes*, by setting aside 'strict jurisdictional or doctrinal considerations' and concentrating on an objective common to the 'various potential causes of action': an objective of compensating a confider for loss suffered through a breach of confidence.[110] Those 'strict jurisdictional or doctrinal considerations' tell against this method and the pursuit of underlying policy objectives over doctrine.[111] Binnie J's 'considerations' are more accurately denominated as 'rules'. In particular, they are the rules according to which compensation is awarded on different causes of action. They are rules according to which the one purpose—of compensating for loss—is pursued differently according to the distinct legal concerns advanced and protected by each

[107] *Cadbury Schweppes* (n 6) [25].

[108] *Strother v 3464920 Canada Inc* [2007] 2 SCR 177, [158]. As to concurrent liabilities in contract and negligence, see B Finlay, M Vermette and B Bethell, 'Convergence of Contract and Tort: Damages in the Age of Concurrent Liability' in Law Society of Upper Canada, *Special Lectures 2005: The Modern Law of Damages* (Toronto, Law Society of Upper Canada, 2006) 379ff.

[109] *Cadbury Schweppes* (n 6) [25]. See *Strother* (n 108) [156]–[158].

[110] *Cadbury Schweppes* (n 6) [24]. Similarly, *Mouat* (n 96) 569 (appeal allowed on other grounds [1994] 1 AC 428 (PC)), quoted by Binnie J at [50].

[111] Compare *Wainwright* (n 64) [31].

cause of action. For instance, while compensatory damages are granted for the torts of trespass, deceit and negligence, and for breaches of contract, the 'policy objective' of compensating the victim of the tort or the disappointed contract party is pursued quite differently in each case. It is not evident why those distinct and valuable objectives should be forsaken, nor that a court (rather than parliament) is institutionally competent to do so.

Equity, too, advances and protects distinctive values. Binnie J's approach and similar approaches ignore those differences or demote them to a level where they are subsidiary to 'considerations' drawn from other, common law or statutory, 'potential causes of action' that lie on the same facts. Why the 'considerations' pertaining, say, to contract or tort law should take precedence over equitable principles is also not apparent.[112]

C. Different Remedies

When expounding principles of relief for breach of confidence, no consideration has exercised the judges more than differences among remedies. The exercise has wasted much energy. Differences among remedies are of great practical interest to litigants but of scarcely any relevance to the principles of equitable compensation for breach of confidence.

It is interesting that differences among the remedies for breaches of confidence should have exercised the judges so. Differences in remedy have featured in common law systems since beyond memory. The common law, narrowly defined as the counterpart of equity, provides 'different' remedies on a given set of facts. A victim of fraud may rescind by self-help and claim money had and received on a failure of consideration[113] or instead affirm the transaction and claim damages for deceit.[114] Again, an owner of chattels may claim damages for the loss caused by the conversion of the owner's goods or instead waive the claim for damages and recover as money had and received the value derived from the conversion by the defendant.[115] And so on. Equity, too, offers 'different' remedies. A breach of trust may lead to an accounting, proprietary relief, an order for administration and an injunction to restrain an apprehended repetition of the breach. Rules requiring a claimant to elect between inconsistent causes of action and inconsistent remedies[116] have developed at law and in equity. So have principles against double

[112] Stuckey-Clarke (n 34) 74; J Edelman, 'The Meaning of "Damages": Common Law and Equity' in A Robertson (ed), *The Law of Obligations: Connections and Boundaries* (London, UCL Press, 2004) 50.

[113] D O'Sullivan, S Elliott and R Zakrzewski, *The Law of Rescission*, 2nd edn (Oxford, Oxford University Press, 2014) [14.36]–[14.38].

[114] ibid [2.03].

[115] *United Australia* (n 20) 11–13, 18–19, 28–30, 34–35.

[116] ibid; *Tang Man Sit v Capacious Investments Ltd* [1996] AC 514, 521–522 (PC).

recovery[117] and a comfortable acceptance that a claimant may choose which of several concurrently available remedies to claim against the one defendant in respect of the one course of conduct.[118]

These remain tenets of the common law systems of Australia and England but are now of lesser status in Canada and New Zealand. They were lessened for Canada in *Lac Minerals*, effectively because the Supreme Court felt that the over-readiness of Canadian courts to deem persons fiduciaries, so as to avail claimants of a variety of equitable relief not hitherto available for (say) a mere breach of confidence,[119] could be redressed by holding that proprietary relief may be awarded for breach of confidence as much as for breach of fiduciary duty.[120] The tenets were diminished in New Zealand when the Court of Appeal in *Aquaculture* felt that the reluctance of courts to grant compensation for breach of equitable obligations should be redressed by holding that all kinds of relief are potentially available for breaches of confidence, irrespective of the cause of action pleaded.[121] The results of not adopting the more conventional solutions of instructing lower courts in the proper application of fiduciary doctrine[122] or of the availability of compensation in equity for breaches of equitable obligations are unfortunate. Differences of remedy were summoned in an effort to justify dramatic changes of the law.

The irrelevance of 'difference' among the available remedies, according to authoritative English decisions, has been contradicted at first instance. In *Vercoe v Rutland Fund Management Ltd*,[123] a contractual obligation of confidence was found to be owed by a registered company, RFML, and a corresponding equitable obligation of confidence was found to be owed by other parties—a Mr Cartwright and several limited liability partnerships described as 'the Rutland Funds'—which owed no contractual obligations of confidence to the claimant. Sales J said:

> [S]ince RFML was the contracting party which assumed the primary obligations of confidence in relation to the confidential information, and in effect represented the interests of the Rutland funds and acted by Mr Cartwright throughout, there is no good reason to impose any wider obligation of confidence or to allow any more extensive remedies against the Rutland Funds and Mr Cartwright than are available against RFML.[124]

117 *United Australia* (n 20) 20; *Tang Man Sit* (n 116) 522F–522G; *Baxter v Obacelo Pty Ltd* (2001) 205 CLR 635, [39]–[40], [46], [55]–[64].

118 Above, text to (nn 77–96); *Tang Man Sit* (n 116) 522D–522E. See also *Spring v Guardian Assurance plc* [1995] 2 AC 296, 325–326, 334–335, 351 (HL); *Ashley v Chief Constable of Sussex* [2008] 1 AC 962, *passim* and esp [56].

119 *Lac Minerals* (n 41) 616, 618.

120 ibid 632, 643–652 (esp 652*g*–652*h*).

121 *Aquaculture* (n 9) 301.

122 The latter approach was preferred in Australia and England: see, eg, *Hospital Products* (n 86) 68–75, 97–100, 102–103, 106–107, 122–125, 142–149; *Mothew* (n 86). See *Strother* (n 108) [34]; *Galambos v Perez* [2009] 3 SCR 247, [37].

123 Above (n 89).

124 *Vercoe* (n 89) [330].

All of RFML, the Rutland Funds and Mr Cartwright were found to have breached their respective obligations of confidence. Sales J was worried by the claimant's argument that, whatever the sum of damages for breach of contract recoverable from RFML, different and more extensive equitable relief could be recovered against the third parties. One problem, Sales J thought, was that it would be 'nothing short of sophistry'[125] to say that an account of profits may be awarded for breach of an equitable obligation of confidence but not a contractual obligation of confidence. A second problem was that it was 'not obvious why the remedies for breach of confidence should necessarily be the same as for breach of fiduciary duty, so as to allow an account of profits; nor is it obvious why they should be more than the remedy available for, say, the tort of deceit'.[126]

And yet the supposed 'sophistry' is not really that. English law recognises a difference of mettle: accounting of profits earned through breach of contract is permitted only 'exceptionally';[127] an accounting of profits earned through breach of an equitable obligation of confidence is available as of course. The contrary understanding of Sales J is mistaken. Further, in Australia different relief would in fact be required against the third party whose obligation of confidence is equitable, since an accounting for profits is not as such a remedy for breach of contract in that country.[128]

The doubt that an account of profits should be available for breach of confidence as it is for breach of fiduciary may also be answered. Accounting for profits is routinely available against defendants who profit from a breach of an equitable obligation of confidence because the equitable liability is founded in conscience.[129] This is no idle musing. To invoke conscience is to describe precisely why a defendant is, as of course, liable to account for the profits he or she makes from breach of an equitable obligation of confidence. Megarry J considered the matter in *Coco v AN Clark (Engineers) Ltd*[130] when analysing the 'springboard' doctrine that a confidant may not gain a head start on commercial competitors by breaching a confidence. He asked: 'How is a conscientious recipient of the ideas to comply with the requirements that equity lays upon him?'[131] He felt that he had not reached the bottom of the matter. However, he inclined to the view that 'as a law-abiding

[125] ibid [338], quoting *A-G v Blake* [2001] 1 AC 268, 285D (HL).

[126] *Vercoe* (n 89) [343], citing J Edelman, *Gain-Based Damages* (Oxford, Hart Publishing, 2002) 214.

[127] *Blake* (n 125) 284H, 285F.

[128] *Hospitality Group Pty Ltd v Australian Rugby Union Ltd* (2001) 110 FCR 157, [157]–[159] (FCAFC). As to Canada: *Micro-Watt Control Devices Ltd v Krohne Inc* 2012 ABQB 503, [93]–[98]; as to New Zealand: AS Butler (ed), *Equity and Trusts in New Zealand*, 2nd edn (Wellington, Thomson Reuters, 2009) 900.

[129] *Moorgate Tobacco* (n 4) 437–438; *Smith Kline* (n 7) 86, 94, 95, 111, 112; *A-G v Observer* (n 5) 215–216 (CA); 256–257, 272, 281 (HL); *R v Department of Health* [2001] QB 424, [24]–[31] (CA); *Hunt* (n 80) [92]; *Skids Programme Management Ltd v McNeill* [2013] 1 NZLR 1, [78]; *Vestergaard Frandsen A/S v Bestnet Europe Ltd* [2013] [2013] 1 WLR 1566, [22].

[130] *Coco* (n 25).

[131] ibid 49.

citizen' the conscientious recipient's duty, under the springboard doctrine, was 'more likely to be that of not using [the claimant's confidential information to gain a head start] without paying, rather than of not using [the information] at all'.[132] A person who commits an efficient breach would not be acting according to conscience.[133]

Since such a citizen 'cannot take advantage' of the confider's confidential ideas until the ideas lose confidentiality, the citizen ought also to account for profits earned by reason of that breach or, alternatively, to compensate the claimant for loss caused by the confidant's lapse of conscience. To that extent, the obligations of the party subject to an equitable obligation of confidence and the obligations of a fiduciary are cognate. In contrast, persons found liable in deceit are found liable because they should not have caused the innocent party loss by procuring him or her to rely upon a falsehood told with the intention that the innocent party should rely on it.[134] Moreover, the liability of the fiduciary is more severe than the liability of the deceiver. A breach of fiduciary duty does not depend on showing that the claimant suffered damage. On a claim in deceit, damage is the gist of the action.[135] It is apt that the fiduciary is therefore liable to account for profits whereas the deceiver is not. And in thematic terms, while it is normal that accounts of profits be available for violation of property rights and for undermining the 'facilitative institutions' of fiduciary and other confidential relationships, actions in deceit are not as such directed to protecting property rights or specially facilitative legal institutions.[136] Deceit addresses a wide class of conduct, namely lying. Accountability for profits addresses forms of misconduct that are more specialised and in significant respects more onerous.

According to the source of their obligations of confidence, differences in the available relief exist in England and Australia for sound reasons.[137] The existence of those differences does not reveal injustice or irrationality that would justify denying claimants their choice of remedy. Indeed, those differences greatly weaken the submission that 'a consistent, coherent, and comprehensible body of law'[138] cannot exist while those differences continue. Arguments against differences of remedy

[132] ibid 49–50. See also *Smith Kline* (n 7) 94 (obligations of government); WR Cornish, 'The Basic Character of Confidential Information in the Common Law' in HG Leser and T Isomura, *Wege zum japanischen Recht* (Berlin, Duncker & Humblot, 1992) 845–847.

[133] C Huston, *The Enforcement of Decrees in Equity* (Cambridge, Harvard University Press, 1915) 5–8. See also *Harris v Digital Pulse Pty Ltd* (2003) 56 NSWLR 298, [184] (Mason P).

[134] The matter is carried no further by *Force India* (n 2) [394], on appeal from which it was unnecessary for the court to consider (*Force India Formula One Team Ltd v Aerolab Srl* [2013] EWCA Civ 780, [97]; compare *Flogas Britain* (n 2) [41], which mistakes the Court of Appeal's decision), or by Toulson and Phipps (n 72) [9–041].

[135] *Pasley v Freeman* (1789) 3 TR 51, 56, 64; *Smith v Chadwick* (1884) 9 App Cas 187, 195–196 (HL); *Bradford Third Equitable Benefit Building Society v Borders* [1941] 2 All ER 205, 211 (HL).

[136] IM Jackman, *The Varieties of Restitution* (Sydney, Federation Press, 1998) 123–127.

[137] See especially *AIB Group* (n 76) [92]–[95] (Lord Reed JSC).

[138] Aplin et al (n 10) [17.08].

tend to exhibit the one-topic-one-legal-category fallacy: the assumption that on any topic of legal concern, there ought to be a distinct legal category made up of rules centred on the core of the topic.[139] According to that assumption, the law is incoherent and questionable whenever a topic of legal concern is addressed by more than one law or set of laws, such as contract and equitable doctrine.[140] Owing to the nature of legal ordering in the legal systems of Australia, Canada and England,[141] that assumption is untrue of the topic 'breach of confidence'. Unless the only protection of confidence is to be contractual, the topic of breach of confidence must necessarily be addressed by more than one source of legal obligation.

IV. Discretion

'[N]ormally equitable remedies are discretionary.'[142] The discretion is applied to fashion specific relief so as to avoid unwarranted oppression or hardship, especially to innocent third parties. Monetary relief, particularly for loss, raises those considerations more weakly, particularly where the relief is compensation. The call for equitable discretion in the grant of equitable compensation is correspondingly weaker. However, in recognition of its equitable pedigree the remedy of equitable compensation for breach of confidence has been described as discretionary.[143] How might discretion operate on this monetary remedy? Little is clear.

Equitable discretion poses the classic dilemma of how a legal system can and ought to furnish certainty by means of regular rules while allowing for the exigencies of the particular case.[144] From the chancellorship of Lord Eldon onwards, in general terms equity responded to that dilemma thus. Equity possessed settled doctrines, principles and methods of adjudication. It was no mere array of innominate equities.[145] Equity was settled in that a case would engage ascertained principles whose application was subject to predictable methods. In some areas, equity had fixed rules. In many other areas, equitable principles and doctrines were settled without being rigidly fixed. The nature of the questions decided in the exercise of equity jurisdiction was unsuited to rigidly fixed answers. Inelastic

[139] This identification of this fallacy owes something to WL Twining, 'Is Your Textbook Really Necessary?' (1970–1) 11 *Journal of the Society of Public Teachers of Law* 81, 83.

[140] See, eg, *Wainwright* (n 64) [15]–[18], [31].

[141] Compare New Zealand: *Aquaculture* (n 9).

[142] *Tito v Waddell (No 2)* [1977] Ch 106, 259 (ChD).

[143] See, eg, *Spotless Group Ltd v Blanco Catering Pty Ltd* (2011) 93 IPR 235, [126] (FCA).

[144] See also HE Smith, 'Property, Equity, and the Rule of Law' in LM Austin and D Klimchuk (eds), *Private Law and the Rule of Law* (Oxford, Oxford University Press, 2014) ch 10; M Harding, 'Equity and the Rule of Law' (2016) 132 *Law Quarterly Review* 278.

[145] Compare WB Perkins, 'The English Judicature Act of 1873' (1914) 12 *Michigan Law Review* 277, 281.

rules of specific relief, for example, would produce regular hardship and injustice. A claimant might avail himself or herself of settled equitable principles so as to establish a prima facie equity or entitlement to specific relief, but could not sensibly be afforded a 'right' to any particular remedy in a strong sense.[146] In this settlement of certainty and discretion, the importance of equitable relief being granted upon terms according to recognised equitable principles[147] cannot be overstated. Tempting though it may be to describe equity simply as 'fixed' or 'discretionary', the reality denied such crude descriptions. 'Equity sought to ameliorate the rigidity of common law remedies not by moving at large but by reference to standards adapted to the exigencies of the particular case.'[148]

Equity of this kind is still the equity of Australia and, substantially, of England.[149] Accordingly, whatever obscurities there may be, in Australia and England equitable discretion must apply to equitable compensation for breach of confidence by reference to settled doctrines and principles applied using familiar judicial methods to meet the exigencies of the case, not at large. If the occasions for imposing terms on a grant of equitable compensation are few, and if some suggestions of how equitable discretion might apply to the remedy are better understood on other grounds, it is, at least, consonant with equity's established nature and operation to suggest that equitable compensation may, for instance, be granted on terms[150] and subject to an equitable defence of delay.[151]

The character of equitable discretion in Canada and New Zealand was significantly altered in the decisions of *Lac Minerals* and *Aquaculture* respectively.[152] Relative to Australia and England, the courts of Canada and New Zealand now possess greater discretionary power with respect to equitable compensation. On an equitable claim for breach of confidence, the 'appropriate' remedy lies perhaps wholly in the discretion of Canadian and New Zealand courts. Where other claims and remedies were or could have been claimed, both countries' courts also hold discretionary power to quantify an award of compensation by reference to common law concepts, as will further be seen below.[153] Where a confidant's breach of an equitable obligation of confidence causes loss to the confider, the confider has no 'right' to recover equitable compensation for that loss: the confider might even lack a prima facie entitlement to such relief. With respect, the reasoning by which

[146] WMC Gummow, 'Equity: Too Successful?' (2003) 77 *Australian Law Journal* 30, 40–41; *Grimaldi v Chameleon Mining NL (No 2)* (2012) 200 FCR 296, [503] (FCAFC).

[147] *Colvin v Hartwell* (1837) 5 Cl & F 484, 522 (HL).

[148] Gummow (n 146) 39.

[149] J McGhee (ed), *Snell's Equity*, 33rd edn (London, Sweet & Maxwell, 2015) ch 1. But see P Finn, 'Common Law Divergences' (2013) 37 *Melbourne University Law Review* 509.

[150] P Stanley, *The Law of Confidentiality* (Oxford, Hart Publishing, 2008) 104.

[151] Toulson and Phipps (n 72) [9–060]. Query whether the authors' suggested illustration of delay may be better understood as an instance of a broken chain of causation. See also *X v Attorney-General* [1997] 2 NZLR 623, 639 (unclean hands) (HC).

[152] Regarding New Zealand, see also *Day v Mead* [1987] 2 NZLR 443, 451 (CA).

[153] Below, text to (nn 221–224).

doctrine has thus been unsettled in Canada and New Zealand brims with difficulties, was adopted without adequate cause, and has had undesirable effects.[154]

An attempt that would translate those difficulties to England was made in *Vercoe v Rutland Fund Management Ltd*, elements of which were approved by Rimer LJ in *Walsh v Shanahan*.[155] It will be recalled that Sales J was concerned in *Vercoe v Rutland* at the possible differences in the relief recoverable in contract and in equity for breach of confidence.[156] To overcome those concerns, his Lordship held the claimant to have no 'discretion' to choose between an account of profits derived by the third parties in breach of their equitable obligations and, in the alternative, 'compensation' or 'damages' for loss suffered as a result of those breaches. Sales J said the court holds what he variously called discretion or power 'to control the choice between those forms of relief'.[157] On the facts, his Lordship confined the claimant to a grant of 'damages' to be calculated using the litigants' agreed method.

The case is anomalous in the English legal setting. Sales J took the Court of Appeal's decision in *Seager v Copydex Ltd (No 1)*[158] as authority that a court may in its discretion refuse an accounting of the profits made by a confidant in breach of an equitable obligation of confidence. It is true that the plaintiff's writ in *Seager* did claim 'an inquiry as to damages by reason of the defendants' breaches of confidence or procurements thereof or alternatively an account of profits'[159] and it is true that the Court of Appeal simply 'enter[ed] judgment for Mr Seager for damages to be assessed' in finding for the plaintiff.[160] Sales J is not the first to have read *Seager v Copydex* as denying a claimant's right to elect an accounting of profits.[161] However, *Seager v Copydex Ltd* is not authority for that proposition, as Arnold J has since pointed out.[162] When the matter in *Seager* returned in 1969 to the Court of Appeal pursuant to liberty to reply reserved in the Court of Appeal's orders of

[154] See Birks (n 63).

[155] *Walsh v Shanahan* [2013] EWCA Civ 411.

[156] Text following (n 123).

[157] *Vercoe* (n 89) [333]–[346].

[158] Above (n 25).

[159] *Seager* (n 25) 924F.

[160] ibid 932E.

[161] See *Australian Medic-Care Co Ltd v Hamilton Pharmaceuticals Pty Ltd* (2009) 261 ALR 501, [674] (FCA); Conaglen (n 101) 96–97, 101, 104, 105; D Davies, 'Restitution and Equitable Wrongs: an Australian Analogue' in FD Rose (ed), *Consensus ad Idem: Essays in the Law of Contract in Honour of Guenter Treitel* (London, Sweet & Maxwell, 1996) 164; Dean (n 32) [8.230]; Edelman (n 126) 214–215; PD Finn, *Fiduciary Obligations* (Sydney, Law Book Co, 1977) [383]; Lord Goff and G Jones, *The Law of Restitution*, 3rd edn (London, Sweet & Maxwell, 1986) 670; Jackman (n 136) 126; North (n 37) 156, 161–162; M Thompson, 'Breach of Confidence and Privacy' in L Clarke (ed), *Confidentiality and the Law* (London, Lloyd's of London, 1990) 79. More recently, *Walsh* (n 155) [57]–[61]; P Goulding (ed), *Employee Competition: Covenants, Confidentiality, and Garden Leave*, 3rd edn (Oxford, Oxford University Press, 2016) [11.116]; N Moreham and M Warby (eds), *Tugendhat and Christie: The Law of Privacy and the Media*, 3rd edn (Oxford, Oxford University Press, 2016) [12.147]; G Virgo, *The Principles of the Law of Restitution*, 3rd edn (Oxford, Oxford University Press, 2015) 517–519.

[162] *Force India* (n 2) [396].

1967, counsel for Copydex informed the Court that at the Court's 1967 hearing 'the plaintiff proffered no argument as to the property remedy'; counsel submitted that '[t]he plaintiff cannot say now that the proper remedy was an account of the profits made by the defendants on the sale of the offending goods'.[163] The Court did not refuse an account in its discretion: the plaintiff forwent an opportunity to demand an account. And the summary of argument in the *Reports of Patent Cases* indicates a shared view of counsel and the court that the plaintiff had rights of election founded on a prima facie entitlement to an account of profits.[164] Other authority supports the existence of such a prima facie entitlement.[165]

Sales J's suggestion that the House of Lords had ruled or reasoned that English courts hold discretion to decide on the type and extent of monetary relief for breach of confidence is unsupportable. Sales J relied on *A-G v Blake*.[166] The House of Lords held there to be 'no reason, *in principle*, why the court must in all circumstances rule out an account of profits as a remedy for breach of contract'.[167] Sales J saw this as altering the foundation of relief for breach of confidence. Whether sourced in contract or equity, Sales J thought, *Blake* confers a discretionary power on English courts to grant or withhold monetary relief. However, the leading judgment of Lord Nicholls of Birkenhead in *Blake* cannot bear that reading. Established rules as to established remedies for breach of confidence, or breach of contract generally, were not taken away. Lord Nicholls disavowed any intention of disturbing the settled expectations founded on that settled law.[168] *Blake* accepted only a much narrower discretion. Where a contractual obligation of confidence is breached and the 'normal' contractual remedies of damages, injunction and specific performance would be inadequate, in 'exceptional' circumstances—and where it would be 'the just response to a breach of contract'—an account of profits for breach of contract may be ordered.[169] Thus, for breach of an equitable obligation of confidence, it would still be that 'the injured party is given the choice: either compensatory damages [sic] or an account of the wrongdoer's profits'.[170] The

163 *Seager v Copydex Ltd (No 2)* [1969] RPC 250, 254 (CA).
164 ibid 255.
165 *Peter Pan Manufacturing Corp v Corsets Silhouette Ltd* [1964] 1 WLR 96, 106 (ChD); *A-G v Observer* (n 5) 161–162, 168 (ChD); 211, 232 (CA); 262, 266, 286 (HL); *Blake* (n 125) 285C; *Optus Networks* (n 88) [31], [37], [41]; *Bluescope Steel Ltd v Kelly* (2007) 72 IPR 289, [83], [160] (FCA); *Mosley v News Group Newspapers Ltd* [2008] EWHC 1777 (QB), [175]; *Vasco Investment Managers Ltd v Morgan Stanley Australia Ltd* (2014) 108 IPR 52, [294]–[296] (Vic SC). Though the position in Canada is obscure, *Islip v SSI Equipment Inc* (2009) 60 BLR (4th) 77, [113]–[114], [147] is consistent with the position apparent from the other cases cited in this note.
166 Above (n 125).
167 *Blake* (n 125) 284H (emphasis in original). This remedy is unavailable in Australia: *Hospitality Group Pty Ltd v Australian Rugby Union Ltd* (2001) 110 FCR 157, [155]–[159] (FCAFC).
168 *Blake* (n 125) 285F.
169 ibid 284F, 284H, 285F. See *Devenish Nutrition Ltd v Sanofi-Aventis SA* [2009] Ch 290, [38], [48].
170 *Blake* (n 125) 285C.

House of Lords only added a discretionary remedy to the array of settled remedies for breach of contract and existing equitable remedies. Relief for all kinds of breaches of confidence was not rendered discretionary.

The reasoning in *Vercoe v Rutland* contains a fallacy encountered elsewhere.[171] When Lord Nicholls announced the discretion to order an account of profits as 'the just response to a breach of contract' where 'the plaintiff [has] a legitimate interest' in such relief,[172] he spoke at what Sales J correctly described as a 'high level of generality'.[173] However, Sales J then said that Lord Nicholls' general statements formed a specific 'test': 'whether the claimant's interest in the performance of the obligation in question (whether regarded as an equitable obligation or a contractual obligation) makes it just and equitable that the defendant should retain no profit from his breach of that obligation'.[174] The step from legal abstraction to legal test, with respect, is false. The purpose of a legal rule is no substitute for the rule itself. That is no less true where the purpose is the pursuit of justice through a legal 'response' to another's default.

While a wide discretion applies to equitable compensation for breach of confidence in Canada and New Zealand, the remedy in England and Australia is discretionary in the settled tradition that has existed since the chancellorship of Lord Eldon.

V. Quantum

The quantum of equitable compensation depends on the object of the remedy and, to degrees varying between jurisdictions, on other matters. The remedy's object is, and ought to be, to compensate the confider for loss suffered by reason of a breach of an equitable obligation of confidence. Attention turns to how that should be done.

The foundation of obligations of confidence in conscience ought to structure the principles of relief, including equitable compensation. Conscience being the foundation of the obligation, damage is not the 'gist of the action' for breach of confidence: actions on the case and their rules are not relevant. In that sense, 'detriment' in the sense of 'damage' need not be shown before relief may be obtained to remedy or prevent a breach of an equitable obligation of confidence.[175] As Gummow J said in *Smith Kline & French Laboratories (Aust) Ltd v Department of Community Services and Health*:[176]

[171] Above, text to (nn 72–76); above, text after (n 109); below, text after (n 179).
[172] *Blake* (n 125) 284F, 285H.
[173] *Vercoe* (n 89) [339].
[174] ibid. See *Devenish Nutrition* (n 169) [60] ('Lord Nicholls offers a general test').
[175] See *Cadbury Schweppes* (n 6) [52]–[54] (*obiter dicta*).
[176] Above (n 7).

> [E]quity intervenes to uphold an obligation and not necessarily to prevent or to recover loss ... The cases dealing with recovery from errant fiduciaries of profits which their principals could not have made illustrate a similar point. The basis of the equitable jurisdiction to protect obligations of confidence lies, as the present case illustrates, in an obligation of conscience arising from the circumstances in or through which the information, the subject of the obligation, was communicated or obtained ... The obligation of conscience is to respect the confidence, not merely to refrain from causing detriment to the plaintiff. The plaintiff comes to equity to vindicate his right to observance of the obligation, not necessarily to recover loss or to restrain infliction of apprehended loss. To look into a related field, when has equity said that the only breaches of trust to be restrained are those that would prove detrimental to the beneficiaries?[177]

The decided cases on compensation or 'damages' cannot all be reconciled with the accepted grounding of the obligation of confidence in conscience.[178] Instead, the pertinent enquiry is what principles of quantification will properly give effect to that equitable obligation.

A. Underlying Principles

In matters of quantification, the discernment of 'underlying principles'[179] is proving inutile beyond affirming the tautologous truism that the purpose of equitable compensation is to compensate. From the premise that compensation for loss is a principle underlying the award of relief on various causes of action, it is illegitimate to deduce that the surface-level principles by which, say, damages for breach of contract are quantified are also properly adapted to quantify equitable compensation for breach of confidence. The reasons were exposed earlier.[180] The discernment of 'underlying' principles may sound preferable to distraction by specious differences between the rules of compensating loss on different causes of action, but those rules are not a diverting artifice. Their differences express the more specific precepts by which compensation is to be awarded in order to advance the objectives of the law regarding particular forms of misconduct and wrongdoing. Attention thus returns to how compensation may be awarded in accordance with the obligation of conscience owed by a confidant in equity.

B. Common Law Analogies

It is improbable that the ways of awarding compensation vary infinitely. Loss is not an infinitely variable concept. Nor are the possible ways of quantifying loss

177 *Smith Kline* (n 7) 112. See Huston (n 133) 8.
178 Above (n 129).
179 Above, text to (nn 72–76); above, text after (n 109).
180 Text following (n 111).

infinitely varied. Unless all rules and principles are to be forsaken for unstructured discretion in the award of compensation in equity, some aspects of the enquiry will inevitably resemble some aspects of the quantification of damages for one tort or another, or for breach of contract. For instance, absent a financial loss, in various situations a claimant's loss may be measured by the method of assessing the lost value of the claimant's legal rights.[181] In seeking principles as to the quantification of equitable compensation, is it therefore fitting to seek analogies with common law relief?

'Any discussion of the application of the remedy of "damages" in breach of confidence cases is fraught with difficulty [from] the outset',[182] because such analogies have been sought unthinkingly. The applicable rules of quantification depend on the purpose and scope of the obligation whose breach is to be remedied.[183] Analogies with contractual rules of mitigation and remoteness of loss, or the rules of contributory fault, foreseeability and intervening cause in the tort of negligence, are inapt to effectuate an obligation of conscience.[184] A contract party may be required to mitigate his or her loss by procuring a contract on equivalent terms with another promisor. A confider cannot sensibly be required to mitigate his or her loss by seeking another confidant to keep the secret. It would also be odd to suppose that an obligation of conscience may be discharged by pointing to unforeseen events or the claimant's own fault in a way that engages common law rules of quantification in, for example, contract and the tort of negligence. On the other hand, such matters may inform a decision as to what obligation of conscience the defendant owed in the first place[185] or what loss the defendant's breach caused to the claimant.[186]

C. Equitable Analogies

Analogies with other equitable relief may be more plausible since conscience itself operates elsewhere in equity. Of course, the *power* to award equitable compensation for breach of confidence has been founded on analogies with the power to award 'compensation' for breach of trust and especially with the power, affirmed

181 See, eg, *Darvall McCutcheon v HK Frost Holdings Pty Ltd* (2002) 4 VR 570, [66]; *Skids Programme Management* (n 129) [89]; *Caves Beachside Cuisine Pty Ltd v Boydah Pty Ltd* [2015] NSWSC 1273, [198]; compare Stuckey-Clarke (n 34) 85. As to trespass to land: JNE Varuhas, 'The Concept of "Vindication" in the Law of Torts: Rights, Interests and Damages' (2014) 34 *Oxford Journal of Legal Studies* 253, 284–289.

182 Aplin et al (n 10) [19.02].

183 *Environment Agency v Empress Car Co (Abertillery) Ltd* [1999] 2 AC 22, 31 (HL).

184 Compare *Flogas Britain* (n 2) [97]; *Vestergaard Frandsen A/S v Bestnet Europe Ltd* [2014] EWHC 3159 (Ch) [111] (in which the reasoning is problematic).

185 See *Coco* (n 25) 422–423; *Smith Kline* (n 7) 110–111; *A-G v Observer* (n 5) 282; *R v Department of Health* [2001] QB 424, [54] (CA).

186 *Mosley* (n 165) [224]–[226].

by Lord Haldane LC in *Nocton v Lord Ashburton*,[187] to award equitable compensation for breach of duty by fiduciaries other than express trustees.[188] Analogies in matters of *quantum* have likewise been sought with the principles applicable to trustees and other fiduciaries.[189]

Upon analysis a sound and, at present, simple analogy lies with equitable compensation for breach of fiduciary duty. Analogies with 'compensation' for breach of trust are prone to collapse since the accounting doctrines by which the losses of a trust are recovered do not translate to an equitable obligation of confidence *simpliciter*: confidential information is not a trust asset. Rooted as they are in conscience, the liabilities of a non-trustee fiduciary provide a better analogy. The analogy is simple in that the principles of quantification of equitable compensation for breach of fiduciary duty, while contested, are currently simple:[190] generally,[191] compensation is payable for all losses that the claimant principal would not have suffered but for the defendant fiduciary's breach of fiduciary duty.[192] The analogy is also simple in that that principle has been applied when quantifying equitable compensation for breach of confidence.[193]

The simplicity of the equitable analogies may be their most telling feature: not because simplicity is a defining mark of superior law, but because simple principles of quantification are what naturally stem from the obligation of conscience which lies at the root of equitable obligations of confidence. The shortage of complication is attributable to the founding of equitable obligations of confidence in conscience. If the obligations were not founded in equity, then quantification might be subject to more complicated rules.

D. Personal Information

Breaches of confidence relating to purely personal (as distinct from commercial and 'proprietary' confidences) pose special difficulties. The analogies compete. Should

187 [1914] AC 932 (HL).

188 Australia: *Concept Television Productions Pty Ltd v Australian Broadcasting Corp* (1988) 12 IPR 129, 136 (FCA); *Smith Kline* (n 7) 83. Canada: *Cadbury Schweppes* (n 6) [59]–[61]. England: *Force India* (n 2) [392]–[393]; *Flogas* (n 2) [37]. New Zealand: *Day* (n 152) 451. See also *Kitechnology BV v Unicor Gmbh Plastmaschinen* [1995] FSR 765, 777–778 (CA) (jurisdiction to 'restrain and, if necessary, award damages for breach of confidence' an equitable jurisdiction); Toulson and Phipps (n 72) [2-078]–[2-083].

189 See, eg, *Ithaca Ice Works Pty Ltd v Queensland Ice Supplies Pty Ltd* [2002] QSC 222, [14]–[16].

190 Heydon et al (n 32) [23-020], [23-620].

191 That is, apart from any special doctrine in or derived from *Brickenden v London Loan and Savings Co* [1934] 3 DLR 465 (PC).

192 Heydon et al (n 32) [23-510]–[23-570]. See also M Conaglen '*Brickenden*', Ch 6 of this volume.

193 *Ithaca Ice Works* (n 189) [16]. See also *Cadbury Schweppes* (n 6) [50] (in an appropriate case, equitable compensation may be awarded unlimited by the rules as to recover for remote losses in negligence).

compensation be awarded—and refused—by analogy to the rules for compensating for loss suffered through breaches of commercial and 'proprietary' confidences? If so, then the claimant may recover nothing: though apprehended breaches of confidence may be restrained by injunction no matter the type of information, nowhere else does equity compensate for harm done to purely personal interests. Equity only compensates for loss suffered through harm to economic and proprietary interests. Or should compensation for breach of a purely personal confidence be awarded by analogy to rules of damages pertaining to the law of torts where purely personal interests, such as to body and reputation, are a specialism?

The former is the better analogy. It is suggested that equity should only confer power to compensate for losses suffered through a breach of a commercial or 'proprietary' confidence. Monetary relief for breach of wholly personal confidences should be recoverable, if at all, only under statute or at common law under a new specific tort, such as a tort of misuse of private information.

Once the judge-made law accepts that compensation is to be awarded for breaches of confidence relating to purely personal information, certain consequences seem inevitably to follow. For example, a defendant may misuse the claimant's personal information without thereby causing the claimant any financial loss.[194] Or the defendant may in addition misuse the claimant's personal information in a manner hurtful or highly embarrassing to the claimant, or so as to offend public morals or terribly misuse public power.[195] In contemporary Western societies, it seems inevitable that monetary relief—particularly aggravated and exemplary damages—should be sought and that courts should occasionally sympathise. It also seems inevitable that demands should be made that equity 'find' power to grant such relief lest equity fail to live up to its reputation for justice and flexibility.[196] The momentum of that reasoning has moved leading writers in England,[197] and has twice moved superior courts of Australia to find aggravated equitable compensation available for breach of confidence.[198] All these eventualities seem likely[199] notwithstanding equity's traditional refusal to award

[194] *A-G v Observer* (n 5) 286E; Stuckey-Clarke (n 34) 85.

[195] Compare *A-G v Observer* (n 5) 286E; *Campbell v MGN Ltd* [2002] EWHC 499, [141], [166]–[169] (and, in the House of Lords, *Campbell* (n 30) [35], [51]); *Douglas v Hello! Ltd (No 3)* [2006] QB 125, [107]–[110], [243], [256]; *Hosking v Runting* [2005] 1 NZLR 1, [138], [246], [258]; *Giller v Procopets* (2008) 24 VR 1, [1], [131], [160], [423]–[424], [442]; *Mosley* (n 165) [214]–[231]; *Vidal-Hall* (n 29) [5]; *Gulati* (n 29) [45]–[48]; *Wilson v Ferguson* [2015] WASC 15, [78]–[85]; *Doe 464533* (n 32) [51].

[196] See, eg, *Day v Mead* (n 152) 451.

[197] Aplin et al (n 10) [17.13]–[17.15].

[198] *Giller* (n 195) [1], [142]–[143], [148], [159]–[160], [408], [423]–[424] (relying on a case of breach of contract, *Cornelius v De Taranto* [2001] EMLR 12, [431]; *Wilson* (n 195). The availability of aggravated and exemplary awards in Canada and New Zealand depends on different reasoning: *Doe 464533* (n 32) [52]–[63]; *Aquaculture* (n 9) 301; *X* (n 151) 630–631.

[199] B McDonald, 'Privacy Claims: Transformation, Fault, and the Public Interest Defence' in A Dyson, J Goudkamp and F Wilmot-Smith (eds), *Defences in Tort* (Oxford, Hart Publishing, 2015) 295.

damages—let alone aggravated or exemplary damages—and equity's leaving of compensation for purely personal harm to the common law of torts.[200]

The boldness of awarding compensation in equity for damage to purely personal interests (including distress) and to punish offensive breaches of confidence hides intellectual timidity. By appealing to equity's flexibility in search of support for such awards,[201] an appeal is made to a form of discretion not found in the settlement between discretion and certainty in equity jurisprudence from the time of Lord Eldon's chancellorship onwards. The appeal is to flexibility and justice at large, unconstrained by settled principles such as equity's refusal to award what in substance or form is common law damages. An examination of equitable discretion in Australia and England shows that equity continues to develop and award flexible relief according to settled equitable principles that deny the undisciplined discretion that would be necessary if such awards were to be legitimate.

Resort has also been made to equity's 'flexibility' in order to evade consideration of whether a reversal of equity's settled attitudes towards damages, purely personal harm, aggravation and punishment would be congruent with the rest of the law. That is significant for three reasons. First, it is proper and far from uncommon[202] for appellate courts to consider the congruence of a proposed alteration or development of a legal rule when deciding how to proceed. Secondly, proposed alterations and developments of equity, as one of the sources of obligation within the legal system, are subject to the same scrutiny. Thirdly, especially close scrutiny is properly given to proposed alterations and developments that would impinge upon the carefully worked out rules of recovery of damages at common law.[203] Those considerations compel the conclusion that a reversal of equity's settled attitudes would be incongruent with the rest of the law. 'Equitable' awards of compensation for purely personal harm or for aggravation or to punish would plainly impinge on the rules of recovery of damages at common law.[204] The judicial technique applied in equity since Lord Eldon is quite misunderstood if it is thought

200 See, eg, *Perotti v Garett* (CA, 12 June 1998); *Mosley* (n 165) [181]–[197]; *Lloyds TSB Bank plc v Markandan and Uddin* [2010] EWHC 2517 (Ch), [42] (point not taken on appeal: [2012] EWCA Civ 65, [57]); Heydon et al (n 32) [23-590]–[23-605]; PM McDermott, 'Jurisdiction of the Court of Chancery to Award Damages' (1992) 108 *Law Quarterly Review* 652. See also *David v Administrator-General* (1964) 14 WIR 111, 125 (Jam CA); *Libertarian Investments Ltd v Hall* (2013) 16 HKCFAR 681, [83].

201 See *Giller* (n 195) [146], [148], [152]; *Wilson* (n 195) [72], [82].

202 See, eg, *Tchenguiz v Imerman* [2011] Fam 116; *Gulati* (n 29) [61]–[62]; M Leeming, 'Theories and Principles Underlying the Development of the Common Law—the Statutory Elephant in the Room' (2013) 36 *University of New South Wales Law Journal* 1002, 1019–1020.

203 See, eg, *Sullivan v Moody* (2001) 207 CLR 562, [42], [55]; *Miller v Miller* (2011) 242 CLR 446, [15]; *CAL No 14 Pty Ltd v Motor Accidents Board* (2009) 239 CLR 390, [39]–[42].

204 M Tilbury, 'Remedies for Breach of Confidence in Privacy Contexts' (2010) 15 *Media and Arts Law Review* 290, 292–293; D Butler, 'Protecting Personal Privacy in Australia: Quo Vadis?' (2016) 42 *Australian Bar Review* 107, 115.

the word 'equity' excuses a court of the disciplines attending judicial development of the law.[205] 'Legal analysis is as important in equity as in the common law.'[206]

If compensation is to be available for harm to purely personal interests suffered through breaches of confidence, then greater congruence would be attained by recognising a tort and permitting the recovery of damages, rather than equitable compensation.[207] In England and New Zealand that is being done by accepting that no 'general' action of invasion of privacy exists,[208] but that a narrower 'wrong' of misuse of private information, increasingly tort-like,[209] has the function of protecting privacy. In Canada, a tort of intruding upon seclusion has been held, in Ontario at least, to exist at common law.[210] In Australia, the High Court's invitation to lower courts to develop such a tort[211] has, surprisingly, not yet been taken up by a superior court.[212]

Arguments that equitable compensation should be available for all breaches of confidence are often made to depend on the following syllogism, or a variant thereof:

(a) personal confidences are 'protected' in equity;[213]
(b) 'the action' for breach of confidence is the basis of that protection;[214]
(c) therefore, compensation (or 'damages') is available for all breaches of confidence, including for harm to purely personal interests.[215]

Of the problems raised by that reasoning, two will be mentioned. First, the reasoning assimilates a 'cause of action' for breach of confidence—a factual situation the existence of which entitles a confider to obtain from a court a remedy against another person—to a form of action, specifically the old action on the case. For, in equity a person can have a cause of action for an injunction and yet no entitlement

[205] PG Turner, 'Equity and Administration' in PG Turner (ed), *Equity and Administration* (Cambridge, Cambridge University Press, 2016) 6–7, 9–10, 15.

[206] *AIB Group* (n 76) [95] (Lord Reed JSC).

[207] McDonald (n 199) 290–292, 295–297. How claims to recover lost or actual profits might be treated when brought on the basis of such a cause of action is a large question that cannot properly be considered here. See Moreham and Warby (n 161) [12.95]–[12.102].

[208] *Douglas v Hello! Ltd (No 6)* [2006] QB 125, [96]; *Tchenguiz* (n 202) [65].

[209] England: *Vidal-Hall* (n 29) [21], [25], [43], [51]; *Gulati* (n 29) [88]; compare *Kitechnology* (n 188) 777–778. New Zealand: *Hosking* (n 195) [117]–[135], [248]–[250], [259]; *Television New Zealand Ltd v Rogers* [2008] 2 NZLR 277, [23]–[26], [98], [144]; compare *C v Holland* [2012] 3 NZLR 672, [65]–[93] (asserting a general tort of 'intrusion upon seclusion', notwithstanding *Hosking*).

[210] *Jones v Tsige* (2012) 108 OR (3d) 241. There are several provincial enactments against invasions of privacy. See also H Delany and E Carolan, *The Right to Privacy* (Dublin, Thomson Round Hall, 2008) 107.

[211] *Lenah Game Meats* (n 66) [40]–[43], [107]–[111], [129]–[132], [328]–[336].

[212] Australian Law Reform Commission, *Serious Invasions of Privacy in the Digital Era*, ALRC Report 123 (2014) [3.53]–[3.58].

[213] *Giller* (n 195) [131], [396], [423]–[424]; *Wilson* (n 195) [81].

[214] *Giller* (n 195) [146]–[147], [431]; *Wilson* (n 195) [44]–[47].

[215] *Giller* (n 195) [143], [159], [408], [422]–[424]; *Wilson* (n 195) [82], [84]. Similarly, *Douglas* (n 208) [115]; R Scott, 'Confidentiality' in J Beatson and Y Cripps, *Freedom of Expression and Freedom of Information: Essays in Honour of Sir David Williams* (Oxford, Oxford University Press, 2000) 267–272.

to compensation in equity: each tort restrained in equity is an example.[216] However, if breach of confidence were an action on the case, 'damage' would be the gist of the action and lead to recovery of damages for harm to purely personal interests. In fact, the equitable action is not an action on the case: it corresponds to an equitable obligation of conscience.

Secondly, it is false to reason[217] that, because equity may 'protect' personal confidences by means of a *quia timet* injunction against the confidant, equity ought to 'protect' the confidence after the event by awarding equitable compensation.[218] That reasoning merely avoids, once again, the question of whether it would be congruent with the rest of the law—especially the law of torts—were equitable compensation to be awarded in respect of harm to purely personal interests. Equitable compensation for harm to economic and 'proprietary' interests is, in principle, available against a defaulting confidant where the confider failed to obtain an injunction in time to restrain a breach of confidence. But to suppose that the same ought to be true of harm to purely personal interests is to use an argument of symmetry to avoid the weighty issues presented above.[219]

The upshot, it is suggested, is that equitable compensation for harm done to purely personal interests as a result of a breach of confidence should not be quantified by reference to common law damages. In terms of the principles of the non-statutory judge-made law, such harm should not be compensated in equity at all. If it is to be compensated, that should be by establishing a relevant statutory liability or tort for which damages are recoverable under statute or at common law, as the case may be.[220]

E. Equity Following the Law

Under their discretion to grant 'appropriate' relief for breach of confidence, the courts of Canada and New Zealand effectively apply the maxim that equity follows the law. Courts of Canada possess discretionary power to award 'appropriate' relief where a claimant suffers loss by reason of the defendant's breach of an equitable obligation, and the claimant also had a cause of action for breach of a contractual obligation of confidence.[221] Courts of New Zealand possess such discretionary

216 Tilbury (n 204) 292–293.

217 *Giller* (n 195) [145], [150], [151].

218 D Capper, 'Damages for Breach of the Equitable Duty of Confidence' (1994) 14 *Legal Studies* 313, 327; McDonald (n 199) 292–293.

219 Compare *O (a child) v Rhodes* [2016] AC 219, [77].

220 See also T Aplin, 'The Future of Breach of Confidence and the Protection of Privacy' (2007) 7 *Oxford University Commonwealth Law Journal* 137, 151, 155–161; M Tilbury, 'Privacy: Common Law or Human Right?' in N Witzleb, D Lindsay, M Paterson and S Rodrick (eds), *Emerging Challenges in Privacy Law* (Cambridge, Cambridge University Press, 2014) 174–178.

221 Above, text following (n 34).

power for all breaches of confidence.[222] The courts of both countries ensure that equity follows the law by, for example, reducing the quantum of equitable compensation to what would have been recovered as damages for negligence in tort. The principle appears to be that where (i) the same 'policy objectives' underlie concurrent causes of action, one of which is an action in the tort of negligence, and (ii) both 'policy objectives' 'support' an award of damages to place the claimant in the position it would have occupied but for the breach of confidence, then the court may limit the award of compensation to the quantum of damages recoverable according to the rules from the law of negligence.[223]

Both of those conditions have been criticised earlier in this chapter, and it may be added that the relevance of negligence to breach of confidence is most obscure. If such discretion is to exist, it is difficult to appreciate why it should be routinely limited by 'following' the common law in this way,[224] especially in order to yield awards at odds with the obligations of conscience owed by defendants.

VI. Conclusion

The comparative recency of developments in the judge-made law of a unitary doctrine of protecting confidences apart from contract explains several of the problems examined in this chapter, even if it does not justify them. At a fundamental level, confusion over the very character of obligations of confidence has led courts and writers to confuse the equitable liability for breach of confidence with other sources of liability in civil law, and thence to elide the differences between an equitable remedy of compensation and compensation granted to satisfy liabilities relating to obligations with roots in quite different principles and policies. The difficulty of finding a clear, accurate and comprehensive statement of the principles applicable to the equitable remedy of compensation for breach of confidence results more from these problems than from any other cause.

Identifying those problems allows the rudiments of the equitable remedy to be stated as follows. In the judge-made law, non-contractual obligations of confidence are equitable obligations of conscience. Conscience here is a settled concept. It denotes an obligation of diligence requiring the confidant only to use the confidential information as the terms of the obligation permit. The requirements of conscience still bind a confidant who fails to discharge that obligation of conscience and thus assumes liability for breach of confidence. These liabilities are

222 *Skids Programme Management* (n 129) [87]–[90], [121]–[123]; *Hunt* (n 80) [74].

223 See *Cadbury Schweppes* (n 6) [50].

224 See J Berryman, 'Recent Developments in the Law of Equitable Remedies: What Canada Can Do for You' (2002) 33 *Victoria University of Wellington Law Review* 51, 88 fn 125; Capper (n 218) 328.

distinct from other species of civil obligations, including contractual obligations of confidence. The relief available to satisfy the confidant's equitable liability—equitable compensation and accounts of profits, in particular—differs in nature and purpose from the relief available in respect of contractual obligations of confidence. The quantum of relief is that necessary to discharge the defaulting confidant's obligation of conscience. The defaulting confidant's obligation of conscience will not be discharged by pleas accepted on various grounds at common law, such as that the claimant failed to mitigate his or her loss or contributed to his or her own misfortune.

The existence of equitable liability to compensate ought not to be affected by the presence of concurrent liability in contract. The availability of equitable compensation ought not to be affected by 'differences' in the available remedies on the concurrent causes of action. Since the forms of action have been abolished, the common law systems of Australia, Canada, England and New Zealand have committed themselves to notions of concurrent liability and concurrently available remedies, subject to elections and principles barring double satisfaction. Discretion properly has a modest role in the award of equitable compensation for breach of confidence. The remedy is discretionary, but the discretion is or ought to be settled. In Australia and England, discretion will probably only apply narrowly given that, relative to specific relief, monetary relief in equity is not prone to inflicting unwarranted oppression or hardship, especially to innocent third parties. Where a confider suffers financial loss by reason of another's breach of an equitable obligation of confidence, the confider ought to have a prima facie entitlement to recover compensation for those losses the confider would not have suffered had the obligation of conscience been kept.

13

Rescission, Restitution and Compensation

ELISE BANT

I. Introduction

This chapter considers the nature of pecuniary awards and adjustments, including 'indemnity' orders, consequent on equitable rescission.[1] Its essential thesis is that notwithstanding that the awards are often couched in terms of 'compensation',[2] they can often be fruitfully analysed as restitutionary in nature or reflecting an implicit application of change of position considerations. This thesis is supported by the approach of courts considering the award of analogous remedies under the Trade Practices Act 1974 (Cth), and its successor the Australian Consumer Law.[3] In the statutory context, as in equity, courts apply broad concepts of detriment and compensation in a manner often consistent with a restitutionary analysis. Further, the approach taken to crafting statutory relief is consistent with the view that when awarding relief consequent on rescission, a key aim is to prevent the defendant from being placed in an unjustifiably worse position than she occupied prior to the impugned transaction. This formulation emphasises the very close relationship between the traditional bar of *restitutio in integrum* as formulated in equity and the change of position defence as recently formulated in the High Court of Australia.[4] The closeness of the association has profound implications

[1] Rescission at common law is notoriously strict, requiring precise *restitutio in integrum* and admitting no consequential or facilitative adjustments between the parties: see *Erlanger v The New Sombrero Phosphate Company* (1878) 3 App Cas 1218, 1278–1279 (HL) (Lord Blackburn); *Alati v Kruger* (1955) 94 CLR 216, 224 (Dixon CJ, Webb, Kitto and Taylor JJ). It is therefore outside the scope of this chapter. Further, the nature of awards made pursuant to s 2 of the Misrepresentation Act 1976 (UK) and its derivatives will be the subject of a further, independent paper.

[2] See, eg, *JAD International Pty Ltd v International Trucks Australia Ltd* (1994) 50 FCR 378, 392 (Keely, Hill and Drummond JJ).

[3] The ACL is contained in sch 2 of the Competition and Consumer Act 2010 (Cth).

[4] *Australian Financial Services & Leasing Pty Ltd v Hills Industries Ltd* (2014) 253 CLR 560, 598–99 [84]–[85] (Hayne, Crennan, Kiefel, Bell and Keane JJ), 625–626 [157] (Gageler J).

both for the future development of the law of equitable rescission and for the cognate statutory jurisdiction.

The chief focus of the chapter is on rescission of contractual arrangements, where the mutual exchanges between the parties often raise difficult issues for courts seeking to unwind transactions. However, it should not be forgotten that the same principles of rescission apply with respect to gifts. Although comparatively rare, courts addressing rescission of gifts also engage in complex adjustments to ensure parties are restored in substance to their former positions.[5] As we will see further below, these cases confirm the close relationship between rescission in cases of contract and gift and the remedy of restitution in simple transfer cases.

The chapter begins by introducing the debate about the relationship between rescission and compensation, in particular whether and when compensatory awards for concurrent torts may be made cumulative to orders for rescission. The chapter then considers when and how pecuniary awards and adjustments made solely consequent on rescission may be characterised as restitutionary, rather than compensatory in nature. It then addresses the insights that can be gained on this issue from the statutory context. The chapter concludes by identifying some ramifications of the analysis not only for the concept of *restitutio in integrum* in rescission, but also for the developing and analogous law of change of position.

II. Rescission and Compensation

It has frequently been said that rescission is independent of, and cumulative with, any right the plaintiff may also have to compensation in tort.[6] On this view, where a defendant has, for example, induced the plaintiff to enter into a contract for the purchase of a business through his fraudulent misrepresentations, the purchaser may avoid the contract and sue to recover her purchase money back from the appellant, with interest, as a consequence of rescission. However, she may also seek compensation for any loss which she may have suffered through carrying on the business in the meantime, on the basis of the tort of deceit.[7] If that is correct, an initial question is why it is necessary to consider whether the nature of the awards given by courts consequent on rescission is restitutionary or compensatory in

[5] See, eg, *Quek v Beggs* (1990) 5 BPR 11, 761 (NSWSC); *Winefield v Clarke* [2008] NSWSC 882, [54] (Barrett J).

[6] *Newbigging v Adam* (1886) 34 Ch D 582, 592 (CA) (Bowen LJ), affirmed in *Adam v Newbigging* (1888) 13 App Cas 308; *McAllister v Richmond Brewing Co (NSW) Pty Ltd* (1942) 42 SR (NSW) 187, 192 (NSWSC) (Jordan CJ); *Yorke v Ross Lucas Pty Ltd* (1982) 45 ALR 299; *Archer v Brown* [1985] QB 401; D O'Sullivan, S Elliott and R Zakrzewski, *The Law of Rescission*, 2nd edn (Oxford, Oxford University Press, 2014) [2.03]–[2.04].

[7] In *Archer v Brown* [1985] QB 401, Peter Pain J would have awarded exemplary damages for deceit in addition to rescission, had the defendant not already been jailed, an option that highlights the independent nature of the claims.

nature? If compensation is in any event available, any award that is potentially different from and, in particular, lesser than the compensatory award will simply be subsumed in the latter.

The first reason is that, even where an independent claim in tort is in theory available, a plaintiff may have failed to make an independent and cumulative claim for compensation, seeking only rescission and financial adjustments consequent on rescission. Some cases provide implicit support for the view that a court of equity may order that a defendant indemnify a defrauded plaintiff for all losses, so as to protect him as fully in equity as he could be at common law for deceit, in exercise of its concurrent jurisdiction and of its own volition.[8] However, it seems that on balance, the weight of authority goes the other way and a separate claim must be brought by the plaintiff.[9] This is supported by the clear requirement in cases of rescission involving duress or illegitimate pressure that any claim for compensation must rest on an independently pleaded tort.[10] On this basis, where an independent tort is not pleaded in cases of rescission for fraudulent misrepresentation, the plaintiff's relief is restricted to whatever consequential or ancillary relief inherently flows from his election to rescind. We will consider in more detail below the case of *Brown v Smitt*.[11] In that case, the plaintiff sought rescission of a contract of sale for fraudulent misrepresentation and certain consequential relief. In a joint judgment, Knox CJ, Gavan Duffy and Starke JJ emphasised that the plaintiff had not relied upon deceit and could not obtain compensation consequent on rescission for consequential losses he had suffered from running a business on the farm which was the subject of the sale.[12] In this context, a clear understanding of the nature and bounds of financial relief that is inherent in, or solely attributable to, rescission is essential.

Secondly, notwithstanding the widespread support in the authorities for the availability of cumulative relief arising from common law wrongs, Australian authorities indicate that claims for compensation in equity for breach of fiduciary duty in entering into a contract are precluded where the contract is rescinded.[13] If

8 *Newbigging v Adam* (1886) 34 Ch D 582, 592 (CA) (Bowen LJ); *McAllister v Richmond Brewing Co (NSW) Pty Ltd* (1942) 42 SR (NSW) 187, 192 (NSWSC) (Jordan CJ). See also *Demetrios v Gikas Dry Cleaning Industries Pty Ltd* (1991) 22 NSWLR 561, 573–574 (Meagher and Handley JA).

9 See, eg, *Sibley v Grosvenor* (1916) 21 CLR 469, 475 (Dixon CJ); *Redgrave v Hurd* (1881) 20 Ch D 1, 12 (CA) (Jessel MR, Lush LJ concurring at 26).

10 *Universe Tankships Inc of Monrovia v International Transport Workers Federation* [1983] 1 AC 366, 385 (HL), cited with approval in *Dimskal Shipping Co SA v International Transport Workers Federation (The Evia Luck) (No 2)* [1992] 2 AC 152, 166 (HL) (Lord Goff). See also *Investec Bank (Channel Islands) Ltd v The Retail Group plc* [2009] EWHC 476 (Ch), [122] (Sales J).

11 *Brown v Smitt* (1924) 34 CLR 160.

12 ibid 166. Followed on this point in *Blackley Investments Pty Ltd v Burnie City Council (No 2)* (2011) 21 Tas R 98 (TASSC).

13 *Aequitas Ltd v AEFC Leasing Pty Ltd* (2001) 19 ACLC 1006, 1087 [432] (Austin J) (NSWSC). His Honour drew from the cases in which an account of profit has been denied where a contract was affirmed, rather than rescinded: see *Re Cape Breton Company* (1885) 29 Ch D 795 (CA), upheld in *Cavendish Bentinck v Fenn* (1887) 12 App Cas 652 (HL), and in the High Court of Australia in *Tracy v Mandalay Pty Ltd* (1953) 88 CLR 215.

that is so,[14] it is difficult to see why compensation for common law wrongs such as deceit are cumulative, as opposed to alternative, to rescission. Consistently with this view Barnett and Harder argue that rescission and compensation are mutually exclusive: a plaintiff cannot both affirm the contract in order to seek compensation for deceit and rescind it.[15] Barnett and Harder draw support for this position from both *Brown v Smitt*[16] and *Alati v Kruger*,[17] which we consider immediately below.

It is certainly correct that claims for compensation for breach of contract cannot be brought where the contract has been rescinded. The contract cannot both be avoided and used as the basis of a claim for compensation that effectively enforces the (rescinded) promise.[18] However, does the same necessarily follow for claims for compensation for torts such as deceit? It is of course right that if compensation for deceit cumulative on rescission is awarded, it must take into account the fact of rescission and its inherent remedial consequences. In some aspects, the awards will be incompatible, being based on different premises. As explained by the High Court in *Alati v Kruger*, the normal measure of damages for deceit involving the purchase of a business assumes and affirms the contract of sale.[19] The primary measure of loss in that context is the difference between the price paid and the 'true' value of the property, an amount that assumes the plaintiff has retained or sold the asset.[20] The compensatory award is premised on the plaintiff retaining the property and seeks to 'make good' the loss sustained through the misrepresentation. Where the contract is rescinded, by contrast, the plaintiff disaffirms the contract and recovers her purchase price on returning the purchased asset to the defendant. The financial adjustments and awards consequential on rescission are premised on unwinding the contract and returning the plaintiff to his or her original position. There cannot, moreover, be double recovery, or over-compensation. This means that, assuming an award of damages is available in addition to rescission, that award of damages cannot compensate a plaintiff for any losses for which adjustment has already been made through the process of awards made as part of the process of rescinding the contract.

However, accepting that the natural incidents of rescission must be taken into account in any pecuniary adjustments or awards following rescission, so as to avoid double-recovery, the question remains whether compensation for *consequential loss* (rather than, for example, for the value of the business asset itself) may be awarded in addition to rescission, or whether the two responses are

[14] Against O'Sullivan, Elliott and Zakrzewski (n 6) [2.11]

[15] K Barnett and S Harder, *Remedies in Australian Private Law* (New York, Cambridge University Press, 2014) 399–400.

[16] *Brown v Smitt* (1924) 34 CLR 160.

[17] *Alati v Kruger* (1955) 94 CLR 216.

[18] ibid 222 (Dixon CJ, Webb, Kitto and Taylor JJ), quotation cited below at text to n 21.

[19] ibid 222 (Dixon CJ, Webb, Kitto and Taylor JJ), see quotation above at text to n 21.

[20] *Potts v Miller* (1940) 64 CLR 282; *Toteff v Antonas* (1952) 87 CLR 647; *Gould v Vaggelas* (1985) 157 CLR 215; *HTW Valuers v Astonland Pty Ltd* (2004) 217 CLR 640.

mutually exclusive? In *Alati v Kruger*, the Court's analysis is rather ambiguous on this point. In their joint judgment, Dixon CJ, Webb, Kitto and Taylor JJ stated:

> On the footing which must be accepted, that the contract had been induced by a fraudulent representation made by the appellant to the respondent, the latter had a choice of courses open to him. He might sue for damages for breach of the warranty ... but he could not do this and rescind the contract for misrepresentation. Secondly, he might sue to recover as damages for fraud the difference between the price he had paid and the fair value of the property at the time of the contract, but that again would involve affirming the purchase. Or, thirdly, provided that he was in a position to restore to the appellant substantially that which he had received under the contract, he might avoid the purchase and sue to recover his purchase money back from the appellant, with interest and also with damages for any loss which he may have suffered through carrying on the business in the meantime...[21]

This passage both seems to present the three possible courses as alternatives,[22] as Barnett and Harder argue, but also to contemplate that consequential losses may be awarded following rescission with respect to losses incurred in carrying on the business. The latter is difficult to reconcile with the High Court's earlier decision in *Brown v Smitt*, given that it appears that the plaintiff in *Alati v Kruger* did not plead an independent action in deceit.[23] But, as we will see below, the Court's final orders in *Alati v Kruger* may also be consistent with a restitutionary analysis, in particular that the plaintiff's detrimental changes of position may be brought into account as part of the process of restoring the parties to the *status quo ante*. On this approach, there is no inconsistency with *Brown v Smitt*, as the adjustment made by the Court was required to ameliorate the plaintiff's liability to make counter-restitution to the defendant of benefits received under the contract, rather than compensate for losses incurred.

As a matter of authority, it seems likely that in Australia[24] the matter is settled by the early High Court decision in *Sibley v Grosvenor* in which Dixon CJ addressed the matter head-on:

> Some confusion seems to have arisen in argument from not distinguishing between the case of a purchaser who elects to disaffirm a contract for the sale of property which he has been induced to enter into by fraud and the case of a purchaser who elects to affirm it. If he affirms the contract he acquires the property, and must allow for all the advantages which he derives from the acquisition. The measure of damages is his loss on the whole transaction. If, on the other hand, he elects to disaffirm the contract, he acquires nothing,

21 *Alati v Kruger* (1955) 94 CLR 216, 222 (citations omitted).

22 See also *Munchies Management Pty Ltd v Belperio* (1988) 58 FCR 274, 283–284 (the Court).

23 *Alati v Kruger* (1955) 94 CLR 216, 223 (Dixon CJ, Webb, Kitto and Taylor JJ).

24 In England, see for example *Redgrave v Hurd* (1881) 20 Ch D 1, 12 (CA) (Jessel MR, Lush LJ concurring at 26) refusing a defendant's counter-claim for 'damages' for costs incurred in reliance on a misrepresentation, because he had not pleaded knowledge on the part of the plaintiff that the statements were untrue, nor pleaded the allegations themselves in sufficient detail to found an action for deceit.

> and is entitled to be put in the same position as if he had not made it. … But, if rescission of the contract will not completely indemnify the purchaser, he is entitled to bring an action of deceit against any person who has knowingly made the false representation on which he acted. This remedy is entirely independent of and additional to the right to rescind.[25]

On this basis, compensation cumulative to rescission may be obtained by a plaintiff, provided that the tort supporting the claim is separately pleaded. The same position should apply to concurrent claims based on breach of an equitable duty.[26]

However, it may be observed in closing this discussion that the marriage of compensation and restitution as cumulative remedies does present some challenges in terms of principle and practice. Notwithstanding the position as a matter of authority, it remains unclear how, as a matter of principle, one can be entitled to relief that entails simultaneously affirming and rescinding a contract. Even if that is somehow a coherent position for the law to take, we saw earlier the challenges this presents to calculating any compensatory award. It may be added that if overcompensation of the plaintiff is to be avoided, then it will be necessary to be very clear on the differing purposes of the awards. Compensation for tort seeks to place the plaintiff in the position she would have been had the tort not occurred. By contrast, notwithstanding Dixon CJ's expression of the purpose of rescission, we will see below that the emphasis in rescission tends to be on returning the parties to their former position. One remedial enquiry is hypothetical and potentially broad-ranging, the other historical in nature and potentially much more limited in focus. If that is correct, then as a matter of practice it will be important to map out the scope of pecuniary awards inherent in rescission before considering what consequential losses not covered by this these awards might nonetheless be compensated though damages.

The third and probably most significant reason for close analysis of the nature of awards consequent on rescission is that, although rescission is a response to wrongdoing such as fraudulent misrepresentation, unconscionable dealing[27] and breach of fiduciary duty,[28] rescission is also triggered by events that do not constitute actionable wrongs, such as innocent misrepresentation and duress. Neither innocent misrepresentation[29] nor duress gives rise to a right of compensation.[30]

[25] *Sibley v Grosvenor* (1916) 21 CLR 469, 474–475 (Dixon CJ).

[26] See O'Sullivan, Elliott and Zakrzewski (n 6) [2.10]–[2.11].

[27] The characterisation of unconscionable dealing as a form of equitable wrongdoing seems unavoidable following the High Court of Australia's emphasis on the need to show a 'predatory state of mind' on the part of defendants: *Kakavas v Crown Melbourne Ltd* (2013) 250 CLR 392, 439–440 [161] (the Court).

[28] This assumes the conventional position that these constitute equitable wrongs. For a contrary, powerful analysis of the no-conflict and no-profit rules that shows them to be independent of wrongdoing, see L Smith, 'Fiduciary Relationships: Ensuring the Loyal Exercise of Judgement on Behalf of Another' (2014) 130 *LQR* 608, 620–625, 628–630. Some potential ramifications of the different views are explored briefly below at n 125 and accompanying text.

[29] See, eg, *Newbigging v Adam* (1886) 34 Ch D 582 (CA).

[30] *Universe Tankships Inc of Monrovia v International Transport Workers Federation* [1983] 1 AC 366, 385 (HL), cited with approval in *Dimskal Shipping Co SA v International Transport Workers Federation*

The same is true of undue influence in equity.[31] Although there may be a concurrent wrong arising on the particular facts of a case which may support a claim for compensation, where there is none, the plaintiff will again be left to whatever consequential relief flows inherently from rescission. In that context, characterising the nature and extent of that relief is essential.

In conclusion, determining the nature of pecuniary awards or adjustments solely consequent on rescission is an essential first step in clarifying the broader boundaries of recovery for rescinding plaintiffs. In that regard, one judge has suggested that many compensation orders made consequent on rescission are orders ancillary to the primary decree, directed to ensuring that the primary decree achieves its restitutionary purpose.[32] On this account, many so-called compensatory orders made pursuant to rescission are properly characterised as restitutionary rather than compensatory in nature. Whether or not that is always correct (and it must be doubted where there is a concurrent claim for compensation for a legal or equitable wrong) the observation reminds us that not all pecuniary awards are compensatory in nature and that, in the context of rescission, the labelling of awards as 'compensatory' cannot be determinative of the issue. With that background, it is appropriate to turn to the nature and aim of financial awards and adjustments made solely consequent on rescission.

III. The Requirement of *Restititio in Integrum* in Rescission

A. Restitution and Counter-restitution

As the authors of *The Law of Rescission* observe, the basic objective of relief upon rescission in equity is to return the parties in substance to their original position.[33] Equity is not overly fastidious as to the degree of precision required to satisfy this aim. As was explained in *Erlanger v The New Sombrero Phosphate Company*, 'the practice has always been for a Court of Equity to give this relief whenever, by the

(The Evia Luck) (No 2) [1992] 2 AC 152, 166 (HL) (Lord Goff); *Investec Bank (Channel Islands) Ltd v The Retail Group plc* [2009] EWHC 476 (Ch), [122] (Sales J).

[31] There may be compensation awarded for the equitable wrong of abuse of influence, as in *Mahoney v Purnell* [1996] 3 All ER 61 (QB); *Nattrass v Nattrass* [1999] WASC 77; *Smith v Glegg* [2005] 1 Qd R 561. There may also be an account of profits awarded for this form of equitable wrongdoing: *O'Sullivan v Management Agency and Music Ltd* [1985] QB 428 (CA). Otherwise, all authorities limit the remedial response for the not-wrong of undue influence to rescission. For detailed discussion of undue influence, see J Edelman and E Bant, *Unjust Enrichment*, 2nd edn (Oxford, Hart Publishing, 2016) Ch 10.

[32] *Aequitas Ltd v AEFC Leasing Pty Ltd* (2001) 19 ACLC 1006, 1087 [432] (NSWSC) (Austin J).

[33] O'Sullivan, Elliott and Zakrzewski (n 6) [13.01].

exercise of its powers, it can do what is practically just, though it cannot restore the parties precisely to the state they were in before the contract'.[34] Critical to this task is to require both parties to restore to the other any benefits obtained under the impugned transaction: there must be a 'giving back and a taking back on both sides'.[35] Thus the courts commonly require plaintiffs, as a condition of rescinding loan agreements, to make restitution of the principal received from the defendant plus interest.[36] Where *restitutio in integrum* in this sense is no longer possible, restitution will be denied.[37] However, in many cases, the process of returning the parties to the *status quo ante* is not so clear-cut and requires close attention not only to the benefits that have initially been transferred pursuant to the impugned transaction, but to subsequent actions by the parties.

The starting point for any discussion of monetary awards or adjustments consequent on rescission to achieve *restitutio in integrum* must, in Australia, commence with the High Court decision in *Brown v Smitt*.[38] In that case, a purchaser of farming land sought rescission of the contract of sale on the ground of various fraudulent representations made by the vendor. In addition, the purchaser sought return of the purchase price and 'damages' including a sum of £854 for the 'expense incurred by the [purchaser] in repairing, working and improving the farm, loss and depreciation of live-stock, and cost of maintenance and other expenses incurred in connection with the live-stock'.[39]

As Knox CJ, Gavan Duffy and Starke JJ explained:

> The parties being relieved of the contractual obligations, each must give back all that he obtained under the contract. Where the property the subject matter of a contract remains unchanged, no difficulty arises. Where it has been wholly or substantially destroyed by the default of the party seeking rescission, there can be no rescission because there can be no restitution. But where the property has been improved or deteriorated by the act of the purchaser, and yet remains in substance what it was before the contract, equity adjusts the rights of the parties by awarding money compensation to one or the other, and so substantially putting each party in the position which he occupied before the contract was made.[40]

Although labelled 'compensation', the financial adjustments contemplated by their Honours reflect what would nowadays be recognised as restitutionary considerations. As their Honours noted, in cases of depreciation, a plaintiff will be required to make good any loss in value in relation to an asset that must, following rescission,

[34] *Erlanger v The New Sombrero Phosphate Company* (1878) 3 App Cas 1218, 1278–1279 (HL) (Lord Blackburn).

[35] *Newbigging v Adam* (1886) 34 Ch D 582, 595 (CA) (Bowen LJ).

[36] See, eg, *Maguire v Makaronis* (1997) 188 CLR 449; *Elkofairi v Permanent Trustee Co Ltd* (2002) 11 BPR 20841 (NSWCA); *Perpetual Trustee Co Ltd v Khoshaba* (2005) 14 BPR 26639 (NSWCA).

[37] *Maguire v Makaronis* (1997) 188 CLR 449.

[38] *Brown v Smitt* (1924) 34 CLR 160.

[39] ibid 163.

[40] ibid 164.

now be returned to the other party. The effect of that order is to require the plaintiff to make full counter-restitution of the value of the benefit received from the defendant, a point to which we return below. By contrast, if the land has been improved, then there is a possibility that rescission will result in the unjustified enrichment of the defendant. Orders therefore must be made to require the defendant to make restitution of the value of the improvements, to the extent that they would otherwise result in the unjustified enrichment of the defendant.

The parallels between the considerations identified by the High Court in *Brown v Smitt* in this respect and the circumstances in which defendants will be found to be 'enriched' for the purposes of the law of restitution of unjust enrichment are striking. For example, Knox CJ, Gavan Duffy and Starke JJ explained that defendants are not expected to pay for improvements made by plaintiffs which were matters of 'taste or personal enjoyment'.[41] The plaintiff could however recover for 'permanent and lasting improvements ... which increased the sale value of the estate in [the defendant's] hands'.[42] This analysis is entirely consistent with the modern approach to claims for restitution of unjust enrichment. It is increasingly recognised in that context that in order to protect defendants' freedom of choice, plaintiffs cannot foist what they consider to be a benefit on defendants and then claim restitution of the value of the benefit. The defendant is entitled to say that he was not enriched by an unwanted benefit, no matter that the plaintiff considered it valuable. Although the principle often bears the unfortunate label of 'subjective devaluation', it is better understood as concerned with the defendant's right to choose the benefits that he will receive.[43] Relevantly for present purposes, where they have not expressly chosen a benefit, defendants will generally only be found to have been enriched where the plaintiff's expenditure saved them some necessary expense or created improvements that are readily realisable in money. The latter example is precisely the instance of 'permanent and lasting improvements ... which increased the sale value of the estate in [the defendant's] hands' given by Knox CJ, Gavan Duffy and Starke JJ in *Brown v Smitt*.[44] Their Honours further explained that no 'allowances [are to] be given for improvements made after the party making them knows, or has reasonable notice, of the defect in title. He must then take the risk'.[45] Again, precisely the same approach has been taken in recent

[41] ibid 165.

[42] ibid.

[43] *Benedetti v Sawaris* [2014] AC 938, 987 [115] (Lord Reed); *Littlewoods Retail Ltd v Comrs for HM Revenue and Customs* [2014] EWHC 868 (Ch), [363]–[374] (Henderson J); *Test Claimants in the FII Group Litigation v Comrs for HM Revenue and Customs* [2014] EWHC 4302 (Ch), [271] (Henderson J). Compare *Benedetti v Sawaris* [2014] AC 938, 956–957 [15]–[17] (Lord Clarke, Lords Kerr and Wilson concurring), 987 [115] (Lord Reed).

[44] *Brown v Smitt* (1924) 34 CLR 160, 165. Compare the minority of Isaacs and Rich JJ, who emphasised that the defendant had not asked for the improvements, which were not necessary to maintain the property, and therefore should not be bound to 'purchase' them: at 170.

[45] ibid 165. See also *McFarlane v Heritage Corp (Aust) Pty Ltd* [2003] QSC 350, [84]-[85] (Chesterman J), affirmed on appeal: see [2004] QCA 183 (no orders for expenses incurred by the plaintiffs in maintaining the property over the period when they had use of that property).

cases applying the analytical concept of unjust enrichment in the context of rescission and restitution for mistake.[46]

Critically, too, their Honours emphasised the significant distinction between the awards possible consequent on rescission on the one hand, and compensation properly-so-called for torts such as deceit on the other:

> [P]utting the parties in the position they were in before the contract, replacing them *in statu quo*, does not involve replacing them in the same position in all respects, but only in respect of the rights and obligations created by the contract which is rescinded. A party, in case of rescission, cannot ask the Court to award him compensation for all collateral losses which he may have sustained by reason of the fact that he entered into the contract, such as losses incurred in carrying on a business (*Newbigging v Adam*; *Whittington v Seale-Hayne*), but only such compensation as will restore the *status quo ante* in relation to the subject matter of the contract. Such losses could, in this case, only be recovered in an action of deceit. That cause of action, if included in the statement of claim, was not relied on below, and in any event it seems to us that it was the contract, and not, in a legal sense, the establishment of the business, which the fraudulent representations induced.[47]

The orders made by the Court required: (1) an account of the purchase price with interest; (2) an account of the costs charges and expenses paid and incurred by the purchaser in consequence of and incidental to the purchase; (3) an account of the sums laid out by the purchaser prior to becoming aware of the fraud in 'necessary repairs and in improvements of a permanent lasting and substantial nature', and an inquiry whether and to what extent the value of the premises had been increased in value by the plaintiff's improvements; and (4) an amount by way of occupation rent to be paid by the plaintiff to the defendant for the use of the land prior to rescission.[48]

The first, third and fourth of the Court's final orders underline the point that the process of restitution in unwinding a contract following rescission is mutual: both the defendant and plaintiff must make restitution of benefits obtained pursuant to the contract. The nature of these awards in relation to the improvements, rent and interest clearly have the effect of requiring each party to return to the other as a consequence of rescission the reasonable value of any benefits obtained as a result of the impugned transaction. In the language of unjust enrichment analysis, the defendant must make restitution and the plaintiff counter-restitution of all benefits obtained as a result of the impugned transfer. In the language of equity, the plaintiff must 'do equity' as a condition of rescission by paying an occupation rent on the premises[49] and the defendant likewise must make restitution

[46] See, eg, *Pitt v Holt* [2013] 2 AC 108, 153 [114] (Lord Walker, delivering the judgment of the Court); *Brennan v Bolt Burdon* [2005] QB 303, 316 (CA) (Maurice Kay LJ), 319 (Bodey LJ); *Queensland Alumina Ltd v Alinta DQP Pty Ltd* [2007] QCA 387, [70]–[72] (Holmes JA); *Re Magarey Farlam Lawyers Trust Accounts (No 3)* (2007) 96 SASR 337, 387–388 (Debelle J); *Lahoud v Lahoud* [2010] NSWSC 1297; *Salib v Gakas* [2010] NSWSC 505, [333] (Ward J).

[47] *Brown v Smitt* (1924) 34 CLR 160, 165–166 (citations omitted).

[48] ibid 173–174.

[49] *Maguire v Makaronis* (1997) 188 CLR 449.

of all benefits received. Whatever the label, the process of reasoning is precisely the same.[50] This same approach has been taken to the award of monetary allowances and adjustments consequent on rescission in innumerable cases since.[51]

The reason why a plaintiff must restore any benefits obtained under the impugned transaction as a condition of rescission has long been understood as resting in the prevention of unjust enrichment. As Lord Wright said in *Spence v Crawford*:

> Though the defendant has been fraudulent, he must not be robbed nor must the plaintiff be unjustly enriched, as he would be if he both got back what he had parted with and kept what he received in return.[52]

On this analysis, rescission as a process conceals mutual cross-claims for restitution: one made by the plaintiff against the defendant on the grounds of induced mistake (innocent and fraudulent misrepresentation), undue influence, duress or breach of fiduciary duty, the other by the defendant against the plaintiff. The latter is best understood as resting on failure of consideration: once rescission occurs, the basis on which the defendant transferred any benefits under the impugned transaction wholly fails. This is so in every case of rescission, whatever the nature of the primary claim (that is, whether the plaintiff's claim of rescission is based on fraudulent or innocent misrepresentation, duress, undue influence or breach of fiduciary duty). In this respect, these sorts of adjustments have much in common with the process courts regularly undertake in awarding allowances for the skill and effort of breaching fiduciaries, where it has been observed that 'the liability of the fiduciary should not be transformed into a vehicle for the unjust enrichment of the plaintiff'.[53]

If this analysis is correct, then the nature of the second order made in *Brown v Smitt* merits further consideration. This enquiry is not obviously restitutionary: the expenses paid by the purchaser in consequence of the contract were not related to improving the property, nor does expenditure incurred by the plaintiff necessarily equate to a benefit to the defendant.[54] The answer may lie in taking seriously the proposition that rescission involves mutual claims for restitution. On this approach, the second order made in *Brown v Smitt* may be best understood as directed to the plaintiff's detrimental changes of position made as a result of entering into the contract. This is not a compensatory enquiry but a particular manifestation of the defence of change of position.

50 *Plan B Trustees Ltd v Parker* [2013] WASC 216, [89]–[91] (Edelman J).

51 See, eg, *Alati v Kruger* (1955) 94 CLR 216; *McAllister v Richmond Brewing Co (NSW) Pty Ltd* (1942) 42 SR (NSW) 187, 192 (NSWSC) (Jordan CJ); *JAD International Pty Ltd v International Trucks Australia Ltd* (1994) 50 FCR 378.

52 *Spence v Crawford* [1939] 3 All ER 271, 288–289 (HL).

53 See, eg, *Warman International Ltd v Dwyer* (1995) 182 CLR 544, 561 (the Court).

54 See also *JAD International Pty Ltd v International Trucks Australia Limited* (1994) 50 FCR 378, 391 (Keely, Hill and Drummond JJ).

B. Detrimental Changes of Position

Rescission case law is replete with examples of financial adjustments and allowances that work as functional equivalents of the change of position defence. In the context of gifts, a number of cases have adjusted or contemplated adjusting defendants' restitutionary liability in the light of their subsequent changes of position. Thus in *Quek v Beggs*, a pastor and his wife irreversibly changed their position in various ways in good faith reliance on receipt of gifts that were subsequently set aside for undue influence.[55] For example, they had taken out a mortgage over one of the given properties and used the money raised to improve the property of a third party. The defendants later discharged the mortgage with the sale proceeds of another of the given properties. Justice McLelland held that it would be inequitable to make the defendants account for the sums used in improving the property, as they would be unable to be returned to their former position.

A similar approach in the contractual context led the High Court of Australia to conclude in *AH McDonald & Co Pty Ltd v Wells* that the plaintiff was not entitled to rescind the contract for innocent misrepresentation.[56] In that case, the defendant had 'unalterably changed his position' in reliance on the transaction by entering into an agreement with a third party.[57]

Conversely, changes of position made by a plaintiff in good faith and in reliance on the contract have in some cases been taken into account to reduce the plaintiff's counter-restitutionary liability. The second order made in *Brown v Smitt*, whereby costs, charges and expenses paid and incurred by the purchaser as a result of the contract were brought into the account, is one such example. In *Alati v Kruger*, the Court similarly made allowances in favour of the plaintiff in respect of conveyancing and stamp duty costs incurred by the plaintiff in relation to the transaction.[58]

The same parallels between the requirement of *restitutio in integrum* and change of position are visible in relation to what could be termed independent or spontaneous changes of position, for example where a benefit received by a defendant subject to a transaction later sought to be set aside is devalued or destroyed. Where the asset has been destroyed, rescission is in general denied completely, affording the defendant a complete defence. However, as noted earlier,[59] in cases of depreciation, a plaintiff or defendant will be required to make good the value of any loss in value in relation to an asset that must, following rescission, now be returned to

[55] *Quek v Beggs* (1990) 5 BPR 11766. See also *Allcard v Skinner* (1887) 36 Ch D 145 (CA); *Cheese v Thomas* [1994] 1 WLR 129 (CA); *Hartigan v International Society for Krishna Consciousness Inc* [2002] NSWSC 810.

[56] *AH McDonald & Co Pty Ltd v Wells* (1931) 45 CLR 506, 512–513 (Rich, Starke and Dixon JJ).

[57] ibid 513 (Rich, Starke and Dixon JJ).

[58] *Alati v Kruger* (1955) 94 CLR 216, 229–230, described as 'damages in respect of the conveyancing costs and stamp duty incurred by the plaintiff in relation to the said contract'.

[59] Above text to n 40.

the other party. As Lord Blackburn stated in *Erlanger v The New Sombrero Phosphate Company*:

> It would be obviously unjust that a person who has been in possession of property under the contract which he seeks to repudiate should be allowed to throw that back on the other party's hands without accounting for any benefit he may have derived for the use of the property, or if the property, though not destroyed, has been in the interval deteriorated, without making compensation for that deterioration.[60]

This order for 'compensation' has the effect of ensuring that full restitution and counter-restitution take place. It may in that light seem entirely contrary to the influence of any change of position considerations. However, the general position is subject to exceptions that operate, again, much like a change of position defence. For example, a defendant will not be held liable to make an adjusting payment for inherent depreciation not due to the fault of the defendant. The point rarely arises in practice: as Lord Wright commented in *Spence v Crawford*, the 'plaintiff who seeks to set aside the contract will generally be reasonable in the standard of restitution which he requires'.[61] However, again consistently with change of position, where a received asset naturally deteriorates but the defendant has been fraudulent, the court will order the defendant to pay 'compensation to make good the change of position'.[62] In these circumstances, the defendant's liability to make full restitution to the plaintiff is undiminished, consistently with denial of a change of position defence. Turning to changes of position made by the plaintiff, it is well established that a plaintiff will not be required to make an adjusting payment where the deterioration of an asset received from the defendant occurred without fault of the plaintiff, such as where the deterioration was inherent in the nature of the asset or was the result of independent market forces.[63] Again, such orders serve as functional equivalents of the change of position defence. The protection afforded to parties to rescission in such cases of non-reliance based changes of position is striking, given the long-standing debates in simple transfer cases over whether the change of position defence should apply to such changes.[64]

The same defensive principle is visible in cases of rescission involving restitution and counter-restitution of the use value of benefits. In general, parties will be

60 *Erlanger v The New Sombrero Phosphate Company* (1878) 3 App Cas 1218, 1278.

61 *Spence v Crawford* [1939] 3 All ER 271, 289 (HL) (Lord Wright).

62 ibid.

63 *Alati v Kruger* (1955) 94 CLR 216, 225 (Dixon CJ, Webb, Kitto and Taylor JJ); *Cheese v Thomas* [1994] 1 WLR 129, 135 (CA) (Sir Donald Nicholls VC); *Armstrong v Jackson* [1917] 2 KB 822; *Balfour & Clark v Hollandia Ravensthorpe NL* (1978) 18 SASR 240, 258 (Hogarth J); *Akron Securities Ltd v Iliffe* (1997) 41 NSWLR 353, 370 (Mason P, Priestley JA agreeing).

64 In England, the authorities clearly support its application: *Lipkin Gorman v Karpnale Ltd* [1991] 2 AC 548, 580–581 (HL) (Lord Goff); *Scottish Equitable plc v Derby* [2001] 3 All ER 818, 827 (Robert Walker LJ), 831 (Keane and Simon Browne LJJ concurring); *Dextra Bank & Trust Co Ltd v Bank of Jamaica* [2002] 1 All ER (Comm) 193 (PC); *Cressman v Coys of Kensington (Sales) Ltd* [2004] 1 WLR 2775; *Test Claimants in the FII Group Litigation v Comrs for HM Revenue and Customs* [2008] EWHC 2893 (Ch), [325] (Henderson J); *Bloomsbury International Ltd v Sea Fish Industry Authority* [2010] 1 CMLR 12, 379–382 [134]–[137] (Hamblen J); *Test Claimants in the FII Group Litigation v Comrs for HM Revenue and Customs* [2014] EWHC 4302 (Ch), [343]–[347] (Henderson J). In Australia, the

required to make restitution of the full market value of the opportunity of using a benefit. Thus the plaintiff in *Alati v Kruger* was required to pay rent for the period of occupation of the premises and the defendant had to pay interest on the receipt of the purchase price.[65] Sometimes, however, a party will not actually have used the asset obtained and in those circumstances restitution is often restricted to the lesser value actually obtained.[66] The result is akin to a change of position defence: the party is effectively pleading that, in reliance on her receipt, she chose not to use the asset to its full potential.[67] By contrast, where the party has been fraudulent, full restitution of the market value of the use of the asset is required,[68] again consistent with a denial of the defence.

While the adjustments consequent on rescission often echo change of position, the cases are not always clear or consistent—even internally. An example is *Spence v Crawford*, where a fraudulent defendant was held not to be entitled 'in bar of restitution' to rely on his change of position in altering the share holdings in the company in reliance on the impugned share transfer.[69] Lord Thankerton left open the question whether a defendant guilty only of innocent misrepresentation would be entitled to plead the change of position.[70] This is consistent with the foregoing analysis. However, the court did allow the defendant to plead in limitation of his liability the fact that he had sold certain stock at a loss as required under the impugned contract. Lord Wright expressed his concern that the result was incoherent, however found that it was unnecessary to decide the matter because the parties had agreed a form of order (which supported Lord Thankerton's order) in the event that rescission proved possible.[71]

C. The Nature of 'Indemnity Orders': Compensation or Restitution?

The previous sections have shown that consequential orders following rescission may use the language of compensation but often reflect restitutionary or change of

position remains open but is increasingly doubted: *Citigroup Pty Ltd v National Australia Bank Ltd* (2012) 82 NSWLR 391, 405 [64] (Barrett JA) but compare 394 [6] (Bathurst CJ, Allsop P, Meagher JA), seemingly leaving the question open; *Australian Financial Leasing Services Pty Limited v Hills Industries Ltd* (2014) 253 CLR 560, 597 [81] (Hayne, Crennan, Kiefel, Bell and Keane JJ), 619 [142] (Gageler J), discussed below at text to n 102 and following.

65 *Alati v Kruger* (1955) 94 CLR 216, 229–230.

66 See, eg, *Coastal Estates Pty Ltd v Melvende* [1965] VR 433, 440–441 (Sholl J).

67 *Sempra Metals Ltd v Inland Revenue Commissioners* [2008] 1 AC 561, 617 [151] (Lord Scott); *Test Claimants in the FII Group Litigation v Comrs for HM Revenue and Customs* [2014] EWHC 4302 (Ch).

68 O'Sullivan, Elliott and Zakrzewski (n 6) [17.09]. See also *Howell v Howell* (1837) 40 ER 722; *Adam v Sworder* (1863) 46 ER 291.

69 *Spence v Crawford* [1939] 3 All ER 271, 291 (HL) (Lord Thankerton, Lords Atkin and Russell concurring).

70 ibid 282–283.

71 ibid 290.

position considerations. A similar need to delve below the surface labels of court orders is apparent in cases where courts in equity order the defendant to 'indemnify' the plaintiff in relation to some loss or liability under a rescinded contract. The language of indemnity suggests a solely compensatory function but, as the following discussion shows, indemnity orders are also made to effect restitution and counter-restitution. A good example is *Newbigging v Adam*.[72] In that case a plaintiff sought to rescind a contract by which he had become a partner in a failing business. The ground of rescission was that the contract had been induced as a result of the defendants' innocent misrepresentations as to the financial state of the business. In accordance with the contract, Newbigging paid more than £9,000 by way of contribution to the capital base of the business and £324 by way of discharge of certain liabilities of the partnership. When the business failed, Newbigging sought (among other things) orders that the defendants be required to indemnify him against all claims and demands, debts or liabilities arising from or in respect of the partnership and that he be repaid the amount of his capital contribution plus interest. The trial judge made orders in favour of the plaintiff. On appeal, the awards were in essence upheld, but for slightly different reasons. The necessity for return (restitution) of the capital contribution and interest in favour of the plaintiff was not disputed. The focus of the appeal was rather on the nature of the indemnity ordered and whether it was in effect, as argued by the defendants, an order for compensation. This would be inappropriate as the case was one of innocent, rather than fraudulent misrepresentation.

It was accepted that, in a case involving fraudulent misrepresentation, equity could exercise its concurrent jurisdiction in cases of fraud to give complete indemnity to the victim 'so as to protect him as fully in equity as he could have been protected in law' in an action for deceit.[73] In this category of case (fraudulent, rather than innocent misrepresentation), the indemnity effects the equivalent of common law compensation. It was therefore critical for the Court of Appeal to distinguish this (compensatory) form of indemnity from the indemnity awarded for innocent misrepresentation, where compensation is not an appropriate or available remedy. Although the precise reasoning of each judge differed, they were unanimous in the view that in the case of innocent misrepresentation, the indemnity award is measured differently, and has a different purpose to, the indemnity that could be awarded in cases of fraudulent misrepresentation.

Cotton LJ distinguished the indemnity in the instant case from an order for compensation on the grounds that the former was less extensive. He posited a scenario in which the plaintiff had given up a valuable commission in reliance on entering into the partnership contract.[74] While compensation for the lost commission

[72] *Newbigging v Adam* (1886) 34 Ch D 582 (CA), affirmed in (1888) 13 App Cas 308.
[73] ibid 592 (Bowen LJ).
[74] ibid 589.

could be claimed in an action for deceit, it would not be included within an indemnity awarded following rescission of the contract for innocent misrepresentation. In his Lordship's view, the latter indemnity only covered obligations for which the plaintiff had contracted under the contract, for example, a contractual obligation to pay third parties, or a contractual obligation to assume the liabilities of the defendant. However, he also put the position rather more broadly: 'In my opinion it cannot be said that [the plaintiff] is put back into his old position unless he is relieved from the consequences and obligations which are the result of the contract which is set aside'.[75] This formulation would extend to any losses causally connected to the fact of entering into the contract, rather than being restricted to losses arising from obligations imposed under the contract. In a brief concurring judgment, Fry LJ approved the broader approach taken by Cotton LJ and added that a plaintiff is entitled to an indemnity in respect of 'all obligations entered into under the contract when those obligations are within the necessary or reasonable expectation of both of the contracting parties at the time of contract'.[76]

By contrast, Bowen LJ emphasised that an indemnity in cases of innocent misrepresentation could not extend to any loss simply arising out of, or causally connected to, the contract. That would allow compensation in circumstances where it was not justified. Rather, the plaintiff in such cases is entitled to be replaced in his position only so far as regards the rights and obligations created by the contract. Critical to the enquiry is identification of the benefits that each party has given and received under the contract:

> Now those advantages [received by a party] may be of two kinds. He may get an advantage in the shape of an actual benefit, as when he receives money; he may also get an advantage if the party with whom he contracts assumes some burthen in consideration of the contract. In such a case it seems to me that complete rescission would not be effected unless the misrepresenting party not only hands back the benefits which he has himself received—but also re-assumes the burthen which under the contract the injured person has taken upon himself. … There ought, as it appears to me, to be a giving back and a taking back on both sides, including the giving back and taking back of the obligations which the contract has created, as well as the giving back of the advantages.[77]

While Bowen LJ was in the minority in this case, his is generally regarded as the leading judgment.[78]

What is the nature of the indemnity as characterised by Bowen LJ? It has already been explained that the Court had rejected the allegation that the award was

[75] ibid.

[76] ibid 596. For criticism of this analysis on the ground that it confuses indemnity and compensation, see *Whittington v Seale-Hayne* (1900) 82 LT 49.

[77] *Newbigging v Adam* (1886) 34 Ch D 582, 594–595 (CA).

[78] See *Munchies Management Pty Ltd v Belperio* (1988) 58 FCR 274, 284–286 (the Court); *JAD International Pty Ltd v International Trucks Australia Ltd* (1994) 50 FCR 378, 392 (Keely, Hill and Drummond JJ).

compensatory in nature. It could be considered that some of the relief granted reflects change of position considerations: the plaintiff for example had changed his position in reliance on the misrepresentation by discharging some £324 worth of the partnership liabilities. However, the better view is that the main focus of the indemnity award in this instance was to effect restitution and counter-restitution of benefits received under the contract. Here, the plaintiff had assumed liability for the debts of and claims against the partnership and, indeed, had discharged some of those liabilities. This relieved the defendants of a considerable legal burden.

There can be little doubt that being relieved from an obligation, or having a liability discharged, constitutes a real and actionable benefit in the broader law of restitution of unjust enrichment. Common examples involving this sort of benefit are found in the law of contribution and subrogation (although characterisation of the latter as arising within the law of unjust enrichment is contentious in Australia).[79] A good, more recent example of a discharge of liability being recognised as a form of enrichment comes from the area of undue influence. In *Winefield v Clarke*, representatives of a mother (who lacked capacity) sued her daughter to recover an interest in the family home.[80] Originally, the mother was the sole registered proprietor. She transferred the property to herself and her daughter as joint tenants. Barrett J emphasised that the daughter was to 'be commended for the way in which she looked after her mother'[81] but held that, as the mother's primary caregiver, a presumption of undue influence arose that had not been rebutted on the facts. In calling for further submissions on the issue of the relevant orders to be made, Barrett J noted:

> [T]he defendant paid (apparently from her own pocket) the mortgage debt of about $6,500 secured on the property in May 2004, being a debt of the plaintiff. Although there is no cross claim in that connection, the just result may be that the defendant should be recognised as having a charge or lien upon the property for that sum, but on a basis that ensures that the charge cannot be enforced except out of the proceeds of a voluntary sale of the property by the plaintiff or her legal personal representative.[82]

That is, Barrett J contemplated that the mother's representatives would be required to make restitution of the value of the benefit (ie the discharge of the mother's debt) received from the daughter.

Viewed against this broader legal landscape, the nature of the indemnity awarded in *Newbigging v Adam* looks decidedly restitutionary, albeit in the rather unusual or 'stretched' sense that, rather than being required to make restitution of the value of the benefit (as was contemplated in *Winefield v Clarke*), the benefit

79 Compare *Banque Financière de la Cité v Parc (Battersea) Ltd* [1999] 1 AC 221 (HL); *Bofinger v Kingsway Group Ltd* (2009) 239 CLR 269.

80 *Winefield v Clarke* [2008] NSWSC 882. See also the complex adjustments considered in *Bridgewater v Leahy* (1998) 194 CLR 457.

81 *Winefield v Clarke* [2008] NSWSC 882, [43].

82 ibid [54].

enjoyed by the defendants of being relieved of liability was reversed by requiring them to re-assume that burden.

In coming to his decision, Bowen LJ placed some reliance upon *Rawlins v Wickham*.[83] In that case, Knight Bruce and Turner LJJ affirmed a decree of Stuart V-C whereby (i) a partnership deed was set aside for fraudulent misrepresentation, (ii) the defendant partners were obliged to repay the premium paid by the plaintiff, (iii) the plaintiff was indemnified against all outstanding partnership debts and (iv) an account was ordered of all sums paid by the plaintiff in respect of the partnership debts (with interest from the day of payment) but with a credit of all profits drawn by the plaintiff (with interest). Again, this mix of awards can be well understood from a restitutionary perspective.

A similar case is *Whittington v Seale-Hayne*, where the plaintiff sought rescission of a lease on the ground of innocent misrepresentation and various consequential orders.[84] Farwell J made orders ancillary to rescission for the defendant to indemnify the plaintiff with respect to the rents, rates and repairs paid for by the plaintiff in relation to the property. These payments could legitimately be characterised either as discharging what would otherwise have been the defendant's obligations, or as being necessary to preserve the asset and its future lease value. However characterised, the orders were necessary to ensure that the rescission of the lease did not result in the unjust enrichment of the defendant. By contrast, Farwell J refused to extend the indemnity to other expenditures, such as modifications made by the plaintiff to the property for the purposes of his poultry business, which he considered would inappropriately extend the award to compensation. This is consistent with the approach taken in *Brown v Smitt*, discussed earlier. Such expenditures, which are tailored to the plaintiff's personal needs and preferences, do not obviously save the defendant any necessary expenditure, nor result in any increase in the market value of the land. In those circumstances, the defendant will not be left unjustly enriched following rescission in the event that no ancillary adjustments or indemnity are awarded in favour of the plaintiff in relation to those expenditures.[85]

In concluding the discussion in this section, it can be seen that the financial orders and adjustments consequent on rescission often appear to be restitutionary in nature, or to incorporate what in recent times have come to be recognised as change of position considerations. This is not surprising: if rescission does indeed involve a process of bilateral or mutual restitution, we would expect to see these kinds of orders and considerations in play. However, the position taken in the cases is not always clear or consistent: for example, the use of the common orders of 'indemnity' to cover both wholly compensatory relief for torts such as deceit[86]

[83] *Rawlins v Wickham* (1858) 65 ER 954, affirmed in (1858) 44 ER 1285.
[84] *Whittington v Seale-Hayne* (1900) 82 LT 49, 51 (Farwell J).
[85] Whether such expenditures should, however, be brought into the account via a defence of change of position is considered in Part V below.
[86] As in *Newbigging v Adam* (1886) 34 Ch D 582, 592–593 (CA) (Bowen LJ).

as well as restitutionary orders, as part of the inherent process of rescission, tends to obscure the true nature of the plaintiff's relief.

Given this opacity, it is useful to consider how the equitable case law has been interpreted and has influenced the crafting of similar orders under the Trade Practices Act 1974 (Cth) (now the Australian Consumer Law). The statutory scheme now dominates the traditional terrain of equitable rescission, both drawing on and, potentially, exerting gravitational force on its neighbouring general law principles. As the following discussion shows, in making rescission-like orders under the Acts, courts repeatedly apply broad concepts of detriment and compensation in a manner that reflects both restitutionary and change of position considerations. This consistency in approach suggests some important possibilities for the further coherent evolution of relief in both areas.

IV. Rescission-like Orders Under the TPA/ACL

As Mason P observed in *Akron Securities Ltd v Iliffe*, s 87 of the Trade Practices Act 1974 (Cth) (TPA) (see now ss 237, 238 and 243 of the Australian Consumer Law (ACL)) offers a veritable 'smorgasbord' of remedies where a person 'has suffered, or is likely to suffer, loss or damage by conduct of another person that was engaged in … contravention' of provisions including the prohibition of misleading or deceptive conduct contained in s 52 TPA (now s 18 ACL).[87] Section 243 of the ACL, which replicates the earlier provision under s 87, provides a non-exhaustive list of the kinds of orders that may be made:

243 Kinds of orders that may be made

Without limiting section 237(1), 238(1) or 239(1), the orders that a court may make under any of those sections against a person (the *respondent*) include all or any of the following:

(a) an order declaring the whole or any part of a contract made between the respondent and a person (the ***injured person***) who suffered, or is likely to suffer, the loss or damage referred to in that section, or of a collateral arrangement relating to such a contract:
  (i) to be void; and
  (ii) if the court thinks fit—to have been void ab initio or void at all times on and after such date as is specified in the order (which may be a date that is before the date on which the order is made);

(b) an order:
  (i) varying such a contract or arrangement in such manner as is specified in the order; and

87 *Akron Securities Ltd v Iliffe* (1997) 41 NSWLR 353, 366.

(ii) if the court thinks fit—declaring the contract or arrangement to have had effect as so varied on and after such date as is specified in the order (which may be a date that is before the date on which the order is made);

(c) an order refusing to enforce any or all of the provisions of such a contract or arrangement;

(d) an order directing the respondent to refund money or return property to the injured person;

(e) except if the order is to be made under section 239(1)—an order directing the respondent to pay the injured person the amount of the loss or damage;

(f) an order directing the respondent, at his or her own expense, to repair, or provide parts for, goods that had been supplied by the respondent to the injured person;

(g) an order directing the respondent, at his or her own expense, to supply specified services to the injured person;

(h) an order, in relation to an instrument creating or transferring an interest in land, directing the respondent to execute an instrument that:

(i) varies, or has the effect of varying, the first mentioned instrument; or

(ii) terminates or otherwise affects, or has the effect of terminating or otherwise affecting, the operation or effect of the first mentioned instrument.

It will be noted that none of the orders listed adopt the language of rescission. Nor do they refer to other related concepts such as counter-restitution or the requirement of *restitutio in integrum*. Further, s 237(2) of the ACL provides that any order made under s 243 'must be an order that the court considers will: (a) compensate the injured person, or any such injured persons, in whole or in part for the loss or damage; or (b) prevent or reduce the loss or damage'. That is, the remedial aim of the provisions appears compensatory, not restitutionary.

Nonetheless, courts have repeatedly held that the statute empowers them to award rescission-like remedies, in particular pursuant to a combination of s 243(a), (c) and (d). In this context, the equitable remedy of rescission has been considered to constitute a powerful albeit not binding guide to the relevant considerations that should inform the making of analogous orders under the provision. The position is encapsulated in *Marks v GIO Australia Holdings Ltd* by Gummow J, who described s 87 of the TPA as creating 'new remedies which have an affinity to the equitable remedies of rescission and rectification'.[88] Thus '[t]he principles regulating the administration of equitable remedies afford guidance for, but do not dictate, the exercise of the statutory discretion conferred by s 87'.[89]

However, our purpose here is to see what insights into the nature of the awards and adjustments made in effecting equitable rescission are offered by consideration of the statutory context. Of critical significance is the way in which courts

[88] *Marks v GIO Australia Holdings Ltd* (1998) 196 CLR 494, 535. See also *Tenji v Henneberry & Associates Pty Ltd* (2000) 98 FCR 324, 329–330 [12] (French J).

[89] *Marks v GIO Australia Holdings Ltd* (1998) 196 CLR 494, 535 (Gummow J) (citations omitted).

have married the restitutionary nature of rescission with the ostensibly compensatory purpose of the statutory scheme. In the context of the 'remedial smorgasbord' set out in s 243 ACL (as opposed to the compensatory orders available under s 82 TPA, or s 236 ACL) courts have emphasised the broad conception of detriment at which the statutory provisions are aimed.

The relationship between rescission and loss under the Act was explored in *Demagogue Pty Ltd v Ramensky*.[90] As Black CJ explained, 'the loss or damage contemplated by s 87(1A) is not limited to loss or damage in the s 82 sense but was intended to include the detriment suffered by being bound to a contract unconscionably induced'.[91] Gummow J agreed that the language of the statute taken as a whole 'emphasises that the phrase "the loss or damage", at least in s 87, may be concerned with more than pecuniary recovery as understood in the law of damages in tort' and may extend to entry into contractual obligations as a result of misleading or deceptive conduct.[92] His Honour later drew further support for that view from the equitable doctrine of rescission:

> It may well be that in a given case the contract is not financially disadvantageous to the complainant. But, at least in Australia, if a contract is rescinded in equity for some vitiating factor in its formation, it is not sufficient for the defendant to show that the transaction to which the complainant was improperly induced to assent, after all, contained terms which, viewed objectively, were not manifestly disadvantageous so that, the complainant should freely have accepted them. … It would be an odd result if s 87 and s 4K were to be read in a contrary sense by giving too narrow a meaning to the phrase 'loss or damage'.[93]

In a short concurring judgment, Cooper J considered that 'loss or damage' in s 87 'means no more than the disadvantage which is suffered by a person as the result of the act or default of another in the circumstances provided for in the section'.[94] On this approach, the conception of loss under s 87 TPA (now s 237 ACL) is much broader than the traditional characterisations of losses the subject of compensation orders in tort and, indeed, those covered by the compensatory provisions in s 82 TPA (now s 236 ACL). His Honour emphasised that relief granted under s 87 to compensate or prevent that broadly-conceived loss or damage must meet the purpose of the provisions and may require the award of gain-based relief:

> That object mirrors the approach of equity in the case of equitable fraud or unconscionability. The granting of equitable relief in those circumstances is not 'to extend sympathetic benevolence to a victim of undeserved misfortune' but 'one which denies to those who have acted unconscientiously the fruits of their wrongdoing.'[95]

90 *Demagogue Pty Ltd v Ramensky* (1992) 39 FCR 31.
91 ibid 33.
92 ibid 43.
93 ibid 43–44.
94 ibid 47 (citations omitted).
95 ibid 48 (citations omitted), quoting *Blomley v Ryan* (1956) 99 CLR 362, 429.

This broad, policy-driven conception of 'loss or damage' under the statute is evident in the orders made by courts effecting the statutory equivalent of rescission. In *Munchies Management Pty Ltd v Belperio*, the Full Court of the Federal Court unanimously drew on the equitable case law concerning rescission to craft orders under s 87 TPA (s 243 ACL) following a finding that the respondents had purchased a business due to the misleading or deceptive conduct of the appellants and its agent, Mr Munro.[96] In that case, the respondents sought rescission of the purchase agreements in a timely manner but by the time the matter came to court, the third party landlord had repossessed the business premises and the business had substantially declined. In particular, much of the plant and equipment for the business had been forcibly sold on the re-entry of the landlord, to satisfy the outstanding rent that had not been paid by the respondents following their purported rescission. These assets therefore could not be returned. The parties, and indeed judge, at first instance had assumed that rescission was unavailable in the circumstances. The Federal Court disagreed, citing *Alati v Kruger*. The Court followed the lead taken in cases such as *Newbigging v Adam* and *Alati v Kruger* to find that rescission was still available notwithstanding the various changes of position affecting the ability of the respondents to restore the business to the appellants. While the case is replete with the language of loss and compensation, we again see the same pattern of restitutionary reasoning present in the cases considered earlier concerning rescission in equity. Thus, the Court refused to require the respondents to 'make good' the deterioration in the value of the business, so as to effect full counter-restitution to the appellants:

> A deterioration in the value of the business occasioned by the landlord's eviction of the purchasers and any fall in value of the plant that may have resulted from disposal of that plant and equipment by forced sale are not matters for which the purchasers may be held responsible, and the extent of that loss must fall upon the respondents. This is not a case in which the purchasers should be required to allow compensation in respect of that deterioration.[97]

This echoes the change of position considerations discussed earlier in the context of *Brown v Smitt*. The Court went on to stipulate as conditions of declaring the contract void under the Act that the appellant make restitution of the purchase price subject to allowances including sums for the use of the plant by the respondents prior to rescission. The Court also awarded sums in favour of the purchasers for; (1) legal costs and associated costs paid on settlement of the sale of the business, (2) demolition cost incurred on the vendor's behalf, (3) net trading losses for a defined period, and (4) interest on the purchase price. In the course of its reasons, the Court noted:

> The orders for accounting and payment of money made in those cases as part of the process of rescission ab initio may be seen as recovery literally of the amount of loss or damage

[96] *Munchies Management Pty Ltd v Belperio* (1988) 58 FCR 274.
[97] ibid 289 (citations omitted).

> within the meaning of s 82, giving 'recover' the sense of *regaining through restitution a position lost* by the conduct complained of. … In any event, orders such as those in *Alati v Kruger* … may properly be considered as reducing the loss or damage suffered within the sense of s 87 of the Act.[98]

In *Akron Securities Ltd v Iliffe*, investors entered into a horse breeding venture in reliance on certain misleading statements of an employee of Akron.[99] At first instance, the trial judge declared the transaction void *ab initio* and ordered Akron to repay all sums received from the investors thus far in the scheme, offset by any distributions made by Akron to the investors pursuant to the scheme. On appeal, Akron argued that, conformably with the equitable remedy of rescission, this order should have been made conditional on the investors making counter restitution of the loan principal received from Akron and which had been used by the investors to fund their participation in the scheme. Mason P (Priestley JA concurring) noted that although '[t]he principles surrounding the remedy of rescission for innocent misrepresentation are clearly available to give guidance in the exercise of the statutory discretion', they could not control the exercise of the court's remedial discretion under the Act.[100] Ultimately, Mason P considered that a rescission-like remedy was not appropriate on the facts of the case, in particular because it could not take into account the taxation benefits which the investors had enjoyed (as intended) under the scheme. Presumably this was on the basis that they were causally-related benefits that could not be 'reversed' or undone in favour of the government. However, pertinently for current purposes, his Honour explained that if rescission had been appropriate, counter-restitution of the loan principal by the investors would not have been required, because, in substance, this had gone directly to Akron and the scheme manager for the purposes of the scheme, rather than having been enjoyed personally by the investors. In those circumstances, to impose a requirement of counter-restitution would add to the loss or damage suffered by the investors, contrary to the remedial purpose of s 87. In other words, to require the investors to make counter-restitution as a condition of rescission would place them in a worse position than they occupied prior to entry into the contract. Meagher JA, although dissenting in the final result, agreed with this analysis of the requirement of counter-restitution on the facts of the case.

In concluding this section, it can be seen that when applying rescission-like remedies in the statutory context, courts have adopted a broad conception of detriment that considers whether the plaintiff would suffer detriment in the absence of, or indeed as a result of, the award. The focus of the enquiry, as for equitable rescission, seems to be whether it is possible to return the parties to the *status quo*

[98] ibid 287–288 (emphasis added); cited with approval in *Demagogue Pty Ltd v Ramensky* (1992) 39 FCR 31, 45 (Gummow J) and *Metz Holdings Pty Ltd v Simmac Pty Ltd (No 2)* [2011] FCA 981, [865] (Barker J). See also *Karmot Auto Spares Pty Ltd v Dominelli Ford (Hurstville) Pty Ltd* (1992) 35 FCR 560, 573 (Heery J).

[99] *Akron Securities Ltd v Iliffe* (1997) 41 NSWLR 353.

[100] ibid 367.

ante and, in particular, whether relief can be fashioned in a way that ensures that the plaintiff is left in no worse position as a result of the misleading or deceptive conduct.

The approach taken to the award of remedies akin to rescission under the statute strongly echoes the recent discussion by the High Court of Australia as to the purpose of the change of position defence in claims for restitution of mistaken payments.[101] It provides a further guide to the potential ramifications and issues of the restitutionary analysis presented in this essay, to which we now turn.

V. Ramifications

The previous sections have explored the restitutionary considerations that commonly inform consequential relief in equity and under statute on avoidance of the impugned transaction. The discussion of the statutory awards in particular shows that courts commonly employ the language of 'detriment' or 'loss' to describe the harm that their restitutionary orders seek to prevent. This might seem counterintuitive. However, a sideways glance at the most recent development in the law relating to the change of position defence suggests that this approach is consistent with the overall development of a coherent law of restitution.

In *Australian Financial Services & Leasing Pty Ltd v Hills Industries Ltd* (*AFSL v Hills Industries*) the appellant, AFSL (a financier) was induced by a fraudster (S) to make payments to a number of businesses, including the respondents Hills and Bosch, for the purchase of what transpired to be non-existent equipment.[102] S advised Hills and Bosch that the payments were for the discharge of debts owed to them by his companies (the 'company debts'). In reliance on their receipts, Hills and Bosch applied the payments in discharge of the company debts, continued to trade with the companies and gave up the opportunity to pursue remedies in enforcement proceedings against them or their directors. Both recipients also gave up the opportunity of taking other steps to improve their position, such as by seeking security from third parties.

When AFSL sought recovery of the payments on the ground of mistake, Hills and Bosch pleaded their changes of position by way of defence. In finding for the respondents, Hayne, Crennan, Kiefel, Bell and Keane JJ jointly explained that the law of estoppel is concerned to avoid the detriment that would be suffered by the defendant if the claimant were to resile from the assumption on which he changed his position. So too, they said, change of position serves to protect a defendant from 'the detriment which would flow from a party's change of position'[103]

[101] Discussed immediately below.
[102] *Australian Financial Services & Leasing Pty Ltd v Hills Industries Ltd* (2014) 253 CLR 560.
[103] ibid 599 [85].

'if the [claimant] were to be permitted to recover payments as mistakenly made where they have been applied by the [defendant]'.[104] Also drawing strongly from the equitable doctrine of estoppel, Gageler J similarly identified as an important condition attracting the defence that 'by reason of having so acted or refrained from acting, the defendant would be placed in a worse position if ordered to make restitution of the payment than if the defendant had not received the payment at all'.[105]

Although their Honours were drawing insights from the law of estoppel, we have seen that these characterisations of the aim of the defence strongly echo the principle of '*restitutio in integrum*' found in the equitable doctrine of rescission.[106] We should not find these parallels surprising: we have seen that rescission commonly involves restitutionary and counter-restitutionary awards made in response to (but not limited to) vitiating factors such as (induced) mistake, duress, undue influence and failure of consideration. Given that these are commonly understood as forming the core examples of claims in unjust enrichment, to which change of position is a key defence, it makes sense that change of position considerations should inform both claims of rescission and restitution.

If we take this seriously, however, then a number of very important issues arise. The first is that it requires us to re-consider the ways in which courts have limited, and sought to justify the limitations placed on, awards and adjustments consequent on rescission. It will be recalled that in *Newbigging v Adam*, Cotton LJ sought to distinguish indemnity orders consequent on rescission from compensation for deceit through a hypothetical example. His Lordship instanced a case where a plaintiff had given up a valuable commission in reliance on the impugned contract. Although, he said, this might count for the purposes of a claim for compensation for deceit, it would not count for the purposes of the indemnity award consequent of rescission. But following the earlier analysis we might well ask, 'why not?' Provided that the opportunity was substantial and not purely speculative, why should it not be taken into account to reduce the plaintiff's counter-restitutionary liability? The giving up of a valuable opportunity is very well-established as a relevant change of position for the purposes of simple restitution cases.[107] Indeed,

[104] ibid 598–599 [84].

[105] ibid 625–626 [157]. On the counterfactual formulation, see above at text following nn 26 and 33 and below at text to n 112.

[106] See also O'Sullivan, Elliott and Zakrzewski (n 6) [18.07]-[18.08].

[107] See *City of Sydney v Burns Philp Trustee Co Ltd (in liq)* (Unreported, Supreme Court of New South Wales, Rogers CJ, 13 November 1992) (change constituted by council's failure to obtain a private valuation of commercial property); *Gilsan (International) Ltd v Optus Networks Pty Ltd* [2004] NSWSC 1077, [260] (McDougall J) (change included failure to withhold amounts by way of provisions or reserve to protect its position in the event of claim for recovery of overpayments), approved on this point on appeal in *Optus Networks Pty Ltd v Gilsan (International) Ltd* [2006] NSWCA 171, [79] (Hodgson JA, Beasley and McColl JA concurring); *Eastbourne Borough Council v Foster* (QB, 20 December 2000) (change included failure to look for work elsewhere, failure to consider suing his legal advisors and failure to bargain for redundancy package), appealed on another point in *Eastbourne Borough Council v Foster* [2001] EWCA Civ 1091; *Hills Industries Ltd v Australian Financial Services and*

one of the accepted changes of position made by the respondents in *AFSL v Hills Industries* was that, in reliance on their receipt of the mistaken payments, they had foregone valuable opportunities to recover the company debts. The same question might be asked of at least some of the detrimental changes of position suffered by the plaintiffs in *Brown v Smitt* and *Whittington v Seale Hayne*, such as the expenditures incurred and losses suffered in running businesses in reliance on the contract.[108] Why did these detrimental changes of position suffered in reliance on their receipt not operate to reduce their counter-restitutionary liability?

We have seen that one reason why courts have been so careful to restrict the considerations that may be taken into the account following rescission is to ensure that the awards (particularly in cases involving not-wrongs, such as innocent misrepresentation) do not become compensatory in nature and, in particular, do not impose on the defendant unwarranted liability for the plaintiff's consequential losses. However, from a restitutionary perspective, this legitimate concern can be re-focused. On the approach taken in this chapter, the true question in these cases is the proper extent of the plaintiff's liability to make counter-restitution to the defendant, not whether the defendant is liable to compensate the plaintiff for her consequential losses. On this approach, a plaintiff's liability to make counter-restitution to a defendant will always be 'capped' at the value of the original enrichment received from the defendant. This is because the greatest effect that the plaintiff's consequential changes of position made in reliance on her receipt of contractual benefits can have is to reduce the plaintiff's counter-restitutionary liability to zero. In other words, the worst possible outcome for a defendant following rescission is not that she will be required to compensate the plaintiff for extended consequential losses, but that the defendant must make full restitution to the plaintiff and receive no counter-restitution from the plaintiff. To that extent, and to that extent only, a defendant may be required to shoulder losses arising from her participation in the transaction. But the defendant is not required to pay compensation to the plaintiff. And the restitutionary liability of good faith defendants will also be limited in respect of changes of position caused by acting in reliance on benefits received from the plaintiff. The balancing of restitutionary and counter-restitutionary interests in this way is both principled and even-handed and importantly does not trespass into compensatory considerations.

This approach also suggests a new way of reconciling and re-drawing the limitations on the scope of indemnity awards identified in *Newbigging v Adam.*

Leasing Pty Ltd (2012) 295 ALR 147, 181 [156] (NSWCA) (Allsop P) (relevant changes included giving up or not pursuing recovery of debts), 149 [1] (Bathurst CJ) and 195 [215] (Meagher JA) agreeing on this point), see also 195 [216] (Meagher JA). The example given in *Sempra Metals Ltd v Inland Revenue Comrs* [2008] 1 AC 561, 650–651 [233] (Lord Mance) of a defendant hiding a mistaken payment under her bed, and thus omitting to invest the money so as to obtain commercial rates of interest for its use, also would constitute a good example of this category of change.

[108] Another example is *Maguire v Makaronis* (1997) 188 CLR 449, where recognition of valid change of position arguments would have resulted in a wholly different outcome for the defrauded plaintiffs.

We saw previously that Cotton LJ and Bowen LJ differed in their conceptions of the detrimental changes of position covered by an indemnity award. Both sought to limit them by reference to the contractual framework, but Cotton LJ's formulation was broader, extending to relief from the 'consequences and obligations which are the result of the contract which is set aside'.[109] These formulations were developed in the context of clarifying how the award of indemnity differed from an order for compensation for deceit. In light of the foregoing analysis, they can be usefully refined by reference to the Court's overall remedial aim. If the defendant must be 'no worse off' as a result of rescission, the question must be 'no worse off relative to what'? We saw earlier that the rescission case law tends to characterise the relevant end-point as the historical position that the defendant occupied prior to the impugned transaction. The case law in that light arguably seeks to ring-fence the relevant enquiry to contractual obligations and, in that way, to focus the enquiry on returning the parties to their former position *vis-à-vis* the contract. In other words, the 'former' position to which the parties must be returned is the position as it related to the contract.

This approach rightly excludes, for example, purely coincidental changes of position that have occurred to the parties, not attributable to the contract, which might otherwise be considered to prevent the parties from being restored to their former position. Again, insight may be drawn from the change of position case law where it is orthodoxy that in order for the defence to apply, the defendant's detrimental change of position must have been brought about by, or be referable to, the impugned transaction.[110] The prime example is *Scottish Equitable plc v Derby*, in which the Court regretfully explained that the fact that the defendant pensioner would suffer undeniable and even crushing hardship if required to make restitution of a mistaken payment was irrelevant, because the mistaken payment had played no role in bringing about his misfortunes.[111] However, while it is clear that the 'no worse off' enquiry in rescission similarly cannot be at large, and must exclude purely coincidental harms, it is less obvious that detrimental changes of position arising from an impugned contract should not be incorporated. To the contrary, consistency with the approach taken to changes of position in the context of simple mistaken payment cases strongly suggests that reliance-based changes of position should certainly operate to reduce the plaintiff's counter-restitutionary

[109] *Newbigging v Adam* (1886) 34 Ch D 582, 589 (CA). See above at text to n 75.

[110] *Ovidio Carrideo Nominees Pty Ltd v Dog Depot Pty Ltd* [2004] VSC 400, [42]–[43] (Kaye J); *Scottish Equitable plc v Derby* [2001] 3 All ER 818, 827 (Robert Walker LJ); *Philip Collins Ltd v Davis* [2000] 3 All ER 808, 827 (Ch) (Parker J) (the change must be 'referable' to the receipt) cited with approval in *Commerzbank AG v Price-Jones* [2003] EWCA Civ 1663, [58]–[59] (Munby J); *Heperu Pty Ltd v Belle* (2009) 76 NSWLR 230, 261 [133] (Allsop P, Campbell JA and Handley AJA concurring); *Bloomsbury International Ltd v Sea Fish Industry Authority* [2010] 1 CMLR 12, 382 [137] (Hamblen J). See also *Colliers CRE plc v Pandya* [2009] EWHC 211, [72] (QB) (Judge Richard Seymour QC), in which the parties had accepted 'a causal link between the receipt of the benefit … and the change of position' as a 'fundamental' requirement of the defence.

[111] *Scottish Equitable plc v Derby* [2001] EWCA Civ 369.

liability. This provides significant support for Cotton LJ's broader formulation of the scope of detriment covered by indemnity orders consequent on rescission.

Relatedly, this discussion highlights the importance of precision in identifying the 'end point' of rescission. We saw earlier that an alternative (albeit rarer) characterisation of the rescission enquiry is that it seeks to place the parties in the position they would have occupied had the transaction never occurred. This is subtly different from returning parties to their former position. The counterfactual formulation is also sometimes found in the approach to rescission-like relief taken under the consumer protection regime.[112] This formulation should, however, be treated with great caution. It strongly resembles the approach taken to compensation for deceit and would likely lead to a much broader enquiry (and hence relief) than its more historical counterpart. We have seen that amongst all the confusion and uncertainty associated with the nature of relief consequent on rescission, the one thing on which all courts agree is that it is and must remain distinct from any independent claim that may be available for compensation arising from a tort.

Re-focussing the enquiry on the proper limits of restitution, rather than compensation, also allows us to avoid some of the dubious distinctions drawn between the award of compensation for deceit and indemnity awards. For example, in *Whittington v Seale-Hayne* (discussed earlier) the Court emphasised that an indemnity award would not extend to damages payable to an employee of the plaintiff, who had suffered loss (in the form of the illness of himself and his eight children) as a result of the plaintiff entering into the contract.[113] It is however not at all clear that this sort of loss would be regarded as sufficiently 'direct' for the purposes of a claim for compensation for deceit, as the Court assumed. Conversely, a number of cases have emphasised that an indemnity award will not cover losses incurred as a result of the plaintiff's unreasonable business decisions; for example continuing with the business when it should have been sold to reduce losses or borrowing money from a third party that the plaintiff could not repay.[114] Courts citing these examples normally do so to point out the relatively limited operation of indemnity orders, compared to claims for compensation for deceit. However, these sorts of losses would be excluded even in claims of deceit by application of its particular remoteness rules,[115] just as surely as they might be excluded pursuant to an 'indemnity' award.

Rather than seeking to draw such artificial and in some cases misleading distinctions between compensation and indemnity orders, the better approach is to reorientate the indemnity enquiry so that it directly addresses the change of position considerations implicit in these cases. On this approach, irreversible changes of position made in good faith, such as running a business at a loss in reliance

[112] But see *Munchies Management Pty Ltd v Belperio* (1988) 58 FCR 274, 287–288 (the Court).
[113] *Whittington v Seale-Hayne* (1900) 82 LT 49, discussed above at text to n 84.
[114] *Munchies Management Pty Ltd v Belperio* (1988) 58 FCR 274, 710 (the Court).
[115] *HTW Valuers v Astonland Pty Ltd* (2004) 217 CLR 640.

on receipt of contractual benefits, may count to reduce a plaintiff's counter-restitutionary liability (so performing the functional equivalent of the change of position defence) in the way discussed earlier. However, those detrimental changes of position will not support an independent order for compensation against the defendant. Further, re-orientating the enquiry to change of position considerations provides a principled reason why plaintiffs may be denied allowances in diminution of their counter-restitutionary liability if they become aware of the vitiating conduct of the defendant and nonetheless continue to run the business. Where a plaintiff is aware of the circumstances supporting rescission, any change of position must be objectively justified by the circumstances of their receipt in order to qualify as good faith reliance.[116] Where a plaintiff acts as caretaker of a business following rescission, pending coming before the court to obtain consequential relief, and the business suffers further losses, the plaintiff's behaviour in continuing to run the business is consistent with ongoing good faith reliance. In these circumstances, as we saw earlier in the case of *Munchies Management Pty Ltd v Belperio*, the plaintiff's change of position should operate to diminish their restitutionary liability. By contrast, where a plaintiff becomes aware of vitiating conduct of the defendant, any decision irreversibly to change their position in a way inconsistent with that knowledge (such as by taking on new liabilities or seeking to expand or alter their business operation) is no longer made in good faith reliance.[117] In those circumstances, any further changes of position are made at their own risk.

A further ramification of the foregoing analysis 'feeds back' into a key debate currently surrounding the defence of change of position. In *David Securities Pty Ltd v Commonwealth Bank of Australia*, the High Court of Australia identified as the core requirement of the defence the fact that 'the defendant has acted to his or her detriment on the faith of the receipt'.[118] Given that *David Securities* concerned a reliance-based change of position, this identification of reliance as a core requirement was entirely proper. It was unnecessary to consider the position of independent changes of position, such as where a received benefit devaluates or is destroyed by some act independent of the defendant. On this view, the decision should not constitute an insurmountable barrier to the principled application of the defence to independent changes of position. However, in *Citigroup Pty Ltd v National Australia Bank Ltd* Barrett JA considered that it was not open to the New South Wales Court of Appeal to adopt a wider version of the defence that took into account non-reliance changes, in light of the High Court's pronouncement.[119]

116 *Perpetual Trustees Australia Ltd v Heperu Pty Ltd* (2009) 76 NSWLR 195, 224 [139] (Allsop P and Campbell JA, Handley AJA concurring) (emphasis added).

117 *Henjo Investments Pty Ltd v Collins Marrickville Pty Ltd* (1988) 39 FCR 546.

118 *David Securities Pty Ltd v Commonwealth Bank of Australia* (1992) 175 CLR 353, 385 (Mason CJ, Deane, Toohey, Gaudron and McHugh JJ) (emphasis in original omitted).

119 *Citigroup Pty Ltd v National Australia Bank Ltd* (2012) 82 NSWLR 391, 405 [64] (Barrett JA), but compare Bathurst CJ, Allsop P, Meagher JA at 394 [6], seemingly leaving the question open.

On this view, and if reliance is always required, independent changes of position must fall outside the ambit of the defence.[120] This conclusion is further supported by dicta in *AFSL v Hills Industries*, influenced both by the approach taken in *David Securities* and the central importance of the element of detrimental reliance in the context of equitable estoppel.[121]

It seems clear that where the benefit received by a defendant has irreversibly devalued, been destroyed or disappeared, an order for restitution would place the defendant in a 'worse position' than she occupied prior to her original receipt.[122] It seems therefore that the category of case falls within the general class of circumstances identified by the High Court as calling for protection by the change of position defence. Further, in terms of the defence's 'fit' with broader authority, the analogy drawn between estoppel and change of position which so influenced the High Court's reasoning in *AFSL v Hills Industries* is neither exhaustive nor exclusive of relevant guiding principles applicable to cases of independent changes of position. In particular, as we have seen, the doctrine of equitable rescission offers many examples of non-reliance based changes which have been taken into account by courts in making orders for restitution and counter-restitution following rescission.[123] Extension of the change of position defence to such circumstances in cases of simple restitution (not consequent upon rescission) will prevent an otherwise meritorious defendant from being put in a worse position than he occupied prior to his receipt through the order for restitution and will promote coherent treatment of like cases. This seems highly desirable.

Indeed, the operation of change of position considerations in the context of rescission may require reconsideration of the common assumption that the defence of change of position is not available to wrongdoers.[124] We have seen that *restitutio in integrum* is a general requirement of rescission, applicable as much to rescission arising from breach of fiduciary duty as rescission responding to innocent misrepresentation. In that light,[125] the defence seems to be a necessary correlation of those remedies, which aim solely to reverse or unwind transactions pursuant to which benefits have been conferred on another party. The defence operates in those contexts to ensure that the restitutionary or counter-restitutionary defendant

[120] See also *Streiner v Bank Leumi (UK) plc* (QB, 31 October 1985); *Euroactividade AG v Moeller* (CA, 1 February 1995); *Credit-Suisse (Monaco) SA v Attar* [2004] EWHC 374 (Comm), [98] (Gross J); C Mitchell, 'Change of Position: The Developing Law' [2005] *Lloyd's Maritime and Commercial Law Quarterly* 168, 178–179.

[121] *AFSL v Hills Industries* (2014) 253 CLR 560, 597 [81] (Hayne, Crennan, Kiefel, Bell and Keane JJ), 619 [142] (Gageler J).

[122] ibid 596 [77] (Hayne, Crennan, Kiefel, Bell and Keane JJ), 625–626 [157] (Gageler J).

[123] See earlier discussion at text following n 58.

[124] *Lipkin Gorman v Karpnale Ltd* [1991] 2 AC 548, 580 (HL) (Lord Godd).

[125] A more radical possibility is that the no-conflict rules are in essence concerned with vitiated consent and, to that extent, align with mistake, duress and other 'unjust factors' within the law of unjust enrichment: above n 28. On this view, change of position again most strongly aligns with the claim in unjust enrichment, rather than the remedy of restitution.

is not placed unjustifiably in a worse position as a result of rescission or restitution than she occupied prior to her receipt. In this manner, it operates to ensure that rescission and restitution do not operate so as to impose loss on innocent defendants, contrary to their remedial purposes. This role for change of position considerations in the requirement of *restitutio in integrum*, is required seemingly as much in cases of breach of fiduciary duty as cases of innocent misrepresentation (where no wrong is committed). If that is correct, then provided the defence does not operate to undermine or stultify the law's prohibition of the particular wrong, the defence may be available in cases where restitution is sought of benefits obtained by 'innocent' wrongdoers (such as an innocent trespasser) who has changed her position in good faith in reliance on her receipt. On this view, the defence is not necessarily limited to claims in unjust enrichment and should be conceptualised in the light of the remedies of rescission and restitution.

The final ramification of this analysis is potentially the most far-reaching and can only be touched on here. It has been argued in this chapter that rescission comprises mutual cross-claims for restitution and counter-restitution of benefits conferred under a transaction. This analysis suggests that rescission should far more commonly be made conditional on payment of substantial counter-restitution by the plaintiff of the value of services performed by the defendant, where services were performed on the basis of the transaction now sought to be set aside, than is currently the case. A burgeoning area ripe for this analysis relates to the role and entitlements of good faith care-givers in cases of undue influence. We saw earlier that in *Winefield v Clarke*, Barrett J had independently noted that some adjustment should be made to orders in that case for the fact that the defendant caregiver had discharged her elderly mother's mortgage over the family home on the basis that the mother had given her an interest in the property.[126] Barrett J recognised that unless this benefit was taken into account, the plaintiff would be unjustly enriched by an order for restitution of the defendant's interest. In the language of unjust enrichment, the plaintiff had been saved the necessary expense of discharging the mortgage herself by the defendant's action and must make counter-restitution of that benefit as a condition of relief. However, what was also noted by Barrett J in that case was that the defendant daughter had acted throughout in the utmost good faith and had provided valuable carer services to the mother, for which she ought to be 'commended'.[127] But one might ask why those valuable carer services were not the proper subject of an order for counter-restitution for their reasonable market value? One basis[128] on which the daughter provided the services (just as in the case of the discharged mortgage) was that she had been given an interest

[126] *Winefield v Clarke* [2008] NSWSC 882, discussed at text to n 80.

[127] ibid [43].

[128] Others might have included filial duty or mutual love and care between the mother and daughter. It is no bar to a claim for restitution for a total failure of consideration that there was more than one basis of a transaction: see Edelman and Bant (n 31) ch 11.

in the mother's property. Her services were necessary for the care and comfort of her elderly mother and in that sense enriched the mother just as much, again, as the discharged mortgage. Had the daughter not provided those services, someone else would have had to and there was no sign that the other children (who later pursued the claim against the daughter as the mother's personal representatives) would have taken up that role. In those circumstances, ordering restitution of the defendant's interest in the house without taking into account her valuable services unjustly enriched the mother (and, more particularly, the personal representatives who regained the interest in the house and had the windfall benefit of the daughter's services for free).

This is not an isolated instance but forms just one example of the many cases in which 'invisible' domestic services are routinely overlooked by defendant legal advisers and courts alike.[129] The failure to appreciate and give appropriate relief in respect of domestic services stands in stark contrast to the position of commercial defendants, whose valuable services are routinely taken into account to condition or defeat claims of rescission and restitution.[130] Once it is appreciated, however, that rescission generally will cause the objective basis for conferral of benefits by a defendant on a plaintiff pursuant to the impugned transaction to fail, there is no principled reason for continuing to ignore defendant's rights to fair counter-restitution of the value of domestic services, where those services have enriched the plaintiff. It might be added that greater appreciation of this point may also go a considerable way to deterring unmeritorious actions by relatives of the elderly or deceased, whose own actions have been characterised by a history of neglect of the plaintiff in whose interests they now purport to act.[131] It is interesting to speculate that in some cases, the value of the counter-claim may well outweigh the value of the benefit initially transferred by the plaintiff to the defendant. In those cases, the plaintiff (or plaintiff representatives) has a choice. The plaintiff may refuse to make counter-restitution, in which case the transaction stands.[132] Alternatively, if the property transferred to the defendant is of special significance, such as may be the case of a family home, the plaintiff may opt to pay the value of the order of counter-restitution to obtain specific restitution of the asset. Neither option is unduly onerous on the plaintiff or her representatives and the approach ensures that neither is left unjustly enriched as a consequence of rescission.

[129] Other prominent examples that fall within this category are *Inche Noriah v Shaik Allie Bin Omar* [1929] AC 127 (PC), and arguably the seminal High Court of Australia decision in *Johnson v Buttress* (1936) 56 CLR 113.

[130] See, eg, *Warman International Limited v Dwyer* (1995) 182 CLR 544; *Streeter v Western Areas Exploration Pty Ltd* (2011) 278 ALR 291; *Grimaldi v Chameleon Mining NL (No 2)* (2012) 200 FCR 296.

[131] Again *Inche Noriah v Shaik Allie Bin Omar* [1929] AC 127 (PC) and *Johnson v Buttress* (1936) 56 CLR 113 are leading examples, but the examples are legion.

[132] *Maguire v Makaronis* (1997) 188 CLR 449.

VI. Conclusion

This chapter has sought to identify and explore the restitutionary and change of position considerations often present in financial awards and allowances consequent on rescission. It has demonstrated that the language of compensation and indemnity that often characterise these awards obscures these features and can lead to further confusion and error. By looking at the substance of the awards, however, it becomes possible not only to understand the complex relationship between rescission and compensation, but to align the law of rescission with the related law of restitution. The result is a more coherent and principled approach to both the conditions for and measure of relief in both areas.

14

Discretion and Equitable Compensation

SIMONE DEGELING*

This chapter considers the ambit of equitable compensation. As an equitable remedy, equitable compensation is given within equity's discretion to grant or refuse relief, or otherwise fashion the remedy, to meet the equity of the case. We know that historically chancery concealed its remedy of compensating loss behind the language of account. So it shouldn't surprise us that the discretionary character of the order which flows after the taking of an account is also bound up in the description of the account itself as being discretionary in nature. Such is implied by Lord Millett NPJ in *Libertarian Investments Ltd v Hall*, who refers to the orthodox approach of taking a formal account prior to considering any subsequent obligation on the defendant to pay equitable compensation in the following terms: '[a]lthough like all equitable remedies an order for an account is discretionary, in making the order the court is not granting a remedy for [a] wrong but enforcing performance of an obligation',[1] and later in the same case confirms that 'the court will always have the last word.'[2]

Equity's discretion is principles based. It lies beyond the remit of this chapter to model the nature of equitable judicial decision making and it is important not to overstate the contingent nature of equitable discretion.[3] Judges and juries tasked

* I am grateful for the comments of Jessica Hudson and Keith Mason. I am also indebted to Maximus Jones for excellent research assistance, which was made possible through generous support of private law research at UNSW Law by Whittens & McKeough. All remaining errors are mine.

1 (2013) 16 HCFAR 681, [167].

2 ibid [172].

3 There are particular sites of discussion and debate on this question, such as in relation to the availability of a remedial constructive trust. See, eg: P Birks, 'The End of the Remedial Constructive Trust' (1998) 12 *Trust Law International* 202; S Evans, 'Defending Discretionary Remedialism' (2001) 23(4) *Sydney Law Review* 463; C Rotherham, 'Proprietary Relief for Enrichment by Wrongs: Some Realism about Property Talk' (1996) 19(2) *UNSW Law Journal* 387; W Swadling, 'Property and Unjust Enrichment' in J W Harris (ed), *Property Problems from Genes to Pension Funds* (London, Kluwer Law International, 1997) 130. Note also the monist and dualist approaches to remedies discussed in Ch 1, in which according to a dualist position once liability has been established, the grant and choice of remedy is in the discretion of the court. One potential consequence of a highly discretionary model

with fact finding may properly bring to bear individual judgment and diverse methods. Similarly, choices are inevitable in much legal reasoning. However, this is not an arbitrary selection between possible facts, principles and outcomes. As stated by Gleeson CJ (speaking of the defendant's and ultimately equity's conscience): '[t]he conscience of the appellant, which equity will seek to relieve, is a properly formed and instructed conscience.'[4] A majority of the High Court of Australia has since reiterated that equitable conscience is properly informed and instructed by 'established equitable principles and doctrines'[5] and that '"[t]he conscience spoken of here is a construct of values and standards against which the conduct of 'suitors'—not only defendants—is to be judged."'[6] Equity's margin of decision making in awarding equitable compensation encompasses two distinct questions. The first is more obviously familiar in equitable analysis, and is concerned with the considerations of factors which weigh in the balance in shaping the availability or appropriateness of an equitable remedy given the facts and circumstances of the case. Such considerations are commonly labelled bars to relief and so called discretionary factors.[7] The second is a distinct exercise of discretion in relation to the calculation of the money sum to be paid to the plaintiff as equitable compensation. These considerations arise in particular since it turns out that many claims for equitable compensation concern the loss of a chance. Each will be considered in turn.

I. Factors Going to Availability or Appropriateness of Equitable Compensation

In traditional analysis, as explored by others in this book, equity deals with a trustee or other accounting party's liability by first taking an account. This is 'the means

of judicial decision making is that a meaningful conceptual distinction between right and remedy is collapsed, arguably leaving the settlement of disputes to unrestrained judicial discretion. This chapter takes the view that the equitable discretion under discussion is not of that quality.

[4] *Australian Broadcasting Corporation v Lenah Game Meats* (2001) 208 CLR 199, [45] (Gleeson CJ).

[5] *Australian Financial Services and Leasing Pty Limited v Hills Industries Limited* [2014] HCA 14; (2014) 253 CLR 560 [76] (Hayne, Crennan, Kiefel, Bell and Keane JJ) ('*AFSL v Hills*').

[6] ibid quoting *Kakavas v Crown Melbourne Ltd* [2013] HCA 25, (2013) 250 CLR 392 [16] (French CJ, Hayne, Crennan, Kiefel, Bell, Gageler and Keane JJ), their honours quoting WMC Gummow, *Change and Continuity: Statute, Equity, and Federalism*, (Oxford, OUP, 1999) at 44–51. See also G Virgo, 'Whose Conscience? Unconscionability in the Common Law of Obligations' in A Robertson and M Tilbury (eds), *Divergences in Private Law* (Oxford, Hart Publishing, 2016) 293; R Havelock, 'The evolution of equitable "conscience"' (2014) 8 *Journal of Equity* 128; R Havelock, 'Conscience and unconscionability in modern equity' (2015) 9 *Journal of Equity* 1.

[7] It must be acknowledged that there has raged a fierce debate as to whether equitable compensation is subject to limiting devices, which may themselves be vehicles for equitable discretion, such as: a doctrine of intervening acts, notions of contributory negligence and a requirement that the plaintiff mitigate her loss. Such questions are not dealt with in this chapter. See generally K Barnett and S Harder, *Remedies in Australian Private Law* (Cambridge, CUP, 2014), Ch 9.

by which a beneficiary requires a trustee to justify his stewardship of trust property. The trustee must show what he has done with that property. If the beneficiary is dissatisfied with the way that a trustee has dealt with trust assets, he may surcharge or falsify the account.'[8] Following the taking of the account, the defendant may then be required to restore or make good losses to the fund, the orders to do so in substance comprising what is now known as equitable compensation. Modern equity, as shown by cases such as *Target Holdings Ltd v Redferns (a firm)*[9] and *AIB Group (UK) plc Ltd v Mark Redler*,[10] has in some instances dispensed with the intermediate step of a formal taking of accounts and instead allows a direct claim for the remedy of equitable compensation.[11] Irrespective of which route is followed, this analysis therefore assumes a court's need to decide whether, and on what terms, equitable compensation or an order following the taking of an account is an appropriate remedy. For ease of reference, these are compendiously referred to in this chapter as 'equitable compensation'. Similarly, the underlying event triggering the plaintiff's recourse to equity is assumed to have been established and any applicable causation rules satisfied. For example, a breach of fiduciary duty or an unauthorised disbursement of trust property.

In understanding the factors considered by a court in deciding on the availability of equitable compensation, there are matters which will disqualify or limit the plaintiff's equity for relief. At the outset it must be acknowledged that it is not the purpose of this chapter to attempt any overarching theory of equity's disqualifying factors. Rather, the discussion reviews their pattern of implementation in relation to equitable compensation, focusing on examples from Australian courts. Professors Bant and Bryan separate the disqualifying items into defences, bars to relief and discretionary factors.[12] On this model, defences are matters which if proved will defeat the plaintiff's suit, and 'tend… to settle the question of the defendant's liability once and for all'[13] such as illegality or a plea of bona fide purchase without notice. Where a defence applies, the court has no residual discretion to permit recovery. Bars to relief include laches, lack of clean hands and hardship and invoke a highly structured model of decision making. In contrast, Bant and Bryan

[8] *Ultraframe (UK) Ltd v Fielding* [2005] EWHC 1638 (Ch) (27 July 2005) [1513] (Lewison J).

[9] [1996] 1 AC 421 (HL).

[10] [2015] AC 1503 (SC(E)).

[11] See generally: J Edelman, '*Nocton v Lord Ashburton* (1914)' in C Mitchell and P Mitchell (eds), *Landmark Cases in Equity* (Oxford, Hart Publishing, 2012) 473, 490–491; JD Heydon, MJ Leeming and PG Turner, *Meagher, Gummow & Lehane's Equity Doctrines & Remedies*, 5th edn (Sydney, LexisNexis Butterworths, 2015), 802–3 [23-030]–[23-035]; M Conaglen, 'Equitable Compensation for Breach of Trust: Off *Target*' (2016) 40(1) *Melbourne University Law Review* (advance), 20–25. However, as noted by Conaglen at 38, simply by dispensing with the formal accounting procedure does not of itself 'affect the fundamental principles which determine the quantum of compensation payable' which are arguably unchanged.

[12] See E Bant and M Bryan, 'Defences, Bars and Discretionary Factors' in E Bant and M Bryan (eds), *Principles of Proprietary Remedies* (Sydney, Thomson Reuters, 2013), 185–186 ('Bant and Bryan'). Note that Bant and Bryan's study concerned the availability of equitable proprietary remedies, but there is no reason to think that equitable discretion is qualitatively different when acting in rem and in personam.

[13] ibid 185.

suggest a third category of discretionary factors according to which a court may engage in relatively open textured decision making. Fact and case specific matters may be relevant in refusing or fashioning relief, although '[t]he identity and ambit of operation of these factors is informed and curtailed by precedent and is not left open to personal judicial preference. … The list of factors … is fairly stable and transparent.'[14] Bant and Bryan include in the list of discretionary factors the intervening interests of third parties.[15] The interrelationship between these three categories of defences, bars to relief and discretionary factors is not fixed. Bant and Bryan acknowledge that even on their own explanation, the borders between categories are porous so that a more useful division might be between two categories, defences and discretionary factors, and an acceptance that 'the exercise of judgment is relevant to both'.[16] In recognition of that truth, this chapter embraces Bant and Bryan's ultimate suggestion of a dichotomy between defences and discretionary factors.[17]

The question of what is a defence is contentious. Associate Professors Dyson, Goudkamp and Wilmot-Smith argue that in order to understand private law defences it is necessary to 'separate the *definition* of a defence from the *consequences* of something being a defence.'[18] This separation reveals a dichotomy between denials and defences according to which denials are the defendant's response to the plaintiff's claim, in which the defendant alleges that the plaintiff's cause of action is incomplete. By contrast, a defendant who raises a defence accepts that the cause of action is complete, but raises some other consideration which justifies reducing or eliminating their liability.[19] On this view, equity's bars to relief and other discretionary factors would all be categorised as defences since their functional effect is to reduce or limit liability. However, for the purpose of this chapter the narrower conception favoured by Bant and Bryan will be adopted. Irrespective of label, the point to observe is that where a defence applies, the court has no or little room to manoeuvre in nonetheless allowing the plaintiff to recover. As discussed below, this is not in substance the phenomenon of concern. Rather, this chapter is principally concerned with the exercise of discretion in awarding equitable compensation.

[14] Bant and Bryan (n 12) 186.
[15] Bant and Bryan (n 12) 206.
[16] Bant and Bryan (n 12) 187.
[17] Bant and Bryan (n 12) 187.
[18] A Dyson, J Goudkamp and F Wilmot-Smith, 'Central Issues in the Law of Tort Defences' in A Dyson, J Goudkamp and F Wilmot-Smith (eds), *Defences in Tort* (Oxford, Hart Publishing, 2015) 3, 5 (emphasis in original).
[19] The distinction drawn between defences and denials in private law continues to be worked through, with at least two edited collections considering the consequences (and more are planned): A Dyson, J Goudkamp and F Wilmot-Smith (eds), *Defences in Tort* (Oxford, Hart Publishing, 2015); A Dyson, J Goudkamp and F Wilmot-Smith (eds), *Defences in Unjust Enrichment* (Oxford, Hart Publishing, 2016).

A. Discretionary Factors

Professor Tilbury when writing about the discretionary nature of equitable relief preferred a functional approach which looks at the court's discretion according to: (a) whether the discretion operates only between the parties or as between the parties and third persons (which further divides into discretions a function of the parties' conduct such as laches, or clean hands and result based discretions such as hardship); (b) discretions involving considerations relating to the administration of justice, such as the need for the constant supervision of the court; and (c) discretions involving general policy considerations.[20] All of the cases considered in this chapter fall into (a) discretions operating between the parties or between the parties and third persons. This can largely be understood as occurring for practical reasons. For example, an award of equitable compensation, which is a one off money remedy, does not as in the case of an injunction raise the same administration of justice concerns.

Recall that all are suitors before the court,[21] and the court applies checks and balances in decision making as to the conduct and conscience of both the plaintiff and the defendant. The discussion below considers the following conduct based discretions: (i) laches and delay; and (ii) clean hands. The chapter then turns to the result based discretions which consider: (i) appropriateness of other remedies; (ii) third party interests; and (iii) clean break considerations. These examples have been chosen as they illustrate the application of these principles in the context of equitable compensation. These discretionary levers operate differentially in the balance of justice. In particular, stemming from its quality as a money remedy, the existence of third party interests and the need for a clean break may tip the balance *in favour* of an award of equitable compensation, as opposed to matters which may justify a court awarding equitable relief at all.

i. Laches and Delay

The plaintiff may delay in instituting or bringing her action against the defendant. Where the effect of the delay is to cause prejudice to the defendant or other third parties laches may be established such that the plaintiff's cause of action may be barred.[22] Modern commentary confirms we now confine laches 'to describe

[20] MJ Tilbury, *Civil Remedies Volume 1 Principles of Civil Remedies* (Sydney, Butterworths, 1990), 289–299 ('Tilbury'). On Tilbury's model any distinction between bars to relief and discretionary factors is unnecessary. All considerations weighing in the court's judgment are relevant.

[21] *AFSIL v Hills* (n 5) [76] (Hayne, Crennan, Kiefel, Bell and Keane JJ).

[22] *Orr v Ford* (1989) 167 CLR 316, 341 (Deane J) citing Lord Selborne LC speaking for the Privy Council in *Lindsay Petroleum v Hurd* (1874) 5 PC 221, 239–240 and *Erlanger v New Sombrero Phosphate Co* (1878) 3 App Cas 1218, 1279 (Lord Blackburn); *Crawley v Short* [2009] NSWCA 410, [163]–[165], [180] (Young JA).

the equitable defence where delay is coupled with prejudice'.[23] Thus the doctrine focuses on the effects of the delay in causing prejudice, such as where through delay evidence or witnesses are lost or where the defendant has to her detriment acted reasonably in reliance on the plaintiff's actions constituting delay. Meagher JA in *Gerace v Auzhair Supplies Pty Ltd* explains the elements of laches as follows:

> …the question is whether, as between the parties, it would be practically unjust to give relief which otherwise would be just. … account is taken of the length of any delay, the nature of the acts done during the period of that delay, whether the plaintiff had sufficient knowledge to justify the commencement of proceedings, whether there has been prejudice to the defendant or others and the nature of the relief claimed.[24]

In *Disctronics v Edmonds*[25] (the precursor to *Howard v Commissioner of Taxation of the Commonwealth of Australia*)[26] Warren J identified delay as an 'important factor'[27] in denying a constructive trust instead ordering equitable compensation. Six joint venturers proposed purchasing a golf course, obtaining a reliable long term tenant and selling the land subject to the lease to a third party. Two of the joint venturers acquired the golf course on their own account and let it to a tenant. The remaining four joint venturers sued alleging, inter alia, breach of fiduciary duty and lodged a caveat on the golf course thus hindering its sale to any third party. Warren J found the two joint venturers (Edmonds and Cahill) had breached their fiduciary duty in diverting a commercial opportunity of the joint venture. Of interest to the present discussion is the observation that 'the plaintiffs did not take legal action until well after the defendants gained title on 14 December 1999. There were legal avenues open to them none of which were pursued.'[28] As explained by Phillips JA in the Court of Appeal phase of the case, *Edmonds v Donovan*,[29] 'the [plaintiffs/respondents] had not moved swiftly to establish their claims.'[30] A formal contract of sale was entered into in October 1999 together with a lease for a long term tenant. It was not until December 2000 that the other joint venturers (through their investment vehicle Disctronics) lodged their caveat. As Phillips JA stated: '[t]hat delay was never really explained.'[31]

[23] JD Heydon, MJ Leeming and PG Turner *Meagher Gummow & Lehane's Equity Doctrines & Remedies*, 5th edn (LexisNexis Butterworths, Chatswood, 2015), 1087 [38-020] ('*Meagher, Gummow & Lehane*'). This contrasts with acquiescence in which the delay is used by equity as evidence of some kind of agreement or acceptance by the plaintiff of the defendant's conduct, such that it would be unconscionable now to require the defendant to provide a remedy. Acquiescence also requires the plaintiff to have knowledge of her rights and the facts on which they are based. The learned authors of *Meagher, Gummow & Lehane* prefer the terminology of 'waiver or release or affirmation' rather than the 'imprecise' acquiescence. See *Meagher Gummow & Lehane*, 1087 [38-020].

[24] (2014) 87 NSWLR 435, [73].

[25] [2002] VSC 454 ('*Disctronics*').

[26] (2014) 253 CLR 83.

[27] *Disctronics* (n 25) [215].

[28] ibid [215].

[29] *Edmonds v Donovan* (2005) 12 VR 513 ('*Edmonds*').

[30] ibid, [66] (Phillips JA) with whom Winneke P and Charles JA agreed.

[31] *Edmonds* (n 29) [517].

Despite the presence of delay, *Disctronics* was not a case about laches.[32] Facts may or may not have been available to establish the necessary prejudice. Certainly, there was knowledge by the defendants, who had 'not merely stood by for nearly two years without attempting to intervene but thereby acquiesced in what was happening, if not indeed to the point of adopting it…'.[33] Leaving to one side the issue of whether in fact the delay could have been evidence of acquiescence, laches may have on the facts been in view. Taken strictly, this would have presented an obstacle to the plaintiff's claim and thus operated in the same fashion as a defence, despite the fact that the effect of laches is not to deny the existence of the plaintiff's substantive right, here a breach of fiduciary duty.[34]

Rather, delay is used in the analysis in *Disctronics* in a more nuanced way in justifying equitable compensation. First, it is arguably employed as evidence in support of the unjust enrichment of the plaintiff which would otherwise remain if a constructive trust were awarded. Thus, in the Court of Appeal, Phillips JA used the plaintiff's delay in intervening as evidence of their opportunism; of waiting to see whether or not the infringing venture proved successful before bringing a claim. On this basis, he preferred a claim for equitable compensation over any gain based award, whether an account of profits or constructive trust. There was no 'warrant for allowing the [defendant] to stand by for nearly two years and then to obtain a remedy which … exposed them to none of the risks but gave them all of the rewards of the business having been run in the meantime.'[35] Arguably, this reflects a concern that to transfer to the plaintiff the infringing venture via a constructive trust would by that mechanism have unjustly enriched the plaintiffs at the expense of the defendants.[36]

Secondly, Warren J at trial employed delay to justify an award of equitable compensation and rejected the claim for a constructive trust over the golf course.[37] The object of the award was to value the opportunity lost by the four joint venturers after various adjustments. Mindful of the plaintiffs' delay in combination with the risk that a constructive trust may afford priority to the plaintiff over third party interests in the property, such as that of mortgagees,[38] Warren J declined to find

[32] An example of an equitable compensation case in which laches *was* pleaded, albeit not made out, is *Herrod v Johnston* [2012] QCA 360, [69]–[72] (Muir JA). Despite extensive delay by the plaintiffs in pursuing their claim, laches was not established as the necessary reliance was not present. The defendants were aware, or ought reasonably to been aware, that the plaintiffs intended to 'vindicate their rights' [71] and if they acted to their 'disadvantage during the period of the dispute … they did so, not in reliance on any conduct or inaction on the part of [the plaintiffs] but despite [their] claims and without regard to [their] rights and interests' [72]. See also *Hodgson v Amcor* (2012) 264 1 FLR 1, [1762]–[1766] (Vickery J).

[33] *Edmonds* (n 29) [82] (Phillips JA) with whom Winneke P and Charles JA agreed.

[34] See further: Bant and Bryan, 199.

[35] *Edmonds* (n 29) [77] (Phillips JA) with whom Winneke P and Charles JA agreed.

[36] I am grateful to Elise Bant for her discussion on this point.

[37] *Disctronics* (n 25) [216].

[38] ibid [212]–[213].

a constructive trust.[39] The impact of delay in this analysis is therefore less specific, although Warren J nonetheless identifies it as a separate factor in her analysis.

Delay may also be reflected in the award of interest, as was applied by Austin J in *Aequitas v AEFC*.[40] Various parties breached the fiduciary obligations of a corporate and financial adviser, promotor or paid a bribe such that breaches of fiduciary duties owed to Aequitas and Aequitas No 1 occurred.[41] Aequitas had purchased securities on receipt of conflicted advice and sought advice on the identification of possible litigation targets and opportunities in September 1986. However, proceedings were not commenced until 6 November 1991. Whilst some securities were realised in the intervening period, no satisfactory explanation was given to the court as to why legal proceedings against the defaulting fiduciaries was delayed. Accordingly, the defendants submitted that an order for interest on all of the losses recoverable by the plaintiff from the time that the losses were incurred until the date of the court's orders would be 'productive of unfairness to the defendant.'[42] Austin J agreed, pointing out that it would not be fair to require the defendant to pay interest for this period.[43] Rather, he awarded interest, calculated on a compound basis,[44] running from the date of incurring each individual loss until 30 June 1987,[45] being the date he identified as that when 'on a fair view of the circumstances, the plaintiffs might reasonable have been expected to have commenced proceedings.'[46]

ii. Doing Equity and Clean Hands

The plaintiff's conduct is also subject to twin equitable maxims that 'he who seeks equity must do equity', which looks to the conduct which the plaintiff undertakes to engage in the future, and 'she who comes to equity must come with clean hands', which requires equity to examine the past conduct of the litigant who seeks equity's assistance.[47]

The requirement that the plaintiff do equity embodies equity's concern with reciprocity. As explained by the authors of Meagher, Gummow & Lehane: '[n]o plaintiff can get an equitable remedy unless that plaintiff fulfils his or her own

[39] *Disctronics* (n 25) [216]. See also *Windemac Pte Ltd v Jada Ex Beverages Pty Ltd* [2013] VSC 1, [28] (Sifris J) in which the 'peculiar and unexplained' delay of the plaintiff in taking steps to protect its interest was a factor relevant to the 'form of relief'. The court ordered equitable compensation but not interest or any proprietary relief, which was also undesirable given third party interests.

[40] [2001] NSWSC 14, [460]–[463] ('*Aequitas*').

[41] Aequitas (n 40) [277].

[42] Aequitas (n 40) [457].

[43] Aequitas (n 40) [460].

[44] Aequitas (n 40) [464]. See also *Herrod v Johnston* [2012] QCA 360, [44]–[49] (Muir JA) supporting the use of compound interest in equitable compensation claims.

[45] *Aequitas* (n 40) [461].

[46] ibid [460].

[47] *Black Uhlans Incorporated v New South Wales Crime Commission* [2002] NSWSC 1060, [159] (Campbell J).

legal and equitable obligations arising out of the subject matter of the dispute.'[48] An example of a case in which the plaintiff was required to do equity, thus effectively sanctioning the enforcement of the transaction despite the breach is *Maguire v Makaronis*.[49] The defendants agreed to purchase a chicken farm and consulted the plaintiff solicitors about obtaining finance to fund the purchase. The defendants assumed the plaintiffs would act for them in obtaining a loan from a commercial lender. In fact, the plaintiffs themselves obtained finance from a bank at 22% interest then on-lent their clients the entire amount to purchase the chicken farm at 24% annual interest rate, secured by a mortgage over the farm. The defendants were unaware that their creditors/mortgagees were their solicitors. The defendants defaulted on loan repayments after meeting only one contracted instalment and the plaintiff's commenced proceedings to claim repossession of the mortgaged property. The defendants resisted, seeking a declaration that the mortgage was 'void and of no effect'. The defendants relied on the plaintiffs' breach of fiduciary duty in seeking rescission. In particular, there:

> had been a conflict between the duty of the [plaintiffs solicitors] to the [defendants] and their personal interests in the transaction, in particular as mortgagee … The conflict meant that the loyalty of the [solicitors] to their clients had not remained undivided, with the result that they could not properly discharge their duties to their clients.[50]

Further, there was no informed client consent to the conflict between duty and interest.[51]

Although not a case in which equitable compensation was claimed, the High Court contemplated that the 'nature of the case'[52] will determine the appropriate remedy which might include rescission but also:

> the further remedies referred to by the Lord Chancellor in *Nocton v Lord Ashburton*, namely an account of profits … or … compensation for that which the plaintiff has lost "by [the fiduciary] acting", to use the Lord Chancellor's phrase, in breach of duty.[53]

In considering the defendant's counterclaim for rescission, the Court required that the defendant do equity and declined to rescind the mortgage:

> [t]o set aside the Mortgage purely in its operation as a security, without conditioning that upon repayment, would be to reform the transaction in an impermissible fashion. It would be to strike down the security interest without ensuring repayment of that which was paid in return for it.[54]

48 *Meagher Gummow & Lehane* (n 23) [3-050].
49 (1997) 188 CLR 449 ('*Maguire*').
50 ibid 465 (Brennan CJ, Gaudron, McHugh and Gummow JJ).
51 *Maguire* (n 49) 466–467 (Brennan CJ, Gaudron, McHugh and Gummow JJ).
52 *Maguire* (n 49) 467 (Brennan CJ, Gaudron, McHugh and Gummow JJ).
53 *Maguire* (n 49) 468 (Brennan CJ, Gaudron, McHugh and Gummow JJ).
54 *Maguire* (n 49) (Brennan CJ, Gaudron, McHugh and Gummow JJ).

The mortgage was therefore set aside on condition that the defendant repay all of the money owing under it.[55] In an action for equitable compensation, the obligation to do equity similarly applies to the plaintiff in relation to her own legal or equitable obligations arising out of the subject matter of the dispute.

The clean hands doctrine rests on the normative position that the wrongdoer should not be permitted to derive advantage from their own wrong. It is said to derive from the judgment of Eyre LCB in *Dering v Earl of Winchelsea*[56] and asks about the relationship between the equity sued for and the plaintiff's impropriety. The court does not look simply to the moral culpability of the plaintiff, but whether there is an immediate and necessary connection between the conduct of the plaintiff and the equity relied upon, and further, notwithstanding this connection, whether the facts indicate that equitable relief should be denied or otherwise moulded to the circumstances. For example, as explained by Campbell J in *Black Uhlans Inc v New South Wales Crime Commission*,[57] prior to trial the plaintiff may have ceased the offending activity and undertaken not to continue it, in which case equitable relief might be available notwithstanding that the conduct in question was immediate and necessary to the equity sued for.

An example of a case in which clean hands was raised, albeit not on the facts made out, is *Australasian Annuities Pty Ltd (in liq) v Rowley Super Fund*.[58] Australasian Annuities (AA) sued the recipient of funds in knowing receipt. The funds had been paid away by one of the directors of AA in breach of fiduciary duty. In awarding equitable compensation requiring the recipient to restore the fund,[59] the Victorian Court of Appeal considered an argument that the plaintiff AA was disentitled to equitable relief on the basis of unclean hands. This was unanimously rejected.[60] On the particular facts, the claim arose following the failure of AA to repay $2.5 million advanced to it by Macquarie Bank Ltd in 2007. Macquarie subsequently appointed a receiver and manager who stood in the shoes of AA and commenced proceedings in the name of AA against the recipient. It was submitted

[55] Ibid 478 (Brennan CJ, Gaudron, McHugh and Gummow JJ).

[56] (1787) 1 Cox 318, 319: 'It is not laying down any principle to say that his ill conduct disables him from having any relief in this court. If this can be founded on any principle, it must be, that a man must come into a Court of Equity with clean hands; but when this is said, it does not mean a general depravity; it must have an immediate and necessary relation to the equity sued for; it must be a depravity in a legal as well as in a moral sense.'

[57] *Black Uhlans Incorporated v New South Wales Crime Commission* [2002] NSWSC 1060, [181].

[58] [2015] VSCA 9 ('*Australasian Annuities*'), special leave to appeal to HCA refused *Rowley Super Fund Pty Ltd (ANC 129 688 455) v Australasian Annuities Pty Ltd (in liq)* [2015] HCATrans 235. See also the following cases which recognised the application of clean hands to equitable compensation, but did not apply on the particular facts: *David Alan Thomson v Golden Destiny Investments Pty Limited* [2015] NSWSC 1176 [90]–[97], [629] (Sackar J); *Sino Iron Pty Ltd v Palmer (No 3)* [2015] 2 Qd R 574, [146] (Jackson J); *Hydrocool Pty Ltd v Hepburn* [2011] FCA 495, 279 ALR 646, [198] (Siopis J).

[59] *Australasian Annuities* (n 58), [136] (Neave JA) and [279] (Garde AJA), finding that the defendant was a liable as a knowing recipient. Warren CJ at [116] dissented on the question of liability, but at [132] did not disagree in the court's finding that the submission that Macquarie lacked clean hands was irrelevant.

[60] *Australian Annuities* (n 58) [132] (Warren CJ), [134] (Neave JA) and [315] (Garde AJA).

that Macquarie had 'facilitated the transaction it subsequently complained about, and knew of the purpose for which the funds were to be advanced.'[61] Thus, the recipient attempted an argument that *Macquarie's* equity was brought into existence by its own wrongful conduct. All members of the court rejected this submission. First, and most obviously, because the equity being asserted was AA's not Macquarie's and Macquarie was therefore not in any sense a party to the proceedings.[62] Secondly, Macquarie's conduct even if relevant, was not improper in any way.[63] Thus AA's entitlement to equitable relief was not impugned.

iii. Third Party Interests

A court will consider the appropriateness of a particular remedy and the impact of that remedy on third parties. Where a proprietary remedy is sought, a court must consider whether there is an 'appropriate equitable remedy which falls short of the imposition of a trust.'[64] This means that a proprietary remedy such as a constructive trust ought not to be imposed if other orders are capable of meeting the plaintiff's equity, and 'care must be taken to avoid granting equitable relief which goes beyond the necessities of the case.'[65] That a trust will bind third parties is also recognised and may tend against its imposition if to do so would be injurious to them.

Equitable compensation may thus be the alternative remedy sought by the parties or ordered by the court. Its nature as a personal money remedy allows the court some flexibility in 'quell[ing] the controversy'[66] between the parties without awarding a constructive trust. An example is *Giumelli v Giumelli*[67] in which the son (Robert) of the family had been promised a subdivided part of their property if he stayed on the property and worked in the family orchard. He subsequently built a three bedroom house on the land and gave up offers of work elsewhere.

[61] *Australasian Annuities* (n 58) [313] (Garde AJA).

[62] *Australasian Annuities* (n 58) [132] (Warren CJ), [134] (Neave JA) and [315] (Garde AJA).

[63] ibid.

[64] *Giumelli v Giumelli* (1999) 196 CLR 101, [10] (Gleeson CJ, McHugh, Gummow and Callinan JJ) ('*Giumelli*'). See also, eg: *Bathurst City Council v PWC Properties Pty Ltd* (1988) 195 CLR 566, [42] (the Court) ('*Bathurst*').

[65] *John Alexander's Clubs Pty Limited v White City Tennis Club Limited* (2010) 241 CLR 1, [129] (French CJ, Gummow, Hayne, Heydon and Kiefel JJ). See also, eg: *Grimaldi v Chameleon Mining NL (No 2)* [2012] 200 FCR 296, [183], [508], [514] (the Court), [681] (The Court).

[66] *Bathurst* (n 64) [42] (the Court); *Angus Carnegie Gordon as liquidator of Lyon Form Pty Ltd (in liq) v Leon Plant Hire Pty Ltd (in liq)* [2015] NSWSC 397, [63] (Black J).

[67] *Giumelli* (n 64). See also, eg: *Windemac Pte Ltd v Jada Ex Beverages Pty Ltd* [2013] VSC 1, [28] (Sifris J); *Angus Carnegie Gordon as liquidator of Lyon Form Pty Ltd (in liq) v Leon Plant Hire Pty Ltd (in liq)* [2015] NSWSC 397, [63]–[65] (Black J); *Ryan v Ryan* [2016] TASSC 4, [46]–[50] (Estcourt J). Recall that in *Disctronics* (n 25) [212]–[213] (Warren J) the impact of a constructive trust on third party interests, including mortgagees, was a factor to consider favouring equitable compensation as an adequate remedy. In *Ian Rodda Pty Ltd v Rodda* [2015] SASC 149, [61] and [67] (Kelly J) the injustice to third parties of equitable compensation itself was considered but on the facts rejected.

After disputation with his parents about his choice of life partner, Robert left the property and his brother Steven lived elsewhere on the promised lot and made substantial improvements to the property. The Supreme Court of Western Australia held that the parents held the lot on constructive trust in order to convey it to Robert. On appeal, the High Court of Australia held that the lower court had erred on the form of remedy since a constructive trust would not recognise Steven's improvement of the land and his continued residence on it:

> [Q]ualification [is] necessary both to avoid injustice to others, particularly Steven and his family, and to avoid relief which went beyond what was required for conscientious conduct by Mr and Mrs Giumelli. The result points inexorably to relief expressed not in terms of acquisition of title to land but in a money sum .... to represent the value of the equitable claim of [Robert] to the [promised lot].[68]

In result, the matter was remitted to a judge of the Supreme Court to calculate equitable compensation.[69] The trust was refused and the order to pay compensation was secured by a lien, defeasible on payment of the equitable debt.[70]

iv. Clean Break Considerations

The desirability of the parties having a clean break may similarly suggest equitable compensation as the appropriate remedy. Leaving to one side the impact on third parties, a separate characteristic of constructive trusts and liens, at least until the trust is performed or the lien defeased, is that it locks together the parties. Whilst there is certainly no relationship in mind requiring performance, such as may be contemplated via a decree of specific performance, in which equity may be reluctant to compel the maintenance of an ongoing personal relationship between the parties,[71] equity nonetheless asks whether the parties need an immediate separation. An example is *Rodda v Ian Rodda & Anor*[72] in which a father and son were in dispute about family farmland and the associated farming business. Title was either held or controlled by the father and the son asserted an equitable interest in the land and claimed that money was owed to him on the basis of financial and non-financial contributions and promises made. Having decided the son was entitled to relief via proprietary estoppel, the court considered, amongst other matters, whether a constructive trust and equitable compensation or in the alternative a larger award of equitable compensation would be appropriate 'pay[ing] sufficient regard to the very real need in this case for remedies designed to assist with a clean break, particularly if, as the [son has] offered, [the father] were to continue to live in the homestead.'[73] The land in question comprised neighbouring

[68] *Giumelli* (n 64) [50]–[51] (Gleeson CJ, McHugh, Gummow and Callinan JJ).
[69] *Giumelli* (n 64) [51] (Gleeson CJ, McHugh, Gummow and Callinan JJ).
[70] *Giumelli* (n 64) [58] (Gleeson CJ, McHugh, Gummow and Callinan JJ).
[71] *Byrne v Australian Airlines Ltd* (1995) 185 CLR 410, 428 (Brennan CJ, Dawson and Toohey JJ).
[72] [2015] SASC 95. See also *Windemac Pte Ltd v Jada Ex Beverages Pty Ltd* [2013] VSC 1, [27] (Sifris J).
[73] ibid [325]–[327] (Nicholson J).

properties. A constructive trust, if imposed, would force shared boundaries and a form of co-ownership on the parties, unless and until one party decided to sell. In result, the need for a clean break was not compelling and the court awarded a constructive trust and a lesser amount of equitable compensation recognising the son's contribution, secured by an equitable lien over the land.[74]

II. Factors Going to Calculation of Equitable Compensation—Loss of a Chance

Loss recognisable in equity includes a lost opportunity or lost chance. For example, the value of a contract not obtained or market opportunity not pursued by the plaintiff. Equitable discretion is shown in the manner by which equity constructs the value of this loss and meets it in an award of equitable compensation. The court's discretion is not explicitly tied to the discrete discretionary factors identified above, but is rather a more particular exercise of judgment in order to address the following structural hurdles which would otherwise exist. First, the plaintiff's loss must be made certain. Certainty of loss refers to the requirement that the plaintiff satisfy the court both as to the fact of damage and its amount.[75] Certainty is a requirement familiar at law in actions for example, for damages for breach of contract or in negligence, and may be taken to include an obligation on the plaintiff to demonstrate according to the civil standard the nature and extent of her losses.[76] Where the plaintiff sues for a lost chance, this loss may be inherently uncertain since demonstrating the extent of this loss depends on comparing the plaintiff's position at trial and the position the plaintiff would have been in without the defendant's breach of duty. Thus, for example, the return a principal would have made on a commercial opportunity had that opportunity not been usurped by a fiduciary might be considered an uncertain loss. As discussed below, there is evidence that equity requires the plaintiff's loss to be made certain before equitable compensation may be ordered, and that this is in part achieved through the exercise of equitable discretion.[77] The second structural hurdle is that in calculating equitable compensation for a lost chance, a court may make adjustments to the award reflecting notional burdens and costs which would have been borne

[74] ibid [319]–[321] (Nicholson J) and *Rodda v Ian Rodda Pty Ltd (No 2)* [2015] SASC 128, [79] (Nicholson J).

[75] H McGregor, *McGregor on Damages*, 19th edn (London, Sweet & Maxwell, 2014), para [10-001].

[76] Tilbury (n 20) 149.

[77] See further: S Degeling, 'Loss of Chance and Breach of Fiduciary Duty: The Requirement of Certainty' (2016) 28 *Singapore Academy of Law Journal* 825 for a more detailed examination of equity's requirements of certainty of loss.

by the plaintiff had the chance been exercised. As explored below, these adjustments are similarly highly discretionary.

A. Certainty of Loss

The discussion above suggests a commercial opportunity usurped by a fiduciary in breach of fiduciary duty. This loss may be characterised as a lost opportunity or loss of a chance to the principal for which equitable compensation will be sought. There is some evidence that in awarding this remedy, equity has employed machinery to make the loss certain. Two approaches can be seen. The first is shown by the approach of court in *Libertarian Investments v Hall*[78] in which equity's underlying moral values imbue the approach to construction of loss. The second is the probabilistic approach taken in *Ramsay v BigTinCan*.[79]

In *Libertarian*, an investor wanted to acquire a 10% stake in a company (TSE). Hall undertook to use his connections and knowledge of TSE to assist the investor to purchase the shares. The investor's company was Libertarian which was the vehicle by which at the end of 2002 the parties embarked on their project to obtain 10% of TSE's shares using EUR50 million (GBP5,949,994) provided to the investor. The money was paid by the investor into a trust account set up by Hall with a firm of solicitors (BLP). Unknown to the investor or Libertarian, Hall designated the BLP trust account the client account of his own company Axdale and transferred substantial amounts in and out of it without authority. On 14 October 2003 Hall withdrew GBP5,463,508 claiming that this money was to purchase 1,777,700 shares in TSE at GBP3.11 per share. This was a lie: no shares were purchased and no explanation was given as to how the money was used.[80] The investor was thus the victim of a breach of fiduciary duty.[81]

Libertarian suffered the loss of an opportunity to on-sell TSE shares in the market. Evidence indicated that subsequent to the notional purchase date, Libertarian would have been able to offer the entire parcel to Softbank and that 42% would have been purchased at GBP13.2005 per share. The remaining 58% were assumed to have been able to be sold at GBP8.84 per share. The court acknowledged the inherent difficulties in finding a basis for valuing the shares,[82] principal amongst these the 'guesswork' and 'evidential gaps' in ascribing a price a potential buyer would have been willing to pay for a hypothetical shareholding in a company whose share register was in a state of flux, the time of the hypothetical transaction being more than 10 years prior. However, adopting an approach in which '…the

[78] (2013) 16 HKCFAR 681 ('*Libertarian*').

[79] [2014] *Libertarian* (n 78) NSWCA 324, special leave to appeal to the High Court of Australia refused [2015] HCATrans 59.

[80] *Libertarian* (n 78) [30] (Ribeiro PJ).

[81] *Libertarian* (n 78) [35], [106], [111]–[112] (Ribeiro PJ).

[82] *Libertarian* (n 78) [137] (Ribeiro PJ).

court is entitled to be robust and do rough and ready justice without having to justify the amount of its award with any degree of precision'[83] the orders made by the courts below were confirmed on ultimate appeal.

According to the approach adopted in *Libertarian*, the inherent uncertainty of valuation was resolved via recourse to equity's presumptions and assumed standards of conduct which apply to the fiduciary. As explained by Millett NPJ the court 'may [first] be able to take the fiduciary at his own word and use his falsehoods to establish the facts as if they were true, even though they are known to be untrue. Secondly the court is entitled to make every assumption against the party whose conduct has deprived it of the necessary evidence.'[84] Everything is presumed against the wrongdoer. Thus, in valuing hypothetical loss equity presumes a state of affairs consistent with performance by the fiduciary of their underlying obligations. The fiduciary's obligation was an obligation of loyalty, being an obligation not to put himself in a situation of conflict or serious possibility of conflict between duty and self-interest. Consistently with this expected standard of conduct, a probabilistic method of making certain the value of the lost opportunity is arguably not relevant because the obligation of the fiduciary is not inherently probabilistic or at least capable of reduction to a level of performance.

The alternative approach is demonstrated in the reasoning of the New South Wales Court of Appeal in *Ramsay v BigTinCan*.[85] BigTinCan (BTC) required capital, a task which one of BTC's directors (Ramsay) undertook during 2009. Ramsay had with others during his association with BTC '…formulated and implemented a plan to acquire BTC assets at a discounted value, to develop and undertake BTC's business through a new entity ('Newco') and to divert funding and business opportunities from BTC to Newco.'[86] Ball J at trial found Ramsay had breached his fiduciary duties as director of BTC and that in consequence BTC had lost the opportunity to raise finance. Equitable compensation of $300,000 plus interest was awarded. Ball J calculated this sum adopting a degree of probability method, by which it was assumed BTC had a 25% chance of raising $1,200,000. A majority of the New South Wales Court of Appeal agreed with the amount awarded, but varied the method by which it was arrived at.

Specifically, the lost opportunity to obtain funding, of itself, could not be treated as a financial loss. Rather, it was necessary for BTC to demonstrate that the funding 'would, or might'[87] have been put to profitable use.[88] Otherwise, it could not be regarded as causally related to a financial loss. On the facts of the case, although

83 *Libertarian* (n 78) [174] (Millett NPJ).

84 *Libertarian* (n 78) [174] (Millett NPJ).

85 [2014] NSWCA 324 ('*Ramsay*'), special leave to appeal to the High Court of Australia refused [2015] HCATrans 59.

86 *Ramsay* [12] (Macfarlan JA); *BigTinCan v Ramsay* [2013] NSWSC 1248, [68] (Ball J) ('*BigTinCan*').

87 *Ramsay* (n 85) [69] (Macfarlan JA).

88 *Ramsay* (n 85) [69] and [72] (Macfarlan JA) with whom at [2] McColl JA agreed. Gleeson JA at [123]–[141] valued the lost opportunity significantly lower at 0.1 x $650,000 = $65,000, taking into

Macfarlan JA held that the trial judge had erred in the approach he took in arriving at $300,000, the same result was reached through different computation as a 'fair assessment of BTC's loss'[89] taking into account the various contingencies[90] involved in the business enterprise, and the fact the parties would not have committed their time and energy had they not assessed the prospects of business success at greater than 10% nor estimated returns in excess of $650,000.[91] Therefore, the original value of equitable compensation was confirmed.

Embedded in this notion of 'put to profitable use' is therefore a judgment about what the principal might have done with the capital had it been obtained, an inquiry which is necessarily uncertain. *BigTinCan* advocates a probabilistic approach to solving this uncertainty, suggesting that the various contingencies, such as the hypothetical conduct of third parties, may be accounted for in this calculation. However, it is important to notice that in exercising equity's discretion in making certain the value of the lost chance, equity's normative commitments about the conscience and conduct expected of the fiduciary or other duty bound party must inform that discretion. So, for example, it should not be permissible in calculating the value of the lost chance to discount for the contingency that the *principal* would not have pursued the chance. Such a discount would run contrary to equity's stated position, which is to require the fiduciary to avoid placing herself in a position of conflict or possibility of conflict between duty and self-interest, or conflicting duties owed to more than one principal, and the obligation not to make a profit.[92] The breaching fiduciary should not be permitted to argue that the value of an opportunity be discounted for the risk that the principal 'was unwilling, unlikely or unable'[93] to pursue it. Despite the fact that the valuation of a lost commercial opportunity at law *would* entail the question of whether the plaintiff would have taken up the opportunity in any case, to be determined according to the balance of probabilities,[94] equity's method of making certain the principal's loss should not be permitted to run contrary to the underlying obligation of the fiduciary. Similarly, when we consider the parallel liability of the breaching fiduciary to account for profits, is irrelevant that the gain in the hands of the fiduciary is one which the principal could or would not have made.[95]

account various contingencies affecting the possible outcome of *Ramsay* in successfully raising funds. Despite Macfarlan JA and Gleeson JA reaching differing figures, both approaches were premised on the view that BTC had to show the 'prospects of success of that opportunity had it been pursued' expressed in the view that '… the funding would have been put to profitable use.'

[89] *Ramsay* (n 85) [83] (Macfarlan JA).

[90] *Ramsay* (n 85) [84] (Macfarlan JA): 'the very significant business contingencies to which the prospect of deriving the anticipated profits was subject'.

[91] Note that this was the figure placed on success by Gleeson JA.

[92] *Breen v Williams* (1996) 186 CLR 71, 135 (Gummow J); *Pilmer v Duke Group Ltd (in liq)* (2001) 207 CLR 165, [78]–[79] (McHugh, Gummow, Hayne and Callinan JJ).

[93] *Warman v Dwyer* (1995) 182 CLR 544, 558 (the Court) ('*Warman*').

[94] *Heenan v DeSisto* [2008] NSWCA 25, [29] (Giles JA).

[95] *Warman* (n 93) 558 (the Court).

B. Adjustments and Allowances

When awarding a disgorgement remedy such as an account of profits, equity adjusts the value of the sum to be disgorged in order to reflect the burdens of making the wrongful gain. Thus the equitable allowances given to a breaching fiduciary[96] and various of the costs of production which may be attributed to the infringement[97] are made. In calculating equitable compensation for a lost opportunity, there is evidence that some adjustments are made to the figure representing the value which would have been realised by the principal in exercising the lost opportunity. Indeed, equitable compensation 'may occasionally be computed by reference to the profit that has been made by the errant fiduciary',[98] not least when the loss *is* the loss of a chance. Despite this assertion, it is not clear that equitable compensation (in the reparative sense) for a lost opportunity to obtain a profit should always be the mirror image of the disgorgement of a gain. In particular, as discussed below, it is not clear whether an equitable allowance for the breaching fiduciary's care and skill may be accommodated.

An example is *V-Flow Pty Ltd v Holyoake Industries (Vic) Pty Ltd*.[99] Former employees of Holyoake, whilst still in that company's employ, acted in breach of fiduciary duty to negotiate the purchase of the business of a competitor (Variflow) via a new corporate entity (V-Flow). The directors of V-Flow were thus the former employees of Holyoake. The trial judge found that the directors/former employees had breached fiduciary and contractual duties they owed Holyoake and ordered equitable remedies, including an account of profits and equitable compensation, for Holyoake's lost opportunity to acquire Variflow's business.[100] Of interest to this discussion is the consideration by the Full Court of the Federal Court of Australia of the quantum of equitable compensation. In calculating the value of the opportunity lost by Holyoake, the court confirmed the defendant was entitled to set against this, as an expense, 'the notional salaries which would have been paid by Holyoake to [the defaulting employees/directors]'[101] had the opportunity been pursued by Holyoake. Further, maintaining symmetry with the position in account of profits, the Court confirmed that, despite no actual remuneration on

[96] *Phipps v Boardman* [1964] 1 WLR 993 (Ch); *Warman* (n 93). These are said to reflect the care and skill of the fiduciary in producing the profit, and may be declined depending on the honesty of the fiduciary in breach. See generally: M Harding, 'Justifying Fiduciary Allowances' in A Robertson and Tang HW (eds), *The Goals of Private Law* (Oxford, Hart Publishing, 2009) 341.

[97] *Dart Industries Inc v The Decor Corporation Pty Ltd* (1993) 179 CLR 101.

[98] [2013] FCAFC 16, [55] (the Court). See also *Hill v Rose* [1990] VR 129, 143 (Tadgell J); *Hodgson v Amcor Ltd* (2012) 264 FLR 1, [1663] (Vickery J); *Links Golf Tasmania Pty Ltd v Sattler (No 3)* [2012] FCA 1418, [22] (Jessup J).

[99] [2013] FCAFC 16 ('*V-Flow*'). See also *V-Flow Pty Limited v Holyoake Industries (Vic) Pty Limited (No 2)* [2013] FCAFC 27 giving reasons as to costs and the parties' election.

[100] *V-Flow* (n 99) [9]–[10] (the Court). These were subject to the need to elect before final orders were made.

[101] *V-Flow* (n 99) [71] (the Court).

the evidence having been paid by V-Flow to its directors, V-Flow was similarly entitled to include these amounts 'as an expense incurred by V-Flow for the purpose of calculating the profits made by V-Flow during the relevant period.'[102] This was because, if the directors had not worked in the business, 'it would have been necessary to pay someone else to do the work that they did.'[103]

In understanding this adjustment it is important to separate, as did the Court in its reasoning, 'an allowance for work and skill … from the calculation of profit actually made or derived.'[104] In calculating the value of the 'profit' a court may thus have regard to the fiduciary's expenses incurred in order to enable the profit to be realised separately to any allowance for 'skill, expertise and entrepreneurial efforts'.[105] It is clear that the Court in *V-Flow* intended this amount on account of expenses to be distinct from any fiduciary allowance. However, this occurs against a backdrop in which the value of equitable compensation for the lost opportunity was notionally aligned with the valuation of the profits. Two complications thereby emerge.

First, the identity of the V-Flow staff for whom an expense adjustment was permitted included Aloe and Matkovic, who were named as directors of V-Flow[106] and had been senior employees at Holyoake.[107] Thus in a sense, it was the very fiduciaries at fault whose remuneration was discounted as an expense of the business, albeit in the hands of a separate entity V-Flow. This brings into view the question of a fiduciary allowance and raises the issue of the extent to which such adjustments should properly be made through expenses or solely through the lens of a fiduciary allowance which would lead to an inquiry into 'dishonesty, bad faith or surreptitious dealing'.[108] The normative purpose of the fiduciary allowance for care and skill is contested.[109] However, to the extent the allowance is within the

[102] ibid.
[103] ibid.
[104] *V-Flow* (n 99) [69] (the Court).
[105] *Short v Crawley (No 30)* [2007] NSWSC 1322, [753] (White J).
[106] *V-Flow* (n 99) [6] (the Court).
[107] *V-Flow* (n 99) [21] (the Court).
[108] *Short v Crawley (No 30)* [2007] NSWSC 1322, [753] (White J)
[109] For example, it is sometimes suggested that the allowance is given because the profit is not sufficiently causally connected to the beach of duty. For example see: J Edelman, *Gain Based Damages* (Oxford, Hart Publishing, 2002), 104–05, 171–72; G Virgo, 'Restitutionary Remedies for Wrongs: Causation and Remoteness' in CEF Rickett (ed), *Justifying Private Law Remedies* (Oxford, Hart Publishing, 2008) 301, 309–10 and 325–26. An alternative approach is to cast the function of allowances as implementing a rule of remoteness by which, notwithstanding the profit is [factually] causally connected to the breach of duty, it is nonetheless too remote from the breach. For example, see: P Birks, *An Introduction to the Law of Restitution*, rvsd edn (Oxford, Clarendon Press, 1989), 351; R Grantham and C Rickett, *Enrichment and Restitution in New Zealand* (Oxford, Hart Publishing, 2000), 486–487. Alternatively, as Harding has argued, the allowance may be justified on the basis of 'desert'. The fiduciary 'deserves' (to the extent that discretion is exercised) recognition for their expended time, skill and labour. See generally C Mitchell, 'Causation, Remoteness and Fiduciary Gains' 17 *King's College Law Journal* 325; M Harding, 'Justifying Fiduciary Allowances' in A Robertson and Tang HW (eds), *The Goals of Private Law* (Oxford, Hart Publishing, 2009) 341.

discretion of the court,[110] and reflects a concern to capture other transfers of value between the parties which may otherwise remain,[111] this similar computation arguably should not be available in equitable compensation awards. The approach in *V-Flow* raises the possibility of a fiduciary effectively obtaining an allowance by the back door.

The second issue raised by the adjustment in *V-Flow* concerns time, and is a function of the claim for a lost opportunity. In attempting to measure lost opportunity by reference to the value of a gain *actually* made by the defendant, a court will be faced by the problem of certainty of loss. In particular, as in *V-Flow*, in deciding which expenses and allowances employed in calculating a gain made in the hands of the defendant to allocate to the value of the lost opportunity, given that this is necessarily a hypothetical loss vis a vis the plaintiff. Thus, the court may require evidence that the expense is necessary to realise the opportunity. However, the same argument logically cannot be made about fiduciary allowances. This is because the principal, in claiming a lost opportunity, asserts a state of affairs pursuant to which there is no breach of fiduciary duty. The fiduciary may or may not have acted in the facts. Thus the occasion for a fiduciary allowance cannot arise. Nonetheless, as demonstrated by the *actual* gain in the hands of the defendant, services, time and skill may be required to realise the value of the opportunity, irrespective the identity of the party providing these inputs. Such value may be reflected in an adjustment for expenses reflecting reasonable remuneration.

For this reason care is required in identifying precisely the adjustment at hand. As shown by the facts of *V-Flow* slightly anomalous results may follow in circumstances where the value of work done by breaching fiduciaries and recorded in the account as an expense is also capable of capture as a fiduciary allowance.

III. Conclusion

This chapter is not intended as a comprehensive study of discretion in equitable compensation. Rather, the purpose is to identify at a more global level the different senses in which discretion is operating in determining both the availability and computation of equitable compensation. The discussion has not distinguished between equitable compensation in the sense understood by some scholars and judges to be substitutive or reparative. This is because, at least in relation to factors going to the availability or the appropriateness of equitable compensation, such as laches, equity's mandate to consider the conscience and conduct of both parties exists across both categories of compensation.

110 Although, as shown by the facts of *Warman* itself, dishonesty is no necessary impediment to making an allowance. See *Warman* (n 93) 560, 568–69 (Mason CJ, Brennan, Deane, Dawson and Gaudron JJ).

111 Reflecting a desire to effect counter restitution between the parties.

INDEX

Introductory Note

References such as '178–79' indicate (not necessarily continuous) discussion of a topic across a range of pages. Because the whole of this work is about 'equitable compensation' and 'disgorgement', use of these terms (and certain others which occur throughout) as entry points has been restricted. Please look under the appropriate detailed entries. Wherever possible in the case of topics with many references, these have either been divided into sub-topics or only the most significant discussions of the topic are listed.

www.ingramcontent.com/pod-product-compliance
Lightning Source LLC
Chambersburg PA
CBHW071305180926
51613CB00001B/130